MAINTAINING SANITY IN THE CLASSROOM

maintaining sanity in the classroom: illustrated teaching techniques

RUDOLF DREIKURS, M.D.,
Professor Emeritus of Psychiatry,
Chicago Medical School,
Director of Alfred Adler Institute of Chicago

BERNICE BRONIA GRUNWALD

FLOY C. PEPPER

HARPER & ROW, PUBLISHERS
NEW YORK   EVANSTON   SAN FRANCISCO   LONDON

Maintaining Sanity in the Classroom: Illustrated Teaching Techniques

Copyright © 1971 by Rudolf Dreikurs, Bernice Bronia Grunwald, and Floy C. Pepper

Printed in the United States of America. All rights reserved. No part of this book may be used or reproduced in any manner whatsoever without written permission except in the case of brief quotations embodied in critical articles and reviews. For information address Harper & Row, Publishers, Inc., 49 East 33rd Street, New York, N.Y. 10016.

Standard Book Number: 06-041758-7

Library of Congress Catalog Card Number: 74-168348

contents

foreword

The purpose of this book is to encourage teachers, who in these troubled times, are beginning to doubt their own ability to motivate children in school, and who are either accepting defeat and are leaving the teaching profession, or who are resigned to a fate of failure and misery until such time when they can retire.

The encouraging spirit prevails throughout the entire book; it is the foundation on which all our practices rest. Teachers who are discouraged are in no position to exercise effective leadership toward a change in their students' attitudes and values. We must, therefore, help them to adopt new attitudes toward others, to change their own goals, and to be more concerned with understanding and helping children than with their own authority.

Our aim is not to tell teachers how to teach any particular subject, but rather how to create an atmosphere conducive to learning and enjoyment. This can be achieved if they share their responsibility with the students, understand what makes them tick, recognize their aspirations, and help them to realize their hopes.

Teachers often complain that their instructors in college and the textbooks they used gave them nothing more than beautiful-sounding but inapplicable theory. Unfortunately, those who write about our present problems in school and who make suggestions for coping with them often discourage teachers further with their emphasis on the insurmountable obstacles caused by social and cultural conditions. We do not minimize the disadvantaged backgrounds of some children, nor do we overlook the need for improving social and environmental conditions. Teachers need to know that there is much they can do for the child in spite of these conditions. More than anything, they must realize that if they accept these factors as a *force majeur* over which they have no control, they automatically negate the possibility for their students to change and to learn. This invariably leads to failure for many capable children.

It is our hope that in this book teachers will find answers to many of their questions. The book deals primarily with practical applications to classroom problems with special emphasis on group dynamics, and on problem-solving through group discussions dealing with discipline as well as with learning.

Our suggestions are easy to understand and to follow, provided that the teacher is sincere in her attempt to learn new approaches and is willing to apply them consistently and with optimism.

preface

We witness a peculiar dilemma in regard to our schools. Teachers, more than any other professional group, are sincerely concerned with establishing and maintaining democratic procedures. This is the result of Dewey's teaching. He established the notion that autocratic methods infringe on childrens' rights and diminish their cooperation. Unfortunately, Dewey had the right ideas but could not put them into practice. School systems that followed his leadership in the so-called "Progressive Education" often went too far in their permissiveness and thereby failed to stimulate optimal achievement and to maintain order and discipline among students. As a consequence, this type of education fell into disrepute, and the pendulum began to swing in the opposite direction. The trend toward strictness and the resumption of autocratic methods culminated in the demand for physical punishment with the paddle. But it did not do much good, since children no longer are willing to be subdued and to submit to punitive action. Now a tragic vicious circle began. The more the schools became determined to impose their will on the students, the more the students rebelled openly and defiantly, which in turn provoked the adults to apply stricter measures. At the present time, the war between the generations is in full force. This is the so-called "generation gap." The flames of this rebellion are further kindled by the intrusion of the fight for racial equality. The black student fights simultaneously against two enemies who try to suppress his rebellion: white society and black adults.

Until now, educational policies were mostly concerned with two alternatives in dealing with children: permissiveness or strictness. But permissiveness leads to anarchy, and strictness to rebellion. Thus, one assumed that a happy mixture of both, or some middle way avoiding either extreme, could be the answer. It is not. Unless teachers learn to stimulate and to influence children from within instead of relying on pressure from without, they are in no position to overcome whatever resistance they may encounter in their classroom. Most of our present corrective efforts are ill advised. Despite reward and punishment, despite criticism and humiliation, children continue their disturbing or defiant behavior. Consequently, in our school systems we raise an increasing number of illiterates—children who never learn to read and write properly. Many children develop a distaste for and opposition to the institutions of learning. We have the underachievers, who flatly refuse to learn, and the dropouts, who usually went to school without deriving much benefit from it. There are few indications that give us hope of averting a steadily worsening relationship between teachers and students. Unless the future teachers learn during their undergraduate study how to understand children and influence them, they may start with a great deal of idealism and hope that will give way to despair when they find that their best efforts and most sincere intentions are thwarted.

At present, teachers are not prepared to understand children. But without an understanding of the child's motivation, the teacher is hardly in a position to change it. As long as the child wants to study and to behave himself, the teacher finds little difficulty in teaching subject matter; but if the child decides not to study, the teacher does not know what to do. For this reason, teachers need practical psychology that can be applied in the classroom, enabling them to help the child who is deficient academically or socially.

We are proposing a psychological model of man—a theory of human behavior that every teacher can learn—that will be helpful in the teacher's efforts to understand motivation. The theory and practice was developed by the Viennese psychiatrist Alfred Adler and his associates.

We see the child as a social being who wants to find his place at home, in school, and in the world. If he misbehaves, he has developed erroneous ideas about how to belong. The behavior of children can only be understood when we know its purpose. All behavior is goal-directed; it indicates the ways and means that each child has discovered as his expression to gain status and significance. The child decides what he intends to do, although he is usually not aware of what he has decided and that he can change his decision.

The child can function fully only if he feels accepted by the group as a worthwhile member. His ability and willingness to function depends on what we call his "social interest." Disturbances and deficiencies indicate a lack of social interest, of concern with the welfare of others. The restriction of social interest is usually due to inferiority feelings, to the doubts of a child to find a place through useful means. It is the task of the teacher to help the child to overcome his mistaken self-evaluation and, thereby, increase his social interest. For this reason, the art of encouragement is one of the most crucial tools that can be used to correct and improve the adjustment each child is making.

Many of the suggestions made throughout the book are based on common sense; others, however, offset present concepts about children and require considerable relearning. One of the first steps a teacher has to take is to give up punitive retaliation. This alone would revolutionize almost any school system that heretofore used punishment, grades, and other forms of patronizing superiority. A new relationship of equality between adults and children is incomprehensible for teachers who were never exposed to such a concept. They may find it difficult to share their responsibility with the children and let them participate in decision making.

An end to the present warfare between adults and children can only come when our schools become truly democratic, governed by representatives of all segments of the school population. Administrators, teachers, counselors, and maintenance personnel must get together with the students to find a common ground of procedure. We can no longer run schools for children; we must let them participate in the process of education. In order to do so, a new relationship between adults and children is needed, one that reflects mutual trust and mutual respect. Without that, the war can go on indefinitely.

It is our hope that in this book we will contribute to an understanding of methods to resolve the conflicts raging in our schools.

Rudolf Dreikurs
Bernice Bronia Grunwald
Floy C. Pepper

August 1971

MAINTAINING SANITY IN THE CLASSROOM

1
theoretical premises

DEVELOPMENT OF THE CHILD'S POTENTIAL

Every successful method that we use in education does in fact reveal some of the latent potentialities of the child. The educator is constantly confronted with the problem of the extent and degree to which he can stimulate the child to learn and, thereby, to make the latent potentiality a reality. Although we assume that many children could achieve more than they do, in many instances we equate what the child *is* doing with what he can do. Educational progress depends on the ability of the teacher to perceive the untapped resources of the student and to develop techniques of using these resources to best advantage. In both regards, our present culture is remiss. We hardly acknowledge the tremendous potential of each child, and we certainly lack in our educational institutions the ability to evoke their latent talents. It often seems that we systematically prevent the development of children while trying too hard to foster it.

While we cannot base our estimate of the child's potential on any reliable proof, we find some agreement among people with vision[1] that we are all operating at about 15 percent of our potential ability. If anything close to this estimate is correct, then we can attribute this general artificial restriction in our functions to the practice of impeding the development of our children. We have advocated for many years the proposition that children could learn within the first ten years everything that presently a college graduate knows. In line with contemporary concepts of childrens' abilities, such a proposition encounters mostly disbelief and often outright opposition. Pessimism and stubborn adherence to the idea that we are living in the best social situation and can be proud of our educational institutions obstructs the educational revolution that is needed to permit a greater usage of each child's potential. It should make us reflect when we see how much very young children learn before they go to school, and what little progress they make thereafter. The artistic ability and creativity of young children is obvious, and very little of it remains when they become mature, adjusted to family life and school. We need a new concept of children, realizing the tremendous power, scheming and persistence with which they become able to manipulate their environment. Such a realization is in stark contrast to a prevalent notion that children are parasites, victims, have not found their identity. It is one of several scientific theories reinforcing a common doubt that little children can take responsibility and can be relied upon in their judgment.

A consideration of a child's potential must first include the realization of what little children really are. Our present concepts of them preclude an accurate realization of the abilities that they demonstrate, but that adults fail to notice. We have to become aware of the wide range of negative influences to which we expose them. Effective methods of stimulating growth and making use of the child's potential cannot be put into practice until the traditional and detrimental influences are clearly recognized and abandoned. Some techniques to stimulate growth and learning are known and many more will be discovered. The greatest progress may come through new learning theories. It is probable that when we discover how very young children learn, this may lead to totally new approaches in teaching.

[1]H. A. Otto, ed., *Exploration in Human Potentialities* (Springfield, Ill.: Chas. C. Thomas, 1966).

Let us now look at infants and examine their relationship with their environment. We have observed that babies can learn how to dominate the family within the first four weeks of their lives. Such a statement may seem outrageous to a person who cannot believe that such a young child could plan or know anything. Naturally, the child is unaware of what he is doing. This is not only true for infants, but for people in general. Conscious awareness is by no means a premise for well-designed activities. Contrary to a widespread opinion, the newborn infant is not just a bundle of uncoordinated drives and needs; he is a social being, not only concerned with physical needs that call for satisfaction, but with the social atmosphere around him —and relating himself to his surroundings to satisfy his social needs. The infant operates on trial and error. When he finds—long before he can think consciously—that he likes to be picked up and to be fondled, and if he encounters a receptive environment that responds to his crying demands, then he will have learned his first lesson, that is the benefit of crying. As long as the social nature of infants is not recognized, the mother is primarily concerned with their physical needs. She is advised that her function is to provide satisfaction for them, which includes physical proximity with her. In doing so, she stimulates the child to exert pressure for social gratification—to be constantly picked up and fondled. There are many experts who consider such demands as natural, and predict bad consequences if they are not met. Actually, the situation is the opposite. By spoiling the infant, by picking him up whenever he cries, the child becomes more disturbed when he is not picked up and therefore increases his demand to which the untrained mother then succumbs. She is not aware of this management by the infant. As early as the first few weeks, she deprives the child of taking care of himself and of adjusting to life as it is.

It does not take the infant very long to find out when crying will be beneficial and when not. It works with mother, but it may drive father away because he can't stand it. Therefore, soon the child will modify his behavior according to the responses he gets.

A typical example is the transaction of an only child with father and mother. Some have called this situation an Oedipus complex, attributing it to instinctual and sexual needs because they failed to see its social significance. If the child is a boy, then the mother may have a special involvement with him. In the past, giving birth to a son provided higher status, greater fulfillment. Today many a mother still prefers to have a son as the first born, another man in her life who is her own. Therefore, she may be more inclined to watch the child's needs and thereby spoil him. The father too, may be very happy to have a son. However, he may not like the fuss that mother makes

3

over him. He may feel dethroned, since his wife's attention may now have to be shared. When he objects, she may only feel closer to her son. It does not take very long before the child discovers the benefit of provoking father who, by his strictness, tries to counteract mother's indulgence. Now, all the little boy has to do is provoke his father who may then overreact. This brings mother on the scene in defense of her son. Behind his indignant fears of his father's abuse, the son watches with enjoyment mother's antagonism to father's behavior. The more she feels sorry for him, the more he feels sorry for himself and the more he provokes abuse from his father. This Oedipal situation can come to a quick end when mother stays out of the fight between the two males.

A normal 6-month-old infant born to deaf-mute parents has a peculiar way of crying. Tears stream down his cheeks, his face is in a grimace, the whole body shakes—but not a peep comes out. These infants, who after birth cry with a normal sound, discover after one to two months that the sound does not help them; therefore, they give it up. It is hard to believe, but the child's behavior is well designed and he will not continue any behavior pattern if it does not get him desired results. The difficulty adults have in realizing this fact is due to their unawareness of the child's purpose and goals in whatever he does.

Contrary to general assumption, the child is not the victim of the parents but very actively influences them. Without being aware of it, he knows how to make the parents conform to his wishes, though he is not always willing to conform to theirs. The child wants to belong and he will do whatever seems to him to be effective to achieve this. As long as he feels a sense of belonging and is not discouraged, he will respond to the demands and needs of the situation. When he does not believe that he can find his place through useful means, and becomes discouraged, then he misbehaves. Parents and teachers, who do not realize that the child's misbehavior has a purpose, fall for it and do exactly what the child wants them to do. If the adults knew what the child's goal was, then they would not assume that he has to be told what to do. Even very young children are fully aware whenever they do something wrong. But that doesn't stop them. Therefore, the endless explanations and admonitions are worthless. In fact, they actually reinforce the child's reluctance to behave as he is supposed to. In our work with parents we have to help them to understand what goes on, how they can be the victims of the child's unconscious planning. They must be helped to become a match for him. One of the reasons why this game between parents and children remains unnoticed is that not only the parents but the child himself is unaware of the planning. When we ask a child why he does some-

4

thing wrong, he doesn't know. But when his unconscious purpose is properly explained to him, he begins to see it and then responds with a *recognition reflex.*[2] This most important aspect of understanding the child's behavior and motivation will be carefully explored in the next chapter.

The child determines the role which he intends to play through life in his transactions with his brothers and sisters; the parents afterwards merely reinforce his decision of being good or bad, conforming or defiant. He depends less on what his mother does to him than his mother depends on what he is doing. The mother does not *cause* the child's disturbing or deficient behavior; she merely makes it possible through her compliance with his unconscious schemes and provocations.

The development of personality, of a life style, is based on the opinions which the child forms about himself and others and of the goals which he sets for himself. He probably begins with random decisions, perceiving and evaluating the reactions. After he has established the frame of reference within which he operates, that is, his life style, the child is free to choose from a great variety of alternatives. He can make full use of this freedom, frequently to the disadvantage of adults who neither recognize the nature of his decisions nor know how to change them.

For instance, he may overestimate the importance of winning his parents' approval; he may find difficulty in accepting criticism; he might be overly sensitive and try to let others make decisions for him. Or, he may try to control and manipulate everything; being right could become overly important; he might feel that he cannot trust anyone or depend on others. Some children may think that being good is the only way to have status. They may be perfectionists, like to sit in judgment of others who are not so good, feel morally superior, over-react to any mistake they or others make. Others rebel in one form or other, convinced that they are entitled to have their own way.

The realization that each child can decide and *is* deciding what he is going to do opens new vistas for child psychology and pedagogy. It implies the child's present ability to determine whether he wants to change, to learn, and to decide what and when he wants to learn. It puts the emphasis on here and now, on his present movements in the social field. It refutes the common assumption that the child is the victim of past experiences. Past experiences certainly have contributed to his development and to his present attitudes, but there is a profound difference as to whether one regards the past as the

[2] The recognition reflex will be discussed later (p. 34).

cause of his deficiency or difficulty, or as antecedents that explain how and why he developed his ideas and concepts. But the basis for his behavior is what he thinks, believes, and intends to do *today*. The child is not the victim of forces that converge on him, hereditary endowment, environmental influences, traumatic experiences, psychosexual development, and so on. What he is when he is born is less important than what he does with it afterwards. The living conditions in which he finds himself are less important than what he does with himself in them. This view opens the way for change through new and more appropriate concepts and goals. It is the basis for a more optimistic outlook.

In order to understand children, we have to keep in mind that whatever the child is doing depends on his decisions and not on his abilities. Thus, deficient behavior may not result from real deficiencies, but from wrong decisions. Present psychological investigations usually try to establish certain qualities and deficiencies of the child, his abilities and inabilities. This is a psychology of possession, of inventory; ours is a psychology of use. We are not interested in what a child is or what he has, but only what he does with it. Consequently, deficient or antisocial behavior is not regarded as abnormal. We find that the good and the bad child often operate on the basis of the same psychological dynamics. An overambitious child who cannot be the best may prefer to be the worst. One is usually inclined to regard outstanding abilities of the child as an expression of his talent. But a special ability may have developed as a compensation for some hereditary or environmental handicap.[3]

On the other hand, many outstanding people experienced in their early childhood intellectual stimulation through some adults who exposed them to knowledge far beyond their age. We underestimate the abilities of very young children. We have evidence now that the proper age for learning to read and to write is probably between two and a half and three years, according to Chauncey, Doman, Moore, Sidi, and others. Many ingenious experiments have been developed during the last few years to indicate a variety of ways by which children can learn skills presently assigned to a much later age. The ability of young children to learn a foreign language within a few weeks is well known. Although many people consider exposure of the child to several languages as a handicap to its development, children can actually learn several languages at the same time. Their capacity for incorporating knowledge is almost unlimited. The artistic ability of almost all very young children has already been men-

[3]Children with eye defects may become painters; children with defects of the ear, composers; and children with weak muscles, athletes.

6

tioned. In recent years we have discovered their abilities in mathematics using such new methods as Cuisenaire.

One of the most important and far-reaching discoveries concerns the alleged ability of newborn infants to swim. A gag-reflex that disappears after the age of six months supposedly prevents them from drowning. If this is true, and if the reports of parents who tried it would indicate that it is, it could revolutionize all aspects of education and even mankind itself. One merely has to imagine the effect on the self-concept of a child as he develops his mobility. Presently, the human infant is one of the most helpless creatures in the world, like the birds, who also need training and development before they can reach mobility. If the infant could be free in his actions, using his muscles and developing his brain, deciding where to go, he would not have to experience passive helplessness. Our whole attitude toward children would change because of their mobility and capacity for self-determination during the first month of life. Such early activity would speed up the child's physical and mental growth.

Why does the proposition of teaching academic subjects to very young children create so much opposition? We can distinguish two main arguments. The first is the fear of detrimental consequences when one expects functions from the child for which he is not ready. The prototype of such objections is the claim by the psychoanalysts that too early toilet training endangers the child's personality development. It has been shown that the necessary maturation in the central nervous system is not a prerequisite for training as has been assumed but rather a consequence of the practice. Similar opposition to premature stimulation is based on the assumption of inadequate cerebral motivation, overlooking the fact that cerebral development is a consequence of use and not its prerequisite. Such fears indicate a protective attitude toward the child which is one form of lack of confidence in his ability.

The second objection is based on the assumption that early learning would deprive the child of his childhood. But why should it be so? Even the most advanced genius who behaves within his work area on a completely adult level functions socially as other young children do. The proposed form of learning is merely a special kind of play. It only promotes intellectual activities of which children today are deprived. One reason why learning to read may become more difficult if it is postponed until the age of six (according to Maria Montessori) is that the child reaches that age feeling that he is unable to do what adults do. He accepts what is planned for him. In many cases a child becomes ready sooner because an older sibling has difficulty in learning. But many children—particularly boys—do not develop a readiness at all. They simply refuse to learn, either because they are

7

discouraged or they try to defeat adults. Some "scientists" attribute that to the slower development of boys, notwithstanding the fact that in many countries (Britain, Israel) many boys learn to read at the age of four. There it is not assumed that boys are slow to develop.

Before we can really help children to fulfill their tremendous potential, we have to change the practices which are presently used in raising children in the family and teaching them in our schools. Without the elimination of many traditional practices, children will continue to be hampered by those who sincerely want to help them. The bankruptcy of our educational institutions, family and school, has to be realized before we can reevaluate all our attitudes and procedures and systematically train parents and teachers in new approaches. We find ourselves in the same tragic situation in which Semmelweiss found himself about a century ago in Vienna. He had discovered the law of asepsis. Until then, doctors treating their patients actually damaged them. A wound was covered with unclean material causing infection and death. The obstetrician coming from an autopsy delivered babies without washing his hands, causing the deaths of many women who came to the hospital for delivery. He simply did not know the need for washing his hands. One can imagine the reactions of his colleagues when Semmelweiss demonstrated to them the harm they did to their patients. Their wrath finally drove him to suicide.

We cannot and do not blame parents for their mistakes. It is not their fault that they do not know what to do with children. Parents are not familiar with the ways children should be raised, because raising children has always been based on tradition, and the traditional form of raising children, handed down from an autocratic past, no longer brings results. Similarly, as long as children behave and want to learn, our teachers are effective. But they do not learn in our colleges what to do with the child who decides not to behave nor to study. From such cases, pressure from without brings no results. Most parents and teachers do not know what to do in moments of conflict or defiance. Discipline by reward and punishment was and is only possible in an autocratic setting. It has to be replaced in a democratic setting with methods to stimulate from within. Without such stimulation, most educational influences actually undermine rather than enhance the development of the child.

The greatest obstacle to growth and development, to learning and to an improved function, or even to continued functioning on the level already reached, is discouragement, doubt in one's own ability. Our present methods of raising children confront them with a series of discouraging experiences. One either does for them what they could do for themselves, protecting and spoiling them, or one scolds

8

and punishes. In either case the child is deprived of the experience of his own strength. He cannot use his inner resources if he is convinced he has none. One cannot use one's potential of creativity if one is afraid. We constantly frighten children in the mistaken assumption that such fright will stimulate growth, learning and adjustment. Parents and teachers, without knowing and without intending, exert considerable discouraging effects on the majority of children and young people. For them the child is never good enough as he is. They are afraid that he will not grow and develop unless they drive him on with fear.

However, this pressure no longer induces the child to submission as it did in the past. Then the child had to perform regardless of what the adults did. This is no longer true. In the democratic evolution, all previously dominant groups lost their power, be it in the relationship between men and women, management and labor, white and black, adults and children. As a consequence, parents and teachers experience an increasing degree of rebellion and defiance in their children. They, in turn, fight back, openly or subtly. There is a war going on in every family, in every classroom, with increasing mutual distrust and diminished cooperation.

The intense competition within our families, our schools, pitches brother against brother, making each one unsure of himself, driving each one to be more concerned with himself, his glory, and advantages than with more general needs. The overambition that we instill in our children does not provide a sense of security to either the one who succeeds or the one who gives up in despair. The strongest motivation to grow and to fulfill oneself in a broader way is missing. This motivation is what Adler called social interest, a feeling of belonging. It, alone, stimulates everyone to contribute to the welfare of all, to increase his function and his abilities, not for his own sake, but as a member of the group.

When we look at the almost unbelievable way in which young children respond to new stimulations, we are impressed with the fact that children learn through play, through the enjoyment of what they are doing. Learning seems to become fun and achievement, pleasure. There is no honor or failure, no grading, no superiority or inferiority, no threat of deficiency; all simply enjoy what they are doing, and progress through pleasant practice. All normal children can learn in this way, not only the gifted. This seems to indicate that learning deficiencies of normal children are artificial and unnecessary.

We do not know to which level of achievement learning through enjoyable activities can be carried out. We are accustomed to believe that high achievement requires strenuous effort. However, some of our best students learn easily and enjoy studying. The question is whether they are enjoying learning because they are talented or gifted, or whether they become talented because they enjoy learning. Many dropouts who were unable to learn, became successes when they later went back to school. Therefore, it seems that the attitude determines the achievement.

Training is required to master any skill. But does this training have to be unpleasant? What takes place when the child, or anyone else, learns? It is always based on a change of concepts, of perceptions. These changes probably occur instantaneously. At a given point, the child suddenly "catches on." Then he knows what to do. In between these periods of sudden progress, a great deal of time is wasted with meaningless practice, supposedly training muscles, movements, or isolated skills. One assumes that mere repetition will teach. It may, but only if at any given moment the child begins to understand. If this understanding is brought about directly, repetitions are not needed, beyond practicing what one has already learned. In other words, repetition is only helpful after the child has learned, and not before. For this reason, demanding homework from children when they hate it does not promote learning, only rebellion.

With proper instruction, children can learn skills far more advanced than those they are now learning. Unusual feats of memory can be achieved. Very young children can learn to compose music. Suzuki in Japan teaches unselected groups of children at the ages of three to five to play violin concertos. Many other skills and abilities, such as time perception, orientation in space, a deeper grasp of people and the perception of new patterns of various kinds of achievements far beyond the reach of our contemporaries, can be acquired. Any new ability would increase the child's, and mankind's, mastery of life.

We may stand on the threshold of a new culture, if we can remove the obstacles to intellectual growth, to social and moral development. It seems that we are on the verge of achieving this. Then we may, in a relatively short period of a few generations, acquire such a high degree of knowledge, skill, performance, and morality that mankind may be as different from us then as we are now from the inhabitants of darkest Africa.

GOAL-DIRECTED BEHAVIOR

Every educational process is based on a certain concept of human nature, whether or not the educator is aware of what this concept is. In most cases, he acts spontaneously without questioning his premises. His behavior usually is accepted by those who share his concept of man. In this sense, education is based on convictions, either through tradition and cultural influences or through personal choice or associations. All school reforms reflect attempts to change concepts and procedures. As long as certain convictions about the reasons for the behavior of children and the means by which one responds to them prevail, there is little chance to improve established educational procedures.

In the contemporary confusion about how one should deal with children, no universally accepted concept exists and we find a great variety of measures advocated to deal with them. In other words, no agreement has been reached about the way in which children should be raised and taught. Educators either stick to the traditional methods which are no longer effective, or hope that scientific research may bring them information about effective ways of dealing with children. Research has been carried on at considerable expense but often with questionable results. As a matter of fact, it seems that contemporary research has as its main goal to provide teachers with justifications for their inability to influence and teach children who refuse to learn and to cooperate. There was first the concern with mental retardation, which explained learning difficulties, although we have no reliable diagnostic test for distinguishing real from pseudoretardation, where children play dumb without being so. Then there was the assumption of the slow development of boys. Next came the effect of sidedness and its confusion, leading to the concept of dyslexia and cerebral dysfunction and of cultural and perceptual deprivation and of minimal brain damage. The significance of all these factors is highly overrated and will have to be objectively evaluated. In the meantime, they are used to justify the failure of the teachers with an ever-growing number of reluctant pupils.

All these considerations take into account certain "causes" for the child's deficiency or maladjustment. They are in line with prevalent scientific notions that all events can only be explained by their causes. Most of our contemporaries are influenced by the adherence to a causalistic-deterministic explanation of events as it was developed by seventeenth century science. It will take a major breakthrough to eliminate this kind of thinking which originally brought considerable scientific and technical progress but has now become an obstacle to understanding people, particularly children.[4]

The model of man which we propose and which seems to hold great promise for future educational approaches would have little

[4]See R. Dreikurs, "The Scientific Revolution," in *Foundations of Guidance and Counseling,* C. G. Smith and O. G. Mink eds. (Philadelphia: J. B. Lippincott Co., 1969).

chance of being accepted were it not for developments in the basic sciences, particularly in theoretical physics. Adler, who developed a very definite concept of man, was more than fifty years ahead of his time. Today, new theories about learning, about decision making and game theory and about motivation support Adler's concept. However, the majority of our contemporaries, certainly the majority of our teachers, have not been sufficiently exposed to these new perspectives. It is, therefore, difficult for them to comprehend and to accept the new concepts which contradict much of what they had thought and believed.

Our new concepts permit the educator to see the child in a completely different light. We are presenting a well-defined theory of behavior and a system of procedures that can lead to general acceptance. These should provide a stable basis for dealing with children and their problems. Historically, a certain stability existed in an autocratic society. Then almost everybody knew what to do with children, because effective educational methods had been evolved through thousands of years of adult dominance. The futility of traditional methods in a democratic society brought on the present educational confusion and with it a great variety of educational procedures which constantly change as one ill-advised approach is replaced by another one equally faulty.

What is the foundation for our new procedures? It is the realization that behavior is purposive. Only if one can accept this premise and recognize the purpose of a child's behavior, can the methods which we recommend make any sense. To correct goals is different from correcting deficiencies. What can one really do if a child is lazy, passive-aggressive, daydreaming, irresponsible, hyperactive? These and similar terms are used to explain the child's difficulties and deficiencies. But do they really explain anything? They are labels which merely describe what the child does, but not why he is doing it. As long as teachers and educators are satisfied with explaining their educational failures with a child's qualities, little progress through corrective efforts is to be expected. The locked door opens as soon as the teacher realizes the child's mistaken goals, for them he can help him to discover better alternatives.

As a social being, each child wants to belong. His behavior indicates the ways and means by which he tries to be significant. If the means are antisocial and disturbing, then the child did not develop the right idea about how to find his place. His mistaken goals, which we will discuss in detail in the next chapter, reflect an error in his judgment, in his comprehension of life and the necessities of social living.

Before we go any further, we will have to explain more clearly the significance of regarding behavior as being purposive. The method which Alfred Adler developed to recognize the goals of people can be called teleo-analytic (recognizing and changing goals). The teleological mode of thought, contradicting accustomed beliefs, found much opposition. First, the term had been used in a religious sense, that man has to fulfill a purpose for which God has created him. (Jung expressed similar ideas, that man had to fulfill the demands of his ancestors, through his collective unconscious.) The strongest opposition came from scientists who rejected teleoanalysis as unscientific. The doctrine of causality permeates our whole society. It is, therefore, very difficult to grasp that it is not the "cause" which explains behavior.

The force behind every human action is its goal. To a certain extent, everybody knows what he wants and he acts accordingly. More frequently, he is not aware of his goals. The consequences of his actions, however, reveal his intentions, whether he is aware of them or not. Particularly, if our intentions are questionable, we can always escape the responsibility for what we were doing by saying we did not intend it in this way, or by pleading innocent, blaming forces in and around us which made us act as we did. But this is mere self-deception. In general, only a small portion of all our intentions reach the conscious level. We do what we feel like doing without really knowing why we felt so inclined.

The individual has the power to move in any self-determined direction. He is not driven through life by his past; he moves of his own accord. All his actions, qualities and characteristics as well as his emotions can be understood by his effort to find a place for himself in society. A child's actions may be based on faulty assumptions about life and about himself. Although his behavior may appear to be inappropriate, it reflects his conviction that this is the only possible way for him to be significant.

He cannot perceive reality as it is, only as he interprets it. We cannot be fully objective in our evaluation of any given situation, because we have a biased perception. To understand how the child looks at life, at others and at himself, and what he decides to do about it, depends on his private logic. Asking a child why he does something wrong is useless; he does not know. The trained educator has to help him to understand himself, his goals, his private logic.

Although the child is born without preparation for the complexity of social living, he is a truly social being, not merely a bundle of instincts or reflex-mechanisms. He is sensitive to the social atmosphere around him, and very early he experiments with his environment to get what he wants, be it only to be picked up and fondled. As he develops his concepts and goals, he needs some guidelines for

13

his dealing with social intricacies. In his transactions with all the members of his family, he develops a so-called fictitious goal for the organization of his life; it is the basis of his life style. The goal is fictitious, because the child assumes that only under certain conditions can he really be sure of his place. Let us illustrate this through the following examples:

At the dinner table the parents were telling each other the events of the day. Father was telling of a new machine he had purchased for his office, and how it worked. Mother asked many questions and seemed to be delighted with her husband's report.

Marlene who was sitting next to her mother broke into the conversation. "I learned how to pedge legence in school today." She waited for a reaction from her parents, but they ignored her remarks and continued with their conversation.

Marlene tried once more but with no more success than before. Suddenly she stood up on her chair, put her right hand on her heart, and in a loud voice began to recite, "I pedge legence to United States of America." At this, the parents looked at each other and then at Marlene, and they burst out into uncontrollable laughter. Marlene started all over again, this time even louder than before.

"So you can recite The Pledge of Allegiance. Did you hear that, Mother? Our little girl can say The Pledge of Allegiance. Say it again, darling."

All the excitement about the new office machine was suddenly forgotten or put aside. Marlene became the whole center of attention.

When Eddie, 3 years old, came into the kitchen, he noticed that his mother was sewing, his father was fixing a kitchen cabinet, and his older sister was making a cake. Eddie wanted very much to do something too, something that would make his mother happy. He took the shoe polish and a shoe brush and started polishing his shoes. When the father noticed what Eddie was doing, he called to him, "That's great, son. Make sure that they shine." Mother smiled at him.

Some time later, Eddie was found polishing the bedspread on his mother's bed. Unfortunately, mother was not as happy this time as she was before, for he had used dark shoe polish on her satin spread. He received a shaking and a scolding for being a naughty boy.

Herbert, 11 years old, is the oldest of three children. He is a very shy boy, speaks inaudibly, has no friends, and avoids people outside the family. He stays in the house except for going to school or

14

when his parents send him to the store. At home he keeps busy either cleaning his room, straightening up the basement, or helping his mother with whatever she is doing.

His sister, Melanie, is two years younger. She is a very outgoing, happy, rather aggressive child. She is popular with the children. At home the parents have to force her to take care of her room and to do whatever chores they assign to her. Usually, Herbert does her work before Melanie has a chance to do it (at times when she wants to do the work). It is not unusual for her to come into her room and find that Herbert had already made her bed, hung up her clothes, and put away whatever she had left lying around.

Although Melanie enjoys this service, she is constantly complaining about her brother to her parents. "Why is he such a ninnie? Why does he walk so slowly?" She never misses an opportunity to call him names, such as "Sissie" or "Stupid."

These basic guidelines permit the child to establish a certain stability and consistency in his movement through life. But, as we will discuss later, his style of life also sets certain restrictions and leads to the possibility of frustration under certain life situations. A crisis situation develops when his life style clashes with the needs of the situation. At this point, his ability and willingness to participate and to contribute end, and antisocial movements of a neurotic or even psychotic pattern may ensue. Even then, the most antisocial form of existence has a purpose; its recognition is an important factor in therapy and reorientation with children and adults alike.

Within the framework of the life style, based on long-range goals in life, are the immediate movements, the short-range goals, as they may be called. While the concept of his life is unique for each person and may distinguish one person from the other, the immediate responses in dealing with concrete life situations is peculiarly similar.

We find that there are four possible goals of disturbing and maladjusted behavior of young children. These are seen in Table 1 and must be considered before we can understand their behavior.

It may seem unrealistic to expect psychological insights from a teacher who is supposed just to teach and to impart knowledge. But any teacher—and for that matter, any adult—can acquire this skill and knowledge in a relatively short period of time. As long as teachers were supposed to teach, and children were supposed to learn, it was not necessary to understand children and to change their motivation. Today, when the pressure from without has lost its effectiveness and has to be replaced by stimulation from within, such skills and abilities are a prerequisite for every teacher.

Table 1 THE FOUR MAJOR GOALS OF CHILDHOOD MISBEHAVIOR

Direction of Maladjustment ⟶ Decreasing Social Interest ⟶

Social Discouragement ⟶

Useful Behavior		Useless Behavior		Direction of Maladjustment
Active-Constructive	Passive-Constructive	Active-Destructive	Passive-Destructive	GOALS
success The "model" child, "teacher's pet," and so on	charm The "cute" child (admired for what they are, not what they do)	The "nuisance," showoff, tattler, pest	shyness, dependency, timidity, functional reading prob. & speech dif.	AGM (1) Attention Getting Mechanism
		The "rebel" (disobedient, subject to temper tantrums, lying, types of sex behaviorisms may be AGM, also)	stubborness (bed-wetting may also be AGM or revenge)	Power Seeking (2)
		The "vicious" child (frequently found stealing, bullying, being violent)	violent passivity (negativism)	Revenge Seeking (3)
			hopelessness (inaptitude, withdrawal giving up)	Assumed Disability (4)

Ordinarily, the child will attempt to achieve the more constructive goal first and will only progress to the more destructive behavior if he feels he is not achieving this goal. These sequences are only attempted by a child when less destructive behavior fails.

16

THE FOUR GOALS OF MISBEHAVIOR

It is natural for an educator to seek an understanding of the reason for a child's behavior if it is necessary to correct it. Our description of the four goals of disturbing behavior offers the teacher an opportunity to understand the psychological motivation of the child, instead of groping in the dark as to why the child behaves as he does. It permits the teacher to develop diagnostic skills and psychological sensitivity.

It may be difficult for many to accept the fact that children who misbehave and fail to cooperate, to study and to apply themselves, are motivated by one or the other of the four goals. We are often asked on what grounds we can make such generalizations, trying to pigeonhole the great variety of children's misbehavior into one of the four goals. As a matter of fact, we did not put them there, we found them there. We would be more than willing to include another goal for the child's misbehavior if one could be suggested and proven. In each case we can find one or several of these goals existing. They explain the child's misbehavior and can be recognized by the child if he is properly confronted with them.

In this chapter, we intend to describe the four goals and their significance. In the next chapter, we will discuss the means by which the teacher can recognize the child's goals. In Chapter 4, we will present the various methods by which the teacher can help the child to change his mistaken goals.

The child may try to get *attention*, to put others in his service, since he believes that otherwise he would be lost and worthless. Or he may attempt to prove his *power* in the belief that only if he can do what he wants and defy adult pressure can he be somebody. Or he may seek *revenge*, the only means by which he feels significant is to hurt others as he feels hurt by them. Or he may display actual or imagined *deficiencies* in order to be left alone: as long as nothing is demanded of him, his deficiency, stupidity or inability may not become obvious; that would mean his utter worthlessness.

Whichever of these four goals he adopts, his behavior is based on the conviction that only in this way can he be significant. His goal may occasionally vary with circumstances; he may act to attract attention at one moment, and assert his power or seek revenge at another. He can also use a great variety of techniques to obtain his goal; and, conversely, the same behavior can serve different purposes.

These four goals of disturbing behavior can be observed in young children up to the age of ten. It is difficult for parents and teachers to recognize that the child's disturbing behavior is directed against them. In early childhood, the status of the child depends on the impression he makes on adults. Later, he may develop different goals to gain social significance in his peer-group, and later still, in adult society. But these original four goals can still be observed in people of every age and period of life; only then, they are not all-inclusive. One must keep in mind that status and prestige can be achieved, frequently more easily, through useless and destructive means than through accomplishments.

(1) The attention-getting mechanism (AGM) is operative in most young children. It is characteristic of our culture that we provide few opportunities to our young to establish their social position through useful contribution. Whatever has to be done in the family is done by parents or older siblings. Seeing no chance to gain status through constructive contributions, the child may seek proof of his acceptance through what he can get from others, through gifts, through affection, or at least through attention. Since none of these increase the child's self-reliance and belief in his own strength, he seeks constant new proof lest he feel lost and rejected. He may try first to get his satisfaction through socially acceptable and pleasant means. When these methods no longer prove effective, when a younger sibling steals the show, or adults expect the child to give up his childish behavior he will try any other conceivable method to put others in his service and to get attention. Humiliation, punishment or even spanking do not matter as long as he achieves his purpose. He prefers them to being ignored; then he is sure that he is lost and has no place.

(2) Parents and teachers try to stop the child from demanding service and attention. He should stop his annoyance and take on responsibility for himself. When they then try to control the child, they reach a deadlock through the child's attempt to overpower them, or at least to resist their control. The child feels accepted and worthwhile only when he can do whatever he wants, and thereby refuse to do what he is supposed to do. Any adult who lets himself be drawn into a struggle for power with a child is lost. In any instance, the child will win out, with the exception of a few short-lived episodes where the adult succeeds in beating the child down. Parents and teachers pay dearly for such successes. They convince the child even more that power is all that counts in life. And he can prove that he has the means to defeat them. He is not restricted in his fighting method by any sense of responsibility or moral obligation. He is creative and inventive. The adults cannot match their wits with him because they have only very limited means at their disposal to overpower him, while the child can constantly create new and unexpected tactics which are deadly in their aim. They know where to hit.

18

Any adult who tries to control and impose his will on the child has been born fifty years too late. He could have done so successfully in a more autocratic society, when society supported adults in their efforts. Today, there is neither a society that lets the adult abuse the child, nor a child who, in his sense of his own equality, lets an adult impose his will on him and control him. Once a power conflict ensues, the relationship between child and adult can only further deteriorate and the child may move to the next goal, revenge.

(3) For children who feel utterly rejected, who have lost their faith in society and in themselves, the problem of having any significance cannot be solved through their getting attention or demonstrating their power. The fight between such a child and adult society is too violent, too painful and at the same time, too entrenched, to permit any other avenue than mutual revenge. The only role that such a child feels able to play is to get even with those who hurt him. And once the child has established such a policy for himself, he proves to be quite capable of evoking from adults the kind of treatment which then justifies his thirst for revenge. He knows very well where he can hurt the most, and he takes advantage of the vulnerability of his opponents. He regards it as a triumph when he is considered vicious. Since this is the only triumph he thinks he can obtain, it is the only one he seeks. The degree to which such a child can stir up everyone in his reach justifies to him the feeling of triumph.

(4) The intense fight between adult and child leads to complete discouragement, either to the full negation of social participation, as in the revengeful child, or to the full denial of any capacity. The child who first became passive and deficient in order to get special service and attention, eventually reaches the point where he is so convinced of his being an utter failure that he does not even try any more. Under these circumstances, the child wants nothing more than to be left alone. As long as nothing is asked of him, he can still appear as a member of the group. Then he hides himself behind a display of real or imagined inferiority, which justifies his resignation. By avoiding participation and contribution, he thinks he can avoid more humiliating and embarrassing situations.

There are no definite rules in regard to the child's choice of a goal, or of the means by which he can obtain it. By and large, each disturbing child has reached an equilibrium, which guides all his actions. In most cases, we find the disturbing child in the pursuit of one of the four goals. Sometimes he has not settled yet, and so we find the child in between attention and power, or in between power and revenge, or between attention through passive means or giving up in defeat. Some children are so rich in their creativity that they can switch from one to the other goal and actually operate on all four of them, to the

19

distress of adults who are dumbfounded by the unexpected changes in the child's behavior. Sometimes the child may have one goal at home and another at school and still another with his friends. In each instance, one has to be able to recognize the child's goal and to deal with it.

When teachers are asked which of the four types of attention-getting they consider to be least disturbing, they naturally will name the active-constructive. Such a child is usually so good that one cannot easily distinguish him from a child who does *not* seek any special attention, who enjoys doing his job without the need for approval. Many teachers do not realize that there is anything wrong with a child who seeks approval through being good. Therefore, they encourage such motivation, since they do not know how vulnerable these children are. When they no longer succeed in getting approval and special attention, they no longer see any reason to be good and might even prefer to be the worst if they cannot be the best. Yet, as far as attention getting devices go, these children are most desirable as they usually respond to the application of logical consequence. But the opinions vary as to who is the worst. Teachers not familiar with the motive behind the child's behavior may be inclined to consider the active-destructive AGM as the worst of the four, because such children cause the most disturbance. Most teachers name the passive-constructive behavior of a child as the second best. These children use their charm and appeal to get recognition, and many teachers like a child who looks up to them and caters to them. Therefore, we find many teachers inclined to regard the active-constructive behavior as the best, the passive-constructive as the next, the active-destructive as the worst and the passive-destructive in between. From a point of tractability and adjustment, they are wrong. The best behavior pattern is understandably active-constructive AGM; the next best is not the passive-constructive, but the active-destructive, provided the child seeks only attention and not power. Both passive types are actually more discouraged. It is easier to help an active-destructive child to find useful means of achieving significance than it is to move a passive child to active participation. Therefore, in this light, the active-destructive child, difficult as he may be at the moment, is less disturbed and can be remotivated to the useful side. The passive-destructive child is most maladjusted, although he may not cause too much trouble. It is this child who can move directly to goal 4, to giving up completely.

While attention can be received through four types of behavior, power permits two. It can either be active or passive; in either case the adult feels defeated by not being able to stop a child or make him do something. Revenge is mostly active. Only occasionally can passive resistance really hurt an over-ambitious parent. Thus goal 4, by necessity, implies utter passivity. (Methods of dealing with these goals are described on pp. 17, 33, 89, 186, 207).

DISCIPLINE AND ORDER

DISCIPLINE OR PUNISHMENT

Maintaining discipline is a part of the educational process. It is the foundation of social living. It is not a subject to be taught and learned nor a thing that is done to someone. Too often discipline is thought of as an either-or proposition; either the children rule the roost or they have to mind at the drop of a hat. The teaching of discipline is an on-going process, not something to resort to only in times of stress or misbehavior.

One of the reasons for the present dilemma concerning discipline is that most people, educators and parents alike, use the word discipline as meaning control through punitive measures. To many, it signifies physical punishment; to some, rigid control of rules and regulations and autocratic authority. The individuals to be disciplined are completely left out of the process of making these rules, and are never consulted about the enforcement of them. In school, the teacher or principal confronts the child with the consequences that they have decided upon, regardless of whether this makes sense to the child or not. Some teachers argue that the child knows why he is being punished, and they usually view the consequences as being fair, in spite of the child's protests. Defiance, sulkiness, and secret resentment is usually the result of the child not understanding or agreeing with the adult decision. Some teachers argue further that fair punishment is good for the child because he learns to distinguish between right and wrong and learns that wrong behavior does not pay off. They disregard the fact that the child begins to hate authority; he considers that being punished gives him the right to punish too, and the retaliation of children is usually more effective than the punishment of adults. Adults believe that when the child grows up, he will actually be grateful to them for their act of love and concern.

Some teachers are beginning to discover the difference between self-discipline based on freedom with responsibility and imposed obedience to authority based on force, power and fear. During the last decade there has been a decrease in corporal punishment only to be replaced with low grades, humiliation, and other forms of discouragement and disapproval.

Discipline does not have to take the form of punishment. Punishment is what some people use when training fails, or in the place of training. Punishment does not necessarily mean corporal punishment

21

although to many parents it does. It may mean isolation, removal, denial of privileges, etc. Punishment teaches what not to do but fails to teach what to do.

In this chapter, we would like to consider discipline without imposed authority by any individual, but imposed by the individual himself and by that of the group; the development of intelligent self-control rather than blind obedience because of fear.

Discipline, as discussed in this chapter, will relate to the kind of behavior through which the child experiences acceptance by others and consequently greater acceptance of himself. The establishment of self-approval is the strongest form of control.

When thought of in this manner, discipline ceases to be a restriction. As teachers, we should no longer think of discipline in terms of an authority who rules with an iron fist and gives a flat "No," and "Either you finish this work or else. . . ." We need to think of discipline in terms of an authority that permits freedom without license or a "Yes, within certain limits."

Early training in the home has much influence on the child's ability to guide himself. The method used to manage the members of the family is called discipline. Children learn self-discipline through the setting of limits and the approval or disapproval of their parents.

As the child grows older, he is confronted with more situations where discipline is necessary and where some authority is present to guide him. In school, the teacher helps to provide the discipline for studying. Of prime concern is helping the child to develop behavior patterns that are conducive to learning. Letting the child experience the natural consequences of his misbehavior is one method of preserving order. (See "Natural Consequences," p. 80.) Logical consequences or utilizing the reality of the situation rather than personal power can usually exert the necessary pressure to stimulate proper motivation. If the child knows that he will have to face the consequences, he may take fewer chances and disobey fewer rules. However, some children are rebellious and may need persuasion to accept rules.

It is necessary to think of learning experiences that the teacher can use in her class which will help to develop self-discipline. These experiences should be determined by the respective stage of growth of each individual child and the behavior that he needs to develop. The decision as to which experience will be used should be made cooperatively by the child and the teacher. Children need areas of freedom to discover the world, to express their feelings, to develop their own ideas and to test their own self-discipline. These experiences should vary from the relatively simple to the more difficult and complex. They should provide experience in solving problems and should help to establish desired behaviors.

The following example demonstrates a very simple exercise in learning to plan cooperatively within certain prescribed limits:

> At the beginning of the school term, the teacher listed the units to be studied for the year as prescribed by the curriculum department. The children and the teacher discussed what units should be taught first and the order of the other units. Through this process, the children were given the limits within which to make decisions and choices.

In this next example, we can see the more complex experiences which would help a child to grow towards self-discipline:

> In health class we were studying the unit, "Is able to discuss problems and growth changes." The general topic to be dealt with was the realization that people of all ages have emotions, concepts, and intentions. The specific topic under study dealt with *anger*.
>
> The class had decided there were three areas that needed exploration. Consequently three groups were formed to research and report on the three areas, each report to be followed by discussion.
>
> The first group reported on "What makes you angry." A listing was written on the blackboard that was added to and discussed by the entire class.
>
> The second and third groups discussed "For what purpose did you get angry" and "Different ways to overcome angry feelings."
>
> As part of their report, the third group did some role playing. (See "Role Playing," p. 136.)
>
> In the general discussion afterward, such points were brought up as, "Why it is difficult to talk with someone with whom you are angry" and "Why I get mad when my parents don't let me do what I want."

> Teacher and group discuss the amount of work the class will have to cover in Mathematics during the week. The children have the choice to work page by page and hand in the work each day, or they may want to skip around instead of following the pages systematically. Each child is then responsible for completing the assigned chapter, or number of pages at his own pace and according to his own decisions. He may decide to do all of the work in one day, in which case, he has a certain number of minutes each day to use as he decides.
>
> At the end of the week there should be an evaluation by the teacher and the entire class group. Children who, for instance, decide to leave most or all of the work for the last day and then cannot finish may have to accept the logical consequences of doing a

23

definite number of pages each day until such time when they are ready and willing to budget the work themselves and have all work in by the end of the week.

Children often write, direct, and produce their own plays. Usually this is done in the classroom after they have completed their work or during recess. The director choses the actors, and all remain in the classroom, rehearsing, preparing costumes, and so on. These children must then give a report to the class in regard to their accomplishments for the day. Children who act up instead of working on the assignment are first encouraged to help do their part, but if their wrong behavior continues, they are replaced by other children who are interested in being in the play and willing to exercise the self-discipline expected by the group and by the teacher. These children are left in class on their honor. There is nobody there to supervise or discipline them.

THE ROLE OF DISCIPLINE IN THE TEACHING ENVIRONMENT

Discipline in the classroom then means teaching the child a set of inner controls which will provide him with a pattern of behavior that is acceptable to society and which will contribute to his own welfare and progress.

As teachers, it is necessary to take time for training and teaching the child essential skills and habits. If this is not done, then the teacher must spend more time correcting an untrained child. Constant nagging and reminders fail to teach the child, for he looks upon such tactics as criticism and humiliation. It is our job to correct and guide children in developing a sense of responsibility and consideration for other people.

In order for cooperation to take place, the teaching environment should be of a positive, accepting, and nonthreatening nature. It is important for the teacher to remember that growth takes place in one direction when the child is having something *done to* him and in another direction when things are being *done with* him. This type of classroom atmosphere calls for the incorporation of teacher-child planning. Children will approach the educational task with an altogether different attitude when they have been consulted about what they are going to do. They then have a feeling of personal involvement, are committed, and feel responsible for success or failure of the venture. The teacher needs to be willing to share the responsibility of developing plans with the class and give support and approval in carrying out the plans.

In such a climate, the children will recognize the need for limitations that are placed upon them and upon the teacher by the reality of school policies. As youngsters grow up in a society, they have to

24

curb many of their personal desires and impulses because of regulations necessary to group life. Every school has rules and regulations that must be followed. Children are more likely to respect them if they have discussed them and understand them.

Sometimes it is difficult for children to understand the necessity for some school rules or regulations, as is shown in this example:

> One week we had a great deal of snow, which was unusual in our part of the country. All teachers received notices from the principal that we were to read to our classes. The note stated, "The southwest area of the playground has been reserved for snowballing. No snowballing is to be allowed on any other part of the grounds. There is to be no snow brought into the buildings. Offenders will be dealt with."
>
> Upon reading the announcement, there were many audible groans among my sixth grade students. We then discussed the "snowball ruling." At first the students viewed the situation as, "He never lets us have any fun." "We must be living in Russia." After some discussion, the class could understand and accept the ruling. Several of the boys and girls were really relieved as they had been pelted with hard-packed snowballs when entering the building. As the discussion progressed, the class came to realize that it was a "fair" rule. Those who wanted had the privilege of having the fun of snowballing while those who did not want to did not have to protect themselves. (But the wording of the ruling was provocative; it would normally incite the disobedience of the students.)

During group discussion (see "Group Discussions," p. 100), the teacher should explain to the children why she must make certain decisions that affect the entire class such as, which tables in the cafeteria are to be reserved for her class. Through this process the children find out what the teacher considers important, good, trivial, or bad.

Setting limits with children is a form of training in discipline. Training children in the everyday routine of living is basic. Whenever teachers induce children to wash their hands before lunch, to complete their assignments within the allotted time period, to get permission to use another child's property; when they help them to recognize that mowing the lawn is sharing family responsibility, that keeping the bathroom straight is everyone's responsibility, that being ready for school on time is the child's responsibility, and so on, then they are really training in discipline. Discipline in this sense means teaching the child that there are certain rules in life that people live by, and one can expect that the child will become accustomed to these rules and adopt them for his own. The goal that needs to be kept in mind in the daily teaching of children is progress toward self-discipline.

The following example illustrates how a child was able to work directly on self-discipline:

> Mason, a 10-year-old boy, was in a special adjustment room due to his educational deficiency and his behavior pattern. After being in this room for a couple of months, he had become quite cooperative, was interested in learning, and was really a delight.
>
> However, he still had a problem of talking out in class without raising his hand. The teacher invariably found herself answering, even if he didn't raise his hand. She told Mason that, since she was not able to help him with that problem, he would have to take care of it himself. She asked, "What do you suggest?" He said, "Each time I talk out without raising my hand, I will have to leave the room for two minutes and make up my time later." They agreed on this procedure and within a week, Mason was no longer talking out.

Some teachers will say that discussing such issues with children is pointless. "Children should obey without questioning," or "You are teaching them to argue." However, if we want our children to become thinking adults, the problem-solving discussion approach not only teaches them fairness, it also teaches them to consider the alternatives of various issues and situations. Fair-minded teachers who make the basic assumption that children are trustworthy are more likely to teach them to have attitudes of dependability and responsibility. If regulations are to be observed, the child must be stimulated to want to conform. If children agree with the teacher about what they consider to be acceptable behavior and what is out of bounds, and if that teacher's response is consistent, they won't feel that she is being unjust. Children will respond in a positive way to those who are kind, but firm, fair, and consistent in maintaining discipline and order.

The rules for classroom behavior, arrived at through the cooperative efforts of the class, not only give the children an opportunity to increase their understanding of some of the laws of our society, but they also help build respect and obedience for them. Discussing such matters as borrowing personal belongings, using the audio-visual equipment, playing with other children on the playground, table manners in the cafeteria, calling other children names, bicycle rules in general as well as on the school ground, getting help from other classmates, is all part of training in discipline.

One of the best ways to insure that the class works cooperatively is to help the children discover and share mutual interests and concerns. Getting acquainted during the first few days at school helps to prevent hostilities from building and brings the group closer together. When a child knows that his classmates are his friends, that they are interested in him for himself, then he does not have to show off or act up to get attention. Children have vast influence over each other and peer approval or disapproval can play a major role in helping the child behave positively. The teacher who has the cooperation of her class can be effective in most situations, with the children as her allies when isolated cases of misbehavior occur. Quite often, the children themselves will provide the control without the intervention of the teacher.

> One day, Randy was transferred back into my class after being across the hall for a couple of months. He was sitting at his desk humming away and gazing out of the window. Dennis leaned over to him and said, "We work in this room and we don't make noise 'cause it bothers us." Randy looked surprised, stopped his humming, and started to work.

In many of the following chapters we discuss factors that deal largely with the prevention of discipline problems, understanding the child in terms of his goal, his need to have status in the group, his response to encouragement and to natural and logical consequences as compared to punishment. Still, it may happen that in spite of our careful planning we may run into behavioral difficulties with some children.

Here are some of the principles that foster individual growth in discipline and responsibility:

1. The structure of the learning activities should leave room for the child to grow. He needs time to correct mistakes, time to think, and time for understanding to take place.
2. The teaching environment should be of a positive, accepting, non-threatening nature.
3. Children should find that joy, delight, spontaneity, and enthusiasm are associated with their experience.
4. Children need limits to help them develop their own capacities, to curb their impulses, but they also need freedom to explore, to discover, and to use their initiative and imagination.
5. Children and the teacher should plan together.
6. The child needs help in placing himself in relationship to all mankind, and in developing a concern for and an awareness of all mankind.

If children are to become autonomous adults, they must gain independence by being encouraged to find their own solutions, have creative ideas, and independent views as well as independence in carrying out assigned tasks. By so doing, self-management can be

27

integrated into meeting the needs of the child and those of the situation.

The children and teacher should have an inner freedom, the result of positive and free cooperation with one another—the freedom to choose, to be responsible for their choices and their behavior, to say what they are thinking, to have mutual respect and trust for each other, to analyze, and to make decisions different from the pattern of the typical school. Included must be:

1. Responsibility for what you are doing.
2. Respect for yourself and your work.
3. Respect for others and their work.
4. Tolerance for the behavior of others.
5. Responsibility, to influence the behavior of others.
6. Understanding of what is happening around you.
7. Developing a "we" feeling.

THE DO'S AND DON'T'S OF DISCIPLINE

What can a teacher do in order to have the kind of classroom order which is satisfactory to her and to the students? Are these two possible? They are if discipline and order are used as a cooperative enterprise, with understanding on both sides and team spirit. In order to achieve this end, the teacher must know what not to do as well as what she must do in a given situation. Let us consider first what she should *never* do:

1. A preoccupation with one's authority may provoke rather than stifle defiance and resistance to discipline. The teacher should not be concerned with her own prestige.
2. Refrain from nagging and scolding as it may fortify the child's mistaken concept of how to get attention.
3. Do not ask a child to promise anything. Most children will promise to change in order to get out of an uncomfortable situation. It is a sheer waste of time.
4. Do not give rewards for good behavior. The child may then work only in order to get his reward and stop as soon as he has achieved his goal. What's more, this will only strengthen his belief that he must be paid every time he acts civil or makes a contribution.
5. Refrain from finding fault with the child. It may hurt his self-esteem and may discourage him.
6. Avoid double standards, one for the teacher and another for the student. In a democratic atmosphere, everybody must have equal rights. This includes the chewing of gum, swearing, tardiness, unnecessary visiting, and talking with members of the

faculty in class when the children are working, sitting when the class pledges allegiance, checking papers or doing any kind of work that prevents the teacher from looking at the child when he is talking to her.

7. Do not use threats as a method to discipline the child. Although some children may become intimidated and conform for the moment, it has no lasting value since it does not change their basic attitudes.

8. Do not be vindictive; it stirs up resentment and unfriendly feelings.

Let us now consider some of the effective measures that a teacher can use in the disciplinary procedure.

1. Because problem behavior is usually closely related to the child's faulty evaluation of his social position and how he must behave in order to have a place in the class group, the teacher's first concern must be to understand the purpose of his behavior. (See "Goals of Misbehavior," p. 186.) Only then will she be in a position to plan more effectively for this child.

2. Give clear-cut directions for the expected action of the child. Wait until you have the attention of all class members before you proceed in giving directions.

3. Be more concerned with the future behavior of the child than with the one he exhibited in the past. Refrain from reminding the child what he used to be or do.

4. As soon as a child misbehaves and tends to threaten the general atmosphere in the class, give him the choice either to remain in his seat without disturbing others, or leave the classroom.

5. Build on the positive and minimize the negative. There is much good in every child, but if you look *only* for academic achievement, you may never find it.

6. Try to establish a relationship with the child built on trust and mutual respect.

7. Discuss the child's problem at a time when neither of you is emotionally charged, preferably in the regular class discussions.

8. Use natural consequences instead of traditional punishment. The consequences must bear direct relationship to the behavior and must be understood by the child.

9. Be consistent in your decisions. Do not change it arbitrarily just because it suits your purpose at that moment. Inconsistency confuses the child about what is expected of him at a certain procedure.

10. See behavior in its proper perspective. In this way, you will avoid making a serious issue out of trivial incidents.
11. Establish cooperative planning for future goals and the solution of problems.
12. Let children assume greater responsibility for their own behavior and learning. They cannot learn this unless we plan for such learning. Teachers who are afraid to leave the room because of what might happen prevent the children from taking responsibility. Responsibility is taught by giving responsibility. Be prepared for children to act up at first. Such training takes time.
13. Use the class community to express disapproval when a child behaves in an antisocial manner.
14. Treat the child as your social equal.
15. Combine kindness with firmness. The child must always sense that you are his friend, but that you would not accept certain kinds of behavior.
16. At all times, distinguish between the deed and the doer. This permits respect for the child, even when he does something wrong.
17. Guide the individual to assume independence and his own self-direction.
18. Set the limits from the beginning, but work toward mutual understanding, a sense of responsibility, and consideration for others.
19. Admit your mistakes—the children will respect your honesty. Nothing is as pathetic as a defeated authoritarian who does not want to admit his defeat.
20. Mean what you say, but keep your demands simple, and see that they are carried out.
21. Children look to you for help and guidance. Give them this security, but make cooperation and eventual self-control the goal.
22. Keep in mind your long-term goal: an independent responsible adult.
23. Children need direction and guidance until they can learn to direct themselves.
24. Close an incident quickly and revive good spirits. Let children know that mistakes are corrected and then forgotten.
25. Commend a child when his behavior in a situation shows improvement.
26. Work cooperatively with the children to develop a procedure for dealing with infractions of the rules.
27. "Do unto others as you would have them do unto you."

As teachers, we need to exercise kindness but also firmness so that our children will know what to expect from us; thus mutual respect between students and teachers will be the result of the democratic educational process. In this way the child will be able to project the inner order that exists in him out into his environment and will be able to make order in his own way, find his own place, and develop self-discipline.

When the students understand what is expected of them, when they have been accepted and respected as equal partners, when the teachers no longer feel threatened, then and only then, are we ready to move into the process of learning in its true sense.

Lack of respect for order is one of the most common complaints of teachers today. Usually, the complaint goes like this: "I just do not know what to do. I spend half of my time trying to keep order in the room. It seems like all I do is to discipline the kids and try to keep order."

Let us now look at the term order. It has many meanings and we often get confused as to what order should mean in the classroom. Too often it means sitting in nice neat rows, feet flat on the floor, eyes straight ahead, no talking or working in groups, no moving around the room, and most of all—silence. It may also mean lining up and marching down the hall to the restrooms, to the cafeteria, or to the gym. Order may also mean that children do not ask questions, that they only do their assignment and do not use their creativeness, initiative, or curiosity. Their classroom is immaculate, every book is in its right place, the art work is arranged in neat rows across the bulletin board with each design the exact replica of the one next to it.

It would be more meaningful if we could substitute the word *orderly* for the word order. Order usually means rigidity. An orderly room could be one in which there is flexibility and also a proper arrangement or sequence of things to do such as keeping the floor free from litter, arranging a variety of art works in an artistic fashion, grouping the children in small groups and working on unit projects. In such a room, there is an animated look on the children's faces and they are free to move about and explore their environment. Chairs are shifted from one activity to the next, the children work together and talk quietly about their project—there is evidence of teacher-pupil planning and cooperation.

It is the responsibility of the teacher to set up a schedule in which the children can function; to establish and maintain a daily routine and let the children fall into line. This sets the basis for self-discipline, the guidelines one must live by in adult life.

A child needs definite limits in order to develop a sense of security

31

and discipline. Order cannot be maintained by pressure from without in the form of punishment, but only by stimulation from within.

Learning can and does take place in a classroom where discipline and orderliness prevail.

If an individual is to become a useful person, he must adapt himself to some orderly pattern of living, learn to think and act in line with social regulations, adjust to his environment, and develop a sense of responsibility. Individuals cannot live with other persons unless they are guided by certain rules and regulations necessary for happy peaceful living. It is this process that we call discipline.

In an autocratic society, freedom and order are mutually exclusive. Order means doing as you are told and there is no freedom of self-determination. In a democratic society, freedom and order are necessarily complementary; one cannot exist without the other. Freedom alone leads to anarchy, anyone can do what he wants. Each one has to restrain his own freedom to permit optimum freedom for everybody else. Without order there can be no freedom, and without freedom there can be no order in a democratic setting because imposed order is rejected.

We need to help young people learn to live successfully in a changing world which involves them in many different kinds of human relationships. They must be able to set up a pattern for living within a reliable frame of reference. This frame of reference must lead beyond absorbing subject matter into developing attitudes, establishing values, realizing the extent of one's own freedom and self-determination, and accepting responsibility. A set of rules which guarantees success or excludes conflict cannot be devised, so each child will have to make decisions according to his own perception of himself and others.

2
diagnostic techniques

THE CHILD'S PRIVATE LOGIC

One may question our efforts to instruct teachers in the use of psychological methods. Such doubts are justified as long as teachers are exposed to psychological explanations that go beyond their training and their abilities. On the basis of our experience, however, we feel that the kind of psychology which we recommend can be utilized by teachers. We do not intend to make psychotherapists or group therapists out of them, but we know that some of the principles developed in these two areas can be applied by teachers without too much additional training. At the present time, training in this area is almost entirely absent on the undergraduate level. Consequently, teachers cannot understand children and therefore do not know what to do with them when they disturb or refuse to apply themselves. It is our intention to provide teachers with psychological sensitivity so that they may understand the motives of children and learn the means by which to improve them.

Many theories exist about the psychological significance of a child's behavior. For us, behavior is the result of cognitive processes, of ideas, intentions, expectations, and rationalizations. Every teacher can learn this kind of psychology. Some may do it quicker than others —some may be more perceptive than others—but all can improve their ability to understand a child.

Nobody is fully aware why he behaves as he does. Only a few of our intentions reach the conscious level. When you ask a child why he did something wrong, he simply doesn't know. Parents and teachers often become furious when the child openly responds to their question of why he did it, with "I don't know," which is actually the truth. If the child gives an explanation, it is usually a rationalization; the child is actually not aware of his own motive. The trained teacher can help him to become aware. When the goal of his disturbance is disclosed to him, the child usually responds with a *recognition reflex.*[1] Not only is it important for diagnostic purposes to solicit the recognition reflex; such confrontation with his goals can be the first step toward a change. This cannot be accomplished when one tells the child what he *is*—lazy, aggressive, or disturbing. Even if that were correct, it does not mean anything for the child. It is different when he is confronted with his goals, with his intentions. Then alternatives appear, because he *can* decide whether he wants to continue or not. All improvements and corrections imply helping the child to see alternatives. But to do so, he must first become aware of what he intends to do. It is usually quite dramatic to see how children respond to their new insight. In many cases they feel as if a big burden was taken off their shoulders. Since he never understood the purpose of his actions, and since adults did not understand him and regaled him with moral exhortations and condemnation, the child himself became convinced that he was bad. He does not want to be bad, but he sees no alternative. He is helped to become aware that he is not bad; that he had merely decided to be bad. Such insight makes all the difference for the child's self-evaluation. It also helps the adult, and for the first time, understanding replaces recrimination.

Since all intentions and goals remain below the conscious level, and because they all are logical, we can speak of a "private logic,"

---

[1]The recognition reflex is a peculiar smile and glint in the eyes indicating that the child has suddenly become aware of his goal, and is beginning to understand why he is acting in a certain way.

as Adler called it. Our actions do not depend on what we consciously know and want, but on our hidden reasons and goals. This does not mean that they are "deep down" in the Unconscious as Freud suggested. The unconscious processes are not due to repressions. They merely mean that one can keep full awareness and consciousness only for a few focal points that one wants and needs to know fully. If we were constantly aware of everything we think and intend, we could not devote much time and energy to what should be done. One can either be an observer or an actor. When a child learns to walk he has to consciously try to move his legs in an appropriate way so as not to fall down. But once he has learned to walk, he does not need to watch his legs anymore and can devote his attention to other things. Let us repeat: conscious awareness as well as memory function on an economic principle. We only know fully what we need to know or want to know at a given moment. For the rest, we are not aware. But this unawareness is just below the surface. Anyone trained in psychological disclosures can bring into the open what goes on in a person.

The knowledge and skill necessary to elicit such revelations may appear to be too great an assignment for a teacher. Many believe it would take considerable advanced studies, far beyond the courses which a teacher has to take. In fact, such "advanced" techniques can be taught on the undergraduate level. As we see it, all student teachers not only can but should be exposed to psychological sensitivity; without it they never will be capable of understanding children and their motivation, nor know how to change them. At the present time, teachers hardly learn a practical psychology which they can apply in the classroom.

The teacher must learn to recognize the immediate goals of the child. This requires a certain skill and sensitivity, but this can be acquired.

Naturally, this would also require that the instructors in teachers' seminars have the skills and ability to impart them to their students. The reason why so few institutions teach this kind of educational psychology is that we have not enough instructors trained in these methods.

The first step in the development of diagnostic skills is the ability of the teacher to observe a child's behavior and its consquences. The behavior reveals its purpose. Even in situations of minimal activity the child clearly expresses his intentions.

Working with the staff of a kindergarten we arranged the following set-up: The teachers sat in a circle, and each child as he came in the room was asked to sit in a chair in the middle of the circle. The

teachers had been told to remain completely quiet and to observe the child and then describe his goals. One child sat down quietly and patiently, wondering what was going on but without showing any objection. He was a well-adjusted child, willing to play the game, although he did not understand it. This was different with the child who wanted special attention. He pleaded for help and sympathy through his glances. The defiant child was angry, while the revengeful child could have killed with his eyes. And the discouraged child sat with lowered head.

If such minimal opportunities to act are so revealing, how much more are the numerous transactions which the teacher can observe in every classroom? She merely has to learn how to observe and how to interpret. At the present time, we find teacher observations written in the accumulative records, but these observations are only descriptions of the child's behavior without any reference to its meaning and purpose.

Sometimes the diagnosis may not be easy because the significance of a certain act may not be obvious. Then the teacher can verify her diagnostic impression by the reaction of the child to her corrective effort. (We call it the *corrective feedback*.) Let us imagine one of the many classroom disturbances which are found in almost any classroom, such as, the child talking to his neighbor, getting out of his seat, disturbing other children, etc. Before the teacher is able to understand these occurrences, she has first to change her thinking about the cause of such behavior. As long as she does not realize that the child's disturbance is for her benefit, as long as she attributes it to restlessness, short-interest span, surplus energy, or whatever such explanations may be, she will not understand the purpose of the child's disturbance. It will become obvious when she tries to correct him. If his purpose was to get attention, he will stop his disturbance when she corrects him—but not for long. If the child tries to demonstrate his power to do as he pleases, then he will respond to her correction by increasing his disturbance, which then usually gets the teacher more deeply involved in a power struggle.

The goals of the children in the following examples are clear:

> One of the authors gave a demonstration of a group discussion with children, 9 to 10 years old. It took place in a room with a one-way mirror. Students and parents were watching on the other side. The children were not supposed to know that they were being observed, but somehow they found out. Somebody had told them that they were being televised, and that people all over the country were watching them.
>
> As the door opened to let the children in, Calvin pushed the two

girls in front of him and ran ahead of them. He ran up to the window, stuck his tongue out, and shouted, "Is everyone watching? That's me, Calvin." He continued making faces and shouting until Sol and Gregory pulled him away. He sat down, but kept waving his hands and laughing.

We may assume that Calvin wants attention, which falls under active-destructive behavior. (See p. 20.)

Sol kept reminding him to be quiet, that what he was doing was not nice. Sol then looked at the group leader with expectation that she do something to stop Calvin.

The behavior of Sol, who wants to please and do the expected thing, may be called active-constructive behavior.

Gregory sat down close to the leader, putting his finger to his lips, he kept saying, "Sh, sh."

He too can be classified as active-constructive.

Marjorie who was first in line before Calvin pushed her out, remained at the door, allowing all children to go ahead of her. She remained standing there even after all children were seated.

Marjorie's behavior appears to be discouraged, having as its goal assumed disability.

Andy ran from chair to chair, trying to find the one in which he could best be seen by the invisible camera. He could find no chair to please him, and went back to the door where Marjorie was still standing. His facial expression showed anger. At one point, he opened the door, and it looked like he was going to leave altogether, but he changed his mind, closed the door, and remained standing there.

Andy wanted his own way and would probably enter into a power contest if he couldn't get it.

Ruth sat down very demurely, pulled down her dress and kept patting her hair, while staring at the window.

Ruth seems to be adequate to the situation, therefore, pursues no goal of misbehavior.

Jill sat down on one side of the leader, covered her face with both hands, and said, "I don't want to be seen on T.V."

We may assume that Jill was bidding for attention, but we are not certain.

Carol who sat next to Jill tried to pry Jill's hands away from her face. Both of them were very persistent and kept up this struggle for some time. Finally, Jill won the battle.

We are more sure now that Jill's behavior was, as was Carol's, a bid for attention. The two cooperated in creating some disturbance in order to get everyone to look at them, and to involve the group leader who, normally, would have stopped them. Both these girls would fall under active-destructive.

At this point, Calvin ran back to the window, and, putting his thumbs into his ears and wiggling his hands, shouted, "Can you see me? I am Calvin!" Gregory was right after him, trying to pull him away.

Our first impression of Calvin's goal is confirmed.

Beatrice, who was sitting very quietly up till now, got up to help Gregory pull Calvin away from the window, pleading with him not to disturb the group because the discussion would never get started.

Beatrice appeared to be a "good" girl. One cannot say from this little evidence how she uses her goodness; whether she uses it with a sense of responsibility or for showing how good she is in comparison with the others. In the latter case, she too is bidding for attention (active-constructive).

Vivian and Sonia were humming and tapping their pencil in rhythm.

Teacher: Vivian, are you starting this again? I have asked you a dozen times today to stop this nonsense of humming and tapping. Don't you realize that it is disturbing to the others, or don't you care? Honestly, how can anyone be so inconsiderate?

Vivian: *(Smiling to herself, stopped humming and tapping.)*

Teacher: Sonia, I told you to stop. Don't force me to take drastic measures.

Sonia: *(Continuing to tap.)*

Teacher: *(yelling)* Sonia, stop this instant. Do you hear me? I won't put up with this another moment. *(Teacher yanks the pencil out of her hand. Sonia quickly finds another pencil in her desk and starts tapping again.)*

Teacher: That does it. Let's go down to the office, Sonia. Come on! *(Sonia doesn't move.)* I said, let's go to the office. If you don't come voluntarily, I'll have to pull you there, and, by golly, I'll do it. Are you coming or no?

> *(Sonia keeps tapping but doesn't make a move to get up. The teacher grabs her arm and tries to pull her out of her seat.)*
>
> Sonia: Ouch, you're hurting me. Let go, I say.
>
> *(Teacher keeps pulling. Sonia bites the teacher in the arm, and the latter lets go.)*
>
> Teacher: You little devil, you. You won't get away with this, not if I have to fight City Hall. We'll see what Mr. Mankiewitz has to say to this. *(The teacher runs out of the classroom. Minutes later she returns with the principal.)*

Both girls misbehaved in the same way; but the reaction of the teachers was quite different, indicating the different goals of the girls. Vivian just annoyed the teacher. She wanted attention, and she got it, naturally. She responded to the teacher in the characteristic way of a child who wants attention. As soon as she got it, she was satisfied and stopped her disturbing behavior.

The situation was quite different with Sonia. From the way she misbehaved and from the reaction of the teacher, one can recognize her goal: to get the teacher involved in a power conflict. Outwardly, it seems that the teacher won the battle. She got the principal on her side. But nobody was able to stop the girl from misbehaving. On the contrary, every step the teacher took escalated the warfare.

The most reliable clue to a correct diagnosis of the child's goal is the impulsive, immediate reaction of the adult. If he feels annoyed, telling the child to stop what he is doing or to do something for himself, then it is probable that the child merely made a bid for attention. When the teacher feels threatened in her authority, trying to show the child that he cannot do that to her, she is only doing what the child wanted her to do. When the teacher feels deeply hurt by a child's action, the child obviously wanted to hurt her. And when she feels like throwing up her arms in despair she does what the child wanted her to do, to leave him alone.

We can see that the adult's reaction reflects the child's goal and can, therefore, be used for diagnostic purposes. Unfortunately, these reactions are used in an attempt to correct him. This is the worst approach an adult can take, because such reactions only reconfirm and reinforce the child's mistaken goals. Before a teacher can effectively deal with a disturbing child, she has to realize her own role in promoting his behavior.

> A young boy could not sit still. He had a "short interest span" and constantly disturbed the group. In counseling with the child and his family, we succeeded in bringing about his adjustment, freeing him from his sense of failure and his consequent acts of disturbance

which always got him a great amount of attention. The teacher admitted the change in the boy. He stopped disturbing her, but only for the first three periods a day. Then he fell back into his old pattern. The teacher assumed that three periods were the maximum for him to sit quietly; the rest was too much for him. Such a consideration is only possible when the teacher fails to realize the purpose of the disturbance. Why should the child stop using it but only for a limited time of the day? It became quite clear that he merely obliged the teacher. *She* did not expect him to be able to sit quietly for more than three periods. There was a mutual agreement between child and adult, and both acted accordingly.

In many cases, when the teacher can catch herself succumbing to the child's goal, the child may give it up immediately if he sees that the jig is up. This is more frequent with younger than with older children. It takes more effort to help the older child change his goals. The first step is always the same: for the teacher to extricate herself from the provocation. That may be easier with the less provocative child who only tries to fight with a child, many teachers find it extremely distasteful not to respond to the defiance of a power-drunk child. They feel obliged to fight it out with him, although experience should have shown them that in the end the child always continues with defiance. The teacher is afraid for her prestige if she does not try to put the child in his place, regardless of how unsuccessful she may be in her effort. She does not know that nothing is as pathetic as a defeated authority who does not want to admit defeat. The teacher only gains status when she openly admits her inability to force the child into submission. Then she can use all the many other ways available to her to influence him, both by direct approaches and, even more effectively, through the use of group approaches. Ways to cope effectively with disturbing children will be discussed more fully later. At this point, we merely wish to indicate the means by which the teacher can learn to understand the child and his behavior.

With young children, the recognition of the child's immediate goals is all the teacher needs to know; they represent the child's private logic. When she can confront him with his goals,[2] he will usually show the recognition reflex. This will confirm her guess, and mark the beginning as the beginning of a reorientation, of looking for different means to find his place. One should never blame the child for his goals, nor refer to them during regular activities. Goals should be discussed only at the proper time, either in a personal talk, or in

[2]See p. 41.

the weekly group discussion. There is a way which has been found most effective in the process of confrontation. One first asks the child why he misbehaves. We know that the child does not know the reason, and, therefore, will either say he doesn't know or give a rationalization. But this question is necessary as a preparation for the next question: "May I tell you what I think?" And then, after the child agrees, one has to present the goal as a hypothesis. "Could it be that . . ." Then follows the reference to the specific goal: ". . . to keep the teacher busy with you; to show her that you can do what you want and she can't stop you; to punish and hurt her because of what she did to you; to be left alone because you cannot do anything." The recognition reflex may not come immediately, because the child may have to think it over first. Therefore, one has to wait for his reaction. It is most dramatic to watch the child, how he first considers it, and then the corners of his mouth begin to expand in a knowing smile and a gleam appears in his eyes. He begins to recognize what he was up to.

A few children fail to show the recognition reflex. They are the poker-faced youngsters who do not want to reveal anything that goes on in their minds, who do not want to reveal themselves. However, even they can eventually be brought to the recognition and acknowledgment of their goal if one finds the one area where they feel proud for doing something wrong.

> A little boy was a liar. When he was asked why he lied, he denied lying. So we proceeded to ask him whether we could tell him the reason we thought he had for lying. He was furious, he had already said he did not lie. How can we then confront him with his goal? In such cases one has to be unorthodox. The main point is to make him reveal his goal. So we asked him whether he knew anybody who could lie better than he. And with a grin he shouted, "No, of course not!" Then he was ready to respond to his power and his pride in defeating all adults.

Recognizing the four goals in their simplicity, and yet in their variety of manifestations makes it easy for the teacher to diagnose a child's motivation. However, it takes experience and training to be sure about one's diagnostic impression. One hint may facilitate the proper diagnosis: It is generally true that the more violent the interaction between teacher and child is, the greater the warfare. In the course of progression, the goal of attention switches to that of power, and eventually to revenge. The hostility increases on both sides, in the child as well as in the adult. The beginner may be inclined to consider all disturbances as a means of getting attention. Naturally, all disturbing behavior succeeds in getting the teacher involved;

yet, one must distinguish the specific intention of the child. If the teacher feels defeated, he wanted to show his power; if a teacher feels hurt, the child was seeking revenge, and if the teacher gives up in despair, the child wanted to be left alone. Only if she merely feels annoyed can she assume that the child wanted her attention.

A mother brought her 4-year-old boy who had never caused any serious trouble. Her sister had given birth to a little girl, and whenever the boy came to visit them, he pinched and scratched the baby. The hostility implied in such action would suggest revenge. Perhaps the boy felt dethroned—he was the only grandchild before—and in his jealousy he tried to hurt the adults for their betrayal, and he could achieve that by hurting the baby. But when the boy entered the room, after the mother had stated her case, it became obvious from his demeanor that he did not feel neglected, nor unhappy. He moved with the poise of a child who is sure of being loved. Nevertheless, in discussing his behavior, we suggested that perhaps he wanted to show that he can do what he wants and nobody is going to stop him, power? He flatly denied this. What else could it be? It obviously was not Goal Four, since he was very active and not at all downhearted. The only goal remaining was attention. Could it be that he wanted to be noticed and be the center of attention when he pinches his little girl cousin? He beamed all over his face. "Oh yes, my mother is telling everybody what I am doing!" If we had asked the mother how she reacted to the boy's behavior, we would have been led to the right diagnosis, since she responded to the child's action by being amused.

The recognition reflex and the adult's reaction are still the best guide to an understanding of the child's goal. But this is only true for the young child. While each of the four goals are observable at any age level, during adolescence many others lend themselves as a means to find a place in the peer group. Some may be developed in defiance of adults' demands. Teenagers like to show their independence by whatever behavior adults object to and cannot stand, in dress, language, favorite music. More serious offenses become means to find antiadult excitement and pleasure as in drugs, drag races, etc. In order to understand youth, one can no longer rely on the four goals exclusively, as observed in young children. Counselors and principals have to become familiar with the student's private logic, and they in turn can help the youngster's teachers to develop the same skill and sensitivity. Considering the many hours of study which student teachers put in without any tangible benefit to their ability in dealing with children, all teachers should spend a small part of their time in acquiring these necessary skills. It is not sufficient that teachers learn merely how to teach subject matter; they have to learn how to teach children. While the form of training and of practice that we propose may constitute an almost revolutionary change in our high schools, it seems to be mandatory if we want to avoid increasing rates of failure and dropouts in our high school population, not to mention the alarming increase of drug users.

What should one know about a student's motivation? There are first his immediate goals, based on his attitude to parent and teacher and to society. Behind every action is a hidden reason which the student generally does not know himself. In the group discussion without which no school system can function effectively, the teacher has a chance to explore the real reasons for a student's behavior. While adults often find it difficult or even objectionable to delve into the attitudes, intentions, and goals of the students, the benefit of such training is tremendous. Some teachers, out of empathy and a general understanding of youngsters, can sense what's going on. But every teacher should and could learn such understanding.

The technique which we suggest can be learned without any hazard. It can be applied both in a private interview with the student as well as in a group discussion. Why did Johnny say that or do something peculiar? Now all can guess. Guessing as a method of investigation has proven its value and its appropriateness. Many are made to believe that making a wrong guess is more detrimental and damaging than making no guess at all. We cannot subscribe to this rule. If one makes a wrong guess, one can always correct it. But if one makes no guess, one remains blind and cannot do anything. Furthermore, our proposed form of guessing cannot possibly do any harm. If one tries to guess what is going on in a person's mind while he does or says something, his reaction is absolutely reliable. If the guess is wrong, the person says so. If he says, "Maybe there is something to it," then one has come close. And if one can put into words what the person has thought, then he compulsively will agree. What is more important, at this moment the youngster has a feeling of being understood. He loses his defensiveness. Regardless of how defiant and hostile he may have been before, he suddenly changes his attitude and becomes cooperative. One has to see that to believe it. Every teacher can learn to do it, as part of her teaching assignment and not as an endeavor to become a psychotherapist. Of course, all these approaches have to be limited to the occasion of group discussion or individual interviews, and never to the regular class hours. It is not true that a little psychological knowledge is worse than none. The danger may only lie in its misuse, that is as conversation or accusation. But every little bit of psychological insight can be useful. To the many who still are worried about doing some harm in trying to apply

43

psychology, we can only say that it is probably difficult for them to do any more harm than they do right now when they do not understand children.

What are typical motivations which the child has when he misbehaves? In many cases, he merely tries to show how smart he is. He either feels like a victim or a hero or he feels entitled to do as he pleases. We have seen the deep impact which such acknowledgement on the part of the peers can have on a very disturbed and disturbing child. He feels understood and realizes that it is he who decides and, therefore, it is he who can change his plans.

Training in these skills should be deliberate, either on the undergraduate level, or in workshops and discussion groups for teachers, preferably with the school counselors and the principal. If none of these are possible, a resourceful teacher can present his ideas to the students and let them all work on the problem of how to understand each other.

There is another approach available for an understanding of the child's personality, not merely his immediate goals. Alfred Adler provided us with a technique to understand the whole personality with a simple investigation.

In his formative years within the family, each child develops, by trial and error, certain ideas about himself, about others and about the possibility of finding a place for himself, first in his family and then in life in general. Very definite convictions are usually established within the first three to four years of the child's life. Neither he nor the people around him are aware of the convictions which he has formed and of the means which he has chosen to put them into practice. All his actions and attitudes are only facets of his general style of life, based on his central evaluation of himself and his abilities. Generally, dangers and disappointments play an important part in the formation of the life style that includes a scheme of action by which the child hopes to avoid future humiliation, setting up a fictitious goal of assumed security. The goals are fictitious, because it is not true that only under specific conditions can he be worthwhile and have a place. It is our neurotic culture which denies anyone the feeling of being worthwhile and belonging as he is, regardless of his failures or achievements; this insecurity drives people to set up a fictitious goal of assumed security. For example, a child who feels endangered by the arrival of a younger sibling may consider himself worthwhile when he can keep ahead and be the first. On the other hand, a youngest child who succeeded in compensating for his weakness and smallness by putting the older and stronger members of the family into his service, may think that throughout the rest of his life he can have a place only through the support, assistance, and protection of others. One child may think that only through pleasing can he get anywhere, while the other may rely on fighting as his way of securing a place for himself. It is obvious that no principle can be sufficient. It certainly is nice when a girl tries to find her place through pleasing. But if that is her basic principle in life, she will be utterly unable to function if she cannot please and then becomes obnoxious in her despair.

One can understand a person's style of life when one recognizes his relationship with the other members of the family in his particular family constellation. The family constellation does not force a child to behave in a certain manner; it merely indicates how he arrived at his convictions. He is not the victim of the others, since he very early participates actively in shaping his relationships with them. The most important person in the development of his personality is the sibling who is most different from him. We will discuss the method of analyzing the family constellation.

THE FAMILY CONSTELLATION

The relationships that the child has within the family contribute greatly to his personality development and to his transactions in the world outside the family. In the family, each child develops his frame of reference through which he perceives, interprets, and evaluates the world. The knowledge, habits, and skills which he acquires in the home determine his capacity for dealing successfully with all life situations. We shall concern ourselves here with what happens to the child in the family, the opportunities and the barriers, the challenges and expectations which are influenced by his position of birth and by his individual relationships with all other members of the family. This insight can aid the parent or adult in understanding the child's goals and convictions.

Personality and character traits are expressions of movement within the family group; they indicate the means by which a child tries to find his place within the family. They cannot be fully explained by either heredity, psychosexual development, past traumatic experiences, or other environmental stimulations. The concept of the family constellation as a dynamic force affecting the child's development must be understood as the result, not so much of factors which converge on the child, but of his own interactions. He influences the group and the other members of the family as much as he is influenced by them, and in many regards, even more, because his own concept forces them to treat him the way he expects to be treated. Each child, in his early relationships to other members of the family, establishes his own approaches to others in his effort to gain a place in the group. All his strivings are directed towards achieving or maintaining a feeling of security, a sense of belonging and certainty that the difficulties of life will be overcome and that he will emerge safely and victoriously. He cultivates those qualities by which he hopes to achieve significance or even a degree of power and superiority in the family constellation.

Human beings often react differently to the same situation. No two children born into the same family grow up in the same situation. The family environment that surrounds each individual child varies. The environment of each child within the same family may be different for several reasons.

With the birth of each child the situation changes. The parents may become older and more experienced, or more discouraged. During the formative years of each child, the financial situation of the family may have changed, the parents may have moved to another neighborhood or city or even country, their marital status may have changed. These and other possibilities may affect one or the other child: a sickly or crippled child, a child born just before or after the death of another, an only boy among girls, an only girl among boys, some obvious physical characteristic, an older person living in the home, or the favoritism of the parents toward a child—all these may have a profound effect on the child's environment. The dangers of favoritism can hardly be too dramatically put.

In the life-pattern of every child, there is the imprint of his position in the family with its definite characteristics. It is upon this one fact —the child's subjective impression of his place in the family constellation—that much of his future attitude towards life depends.

The only child has a decidedly difficult start in life as he spends his entire childhood among persons who are bigger and more proficient. He may try to develop skills that will gain the approval of adults or he may solicit their sympathy by being shy, timid, or helpless.

Usually, he is a pampered child; if he is a boy he may develop a mother complex. He may consider his father as his rival and become convinced that he never will be able to be as strong or masculine as his father. He usually enjoys his position as the center of interest, and often is interested only in himself. He has few chances to gain things by his own effort; he depends on others doing things for or to him, and often succeeds in having his own way by playing mother against father; he may provoke father to abuse him so that mother comes to his rescue. If his requests to have his own way are not granted, he may feel unfairly treated and refuse to cooperate.

The first child has a precarious position in life. Being the oldest should entitle him to the favored spot, and frequently does. However, he may become discouraged upon the birth of the second child, and refuse to accept responsibility. He had been an only child for a period of time and has therefore been the center of interest. He may believe that he has to be first—in the sense of gaining and holding superiority over the next children. As a dethroned child with the birth of the second child, he may feel unloved and neglected. At first, he usually strives to keep or to regain his mother's attention by positive deeds. When this fails, he quite often switches to the useless side and may become obnoxious. If his mother fights back, the child may become a problem child. If he does not succeed in developing a good, competent behavior pattern, he may become extremely discouraged. He sometimes strives to protect and help the baby in his struggle to keep the upper hand. Sometimes he may go to the other extreme and express death wishes or hate directed toward the second child.

If the first child is a boy followed by a sister, their personal conflict may become a pattern of sexual discord. Girls usually try to be good, while boys capitalize on the assumption that "boys are boys" and one should not expect or demand too much of them. Or a boy tries to assert himself if there is a preference for boys in the family and may take advantage of his "masculinity."

The second child has a somewhat uncomfortable position in life and usually takes a steam engine attitude, trying to catch up with the child in front and feeling as though he is under constant pressure. He never has his parents' undivided attention. There is always another child in front of him who is more advanced. He may feel that the first child cannot be beaten, which defeats his claim for equality. The first and second child are usually the opposite in character, temperament, and interests. Where one succeeds, the other gives up, and where one has a weakness, the other one may develop strength. When a third child is born the second child becomes a middle child.

The middle child of three has an uncertain place in the family group and may feel neglected. He discovers that he does not have the privileges of the youngest nor the rights of an older child. Therefore, he may feel unloved and abused, become a "squeezed" child and believe that people are unfair to him. He may become extremely discouraged and more prone to become a problem child, or he may push the other two down and elevate himself over them. This is particularly frequent when the middle child is a girl and the other two are boys. After all, girls have to be good and boys are boys!

The youngest child has quite a special place in the family constellation. He may become the most successful, or he may become discouraged and feel inferior. He is often like an only child, usually has things done for him—decisions made, and responsibility taken. He often is spoiled by the whole family. He finds himself in a special position being the smallest, the weakest, or the most admired. He may even become the boss in the family. He either attempts to excel his brothers and sisters or evades the direct struggle for superiority. He may retain the baby role and place others in his service.

In large families, we find groups of the oldest, the middle, or groups of the youngest in characteristic relationships. As each member strives for his own place within the group, the competing opponents watch each other carefully to see the ways and means by which each succeeds or fails. Competition between two members of the family is always expressed through differences in character, temperament, interests, and abilities. Conversely, the similarity of characteristics always indicates alliances. Sometimes, the two strongest competitors show no sign of open rivalry, but rather present a close-knit pair. Nevertheless, their competitive striving is expressed in personality differences. One may be the leader, the active and powerful protector, while the other may lean and get support by weakness and frailty. There are cases where strong competition does not prevent a mutual agreement, but rather permits each competitor to feel secure in his personal method of compensatory striving.

If there are quite a number of years between the birth of children, each child will have some of the characteristics of an only child. Perhaps there will be two families—one set of children, then a space of years, then another set. Whatever combination may first exist, with the space of years the situation changes and shifts, but basically the above characteristics remain the same.

The development of an only girl among boys or of an only boy among girls presents a ticklish problem. Both usually tend to go to extremes, either in a feminine direction or a masculine role. In most cases, both feel isolated and have mixed emotions. Whichever role seems to be the most advantageous will be the one adopted.

Every deficient development is caused by early discouragement and lack of cooperation in the family. If we look around at our social relationships and ask why rivalry and competition is so rampant, then we must recognize that people everywhere are pursuing the goal of being conqueror, of being superior and surpassing others. This goal begins in early childhood, in the rivalries and competitive striving of children who have not felt themselves an equal part of their whole family.

From the moment of birth the child acts, thinks, and feels in response to his world in accordance with how he experiences or perceives it, and the way in which he experiences or perceives his world is to him reality. What actually happens to the individual is not as important as how he interprets it. With this in mind, we must remember that it is not the position in the family sequence that affects his development, but rather the situation as the child interprets it.

EARLY RECOLLECTIONS

Once we know the child's position in the family, we can confirm our guess about his outlook on life through his early recollections. One remembers from the abundance of childhood experiences only those which fit into one's outlook on life. The early recollections are highly reliable, but their collection and interpretation require some skill. The teacher can have access to early recollections through innumerable means, through written assignments, personal conversations, or group discussions.

Although it is essential for everyone dealing with children to have the skill to recognize the form of the family constellation in which the child grew up, an extensive knowledge about the diagnosis of early recollections is not essential. Here we can clearly see delineation in the use of psychological means. Which techniques are constructive and permissible and which are not? Once the teacher recognizes the family constellation of the student, she can, in class discussions, bring this knowledge to the attention of the student. As a matter of fact, the discussion of goals and relationships at home could and should be part of regular classroom discussions. Such discussions yield psychological knowledge which the teacher can use for explanation of student behavior. Each child can benefit from learning more about himself in this way, and will learn to understand others as he recognizes similar trends and approaches in the behavior of his peers.

The teacher can make quite different use of early recollections. To recognize their diagnostic significance, however, more study is required. Therefore, interpretations of early recollections should be reserved to the counselor or therapist. If the teacher should not be encouraged to interpret early recollections, what benefit does she then derive from knowing them? This is the crucial point. The teacher can gain some insight about a child's outlook on life through his early recollections. Some teachers will be successful in perceiving the pattern of early recollections and their symbolic meaning about life as the child sees it. Others will barely get an impression. As long as the teacher does not discuss her impression with the student, her insights, be they great or limited, even be they right or wrong, cannot do any harm, but only some good. Allowing children to relate experience from their early childhood is interesting for all. One gets a glimpse of the personality of each child. Children love to write about their early experiences in life too. But the teacher must refrain from attempts at verbal interpretation herself and must also discourage the students from making them.

Here are some points to keep in mind: It is not important that a certain event actually took place in a child's past. It is only important that the child remembers it. This indicates how he looks at life and himself. It is often significant when a movement, up or down, is remembered. It usually indicates the benefits of being high and the dangers of being low. Usually, unpleasant recollections indicate the dangers of life to be avoided, and the pleasant, usually found in idealists, indicate how life could be beautiful, "if only. . . ." A teacher who lets these recollections speak to her may eventually develop considerable sensitivity to their true meaning.

As was stated before, recollections become important with older children, teenagers, and also with adults. The trained psychologist can clearly recognize the person's life style, his basic attitude toward life. This competence is naturally not expected of the teacher. But, within her limitations, she still can benefit from early recollections provided to her by the students. Here are a few characteristic examples:

Christine is a pretty girl of 9. She is always dressed immaculately. Her long hair usually hangs loosely; she likes to have other children play with it. She carries a mirror with her which she takes out ever so often and looks at herself in. She daydreams a lot, rarely hearing what the teacher is saying. She is the youngest child of three, having two older brothers. Her brother next to her, two years older, is excellent in sports, very alert and a good student. He is father's favorite child.

Recollections: I remember when I was very little, maybe 3, when my aunt came to visit us. I was dressed in a pink dress which had three red roses in front, and I looked very pretty in it. And my aunt, Aunt Nancy was her name, brought me a doll with real blond hair. I kissed it over and over because it was so pretty. Then I had an accident because I couldn't stop playing, and I didn't want to stop and go to the bathroom. Then my father spanked me and took the doll away. I cried and cried. Then my father gave me the doll back and carried me to bed.

I remember when I was a little girl, we went all to church on Sunday, and I wore my best white dress and white shoes and a white hat with flowers. My brother John and my father walked in front of me, and my mother walked with me in the back. Then a car came by and splashed my dress, and I cried so much and I didn't want to go to church. My mother told me not to cry, because I still looked nice, and then she picked me up and carried me in.

50

Interpretation: Here you have a girl who obviously is very much concerned with how she looks because this seems to be her main way of finding her place in the group—to be pretty and be admired. As a youngest child, she depends on others for her place, not only through her good looks, but—as the recollections indicate—also through crying, making others feel sorry for her. Her daydreaming is her way of avoiding participation and tasks. The recollections indicate clearly how little confidence she has to take care of herself. Others have to take care of her. And one can see her doubt that even her good looks will suffice in life. She is a pessimist, and is convinced, as the recollections indicate, that life is unfair and destructive. It is probably this pessimism, this assumption that something will go wrong anyhow, which stops her from playing her part and participating. On the contrary, she feels entitled to do whatever she likes to do (in the recollection, playing with the doll) so that she cannot see how she herself provokes her misfortunes. Being spanked and punished by the father seems to be unfair to her; but that she refused to go to the bathroom in time, was, in her eyes, justified because she did not want to stop playing with the doll.

Without explaining this to the child in as many words, the teacher can observe how she feels entitled to do what she wants and to get special attention merely by appearance and by suffering.

Cathy, age 8, is a very pretty child. Her brother Donald who is two years older is almost homely, wears thick glasses. She is dainty and graceful, average in intelligence. Donald is a behavior problem at home and in school. The father is strict, but only with the boy. Cathy is very polite, speaks almost in a whisper. She comes up with her work every few minutes asking over and over, if it is all right, and if the teacher is pleased. "Would you like me to do this for you?" She is always the one who finds faults with children and reminds them how they must behave in order to be good.

Recollections: Well, I remember when I was 4 years old, we had to go to a birthday party, and it was my cousin Mike's party. My brother and I went together. He behaved very badly. He laughed so loudly that everyone looked at us, and then he stole some cookies. I told him that it wasn't nice, and that he was embarrassing me and my parents by behaving that way, but he only laughed. Then he got in a fight with another boy who had the same name as my brother, but was bigger. Then Mike's mother told him to go home, but I had to go too because my mother told us that we must go and come home together. So I didn't get any ice cream or any of the other things the other children got. And it was all my brother's fault.

I was about 4, at least I think so, but I don't know for sure. One

51

day I was playing outside with a girl named Mary. We were jumping rope when her mother called her from the window and asked her to come into the house. But Mary pretended that she didn't hear. Then I said, "Your mother is calling you, why don't you answer her?" But Mary said she didn't hear. I told her that this was not nice, not to listen to one's mother, and that I wouldn't play with her again unless she went upstairs right away. Mary must have gotten mad at me because she scratched my face and she bit me. I ran home crying and told my parents what had happened. My father said I was right, that I shouldn't play with her again. And then he gave me a dollar.

Interpretation: Cathy is not only a good girl, she wants to be better than others. She looks down on the others because they are bad so that she can shine and show how good she is. In her mind, it is unfair that she has to suffer when she only tried to be good. Actually, she sometimes even provokes suffering only to show her martyrdom, how she has to suffer because others are bad. Here is a case of an active-constructive form of attention-getting, which is clearly distinguishable from a girl who just wants to be good, without using her good intentions to get special attention and status.

Fred, age 11, is the youngest of four. A sister is five years older, one brother three, the other two. He is big and heavy for his age, walks and talks with a self–assured manner. He is the leader of the boys and ignores girls. He must have the last word. He argues with adult logic, based on facts alone, refuses to see the human element. Example: A boy took cuts, so he pushed him back roughly, "Back where you belong." When this was discussed, his argument went as follows: "Before we can discuss this, let's talk about certain facts. Do we allow cuts? Yes or no? No arguments please, just yes or no. All right, you say it is not allowed. So that is exactly what I said to him. 'No cuts, please, and back where you belong.' Don't try to make a case out of something when you know darn well that I did only what is right."

Recollections: I remember one day when I was playing with my brother (the one two years older than me) and a boy who lived down the street. We were playing cops and robbers. I was a robber and I held up my brother. He fought with me and I hit him on the neck with my fist. He looked very funny, and then he was out on the ground. I guess I hit him too hard, but what do you expect of a robber?

I remember an incident in kindergarten. One day the teacher accused me of taking a dime from another kid. Well, I didn't, and I told her so. But she didn't believe me and made me give my own dime to this kid. I just wouldn't do it, and when she tried to take it from me, I cupped the dime into my mouth and swallowed it. Well, that scared the daylights out of the teacher. She rushed me to the nurse and they tried to make me throw up, but I wouldn t throw up. The teacher was more scared than I, and that served her right.

Interpretation: Here we have another child who wants to be right and uses his righteousness, not only to push others down, but to have his own way in whatever he wants by always finding reasonable justifications for it. Despite his conviction that he is always right, he seeks power and doesn't mind playing for revenge, too, if others try to overpower him. Whenever he is wrong, it is the fault of someone else. The recollections show this basic attitude more clearly than could be guessed merely on the strength of his overt behavior.

The above examples were taken from written assignments. A comparison of the reported incidents with observations of the child in class will give a teacher a stronger and clearer impression than can be achieved merely from the identification of the mistaken goal upon which each disturbing child may focus.

3
effective democratic methods

WINNING THE CHILD

THE FIRST CONTACT WITH THE CHILD

Most children are concerned about the kind of teacher they will have the next school year. Some children are very apprehensive when they change teachers, especially those who have had unhappy associations with school in general. When a parent brings a child to school on the first day after the summer vacation (which is not uncommon with younger children) his teacher may observe the fearful expression on the child's face; his clinging to his mother's hand, and sometimes crying when she has to leave. Often, the parent explains that the child has become tense with the approach of a new school year. Therefore, the first contact the teacher has with the student is of great importance. In order to win him, she must try to get a positive reaction. This calls for an immediate personal interest which would reassure the child that his teacher is friendly and is interested in him individually.

However, some children do not respond quickly, and it may take a child six weeks or longer before he is able to establish a working relationship with his teacher. The teacher needs to demonstrate that she is interested in and willing to work with him. She needs to convey to the child the idea that, "When you are ready, I am ready."

It helps if the teacher knows something about her new student, for then she can greet him in a more personal manner as:

> "Why, Leo, I am so glad that you are in my class this year; I remember you from last year. I used to watch you on the playground, and I liked the way you always waited for your turn on the swings."

The teacher could say to the child who is from a different school:

> "I know just how you feel, Helen. Everything is so new and strange to you here, and that frightens you. Would you like to sit close to my desk for the time being, or would you prefer sitting next to Sharon, over there? She has been here for several years and can show you around the school."

These examples illustrate how an initial contact may be made with an apprehensive child. Light, friendly but sincere conversation and interest may help to soothe the child and make him feel that he belongs.

TECHNIQUES OF WINNING THE CHILD

A teacher should acquaint herself with the backgrounds, personality traits, or special incidents, of her new students long before she meets them. As soon as the class list is published and she knows who is going to be in her class, she should begin studying the records if they are available. Sometimes she may call on a child's previous teacher for more information if she realizes that the child has had serious difficulties. It is important to discover the positive qualities of each student, so that she may greet a child with a realistic, or encouraging, remark, such as:

> "How are you, Danny? Did your dog's leg get well and is he able to walk without limping?"
>
> "So you are Arlene. I have heard many nice things about you from Mrs. Hanson."

It is very difficult to find the right things to say, especially during the first few days of school when veiled or half-promises slip out so easily. Sometimes the teacher may not realize that the personal exchange with one child may have a dampening effect on another. One needs to speak with caution and be careful not to make false statements and to be constantly aware of the complications which could arise.

Children may inquire how teachers become acquainted with the children's problems or interests. She could tell them that each teacher received a list of the names of the children who would be in her class , and that the teacher then looked up their personal records and asked questions about them from their former teacher.

Sometimes a child may ask, "Didn't you hear any bad things about me? I did some bad things last year." This is usually more than just a statement. Very often, it is meant as a challenge and a warning as to what the teacher may expect of him, and she will have to be careful not to fall into his trap. A possible reply is:

> "Oh, I did hear something, but I wasn't really interested in anything bad that you might have done last year. Why should I worry about last year? Are you concerned about the bad things I did last year?" Sometimes a child may ask, "Well, *did* you do anything bad?" One could reply, "Of course I did. Everybody does something wrong now and then."

Invariably, such incidents end in laughter. However, sometimes a child will question such a reply.

Since the first morning is not the proper time to get into a long discussion, the teacher could suggest that this matter be discussed with the entire class at a later time. This promise should be carried out.

A humorous remark may take the edge off a challenging situation, as shown in the following example:

> The teacher invited Anna to take any seat she wanted, explaining that at a later time the seating would be rearranged. Anna took a seat next to a girl and remarked, in a voice loud enough for everyone to hear, "If she should ever take this seat away from me, I'll slap her face." It was obvious that the children were shocked. They looked alternately at Anna and at the teacher. Anna seemed to have frightened herself with her daring remark. She looked pleadingly at the teacher, who realized that something had to be done quickly. She said, "Anna, you must smile when you joke, otherwise the children will take you seriously. Can you see how shocked they are? They think you have no manners. I know that you do, so why don't you smile to show them that you were just joking." The teacher laughed, and soon the children's faces relaxed, including Anna's.

56

Everyone smiled after a while. This could have backfired if Anna had chosen to test the teacher or to impress the class further.[1]On the playground, Anna came over to the teacher and said that it was nice not to be punished. The teacher won her confidence the first day of school. Anna became a most cooperative and helpful student. Years later, she persuaded her mother to go to the principal and insist that Margaret, her younger sister, be placed in this teacher's class.

To gain and maintain the child's full confidence requires constant deliberate thought and consideration on the part of the teacher. The initial contact is usually the basis for future relationships, for the child often evaluates his new teacher and establishes an attitude toward her according to his first impressions. If the child's attitude should be a negative one, it may take months before the teacher can change it and establish a good relationship. On the other hand, if the initial contact is favorable, the teacher has her foot in the door, her chances of entering are much greater, and the child's chances of learning have been increased.

The technique of winning a child takes in many considerations: the age of the child, the general atmosphere of the classroom, any previous encounters the teacher may have had with the child (directly or indirectly), the amount of time she can devote to the child during the first day of school, any knowledge she has as to the child's general attitude toward himself and toward school—to mention but a few. If the teacher has some previous knowledge about the child, she can plot the first encounter with considerable assurance that it will be pleasing to the child. But, generally speaking, there is no definite technique of winning a child. Each teacher must find her own technique. What may work with one teacher or child may not work with another. Winning a child does not depend solely on words but on the inflection of the voice, the facial expressions, the physical proximity of the teacher, the timing, others who are present in class, and her general personality.

THE FIRST DAY OF SCHOOL

The first day of school may be just as frightening to the new teacher as it is to the child. The teacher, as well as the children, needs time to adjust to the new situation. The teacher faces many problems. She needs to help the children to establish satisfying interpersonal relationships with each other, as well as with herself.

[1]Had Anna challenged the teacher by saying, "I am not kidding," she could have replied, "I will wait until you ask me for another seat," or, "I am sure I couldn't stop you."

By careful planning the teacher can help to alleviate many feelings of anxiety and insecurity. It is of utmost importance that the teacher have a variety of activities planned so that the children will have time to adjust to a new grade and have a favorable impression of what school is going to be like this year. It is important that the teacher should have looked over the class roll and know how to pronounce all names correctly. This gives the children a feeling of belonging.

It is a great help in establishing discipline and routine for the teacher to be in her room or at her door when the children arrive. It also helps for the teacher to have her name on the blackboard and to pronounce it for the children.

It is important for the teacher to establish some control of her class on the first morning, to get acquainted with the children and to establish some kind of routine. Children should be in a cheerful, relaxed atmosphere as they tell of their summer experiences and discuss classroom procedures. As the children plan with the teacher, they will learn to accept some responsibility for their own behavior and the teacher can then begin to relax and enjoy the children.

INVITING TROUBLE

Some teachers believe that they can avoid trouble if they tell the problem child that they are familiar with his history, and that he had better watch his step. With this approach, the teacher may evoke resistance and open defiance from the child. If he feels humiliated, he may be determined to defeat her. If his antisocial behavior is a means to get status in class, she has helped him achieve his goal the minute he enters the classroom. He now must live up to his reputation. The following example may illustrate such a case:

> During my second or third year of teaching, I thought that I would avoid difficulties by taking the bull by the horns. I told Antony that there would be no monkey business in my class, and that he had better watch his step. As it turned out, it was I who did not watch my step, for a few minutes later he tripped me as I walked through the aisle and I fell full length. The class roared. I sent Antony to the principal, who in turn sent for his parents. Thus, I antagonized both Antony and his parents on the first day of school.

AVOIDING DISCOURAGEMENT

The teacher should not become discouraged if all children do not rally to her side within a few days. Children who have had unsatisfying relationships with adults will be quite distrustful. These children are usually the ones everyone has heard about from year to year—the holy terrors!

When a teacher is faced with them, it is possible to discipline

58

herself and to transform resentment into positive action, as the following example indicates:

> I knew for two and a half months that I was going to have Larry in my class when high school opened. I thought of resigning, getting sick or moving away—then I thought of Larry. How did he feel? He really must be miserable to make life such a hassle. What could I do to help him so that we both could survive, and maybe even have some fun? I planned a course of action:
>
> 1. Be certain he had some success experiences.
> 2. Let him know I liked him—by action, by attitudes, and by telling him.
> 3. Give him a trustworthy job, in a matter of fact way.
> 4. Raise my expectations of Larry and of myself.
> 5. Arrange time for weekly conferences with Larry.
>
> Larry and I both learned to build on our successes together—slowly, step by step. It was a difficult task, but a rewarding one. I shudder to think what might have been had I not plotted and planned!

A good relationship between teacher and pupil calls for mutual respect and confidence. Children who are treated with dignity and friendliness (not just for the moment, but consistently) respond sooner or later, and accept order and cooperation, which is necessary for any social existence. One can and must establish mutual respect and confidence.

WINNING THE TEENAGER

It is sometimes impossible for the high school teacher to have background information on her students. Then the teacher has to adopt her technique to the situation. With teenagers the approach has to shift from an individual talk to a class discussion. Winning a class is a tremendous task and a wonderful experience. The following technique was successfully used with high school students:

> At the first meeting of the class I asked the students to fill out a form answering the following four questions: What induced you to take this class as an elective? How would you like this class to be run and what would you like your part to be in helping the class to function in this manner? What do you expect from the teacher? What do you expect from yourself? Most of the answers were concerned with questions two and three. They would like the class to be orderly, to be able to hear, and to have some freedom. They would like the teacher to be kind, considerate, fair, affectionate, obedient, punctual, understanding, friendly, to give them a break, to maintain disci-

pline, and to treat them with respect. For themselves, they expected to come to class and act as seniors should! As a group, we explored what they meant by an orderly class. Since very few had included on their paper what their part was in relationship to the organization and operation of the class, we discussed this problem. The group clarified their responsibility for maintaining an orderly class. We then discussed their expectations of the teacher, stopping to define in their own terms the meaning of the various qualities with particular attention to the words "fair" and "give them a break." After this was accomplished, we looked at the expectations of themselves. It was a real eye-opener to them to realize they were asking many things of the teacher that they were not asking of themselves. They concluded that perhaps it was the teacher who really needed to be "given a break" and they decided that it was the students who needed to be fair! As one boy laughingly said, "What a revolting development this is!" The students were cooperative, responsible and receptive.

Children readily accept the adult's superior experience and skill, provided she does not flaunt her superiority or take special privileges which are denied to them. All of us probably remember overhearing a child complain to his friend, "She always talks to another teacher in assembly but when we do, she punishes us. Why can't we talk if she can?" A teacher who sets aside special rights for herself has little chance to help the children develop character and right values. The children may obey the teacher out of fear, but they will not respect her.

We must not confuse kindness and understanding with indulgence or giving children free rein. The former is related to the basic rules of respect, trust, and cooperation, while the latter is based on disorder and lack of self-respect. To be effective, a teacher must be kind and firm.

DAVID, A CHALLENGE TO THE TEACHER

On the first day of school, one of the teachers stopped me in the corridor to express her sympathy for having in my class David, her student of last year. She claimed that he was the laziest, most obnoxious, and slowest child one can imagine. In David's personal records, I found that all of his former teachers shared this opinion. His second grade teacher had kept him after school almost daily in order for him to finish his work. His parents punished him a great deal. Yet nothing seemed to change David's attitude or behavior.

Having spoken to his former teacher, I went into my classroom and sought out David. I beheld a pale blond boy of 9, too small for his age, with a dirty face and altogether dishevelled appearance. I

asked him if his name was David Jones and he replied,
   "Who, me?"
   I pointed to a boy next to him and said, "No, not you, he."
   David looked somewhat puzzled but quickly replied, "His nam
isn't David Jones. This is my name."
   I asked him if he liked the seat where he was sitting; if not, h
could move up to a seat in the front.
   Again, he replied, "Who, me?"
   I didn't answer and walked away.
   A minute later he came up to me, asking if he could take th
empty seat in the front row. I said that I didn't know yet, that I woul
like to think about it. He was quick to remind me that only a minut
ago I had told him that he could have the seat. I laughed and replie
that if he takes the right to "not hear" I take the right to change m
mind. I quickly added that I was just kidding about changing m
mind, that he could take any seat he wanted.
   When I distributed pencils to the children who did not have any
and when I asked David if he needed one, he replied as before,
   "Who, me?"
   I ignored his question and passed him up whereupon he began
to shout, "Hey, teacher, what about me? You didn't give me a pencil."
   I replied, "Who, you?"
   The class laughed, knowing what I was referring to, but David
looked puzzled. I asked one of the children to explain to David why
we were laughing.
   David assumed more and more responsibilities in helping to keep
the class orderly. He even brought a small broom from home and
proceeded to sweep the floor. When I told him that this was the
janitor's work, he said that he would only sweep the corners.
   One morning, I asked David to see if he could find a certain book
among the class library books. I mentioned the title, deliberately
choosing a title easy to read. David found the book in no time. I
proceeded asking for books with more complicated titles. To my
surprise and delight, he found almost all of them without any difficulty. When I questioned David about this, he insisted that he could
not read the titles; that he just "found" the books. I opened one of
the easier books, asking him to read to me, but he shook his head,
insisting that he couldn't. I asked him who had told him that he
couldn't, and he answered that Mary, his sister said so. "Who else
said that you can't read?" I inquired.
   He mentioned his mother, his former teachers, and the children.
He concluded by telling me that he himself knew that he couldn't
When I asked him if he considered himself a smart boy, he shoo

his head in the negative. During all this time, David's face was serious but unperturbed.

During our next class discussion, I asked the class if anyone who cannot read could just "find" the right books among the many books we have on our shelves. The children said that this would be impossible. I told them that we have an extraordinary boy in our midst, one who can find any book if we tell him the title, without being able to read. I did not mention David's name nor did the name come up for quite a while. We discussed this question from the point of possibility. The children insisted that this was impossible, and all agreed that this child must be able to read some, at least. I turned to David and asked him to bring me a book, naming the title. He went to the bookshelf and brought the book within a few seconds. There were "Ah's" and "Oh's" in the class. I told the children that now it was up to them and to me to help David to want to join us in reading. I explained that their open lack of belief in him may have discouraged him, and now he believes himself what they believed for so long. I appealed to them to undo the damage they may have done.

The children's new attitude toward David was the beginning of his change. Gradually, he began to participate in class activities. I put no pressure on him but expressed my delight. I encouraged the class to show their appreciation. I asked the parents who had given up David as a lost cause to show their happiness in David's willingness and effort. David's life changed at school as well as at home. This marked the beginning of the end of David's "Who, me?", for, whenever he started this game, he caught himself in time, and then answered my questions.

David spent most of the day playing with some object, going to the washroom, or just staring into space. Since he did not disturb the class, I ignored his behavior.

I started my first group interaction with a discussion and the planning of a school party. The children plan the kind of program they want to have, how they want to decorate the class, while I donate the treat. I decided to give David the money and let him buy the treat.

This time, his, "Who, me?" was due to genuine surprise. He seemed happy when I gave him the money but after a few moments, his face fell. I asked him if anything was wrong and he said that he didn't know how much candy costs nor how much to buy for all the children. I told him to look around and find out what things cost. I also told him that it didn't have to be candy unless this is what he really wanted. One of the girls said that somebody ought to go with David because he would not know what to buy. I said that

I was sure that he would know what to do with the money or I would not have given him this job, but that he did not have to take the job if he did not want to. He thought for a minute and replied that he knew a store where he sometimes bought candy and that he would go there.

After lunch, David returned with a bag of chewing gum, lollipops, and change. He said that he didn't have enough money left to buy enough of anything for the entire class. He then asked the class if gum was all right. Some children said that they preferred gum to candy because it lasted longer. This pleased David. I thanked him for his help and complimented him on his choices.

The next day, David asked me if we were going to have another party some day and if he could do the shopping again. I told him that we wouldn't have a party for a while but that there were other things he could do. I put David in charge of the shelves. He had to keep them neat and dust free. David spent half the day at the shelves, paying no attention to what was going on in class. He refused to join a group in reading, saying that he did not have to. When I asked what he meant by "Didn't have to" he could only repeat the same phrase without any further explanation. The children who were in the same class with David the previous year told me that he hardly ever participated in any of the school activities. When I asked the reason for his nonparticipation, some shrugged their shoulders while others felt that he probably couldn't do the work.

I asked David if he agreed with what the children said. First, he replied that he didn't know, but after a moment he said that the children were right—that he couldn't. He said this in a most matter-of-fact way, betraying no emotions. I expressed my doubt as to their and his convictions. "After all," I said, "none of us have ever heard or seen what he can do. How can any one of us say with certainty that *he can't* do anything you can do? If he tried, he might surprise himself and all of us."

The teacher had indeed gained David's trust and through her efforts he was able to develop his capacities.

GOOD RELATIONSHIPS MUST NOT BE TAKEN FOR GRANTED

The teacher cannot afford to take the good relationship she has established with the child for granted. If she does not nourish it and be sensitive to new situations, she may suddenly discover that she has lost the child's confidence without knowing when or how. Children like David respond strongly to their teacher's bad disposition. Some children feel threatened, while others regard it as a personal affront, especially those who have been distrustful of people and have never before formed good interpersonal relationships with adults. They wait for such signs of rejection. This is not to say that a teacher could never be in a bad mood or feel irritable. Like anyone else, teachers do have their bad days. However, it helps when she has the courage to admit to her students that she feels crabby that day.

A teacher could say, "Children, I don't feel well this morning. Don't feel hurt if I say something that upsets you."

A teacher could also write on the blackboard, "Sh-h-h, Teacher has a headache." By so doing, one can often prevent misunderstandings. Nevertheless, they may occur, not just on days when the teacher is out of sorts, but at any time. The following example illustrates how much on the alert a teacher has to be.

> I recall an unfortunate experience I had with a student some time ago. Mitzi was a withdrawn child when she entered my class. It took me months to gain her confidence, and then I ruined it with one sentence. One day she asked me why I never wore anything brown. I replied that brown was not "my color," meaning that it was not becoming to me. Mitzi took it that I disliked the color. As it happened, she had on a new brown dress that day, which I had not noticed. Mitzi cried bitterly, and pushed me away when I tried to console her. I could not reach her for weeks.

It is not enough to show occasional interest in the child. Children's needs are ever present and we must be aware of them. Had the teacher noticed Mitzi's new brown dress, she would not have had to renew her energies and devote so much time to winning Mitzi over again. With Mitzi it was a matter of commenting on the dress, with another child it might be encouraging him in his progress in writing or drawing, with a third, it might be showing interest in his problems at home. It takes continuous awareness of the child's situation.

Children usually test each teacher, especially during the first week or so, to find out what the limits are and the consequences of transgression. The teacher needs to look at this testing period as an academic exercise rather than a personal affront and then she will be more able to cope with the situation. She should avoid making a value judgment of a child; the child will interpret this as "you don't like me," or "you hate me," or "you really don't care." It is important for the teacher to separate the two, "I like you" and "it is your behavior that is unacceptable." For example:

> Darrel was a hyperactive boy and usually screamed all of his demands and his displeasures. The second day in class I said, "I like Darrel very much. I would be so happy if he would leave all those words outside the door when he comes into the classroom."

Several days later, Darrel let loose with another torrent. I happened to be involved in a game with him and I quietly moved away. He looked up, walked over to the door, opened it, wiped his mouth and 'threw it' outside and said, "The teacher likes Darrel. You old words, stay out there."

A trusting relationship should exist between the child and the teacher, with the teacher being able to make some demands for acceptable behavior and an appropriate amount of school work. The teacher is the key person who is responsible for the child having successful school experiences.

ENCOURAGEMENT

HOW AND WHEN CHILDREN LEARN

Most teachers are aware of the range and complexity of learning required in the school curriculum, but not all teachers are as certain about the part played in the child's learning by the process of encouragement or reinforcement. The child who enjoys doing his school work consistently does a better job than the child who is not satisfied with his work. Through the process of encouragement, and by careful planning and organizing, the teacher can make school work seem more worthwhile, and thereby help the pupils stimulate their own learning process.

No one learns unless he makes a commitment to the learning process. We learn from success and we learn from failure. A commitment to learning cannot be made unless the child has a proper self-evaluation and is willing to take his chances with success or failure.

Teachers have a responsibility that goes beyond imparting facts and teaching skills. There is an even greater responsibility to reach each child and help him find a place in the group where he can find satisfaction and acceptance as a human being, regardless of how well or how poorly he performs scholastically. If the teacher succeeds in this endeavor, the child will most likely be able to respond to all learning situations in a positive receptive manner and progress toward developing true knowledge of the learning process. If she fails, he may assume too narrow limits for his capabilities and become a problem socially or scholastically, or both.

WHAT IS ENCOURAGEMENT?

The role of encouragement or reinforcement is paramount in building the child's learning ability and developing his commitment to the learning process. Encouragement is a complex process, not a unique event; its development is dependent on a number of gross and minute circumstances which shift continuously. As a result, a precise definition is impossible. At best, we can say that it is an action which conveys to the child that the teacher respects, trusts and believes in him and that his present lack of skills in no way diminishes his value as a person.

An effective process of encouragement demands continuous alertness for the right moment, tone of voice, and choice of words. Constant opportunities for encouragement appear in many areas and shades of student effort, whether the effort is altogether successful or not.

Recognition must be given for real trying, even if there has been no visible accomplishment. A teacher may say, "You have been working so hard on spelling this morning. I have been watching you and I am happy to see your determination." Or she may say, "Would you like to take a few minutes rest? You have been working so hard that you deserve it." Recognition should never be overdone. A few words will suffice.

A teacher may encourage a child without using any words. For example, a child's paper is checked as soon as he completes the assignment. Each correct answer is marked with a capital C. Each incorrect problem is left unmarked. The paper is immediately returned to the child, who then reworks the incorrect problems. Then, an OK is written on the correct response. Thus, the completed paper has only positive markings, which is encouraging to the child, and another step has been taken in bringing even more academic performance to full strength. Minimizing mistakes will have an encouraging effect if the child is still struggling. That does not imply that a teacher must overlook them or even deny that the child made mistakes.

If the teacher says, "That's pretty good for a first trial; don't worry if you notice any mistakes. In time they will disappear," she builds on the child's strength.

Encouragement can be applied systematically to the slow child by dividing the assignments into many short tasks. This type of programming provides experiences which are "built in" to stimulate the child's positive attention. His concentration span is lengthened, his enjoyment of the tasks is raised, and his self-respect is enhanced. These results have the effect of eliminating many of his old forms of misbehavior. With this method, during a 45-minute period, a child has a chance for ten to fifteen accomplishments. It also produces spiral effect in learning as the teacher is able to reprogram the problem, and the child is able to correctly mark his paper and thereby reinforce his learning of that concept.

WHEN SHOULD WE BEGIN TO ENCOURAGE THE CHILD?

Encouragement is most effective if it starts at the very beginning of the school year. No doubt a sudden change in the teacher's attitude will have an effect on the child's response, particularly if the teacher is persistent in her new approval. However, she could save herself a great deal of time and energy if she demonstrated her belief in the child from the first encounter she had with him. This presupposes the teacher's genuine belief in children and in the process of encouragement.

Since no two children are alike, the teacher will need to be sensitive to the feelings of each member of her class in order to know when and how to encourage him. The effect of her encouragement will also depend on the child's relationships within the group. A child may well be skeptical of the teacher's recognition if he has been in her class for a considerable time and she has never before expressed any appreciation or belief in him. The following example will illustrate this point:

> Doug, a senior in high school, in four months had never received attention or recognition from his teacher in drafting class. Although Doug never completed an assignment, the teacher merely gave him a failing grade without commenting. One day, the teacher passed his table and gently patted him on the shoulder, saying that he was doing a good job on his project. Doug was too startled to respond, but after class he was overheard making the following remark to one of the boys: "Did you hear what old B—— said to me today? What do you suppose he wants?"
>
> It never occurred to Doug that the teacher was serious in his compliment.

THE OVERAMBITIOUS TEACHER MAY FAIL
IN THE PROCESS OF ENCOURAGEMENT

Some teachers may start the year out using encouragement; but if they do not see immediate results, they themselves may become discouraged and either revert to autocratic disciplinary measures, or lose confidence in their own ability to exert an influence on the child and let him do as he pleases. How often do we hear teachers say, "I have tried everything, but all in vain." "I give up, because I don't know how to get through to this child." Such a reaction is very unfortunate for both child and teacher. A teacher has to develop techniques and abilities and with them patience and self-confidence in order to help the child overcome his difficulties. This may require altering her own viewpoint. Instead of seeking academic accomplishments, she may have to look for commendable performances in the everyday activities of the child. He may be a good runner or good in sharpening the teacher's pencils.

DANGER OF COMPETITIVE ENCOURAGEMENT

The teacher must be very cautious in using the term *being better* than others. Many children get the impression that they are important only if they are "better" than others. Such misconceptions are often fostered by parents and teachers. It is advisable to say "I like the way you sharpen my pencils" in preference to "You're the best pencil-sharpener I have ever had."

CONSISTENCY IN THE RELATIONSHIP

Inherent in the process of encouragement is the concept of developing a basic trust between the teacher and the child, as mutual trust is the foundation upon which good interpersonal relationships are built. A child's trust often precedes his gaining confidence in himself. Trust implies that the child has learned to rely on the sameness and continuity of the teacher and that he may trust himself in his transactions with the teacher. Then he is able to consider himself trustworthy enough so that the teacher will remain constant in her relationship. A child's trust in his teacher implies assured reliance on the teacher's integrity and sincerity. The child may constantly test the relationship.

The development of a child's abilities may grow at varied rates. His learning situations change with time, as well as his view of his relationships with the teacher. As a result, some children may test the relationship constantly, others only occasionally.

A child who has not learned to trust others will quite often not trust himself in his relationship and functions. He will relate to very few people and his academic process may become stymied. The establishment of trust is a necessary step in the process of encouragement.

> Barry was an 11-year-old boy who trusted no one, who did not like himself, and who refused to try anything academic. He was not allowed to go through the halls alone as he constantly bothered the other rooms. I had Barry for several days and had been instructed to accompany him through the halls, which I had been doing.
>
> One day, Barry asked to leave the room and I talked with him, saying that I believed that I could trust him to go to the lavatory and return alone and would give him a pass so he would not be questioned. Big tears came into his eyes as he said to me that no one had ever trusted him before. I said that I trusted him. He asked if I was going to stand at the door and watch him and I told him, "No," that he could go to the bathroom and return alone—that I would trust him to do this.

68

Barry lived up to my expectations. Then Barry and I discussed other places and ways in which he might be trusted. I told him I would make no promises and would not ask him to make promises as there might be an oversight and one might forget or break one. This was important to Barry as many people had extracted promises from him that he usually broke. For the first time, Barry found an adult who maintained the same kind of relationship with him during his good times as well as his bad times, one who accepted him as he was and let him grow and develop at his own pace.

One morning, I loaned Barry some books to read. Later in the day, he became angry and ripped some books and papers apart. There was speculation among the faculty about Barry tearing the books that I had loaned him. I said that he would not tear them and that he would return them intact. Later that day, Barry came into the room and handed me the books and said, "I wouldn't tear these books."

I told him that I knew he wouldn't and had said so earlier. He was quite emotional about this bit of information as he blurted out, "You really do trust me—all the way, don't you!"

From this point, Barry was able to cooperate and funnel his energy into the learning process.

RIGIDITY MAY BE AN OBSTACLE TO ENCOURAGEMENT

There are always exceptions to each rule. What is said is often less important than how it is said. Anything that strengthens the child's belief in himself, without damaging his relationship with others, is highly recommendable. Let us examine this more carefully. It would be perfectly in order to fuss over a child who has, at last, mustered up enough courage to participate in some activity, academic or other. If Sally has been afraid to play ball because she may get hurt in catching it, and has, at last, decided to join in a game, it would greatly encourage her if everybody, not just the teacher, would show appreciation. However, the teacher may have to maneuver the situation so as to stimulate or influence the group to praise Sally for her action. The teacher may say, "Look, children, Sally is playing ball with us today. I am so glad, aren't you? Let's show her how glad we are." The class may applaud, or they may give her the ball to be first in throwing it. There are numerous other ways by which other children can express their confidence and their pleasure. Most children will have compassion for those who are not successful if the class is cooperative and not competitive. It is necessary to develop this quality in children; of making them aware of other people's needs and of the power children have to help others.

Children must be helped to understand that people are different and that it is good that all are not alike. This way, the teacher can help them to accept their own personal capacities and difficulties, as well as to understand that others have talents as well as troubles. To encourage a child by comparing him with another defeats such efforts. Supposing Danny too is frightened of playing ball, and has not yet made an attempt. It would be highly discouraging if we were to point out Sally to him as an example. We may help Danny by letting him carry the ball, perhaps throw the ball to somebody and comment on his throwing, and look for an opportunity to encourage him to catch a ball.

AN ACCOMPLISHED SIBLING MAY BE A CLUE
TO THE CHILD'S DISCOURAGEMENT

What can a teacher do if she realizes that a child is discouraged because of a sister or brother who is a better student in school? She can use various approaches. She may help the child through discussions with the entire class about the differences we find in people. She can stress how all of us have some problems, and that we are not alone in our inferiority feelings and difficulties. She might speak to the parents and point out the mistake they make by comparing the two.

Most important is the teacher's constant alertness to situations which present chances to raise the self-esteem of the child. She must provide opportunities to make him feel important and respected by the group. Janek's case might well illustrate such a situation:

> He was the second child in a family of four. His older sister as well as his younger brother were excellent students. The parents, having little education placed great value on academic knowledge, and were determined to give their children an education. They depended on their oldest daughter to do all the writing for them, and promised to send her to college because she was doing so well in school. They loved Janek, but they were disappointed and hurt because of his poor performance. They were constantly holding up Sonia, his sister, as an example.
>
> In spite of all the affection he got from his parents, Janek was convinced that they did not love him, and that he had no place in their hearts. It was difficult for the parents to understand what they should do, especially how to encourage the boy. Janek had never known any adult to take a genuine interest in him. He was withdrawn from the group and showed no interest in any activity except music. He had a lovely voice, but he would hold back in group singing. My first break with him came when we were discussing the different kinds of names people have. Someone asked me what name I liked best. I replied that one of my favorite names is Janek;

70

it has a musical sound, and it looks interesting when written. Everyone's eyes turned to Janek, who blushed, but for once looked straight at me. I added casually, "Sometimes we like certain names because they remind us of people we like. Maybe that's another reason why I like the name "Janek." He said goodbye to me when he left school, something he had never done.

Soon after that, I asked him if he sang in the church choir, and when he said he didn't, I told him that they would be delighted to have someone who could sing as he can, and that he should join. When I asked if he would like to, he shrugged his shoulder as if he were indifferent, but I could detect a gleam in his eye. I asked him if he would object if I were to find out how he could join, and he replied that he didn't care one way or another. At least he did not say "No."

The parents were not aware of Janek's voice; he seldom sang at home. I was very glad to learn that nobody else in the family could sing well. They were less impressed with the discovery of their son's voice than with the possibility that he would sing in the church choir. Both parents could understand that this would give Janek prestige, and that they should make some fuss over his talent. Soon after, Janek sang at church. This was the beginning of his general change toward better adjustment at school and at home.

Janek was now willing to sing for the class, and he even agreed to sing by himself at a school party where parents were present. During class singing, I asked him to sit next to children who had difficulty carrying a tune, so as to lead them. He accepted readily. He was easier to talk to, for he did not hang his head as he did before. He was willing to read his compositions to the class, and often volunteered to lead in an activity. As Janek improved at school, it was also easier to direct the parents in their handling of the boy, for now their belief in him had also grown. Thus it happened that Janek established a closer relationship with the teacher, the group, and his parents.

ENCOURAGEMENT VERSUS PRAISE

It is crucial that teachers recognize the difference between praise and encouragement. Praise is usually given to a child when a task or deed is well done, or when the task is completed. Encouragement is needed when the child fails. Encouraging the child during the task or for trying is as important as giving the child recognition at the completion of the task. If the child is once rewarded with praise, then the withholding or lack of praise signifies failure. Flattery may promote insecurity as the child may become frightened of the possibility of not being able to live up to expectations or not sure of always getting the same kind of praise again. The child has the mistaken idea that *unless he is praised, he has no value,* and therefore he is a failure. Praise puts the emphasis on the child, encouragement emphasizes the task.

Vicki Soltz, in an article entitled, "Why Not Praise" in her book, *Study Group Leader's Manual,*[2] states:

> Most of us have grown up believing that praise is desperately needed by all children in order to stimulate them into "right" behavior. If we watch closely when he is receiving praise we may discover some astonishing facts. Some children gloat, some panic, some express "So what," some seem to say, "Well, finally!"
>
> We are suddenly confronted with the fact that we need to see how the child interprets what is going on rather than assume that he regards everything as we do.
>
> Examination of the intention of the praiser shows that he is offering a reward: "If you are good you will have the reward of being high in my esteem." Well, fine. What is wrong with this approach? Why not help the child learn to do the right thing by earning a high place in parental esteem?
>
> If we look at the situation from the child's point of view, we will find the mistake of this approach.
>
> How does praise affect the child's self-image? He may get the impression that his personal worth depends upon how he "measures up" to the demands and values of others. "If I am praised, my personal worth is high. If I am scolded, I am worthless." When this child becomes an adult, his effectiveness, his ability to function, his capacity to cope with life's tasks will depend entirely upon his estimation of how he stands in the opinion of others. He will live constantly on an elevator—up and down.
>
> Praise is apt to center the attention of the child upon himself. "How do I measure up?" rather than "What does the situation need?" This gives rise to a fictive-goal of "self-being-praised" instead of the reality-goal of "what-can-I-do-to-help."
>
> Another child may come to see praise as his right—as rightfully due him from life. Therefore, life is unfair if he doesn't receive praise for every effort. "Poor me—no one appreciates me." Or, he may feel he has no obligation to perform if no praise is forthcoming. "What's in it for me? What will I get out of it? If no praise (reward) is forthcoming, why should I bother?"
>
> Praise can be terribly discouraging. If the child's effort fails to bring the expected praise, he may assume either that he isn't good

[2]Vicki Soltz, *Study Group Leader's Manual* (Chicago: Alfred Adler Institute, 1967).

enough or that what he has to offer isn't worth the effort and so give up.

If a child has set exceedingly high standards for himself, praise may sound like mockery or scorn, especially when his efforts fail to measure up to his own standards. In such a child, praise only serves to increase his anger with himself and his resentment at others for not understanding his dilemma.

In all our efforts to encourage children we must be alert to the child's response. The accent must move from "What am I?" (good?) to "How can I help the total situation?" Anything we do which reinforces a child's false image of himself is discouraging. Whatever we do that helps a child see that he is part of a functioning unit, that he can contribute, cooperate, participate within the total situation, is encouragement. We must learn to see that as he is, the child is good enough.

Praise rewards the individual and tends to fasten his attention upon himself. Little satisfaction or self-fulfillment comes from this direction.

Encouragement stimulates the effort and fastens attention upon one's capacity to join humanity and to become aware of interior strength and native capacity to cope.

Praise recognizes the actor, encouragement acknowledges the act.

PRAISE	ENCOURAGEMENT
Aren't you wonderful to be able to do this!	Isn't it nice that you can help?
	We appreciate your help. Don't the dishes shine? (after wiping)
	Isn't the carpet pretty now? (after vacuuming)
	How nice your room looks!
	Thanks for watching the baby. It was a big help.
	I like your drawing. The colors are so pretty together.
	How much neater the room looks now that your toys are put away.
	How nice that you could figure that out for yourself. Your skill is growing!
I'm so proud of you for getting good grades. (You are high in my esteem.)	I'm so glad you enjoy learning (adding to your own resources).

73

I'm proud of you for behaving so nicely in the restaurant.	We all enjoyed being together in the restaurant.
I'm awfully proud of your performance in the recital.	It is good to see that you enjoy playing. We all appreciate the job you did. I have to give you credit for working hard.

A teacher often tends to put her faith mainly in the child's intellectual potentialities which she measures by his performance. If he performs well, she is pleased with herself as well as with him. Her attitude has a very definite influence on the child's regard for academic achievement per se; for he senses that the degree of his performance may determine his position in class.

> I recall a conversation with a boy, not my student, who was extremely nasty to other children on the playground. When I confronted him with this fact, he replied, "I know. My teacher always calls me a pest, but she never does anything to me because I am the best student in her class."

This boy felt protected because of his scholastic standing in the class. However, his need for belligerence would indicate a lack of confidence in himself, at least in social relationships. His academic success was obviously not helping him toward a better social adjustment.

ENCOURAGEMENT VERSUS DISCOURAGEMENT

All children need approval, and all seek approbation, regardless of the status they occupy in the group. The lack of appreciation may easily discourage even a very gifted child, and he may withdraw from participation.

If the teacher expects failure, convinced that the child will have to be coaxed or punished, he will most likely respond to these expectations which, in turn, will convince her that she was right in the first place.

On the other hand, if the child has been helped to have the courage to take chances, even at the risk of failure, he will probably do better than he expected. For a discouraged child, even the slightest proof of success is a great booster, for he had never experienced success and was convinced that he never would. Even this little success can be a tremendous help to the teacher and to the group to build on, for it is really the foundation on which all can stand firmly without feeling hypercritical in giving recognition.

Teachers who lack this understanding tend to discourage their children by means and gestures which they think are encouraging.

74

A teacher discourages a child by her actions—perhaps even more so than by her words. She may act as if he were ignorant or stupid or incapable.

> Mike was working on a sixth grade social studies assignment. He asked his teacher for help in locating the answer to a particular question. The teacher helped him locate the material and hovered over him until he had written the answer. She then read the next question aloud and began to look through the book for the answer. Mike at this point said, "Go away. I can do these by myself. Do you think I'm stupid or something?"

The act of hovering has a discouraging effect in itself as it tells the child that the teacher does not think he is able to continue alone. To another child it may seem that the teacher does not trust his reasoning or thinking abilities or cannot do the work correctly.

One of the most frequent and deadly means of discouraging a child is pointing out to him how much better he could be. Instead of spurring him on to greater efforts, it usually stops him from even trying. Has he not been told that he is not good enough as he is? This is the worst thing one can tell a person.

The way a teacher asks a child to do something may have an encouraging or discouraging effect. Usually, she gets better cooperation if she refrains from negative commands. "Try to hold your pencil like this and your hand won't get tired," instead of "Don't hold your pencil at the top. Whoever writes like this?" "Don't you think it would be better to do the workbook first since your group is going to check it soon?" instead of "I told you to do the workbook first. Why don't you do as you are told?" "Please" and "thank you" are always great assets.

The teacher must not confuse encouraging a child with inspiring him to show courage. Showing courage does not always imply self-confidence. A child may show courage if his desire for approval is very strong. A student who was afraid of playing ball because he might be hurt, climbed the outside ledge of a window on the second floor, causing everyone to look at him. A child may force himself to show courage in order not to be called a sissy. Many people believe that such daring acts are indications of courage, manliness, and do not realize that this same child may be really frightened and insecure. It is not unusual for a teacher to hear a parent say "How can you say that my child is discouraged? You should see him climb trees and ride his bicycle without using his hands." This same child may lack the confidence to participate in academic work or in any other group activity. He may feel that nobody likes him; that the only way to get any attention is to do daring deeds. Encouraging such displays of bravado may even become dangerous, for the child may become foolhardy or belligerent.

A child does not feel encouraged if the teacher gives with one hand and takes away with the other. Complimenting a child with a "but" kills any encouraging words. "Buts" easily slip into our good intentions. "I'm very proud of your reading, but you must watch your punctuation." "Your spelling is improving, but you're neglecting your English." Acknowledgments must stand by themselves, with nothing to mar them, if they are to be effective. At another time she may discuss the child's need for improvement in his English.

Comparing children is another important factor to be considered. Parents and teachers often believe that they can induce a child to do better if they point out how much better another child is doing, or how much better a student his sibling was. How many times do we hear, "John is doing better and we are pleased, but at his age Michael, his brother, was much further along in school than he is." Or, "Why don't you do as well as your brother? I had no trouble with him when he was in my class." Comparing children unfavorably creates defeatism, adds to sibling rivalry, and lowers the child's self-respect. Always keep in mind that each child is different, and that each must get respect for what *he is*.

WHAT CAN A TEACHER DO?

An important factor in encouraging a child is the teacher's understanding of the goal the child has set for himself in a particular situation (see Chapter One, Part 3, "Four Goals of Misbehavior"). What may be encouraging for one child may have the opposite effect on another, depending on the child's reaction. In most cases, recognition of a child before the entire class carries more weight because approval of peers is often more important to the child than approval by the teacher.

In *Encouraging Children to Learn*,[3] Don Dinkmeyer and Rudolf Dreikurs list nine things to keep in mind when encouraging children:

1. Place value on the child as he is.
2. Show faith in the child and enable him to have faith in himself.
3. Sincerely believe in the child's ability and win his confidence while building his self-respect.
4. Recognize a job "well done" and give recognition for effort.
5. Utilize the class group to facilitate and enhance the development of the child.

[3]Don Dinkmeyer and Rudolf Dreikurs, *Encouraging Children to Learn* (Englewood Cliffs, N.J.: Prentice-Hall, 1963).

6. Integrate the group so that each child can be sure of his place in it.
7. Assist in the development of skills sequentially so as to insure success.
8. Recognize and focus on strengths and assets.
9. Utilize the interest of the child to energize constructive activity.

To further illustrate the process of encouragement, Clint Reimer, in his paper entitled, "Some Words of Encouragement,"[4] lists ten ways of approaching the child. They are as follows:

1. "You do a good job of . . ."
   Children should be encouraged when they do not expect it, when they are not asking for it. It is possible to point out some useful act or contribution in each child. Even a comment about something small and insignificant to us, may have great importance to a child.
2. "You have improved in . . ."
   Growth and improvement is something we should expect from all children. They may not be where we would like them to be, but if there is progress, there is less chance for discouragement. Children will usually continue to try if they can see some improvement.
3. "We like (enjoy) you, but we don't like what you do."
   Often a child feels he is not liked after he has made a mistake or misbehaved. A child should never think *he* is not liked. It is important to distinguish between the child and his behavior, between the act and the actor.
4. "You can help me (us, the others, etc.) by. . . ."
   To feel useful and helpful is important to everyone. Children want to be helpful; we have only to give them the opportunity.
5. "Let's try it together."
   Children who think they have to do things perfectly are often afraid to attempt something new for fear of making a mistake or failing.
6. "So you do make a mistake; now, what can you learn from your mistake?"
   There is nothing that can be done about what has happened, but a person can always do something about the future. Mistakes can teach the child a great deal, and he will learn if he does not feel embarrassed for having made a mistake.
7. "You would like us to think you can't do it, but we think you can."

---

[4]Clint Reimer, "Some Words of Encouragement," in *Study Group Leader's Manual,* by Vicki Soltz (Chicago: Alfred Adler Inst., 1967), pp. 71–73.

This approach could be used when the child says or conveys the impression that something is too difficult for him and he hesitates to even so much as try it. If he tries and fails, he has at least had the courage to try. Our expectations should be consistent with the child's ability and maturity.

8. "Keep trying. Don't give up."
   When a child is trying, but not meeting much success, a comment like this might be helpful.

9. "I'm sure you can straighten this out (solve this problem, etc.), but if you need any help, you know where to find me."
   Adults need to express confidence that children are able and will resolve their own conflicts, if given a chance.

10. "I can understand how you feel (not sympathy, but empathy) but I'm sure you'll be able to handle it."
    Sympathizing with another person seldom helps him, rather it suggests that life has been unfair to him. Understanding the situation and believing in the child's ability to adjust to it is of much greater help to him.

What else can a teacher do to encourage a child?

1. If a child expresses doubt in his abilities in spite of the teacher's reassurance, she may show him reports of other teachers concerning him, if they are favorable. She may say, "I don't do this very often, but I should like you to see for yourself that I am not the only one who believes in you. Listen to what Mrs. X said about you.

2. If a child is unsure and therefore does not start an assigned project, the teacher may sit down next to him and do part of the work with him. This may, in some cases, be enough to motivate him.

3. Let a child teach the entire class something he knows how to do well, no matter how insignificant it may be.

4. If the teacher senses that a child is unhappy because of his size —being too big or too small for his age, she may read to the class about the achievements of great people who had the same problems. In this way, the child learns to evaluate himself and others not by size but by the person's personality.

5. Let a poor speller be the spelling teacher now and then, allowing him to use the book. The same may apply to any subject from which the child shies.

6. Find special jobs for the child—jobs which give him status.

7. Let a child with poor writing habits write the teacher's assignments on the blackboard.

8. Ask a child who feels rejected to be master of ceremonies at a party.
9. Invite to speak to the class a member of the child's family who might make an impression on the others in class, if, for example, the child's father or brother is a policeman, fireman, or does work which is usually admired by children.
10. If the teacher knows of some special contribution a child makes at home, tell it to the entire class.
11. Display the child's work for everyone to see.
12. Invite the parents, and say in his presence something positive about the child to them.
13. Send a note home commenting favorably on the child's behavior, performance, or both. Teachers tend to send notes home only when children have difficulties.

Teachers must provide opportunities for children to experience success. Merely telling a child that "he can if he tries hard enough" is not enough. "He can" only if the teacher plans situations where he can succeed. It entails planning, which is work for the teacher—additional work to the already heavy load that teachers carry. However, in the long run, such work is rewarding not only because the children do better, but it cuts down the amount of time the teacher will have to spend on children for their antisocial behavior.

Some teachers may argue that despite their best intentions, they cannot find any area in which a certain child can do well or experience even minute success. If one assumes that these teachers refer to academic work, it may be true. However, one cannot be merely concerned with academic success if it is a question of helping a child to raise his self-esteem or his own evaluation of himself.

Merril was a first grader who had difficulties with his visual motor skills. In order to help him to obtain better coordination, a part of each day was devoted to teaching Merril to play Jacks. Day after day, Merril practiced bouncing and catching the ball and picking up Jacks. After several weeks, the teacher noticed that Merril was able to catch the ball and pick up the Jacks at the same time. What a happy time that was—the class applauded as they wanted to show Merril that they valued his achievement.

Therefore, any situation that lends itself to put in a good word for a particular child should be utilized. He may be a good whistler or even a good bubble gum blower. If the teacher realizes this, the child should be given an opportunity to show off his skill and be recognized for it. One must remember that this is just a stepping-stone toward further achievement. In time, as the child feels more accepted, he will become interested in other achievements.

One must always remember that no technique in itself is applicable in every situation. Each child and each situation is unique.

NATURAL AND LOGICAL CONSEQUENCES: A SUBSTITUTE FOR REWARD AND PUNISHMENT[5]

It is possible to stimulate children to proper and acceptable behavior through the use of natural and logical consequences. Through natural consequences the child experiences the consequences of his own behavior in such a way that he will relate pleasure or pain only to his behavior and not to the intervention of anyone else.

Natural consequences represent the pressure of reality or the natural flow of events without interference of the teacher or parent. The child who refuses to eat will go hungry. The natural consequence of not eating is hunger. The parent stands aside and does not become involved.

Logical consequences are arranged or applied. If the child spills his milk, he must clean it up. In this situation, the consequence is tied to the act. A power-drunk child will only respond to natural consequences; he will respond to logical consequences with rebellion.

When logical consequences are used, the child is motivated toward proper behavior through his own experience of the social order in which he lives. Only in moments of real danger is it necessary to protect the child from the natural consequences of his disturbing behavior.

Natural and logical consequences should be discussed with, understood and accepted by the child before their application, otherwise the child may rightly consider it just another name for punishment. The technique of logical consequences can be used effectively only when a good relationship exists between teacher and child. In a power conflict they become punishments. Although the teacher is responsible for what is taking place, she acts not as a powerful authority, but as a representative of an order which affects all children alike. In using this technique, the teacher allows the child to experience the logical consequences of his own behavior as is shown in the following example:

> In home economics class, the girls with their teacher had decided on the rules for cooking class. Any girl who did not bring her apron

[5]Dreikurs and Gray, *Logical Consequences: A New Approach to Discipline* (New York: Hawthorne Press, 1968).

80

would be unable to cook or to share the goodies. Jessie forgot to bring her apron and consequently could not cook. She gave a big sigh and said, "That's life—and to think that I helped make up that rule." She remembered to have her apron at school for the rest of the foods unit.

Natural and logical consequences will be effective *only* if they are applied consistently. If teachers apply them once or twice only, and then allow the *same* situation to go by unnoticed, the child will soon take advantage of the teacher's inconsistency. The student will gamble on the teacher's good mood and on his good luck for he sees a chance to get by with his misbehavior. The teacher needs to be alert and not fall for a side issue if she wants to impress the child with the consequences of his behavior. Natural and logical consequences must be applied so that the child becomes convinced they will follow his misdemeanor just as he is convinced that if he were to put his hand in water it would come out wet.

> Rafael did not answer to the roll call on the first day of school. I called his name a second time without getting any response. I decided to ignore it and went on with the roll call. The next day when Rafael did not respond when I called his name, I ignored the issue again. On the third day I omitted his name. When I had finished, Rafael called out, "You did not call my name, teacher." I told him that I thought that he wouldn't mind, but if it mattered, I'd call his name the next day. The following day when his name came up, he shouted at the top of his voice, "Present." The class laughed so hard, it took a few minutes to quiet them down. The following day when I omitted Rafael's name again, he stood up and yelled, "You did not call my name again." I ignored his outburst and continued with the roll call. I omitted calling his name for several days. Rafael watched me, but said nothing. After a week of this procedure, I decided to try once more. When I called his name, he looked pleased, and in a pleasant way responded with, "Here." I had no trouble with Rafael again on that score.

Teachers and parents often expect that miracles will take place after they have applied some natural and logical consequences for a day or two. Since in most cases it takes much longer than a few days for a child to give up a pattern of behavior which has proven successful for a long time, teachers and parents may become discouraged when they see no drastic changes, and they then resort to their old methods of dealing with the child. To them, the method of using consequences appears an unworkable form of discipline. The following example illustrates this point:

81

Mrs. D. complained to the teacher that her son, Joe, 8 years old, played near and on the railroad tracks after school. He was well aware of the danger, but this precisely added to the thrill. Although his parents had punished him severely a number of times, he still persisted in playing on the tracks. Mrs. D. was desperate and asked for advice. The teacher suggested that the mother tell Joe that if he should play again on the tracks, he could go out to play only on days she would have the time to go out with him, as she does with her 3-year-old daughter. They would all go together. She may even have to hold Joe's hand just as she does her daughter's, because his outdoor behavior is not on a par with an 8-year-old. So, both of the children would have to be treated alike.

On the first day, Mrs. D. was very firm. When Joe was seen playing on the tracks, she took him by the hand and led him back into the house. The next day she walked him to the park where he could play in the sandbox or slide and swing. Joe cried; he promised that he would not go near the tracks again. He was allowed to go out alone the following day. He kept his promise that day, but on the day after, he joined his friends on the tracks.

Mrs. D. came back to school very much discouraged, convinced that using consequences were just a waste of her time. The teacher persuaded her to try it once more. However, this time she was to go out with Joe for an entire week, regardless of his entreaties and promises. After two days, Mrs. D. came back asking the teacher whether she could now let Joe go out by himself since he had promised on oath that he would stay away from the tracks. The teacher asked Joe if he would compromise, making it three days. However, if he failed to keep his promise, he might have to be restrained for a whole month. Joe agreed and after the third day, he was allowed to go out by himself. He was not seen on the tracks again.

Had this mother allowed her initial discouragement to motivate her actions, her child's behavior might have gone on for an indefinite period.

The concept of natural and logical consequences is not clear to many people. Some insist that it is only a different word for the same thing, namely punishment. This is not the case. Punishment is administered by others. The child feels humiliated, and angry at the punisher who displays his power; invariably the child hopes for a chance to get even.

Rewards as well as punishment induce false values in the child. Many children desire to do well only because of the reward that parents or teachers promise. If no reward is foreseen, the child's incentive toward doing well is also gone. We often hear of parents who promise their children money, toys, or grant them special favors for good grades or good behavior. Both parents and teachers bribe the child instead of encouraging him to take pride and pleasure in his functioning. The case of Paul may well illustrate such a situation:

> Paul did very poorly in school until his mother promised him money for every good grade on his report card. As long as he expected the reward, Paul did extremely well at school (which indicates his ability). Yet, when this reward was no longer offered, he not only became worse in his school work than he had ever been before; he came late to school, fought, scribbled in the textbooks, etc. Prior to his mother's promises, he had only been a poor student.

This example takes into account the following points: (a) Paul had the ability; (b) he worked only for the reward; (c) he had to get even, as many children do, by punishing his parents through school failure; and (d) it shows the emphasis that parents put on school. The more they do, the less will the antagonistic child do.

A similar thing happened with Carol who completed two years' work in one semester because her mother had promised her a trip to Florida if she did well in school. When Carol returned from Florida, there was no further incentive for her to work. She assumed her old pattern of indifference, and within a few weeks, she had fallen behind in her work. After the trip to Florida, her mother's bribes of money or taking her to the show were not enough incentive.

Children who work only for reward derive no pleasure from personal growth or achievement of any kind. Very often they display the same kind of attitude toward activities such as art, music, or physical education and refuse to participate unless a reward for their efforts is in sight.

The same holds true for punishment; it underlies the same principles. Very frequently, the child does not associate the punishment with his action, but with the punisher. Since the child's main objective is to emerge the winner in every situation, he refuses to associate his action with antisocial behavior; all he can see is that he is caught and this is humiliating. His entire thinking then revolves around means to win the upper hand in the situation. Not only does he want to continue his offensive behavior despite any form of punishment, but very often he tries to assume the role of the punisher. If others can punish him, then he feels he has the same right to administer punishment to those who punished him. Such children may go out of their way to find an opportunity to retaliate; our homes and classrooms are filled with such acts of mutual retaliation.

The case of Cedric will illustrate the child who does not associate his antisocial action with punishment, but sees himself pushed down by the punisher and therefore feels unfairly treated:

> Cedric's mother had requested that the teacher allow him to take his arithmetic workbook home in order that he might catch up with his work. Permission was granted. The teacher sensed that Cedric was reluctant and asked him if he really wanted to do his work at home. Cedric hesitated and then replied, "I'd better bring it home because my mother said I must." On the way home, Cedric changed his mind about the workbook and threw it into the street and left it there. His friend, walking home with Cedric, told his mother of the incident. She in turn called Cedric's mother and reported what she had heard. Cedric had told his mother that a boy had snatched the workbook out of his hands and had run off with it. When the truth came out he was punished by both parents. His father whipped him with his belt and his mother sent him to his room without supper. Cedric took the punishment without crying or complaining, but when his younger brother came into their bedroom, Cedric whipped him with his belt. When his parents questioned him about his behavior, he replied, "If I can be punished when I did nothing, why can't I do the same thing to somebody else?"
>
> He failed to see that he had done any wrong by throwing away his book and later by lying about it. All he could see was the power his father had over others because he was stronger. Since he was older and stronger than his brother, he felt that he had the same prerogative.

In comparing Cedric's reaction to the same incident when a logical consequence was applied at school, we see that he responded differently:

> The following day, Cedric's mother brought him to school and told the teacher what had happened. The teacher in turn asked Cedric to tell his side of the story. He admitted he had thrown the workbook away, but only because he wanted to play with his friends after school and could see no other way out.
>
> The teacher then said, "I think Cedric, you could have found another way out if you had used your head instead of your temper. Do you suppose you could think for a few seconds and tell me how you might have been able to play and yet work on your workbook? You have always been so wonderful in helping other children with similar problems. I think you could solve your problem as well."
>
> Cedric first thought that he could have taken home the workbook and worked on it; but after further questioning for a still better solution, he replied, "I might have told mother that I will first play

for some time and then work in the workbook, or I might have asked her to let me take it home only over the weekend."

When asked what he proposed to do about the workbook now, he shrugged his shoulders.

The teacher suggested that the problem be discussed during the class council and he agreed.

The class made three suggestions: (1) that Cedric pay the teacher for another workbook, (2) that he take it home over weekends, and (3) that he should try to catch up with his work in four weeks. Cedric agreed without reservation. All he wanted was to be permitted to pay in small payments since his allowance was only twenty-five cents a week. This request was granted. Cedric took his workbook home religiously, without being reminded, and he completed it on time.

This is but one example to show how one can avoid fighting and apply logical consequences instead of punishment.

Let us elaborate this point a bit more carefully. If the teacher does not permit John to draw during the period when other children are drawing, because he was dawdling when he should have been working on his arithmetic, John may well feel abused because he feels deprived of his right without any good reason. If, on the other hand, during the class meeting, the group establishes the rule that anyone who chooses to dawdle during the time when others work, must do the work assignment during art time, John no longer can feel resentful toward the teacher who is only putting into practice the very principle that he helped to establish.

John was the only boy and the youngest of three children. His sisters were 12 and 8. His older sister was very intelligent, a grade ahead of her age group, was musically talented and did well academically. The second girl was mentally retarded and attended a special school each day. The parents described themselves as nonconformists and perfectionists. The mother further described herself as being very conscientious in spending much time with her children.

John's first day in kindergarten went smoothly. When his mother left him, she also left a note for the teacher with a brief review of his character (as she saw it) and stating that if a problem arose she would talk it over with John. She stated that after the discussion, John would usually choose the right way. On the second day of kindergarten, another child sat in the place John wanted. John refused to sit in any of the vacant places and was given the choice of sitting down at another place or standing. He chose to stand.

His parents came to school several times in the next few weeks, very distressed that all John did in school was stand. They tried to change teachers, but were not successful. One day, John asked his mother what she and the teacher were going to do to make him sit. She answered, "Nothing." About the same time, she stopped discussing the matter with John.

Little by little, John began to join in those activities which did not require sitting at a desk. Eventually, he began to return the teacher's greeting and would occasionally converse with her. His efforts in gym brought commendation several times.

On the first day of each month, the children could select a different place to sit. When the children changed places again, John found a place and took part in all activities. John had told his father the previous evening that he just might sit down the next day. From then on his work and behavior were satisfactory.

John received no reinforcement in the classroom for his mistaken ideas. His teacher neither gave in nor struggled with him. He was allowed to make his own decision, and his choice of action was respected. This would encourage a sense of equality by mutual respect for each other's decisions. The morning greetings and the commendations in gym served to make him feel that he, as a person, was welcome and worthwhile. His teacher also showed that she believed he had the ability to solve his own problem.

The parents were encouraged to discover that there was a way out of the dilemma without pressure or loss of face on their part, and that left to himself, their son could really make a sensible decision. The teacher's beliefs in the methods used were reinforced and she was satisfied that John could now turn his abilities into more useful and productive channels.

There is no pat formula for logical consequences. What will work in one situation may not help in another. Jack, who likes to go outdoors, will be differently affected by being kept in during recess time than Mary who hates to go out. Therefore, by treating Jack and Mary in different ways, similar results can be obtained; and since they have participated in setting up the logical consequences, they do not feel that they are punished by the teacher. It must be remembered that the use of logical consequences requires an understanding of the child and of the situation. When to do What and to Whom requires judgment about a very large number of imponderables because every situation is unique.

Adults frequently find it difficult to understand the concept of logical consequences, but it is readily accepted by children. Very often they try to apply it to their out-of-school lives, as the following cases illustrate:

Susan's younger sister had to be coaxed and helped to dress in the morning in order to be ready for the school bus. One day, Susan asked the teacher if she would be permitted to be late to school for a few days. When asked for the reason, she replied, "I have finally convinced my mother that she should let my sister take the logical consequences and miss the school bus if she refuses to get ready on time. She would have to walk to school, and I would have to walk with her. I don't mind, but she hates walking. I am sure that after a few days of walking, she will get ready on time." Susan's plan, it may be interesting to know, worked.

One day, Bobby said, "Will you, please, call my mother and tell her how to handle temper tantrums? She won't believe me when I tell her, but she will believe you. My brother throws tantrums every time he can't get what he wants. Mother gets terribly upset and gives in to him. I told her to either send him out of the room or leave him to have his tantrum all to himself just as we do at school, but she is afraid that something might happen to him." Bobby used to throw tantrums in school. He had learned how to handle this kind of behavior from his own experience.

Most class situations lend themselves to the application of logical consequences. However, some situations require greater skill and ingenuity than others. Often, when the teacher is at a loss as to a possible logical consequence, the child himself may have a suggestion that is appropriate. This may be surprising to some, but teachers who use this approach will confirm the frequency of such occurrences. The following example illustrates this point:

For several days in succession, Ronny returned late to class after recess. The teacher first talked to him about it and told him that he would have to stay in class during recess if he failed again to return on time. He said that he would return with the other children, but failed to keep his word. Ronny had to remain in the classroom for three days while the other children went out to play. The day he was allowed to go out, he was again ten minutes late in coming back to class. He claimed that he did not hear the whistle. This situation was discussed with the entire class. No one could think of a consequence which would be logical and yet effective.

At this point, Ronny himself suggested a logical consequence. He suggested that he go out during recess, but that he should not be permitted to play. He would have to stand somewhere on the playground where the teacher could see him. He claimed that this would be even harder for him to take than being alone in class because in class he could read or play by himself. If he couldn't see the other children playing, it wouldn't bother him quite as much as

87

when he actually sees them and can't participate. It was also easier for him to come back on time when he was not sidetracked by some activity. The class and the teacher decided to try Ronny's plan, and Ronny stood in one spot during recess for an entire week. After that, Ronny returned to class on time.

Natural consequences should apply to everybody, not just to the student. Piaget distinguishes between distributive justice which pertains to all and retributive justice, which is punishment and retaliation. Sometimes, the teacher may have to face the consequences of her behavior. If a democratic spirit is to prevail in the group, the teacher must take such consequences graciously. Two examples may illustrate such a situation:

> Once, after having hastily written an assignment on the blackboard, I left the class alone for a few minutes. Upon my return, I found several words on the board which were circled with colored chalk. At the bottom was written, "Careless writing, please do over." I made the corrections without any comment. Since there was no reaction from the class, it was obvious that the children took this as a matter of fact.
>
> Another time, I forgot to announce that a movie would be shown in the afternoon. Since my class missed it, they asked for a twenty minute-activity period as compensation. They felt this was their perfect right.

When the teacher mentioned these incidents to some of her colleagues, they were horrified at the "insolence" of the students. In their opinion such "permissiveness" leads to disrespect and disorder. We cannot share this pessimism. Children have greater respect for elders who do admit their mistakes, who respect the child's opinion, and who share equally in privileges.

As was already pointed out, before we apply a natural consequence, we must consider the particular child, the goal of his behavior, and his method of obtaining it. Then we must apply the kind of logical consequence which is most likely to be effective in this specific case. Sending a child out of the room for a few minutes may be a very effective consequence for Nancy who seldom disturbs; but if it concerns Arden who is constantly disturbing through talking and other noises, sending him out for a few minutes will only be another feather in his cap.

What then should we do with Arden? One thing is certain, we cannot and must not allow him to disturb the class. There are several consequences which may impress him. Let us consider two of them:

One way of handling this problem is for the teacher to put a mark on the blackboard every time Arden talks out or makes noises with the obvious intention to disturb others. Each mark may count two to five minutes dependent on the extent of his disturbance, then the time will be deducted from Arden's talk time during group discussion. The Ardens are usually the kind of children who actively participate in every discussion. Not being able to talk when all the others can, may be a hard pill for him to swallow.

The teacher could approach the situation in another way. She could have a private talk with Arden asking him whether he knows why he talks so much. Then she could, in the usual way, confront him with his goal, that is, that he wants her attention. He probably would acknowledge that with a recognition reflex. Now comes the crucial question. "How many times do you think you will want my attention during the next hour?" To that the child usually answers, "I don't know." This is correct. He really does not know what to say. So the teacher may ask him whether fifteen times would be enough. Again, the child, not being aware of the extent of his interruption, will think it is too much. But the teacher still may suggest fifteen times. As soon as Arden disturbs, all she has to do is look at him and say, "Arden No. 1, Arden No. 2." It usually does not take fifteen times. There is no fun in this kind of attention.

For a few days, Allain refused to do any work. He refused to answer when I asked him if he needed any help or if anything bothered him. He hummed or tapped his foot when I tried to teach. Several children complained that he pushed them as they were going down the stairs. The class then decided that Allain was to sit in the back of the room where he could do anything he wanted as long as he stayed there. He was also told that he could not return to his seat unless he decided to participate in class activities and stopped disturbing.

Allain sat in the back for several days without making any attempt to return to his seat. Everybody ignored him. On the day when the class lined up to go to gym, the children noticed Allain in the line. Several children protested. They asked for a short student council meeting right there as they stood in line. They decided that Allain could not be free to participate whenever he felt like it and then go back to disrupting the class. He must decide either to participate as a full member of the class, or do as he pleased in the back of the room. In any case, he had to stay in class and think it over while they went to gym. When we returned, Allain was in his seat and had almost finished the arithmetic assignment. The children surrounded him, but said nothing. Allain had made his choice.

No doubt, some teachers will consider this a waste of good time; they may also ask if this is fair to the other children. Everything is "fair" if it helps the class and if, in the long run, it promotes greater cooperation. As long as Allain was disturbing, most of the children could not work. Doubting teachers are invited to try this method consistently for one week; they will find that time will not be wasted. If a mother or teacher does not take the time to train a child, she will spend much more time with the disturbing child.

Thus, we see that there are various possibilities for a child to experience a consequence which is closely related to his behavior, and which he usually accepts without reservations and without considering himself maltreated. No matter how much an Allain may want to participate in the group discussion, he will respect the decision of the class since he is a part of it. He would not react in the same way if the teacher were to put tape on his lips to keep him from talking (as some teachers do) or if he were paddled.

In all cases, we must remember that the application of natural and logical consequences is only a correctional method to deal with the immediate situation; it is not an end in itself. In every case, the child must be helped to understand *why* he is behaving as he does, how this kind of behavior has brought him "success" (from his point of view) until now, how it affects other people, and last but not least, how he may obtain status through more acceptable methods of behavior.

The section on group discussions (see pp. 100–136) explains how we arrange such discussions with young children.

THE STRUCTURE OF THE GROUP

From the moment of his birth, an individual is a member of a group and continues throughout his lifetime in some form of group membership. One of the characteristics common to all human beings is the need to feel that he belongs—that is, the need and capacity for association with other persons.

Whenever human beings get together, their associations with one another set up a process of transaction. The resulting pattern of interpersonal relations has many subtle movements and defines the role and the activities of the individuals in respect to each other, in respect to the main subgroups, and to the group as a whole. An individual may be assigned a role by the other members of the group, or it may be one he has chosen for himself and maintained by his particular behavior. His role is thus, indirectly, assigned by the group. On the other hand, if a child is a bully, he has a good chance of maintaining his role even though the others in the group do not like his behavior. This child forces his behavior on the group.

In the group, some individuals develop status and admiration while others may be completely ignored or rejected, thus reflecting their social participation. Some individuals may be loners by choice, others may be loners by rejection of the group.

Billy, going on 11, was one of the oldest students in the third grade class. He was a handsome fellow, tall and well built. However, his stooped posture, shuffling walk, dangling long arms, and drooping eyelids gave him the appearance of a mentally retarded child. One had to call his name several times before he responded. Billy did not seem to be interested in any of the children or they in him.

Billy spent most of the school day daydreaming, playing with some object, looking out of the window, or in the washroom. It was not unusual for him to disappear into the washroom for as long as half an hour. Usually someone had to go after him. He showed no interest in any of the school activities, not even in art or in physical education.

Billy had failed twice in school—in first grade and in second grade. During these four years of school he had learned virtually nothing, for he could not write his full name, did not know the letters of the alphabet, could not distinguish between the tall and the small letters, and could not count in successive order.

The teacher learned that the family had moved around a lot; that he had lived with his grandmother for a year, and that an uncle lived with them on and off. It was difficult to tell what was true and what was distorted or imagined, for Billy never replied directly to any question. When asked, "Billy, where is your father?" he would reply, "Sometimes my uncle buys me candy." When the teacher replied, "Oh, you have an uncle? Does he live with you?" he would answer, "Sometimes he lets me ride on his shoulders." It was impossible to get a straight answer from him, since he followed his own trend of thought.

One day, the teacher noticed that Billy was watching with fascination two boys playing checkers. She asked him if he knew how to play the game, and he said that he didn't. When she asked him if he would like to learn, he seemed most eager. The teacher presented this situation to the class during group discussion. It was decided that, for some time, the teacher should play checkers with Billy for ten minutes every day, and one of the students would then play with him for ten more minutes. This pleased Billy immensely. The next morning, he came straight to the teacher, asking her when she would play with him. She asked him to watch the clock until the big hand would point to a certain number, and then call her. (He "could not" tell time.) Billy's eyes were glued to the clock, and the second the hand pointed to the specified number, he reminded the teacher that the time had come.

Billy did not learn easily, but he seemed very happy in the process. After a few days, he understood the fundamental principles, and could move his checkers along the black squares without getting off onto the red. (This principle helped him later in his understanding of keeping on the line in writing.) Melvin, the boy who played checkers with him most of the time, showed great patience and was most encouraging. He praised Billy's attitude and pointed out his progress during one of the group discussions, thus raising Billy's prestige in the eyes of the other children. It was in response to Melvin's praise that Billy summoned the courage to walk up in front of the class and thank Melvin for his help. This was his first real contact with the entire group.

One day, Billy asked the teacher if he could sit next to Melvin. The latter said that he would like to have Billy as a neighbor and that he would like to help him with his work. The teacher was pleased with this new development because nobody had chosen Billy in the sociometric test that the class had taken a few weeks before. He had chosen two girls who were equally behind in their achievements, and who could not help him with the work. Thus, a new chapter started in Billy's life. He practiced writing for hours. When he could write legibly, he began working on simple spelling and arithmetic. Melvin helped him by checking his work, and by practicing with him at the blackboard. It was not necessary for the teacher to play checkers with Billy any more, and she devoted this time to helping him with reading. He was still reluctant to join the reading group but was pleased to receive ten minutes of daily reading instruction.

As Billy progressed in his studies he became more out-going and eager to make friends. This was expecially noticeable during recess. He was no longer isolated but participated in the activities of the other children.

For many children, the school is the first place where they are exposed to association and interaction with more than a small circle of family and neighborhood friends. The classroom, therefore, provides the first intensive group living for the child.

Every class has its own particular qualities. Although in many respects the group resembles other groups of similar size, each class has its unique character. This characteristic of each group explains why teachers express astonishment at the differences in the children they had last year as compared to those they have this year. One group was "just a delight to work with," while the other is impossible. What makes the difference? The children come from the same community and have similar backgrounds; they are equally intelligent or slow—and yet, as compared to last year's children who were cooperative and eager to learn, these fight and show no interest in learning.

The class reflects the characteristics of the individuals who play a leading part. Everyone in his own way, through his behavior, contributes toward the particular climate that eventually prevails in the classroom. There are those who promote easy contact with others and those who are peacemakers; the lazy, and the overambitious and industrious; the heroes, and the rejected; the beautiful, and the unattractive; and a score of others. Each one of those has a strong impact on the structure and the atmosphere of the group. Thus we may find an altogether different group behavior in a class where there is a great deal of mutual attraction, while in another group, antagonism prevails. The tone of the class is usually decided by a few who are the natural leaders. Here is an example:

> Three second grade boys were regarded with horror by the others in class, including the teacher. They were noisy, they beat up any child who did not go along with their demands, or beat up those who were admired because of their academic achievement. These boys dictated to their class and literally controlled it. When they entered third grade, they met with a new teacher but with the same group of children. The old atmosphere that had prevailed in second grade was automatically passed on to the third grade. Had these boys been separated, each assigned to a different room, the situation might have been altogether different at the start of school, and it would have influenced the initial setting of the classroom climate.

This example illustrates that the pictures the children have of one another are important for the class. The same type of behavior of two different children may be seen and interpreted differently by the members of the same class. It is the attitude the group takes toward the behavior of the individual that will determine his position in the class. It may bring him status and satisfaction, or it may develop or increase his loneliness and unhappiness.

The classroom must be regarded as more than just an accumulation of many individuals. Some teachers cannot understand why certain classes give them so much trouble and why the students do not learn as they should. They complain that each year the students are more difficult to discipline, and that the effective teaching and disciplinary methods which they previously used to not work.

The skilled teacher, sensitive to the group atmosphere, will sense the type of atmosphere her new class has and plan a constructive program through which she can gradually change the children's attitudes. The climate of the classroom reflects the personal characteristics of all and influences in turn the development of each child emotionally, academically, and socially. Therefore, the teacher must know not only the individuals in the class but also how they interact with one another; for this determines how the child feels in the class. Without some knowledge of group dynamics, a teacher cannot have the necessary insight into the group's problems. She should never lose sight of the fact that children grow and develop within a context of interpersonal relationships. The explanation of what goes on, of how and what the child learns, can be found in certain relationships that further or retard progress. The function of the group can be understood only by examining the interactions that take place and the perceptions, goals, and frustrations of the individual student.

Sometimes a teacher is faced with a class which does not respond or cooperate. She needs to remind herself that it is not she alone who determines whether the group process will be satisfactory or chaotic. There are other factors which make the integration of a group difficult. Of major importance is the presence of various clique leaders within the group. The teacher needs to ask herself these questions: "Is there a clique structure in the group?" "What values do the cliques hold?" "Is there a hierarchal leadership structure?" "Is there a pattern of clique rivalry and competition?" The teacher who is confronted with such a class may very well wonder how she will be able to teach these children to live together, to share together, and to use their varying abilities and interests for the common good.

How can a teacher learn to know each student as an individual as well as a member of his group? How can she learn about the antagonisms and competitions among cliques and other such groups? A great deal can be learned from direct observation in the classroom and on the playground. It is important to observe who plays with whom, who takes the lead, who refuses to participate unless he has his way, who teases, and how others respond to it; who is left out at all times, and who is left out just in certain activities; who appears clumsy; who gets easily angry; who retaliates; who deliberately withdraws; who runs to the teacher for help; who disregards the rules of the game; who is boasting; who fights other people's battles; and scores of other types of behavior. The teacher needs to be aware of who sets off a contagion, who eggs others on in their misbehavior, and who starts enthusiastic volunteering.

Equally important is to know who walks home with whom; who plays with whom after school; who goes to the same Sunday school; who visits whom at home; who east lunch together; who whispers or sends notes to whom; and who copies his work from others.

Teachers often get information about their students from other students, even though they do not ask for this information.

> Lanny came up to his teacher on the playground and asked if she had given Millie some candy canes for straightening out the closet. The teacher indicated that she had not. Lanny said, "Well, she has a whole bunch of them and is passing them out." The teacher checked the closet and a number of candy canes were gone.

All of this information can provide some degree of insight; but, at best, it is only a section or a narrow view. It does not tell a teacher how a child feels about his position in class, nor how he would like to change it if he could. It does not tell whom a student admires or envies or with whom he would like to associate. However, the teacher forms certain opinions regarding individual students. In some respects her opinion may be correct, but often discrepancies occur. For instance, a teacher may be impressed with Mary, who is always neat, polite, and a good student; therefore she cannot understand why the other students reject her. Bill, on the other hand, who is rough, untidy, and a poor student, is very much liked by his peers. The role the child plays in the class is not always immediately obvious. Nor is it always easy to know who is the real leader, who determines acceptance or rejection of each child. However, through the use of sociometric methods, the teacher is able to perceive the interpersonal relationships between the children in her class.

SOCIOMETRIC METHODS

Sociometry is the study of the relationships among people. A sociogram points to the attractions which individuals have toward each other, and it discloses the role they occupy in the class. H. H. Jennings[6] refers to it as a test of friendship constellations.

Sociometric tests or questionnaires are a method of testing the teacher's judgment. They are part of a technique of learning how individuals perceive themselves in relation to others. A sociometric test allows each child to express his personal feeling for others in the form of choices for functioning with them, within the group of which he and they are members. After the tests are given, then the data need to be tabulated. Two methods that are frequently used are the grid system or sociometric matrix, and the sociogram, which is a diagram used to show clearly the network of acceptance and rejections in a graphic way.

There are various forms of sociometric methods, but in school,

[6]Helen Hall Jennings, *Sociometry in Group Relations: A Work Guide for Teachers* (Washington, D.C.: American Council on Education, 1948).

especially in the lower grades, a simple sociometric questionnaire may be sufficient to obtain the information a teacher needs in order to know the sociological structure of relationships. Such a device will provide her with the information needed to deal with children's problems effectively. The teacher who collects sociometric information is well equipped to plan for desired cooperation.

A sociometric questionnaire could be made on a variety of social functions, such as sitting next to, eating with, going to the show with, visiting, playing or studying with, borrowing from or lending to, talking with or telling secrets to, and so on.

A sociogram will help the teacher to know the child's position in the group. Knowing who the individual chooses to associate with may provide a clue to his attitudes and to his values which may explain his difficulties in class. In addition, it provides insight into the kind of position the child wants to occupy. Thus the teacher can find out which of classmates can influence the behavior of a particular child. Seating him next to children he chooses assists him to gain greater acceptance among the class members and may change his past poor associations for better ones. The child gains increasing ability to establish mutual relationships with other children to whom he is drawn.

Through this sociometric device, a teacher may discover that timid Larry wants to sit next to boisterous, bullying Jim. Evidently, Larry considers Jim strong and powerful and worthy of admiration. This permits the teacher to plan activities which may induce Larry's independence and get him to join children with more "healthy" values. In new contacts he can come to a reappraisal of himself. Furthermore, the teacher can use her understanding of their relationship to help both Jim and Larry.

She may assign a project to these two boys for which each would be required to give a report. The chances are that Jim's support would help Larry, who was always afraid to talk in front of the group, to get up the courage to face his ordeal. He may do better than he expected. The group could then give Larry realistic encouragement by showing their understanding of his problem and their appreciation of his delivery.

Jim, on the other hand, might be helped in a reversed way. Larry's admiration for him may help him feel more secure in his social relationships and he may, as a result, have less need to be boisterous. Chances are that he may give his report in a manner which will not diminish the effectiveness of Larry's report. The group has a wonderful opportunity to give him attention by praising his modest and considerate manner.

In the same class, the teacher may discover that a gentle child was regarded with the highest favor by a number of problem children. This would give the teacher a clue to the inner wishes of many of the "tough" ones, and this relationship could be used to influence them.

The information necessary for making up the sociometric matrix in the following example can be obtained by asking each child to indicate which classmates he would like to have sit next to him in the classroom. Two choices were allowed each child; they were asked to indicate with a number 1 their first choice and with a number 2 their second choice (see Table 2, p. 98).

The individual's choice must be taken seriously regardless of how the teacher may feel about this particular constellation. Teachers must give special attention to those students who were not chosen by anyone, placing them with one of their choices. Since the unchosen ones are usually discouraged and unhappy children, putting them together with members whom they admire and envy automatically raises their self-esteem as well as their status in the group. Each sociogram is only a starting point for further investigation to gain understanding of the motives and values underlying the choices and rejections.

Sociograms should be given at specific intervals, for attractions and rejections change as the class works together. These changes occur more frequently in the lower grades where children are more easily influenced. Such tests may be given once a month during the first three months of the school year, and reduced to every two months. However, there is no set pattern as to how and when to give a sociometric test. Each teacher must know her group and use her own judgment.

There are times when a teacher is very much tempted to separate children who show a great interest in each other because it interferes with the work. Separating these children may be a temporary solution to the teacher's problem, but it is not an effective method that will help them toward self-discipline and learning.

Usually seating arrangements, working committees, and other groupings are set up without consideration of the children's wishes. Although such arrangements are made with the best intentions in the belief that this will produce the best working atmosphere, the opposite is often the case, for the best conditions for learning are thereby destroyed.

The following example illustrates how a sociogram helped the teacher understand the problem a child had and how it helped the child as well:

> Maxie, 10 years old, was the only Jewish child in a class of thirty-two. His parents were orthodox and associated only with people whose religious belief was as strong as theirs. They decided that he

97

Table 2

Chooser\Chosen	Ann	Gary	Tom	Helen	Susan	Peter	Barbara	Keith	Danny
Ann		X		1	X		2	X	
Gary		X	2		X	1		X	
Tom		X			X	1		X	2
Helen	1	X			X			X	
Susan	1	X			X			X	2
Peter	X	X	X	X	X	X	X	X	X
Barbara	2	X		1	X			X	
Keith		X			X	1		X	2
Danny		X	2		X	1		X	
Totals	3	0	2	2	0	4	1	0	3

X = Not chosen or the child made no choice himself.

Not chosen: 1. Gary. Put him next to one of his choices Peter or Tom. 2. Keith. Put him next to Peter or Danny. Helen chose only one girl but she was chosen twice. Peter chose no one but he is most popular in class. Why? Probably an operator. If he were popular for being a good student, most likely he would have chosen someone. Telling somebody that he likes him is beneath Peter, or a sign of weakness, but he succeeded in impressing this class with his "strength". Next popular is Danny. Ann is the most popular of the girls. No one chose Susan — put her next to Ann or Danny. Notice she is the only girl who picked a boy. Could she show too much interest in boys and this may be the reason the girls don't want her? Observe her and observe the attitude of the girls toward the boys. Barbara is not popular. Why are she and Helen not popular?

was to become a rabbi. In fact, they felt that he was destined to become one. Maxie was well aware of this and he conducted himself in a manner befitting his destination. He dressed somewhat more conservatively than the other children and he wore a skull cap. This alone was enough to set him apart from the others even if other mannerisms had not made him conspicuous. Maxie kept to himself in class and on the playground. He worked conscientiously and was very much disturbed when he performed poorly on a test. He would then try to convince the teacher that he either misunderstood the problem or that he did not hear her when she dictated. He would plead for another chance, etc. He would ignore the teacher's and the other students' reassurance that his score was of no great importance since he was performing very well most of the time. Maxie nagged, following the teacher wherever she went, repeating over and over, "Please give me another chance."

Maxie was one of the first in class to finish his work. When he finished, he would quietly walk to the library table and read or he would study the globe. He never disturbed. He never joined the other children who had also finished their work and who were engaged in an art project. Maxie disliked going out at recess time. Almost every day he would plead with the teacher to be allowed to remain in class where he could study or read for pleasure. He considered going out a waste of time. When the teacher insisted that he go out because he needed the fresh air and the exercise, he accused her of being undemocratic and inconsistent in her principles, which she had discussed in class; he preferred to stay in, and since this did not hurt anyone, it should be his privilege.

When the first sociometric test was administered, Maxie returned a blank sheet of paper. However, he was chosen by a number of children who carried prestige in class. Maxie was seated next to two of these children, one on each side of him. He neither protested nor showed any enthusiasm.

For several days after, Maxie continued working and keeping to himself as before. He still begged to be allowed to remain in the class at recess.

A few days later, the teacher noticed Maxie explaining the morning assignment to his neighbor who had come late to school that morning. A day later Maxie was pointing out places on the map with a pointer, explaining something to his neighbor. The two boys then sat down at the table and studied the dictionary together. Soon after, Maxie did not ask to be allowed to remain in class during recess. On the playground, Maxie and his friend talked. The teacher noticed that Maxie took off his cap and allowed his friend to try it on.

When the second sociometric test was given, Maxie returned his paper with the names of the two boys who were sitting next to him. As it happened, he was also first choice of the boy with whom he spent most of his free time at school. Several other children had chosen him also.

This was the beginning of a great change in Maxie's social adjustment in class. Gradually, he began to participate in nonacademic activities, and even accepted a part in a play. In time, he joined the boys in playing ball and other games. He talked more freely with the other children. When asked why he wore the skull cap, he explained its meaning and significance. He also talked about his future as a rabbi and what that meant to him.

The use of sociometric methods gives the teacher insight and knowledge as to the composition of her classroom and the sub-groups therein. It allows her to succeed in breaking down the antagonistic forces and to build on the positive elements so that isolated children and oppositional leaders are integrated into a cooperative cohesive classroom.

GROUP DISCUSSIONS WITH CHILDREN

THE PRIMARY SOCIAL GROUP

The child grows up in a world of things and a world of people. From the moment of birth, the child is a member of his family group. In his early relationship to other members of the family, he establishes his own approaches to others and develops his orientation to life. His experiences within the family set the frame of reference through which the child perceives, interprets and evaluates the world around him. In learning to perceive himself and the world, he is guided by his family. This is part of a process of socialization through which the child becomes part of many groups.

The family is often called the primary social group, which provides close, intense, and enduring attachments; it acts as a link between the child and other groups which he joins when he enters school. Bit by bit, piece by piece, the child establishes his own pattern of life which is the integration of all his reactions to his experiences. He fortifies his impressions by watching others and experimenting with them in constantly shifting interpersonal settings or groups that form his social world.

THE SECOND GROUP

The second source of the child's orientation to society is the play group. From this group of peers he learns how to get along with other people. As the child enters school, he has to deal with children from

100

different families, and with a greater variety of experiences and more difficult situations. He learns to establish social relationships outside the family setting and to accept general rules regarding work, order, and regulation. The child learns to play different roles in the community and learns how other people think. Functioning as a group member is one way of learning to cope with his environment. One of the best methods of learning is through group discussions which may bring about changes of behavior.

What is a group discussion? Group discussion involves a group of people talking and thinking together about some problem or topic. Group discussion is not just conversation. It differs from conversation in that it has direction, it examines problem areas and also faces unpleasant facts which normally are ignored or sidetracked. Group discussion is the democratic interchange of ideas guided by the needs of the group.

GROUP DISCUSSIONS AS LEARNING EXPERIENCES

What is the purpose of a group discussion? Using group discussion not only helps children to develop better interpersonal relationships but enhances learning through accumulated information. Effective communication of ideas leads to problem solving. Children learn through discussions to explore controversial matters and to deal with people of different backgrounds.

In a discussion group, children form attitudes and set values which may influence them for their whole life and may affect their behavior inside and outside of school. Group discussions provide opportunities for emotional and intellectual participation and a feeling of reassurance that one is not alone. Difficult tasks seem lighter when we have shared our ideas, aspirations, successes, problems, and anxieties. The child learns to evaluate and profit from another classmate's experience as well as from his own. He feels supported and becomes more responsive. He can learn constructive ways of handling frustrations and of working through upsetting problems.

Communication is the cement that ties individuals to a group. In the group, they communicate their ideas and feelings. Group discussions are probably the most effective means by which a teacher can integrate all children into one class for a common purpose. Through effectively directed group discussions, the teacher may succeed in raising the morale of the group and change the atmosphere of the room. In this way, the learning process is facilitated by a common goal of all pupils. The teacher learns what each child feels and thinks, how he relates to others and what his attitude is toward school. For many children, talking in an atmosphere of mutual understanding stimulates thinking. As a child mulls over and talks about some problem, he may find a solution. In group discussions we have a class of children working on the same problem at the same time, and the results are usually good. Quite often the children will realize there are a number of solutions to the same problem.

These purposes or values of group discussions are achieved by exploring the feelings, the beliefs, doubts, fears, and concerns of those involved and by helping each member to gain an understanding of and respect for each other by collectively solving the problems of the classroom. The first task of group discussion is to stimulate each child to listen to the others.

Frequently, people do not listen to others who express different opinions. In the group discussion, everybody has the right to say what he thinks, and is obliged to listen too. Here everybody is equal and treated with respect.

THE TEACHER'S ATTITUDE

Some teachers have difficulty with group discussions and feel that they are not effective. Usually, the main problem of the teacher stems from doubt in her own ability. She may believe that she is not ready, or the group is not prepared, but usually it is her own feelings of inadequacy.

Teachers must learn how to lead a group discussion. There are two pitfalls into which they quite often fall. First, they may use such a discussion to impose their own ideas, to explain and to preach, and to get some confirming remarks from their students.

The following example shows how a teacher could mistakenly use group discussion to preach to her students:

Teacher: Put your money away and we'll have a discussion.
    Child: I have something I want to bring up.
Teacher: First, there is something I want to talk to the class about. This morning when you went to gym, I was utterly ashamed of you. You know better than to run down the stairs. We have talked about it dozens of times. How often have I told you that you must not run through the corridor and on the stairs? Honestly, one would think that I have never talked to you about it. I don't ever want to see this again. Do you understand? And if this happens again, I just won't let you go to gym. I don't like to have to punish you like this, but I'm sure that you will agree that you're forcing me to do this.

A trained leader in group discussions might have conducted this incident in the following manner:

Teacher: Boys and girls, I would like to discuss with you what happened this morning on the way to Gym. I'd appreciate it if you would carefully consider this matter and comment on it.

With such an approach, the chances are that most of the children would want to talk about it. Should no one respond, the discussion might be channeled in this direction:

Teacher: I need your help, children. I don't want to make any decisions without discussing it with you first. In fact, I hope that you will make the suggestions as to what we should do. Does anyone know what I'm referring to?

Child: I think you are talking about the way we went to gym this morning.

Teacher: That's right. How do you feel about the way the class behaved? The child may say that the class ran and shouted.

Teacher: I recall that we have discussed this matter before. How many of you remember:

Children: *(Hands go up.)*

Teacher: What do you think we should do now? This kind of behavior may bring us into trouble with the principal and with other teachers.

Jimmy: Next time our class should walk down quietly.

Teacher: How do the others feel about Jimmy's suggestion?

Child: Most of us would walk down in an orderly fashion but that there are some who won't.

Teacher: What shall we do about these children? Please, don't think of punishment, but try to think of a solution that would give these children some choices.

Child: Maybe they should be given a chance to walk down with the class, but if they should run or shout, they would have to return to class. They would be deprived of gym that day.

Teacher: How many think that this is a good solution to this problem? *(If the majority of the children should agree to this solution then the possible solution may be tried.)*

Teacher: Let's try it, and if it doesn't work out, we'll have to try something else.

This is but one of a number of possible approaches by which the teacher and the class try to find a solution to a problem. The teacher's appeal for the children's help raises their feeling of importance and unites the class in a common goal. The teacher who uses the class to help her with whatever problem she may have will find that most children will respond in a positive manner.

The following example is especially typical of how many teachers use group discussions to talk to children.

Teacher: I'd like to talk to you about our basketball. I repeat, "a basketball," not "a football." I am sure all of you know the difference. A basketball is meant to be thrown into a basket. That's why it is called "basketball." This afternoon I saw some of you kicking it. Do you know what may happen when you kick it? It may get a hole in it and then we'd have to have it repaired. Do you know how much it costs to have such a ball repaired? It's not cheap, and the school will not pay for it. You know who will have to pay for it? You will. I know that you enjoy that basketball and wouldn't want anything to happen to it, so let's all be very careful how we use it. All right? *(Children nod their heads.)* I knew you'd see it my way, and I'm very proud of you.

This teacher is trying to convey friendliness and confidence in the children. However, she still resorts to "preaching." Chances are that the children pay little attention to what she is saying. She might have said:

Teacher: I must talk to you about our basketball. I know that you enjoy playing with it, but before we can take it out again, we'll have to make some decisions. Whose ball is it?

Child: Ours.

Teacher: I am afraid it is not.

Child: It belongs to the school.

Teacher: That's right. We may use it, but we are responsible if anything were to happen to it. How can we prevent this?
(The children will now discuss various possibilities of how to use the ball so that no damage should occur.)

Teacher: What should we do if any of the children should kick it?

Children will then suggest a number of consequences that will make sense to the possible offenders. They may suggest that these children not be permitted to play basketball for a week or two. They may suggest that these children should pay for any damage they have done. The important thing is that the students need to be involved in the discussion and decision making.

The second pitfall in conducting a discussion is allowing it to become a free-for-all, unrestrained and unstructured, letting each child express himself as he wishes without taking any leadership. Then when things get out of control, the teacher becomes autocratic and overpowering. Children want and need leadership, not *bosses*.

Some teachers voice other objections to the use of group discussions. They have the mistaken idea that children are not capable of understanding the behavior of others, the roles they play within the group, or the ways in which they influence each other. Some teachers feel that discussions take too much time, and that they cannot afford to take this time away from the teaching of subject matter. In reality, much time is saved as the pupils become more willing to learn and are more cooperative.

PRINCIPLES FOR GROUP DISCUSSIONS

There are a number of different ways to use classroom discussions. However, the principles for carrying on good group discussions remain constant, only the format may change. Here are five ways group discussions may be used to good advantage:

1. Group discussions may be held on any subject at any time of the day. For example, in social studies, the discussion may be on Cuba, Vietnam, the United Nations, etc. There may be discussions during the day involving different subjects.
2. Sometimes it is valuable to stop everything and have a discussion concerning a particular child's actions or to share a particular event or happening, such as Kennedy's assassination, results of an election, or other items of importance. This may take only a few minutes and could alleviate the emotional stress of the classroom.
3. Certain discussions should take place at a definite time and place. For example, the last period on Wednesday afternoon could be set aside to discuss classroom problems, personal problems and/or share thoughts and feelings.
4. Teachers can use stories as a basis for discussions in helping children to understand behavior.
5. The class council may be used as the framework for group discussions.

IMPORTANT CONSIDERATIONS

Teachers need to know how to use group discussions for mutual understanding and help. Therefore, she needs to know the purpose and goals of behavior. The four goals of disturbing behavior of children have been described (p. 17). If a teacher uses common sense, induces the children to express themselves freely, and makes interpretations about possible goals, she is on safe ground. Every teacher should be encouraged to try this kind of group discussion. She may make mistakes; if she dares to be spontaneous, she is bound to make mistakes! But despite mistakes, she can help children to understand their own behavior and to solve their own problems.

Usually, when group discussions are undertaken, the expected difficulties do not pose serious problems. Indeed, merely talking things over has strong corrective value. Children have a deep need to discuss with adults what really matters to them. They have too few opportunities to do so. Not only is the content of the discussion important, but also the feeling of acceptance and the freedom to talk without being hushed, ridiculed or threatened. This process encourages spontaneity and self-expression.

WHAT PREVENTS CHILDREN FROM PARTICIPATION?

The child who cannot share his thoughts and feelings is usually a lonely child, one who is constantly on guard, afraid of being hurt. To him, sharing means giving of himself, and since he is only getting and not giving he will find it difficult to involve himself in a discussion. However, if he can be involved in discussions, it will teach him how to give as well as receive.

Many children would like to participate in group discussions, but do not know how. They may have never experienced a friendly discussion. At home, these children are either the ones who rule or the ones who must obey without question.

Some children may use the group to compete with others for having the best idea or to talk the most. Still other children may use the group to criticize or to blame others, to seek sympathy or to gain favor.

With such a variety of problems, how can a teacher unite the class into one group with a common goal? How does she get the children toward this end? How does she conduct a group discussion?

GETTING DISCUSSIONS STARTED

Group discussions should start as soon as the teacher becomes acquainted with her class and the class is comfortable with her. It may start on the very first day of school. (See "Winning the Child," p. 54.) She may invite the class to suggest how their room should be decorated or how they would like to spend the first two days in class. Most of the children will respond favorably to suggestions which do not involve them in a personal way. A discussion develops during the process of planning, organizing committees, and assigning responsibilities. Planning bulletin boards is a suggested beginning. The project should be planned for the following day, if possible, in order to go to the next step, which is an evaluation of their project.

FIRST DAY DISCUSSION—GRADES 3-7

Teacher: As you see, our room is pretty bare. I was wondering if I should put up pictures, but decided to wait for you to help me decide how we should decorate our classroom. Would you like to take a few moments and think about it? Then, if any of you has an idea, raise your hand.

106

Ted: Last year we brought plants to school to put on the window. Maybe we could do that this year.

Nancy: Yes, that looked nice. I brought a geranium.

Alex: I think that we could draw some pictures and put them on the wall.

Teacher: Both of you have good ideas. But let's first see how the children feel about plants and then we will talk about pictures. All right?

Helen: Maybe everyone can bring a plant to school.

Joe: I can't bring a plant because we have only two plants and my mother will not let me have one.

Teacher: Of course not, I know that not everyone can bring a plant. But let's see if most children like the idea of having plants. How many of you would like to have plants? *(Many hands go up.)* It seems that most of you do. So do I. Would you like to find out if you can bring a plant to school, and those of you who can, bring it as soon as possible.

Tommy: I don't know if I can bring a plant, but I have a fish bowl with five guppies that I can bring.

Teacher: Who would like Tommy to bring his guppies? *(Many children raise their hands.)* Tommy, do you know how to take care of the fish? You see, I don't know if I am good at such things. I don't have much experience.

Tommy: Oh, I know what to do. I always take care of the fish.

Jim: I can help him. We have an aquarium at home, and I know all about it.

Teacher: That sounds wonderful. Maybe I'll learn from both of you. Somebody mentioned pictures. I'm sure that most of you like to draw pictures. What kind of pictures should we have?

Alex: I would like to make a picture of the beach, because that's where I was this summer.

Maria: Me too.

Pat: I want to make a picture of horses because I always like to draw horses.

Teacher: What about you, Mary? What kind of pictures do you like to draw?

Mary: I don't know. What would you like me to draw?

Teacher: Well, I'd like you to draw a picture of yourself, if you like. But you may draw whatever you like. How many of you like to decide for yourselves what to draw? *(Hands up)* All right, you draw whatever you like. All the others may choose any of these suggestions: Where you spent your vacation; what your street looks like; a house in the country by a lake; a design; or children going back to school. So far, we decided on plants, fish, pictures. Are there any other suggestions?

Liz: Maybe we could change the desks. I think it looks nicer when several desks are together as if it were one big table instead of the way we have it now.

Sally: Or maybe just four desks together and so four children would all sit together.

Teacher: We have three choices:
1. Stay as we are.
2. Arrange the desks so as to make two large tables.
3. Arrange four desks together.
(They vote.)

Teacher: Shall we try *(whatever they decided to do)* and in a few days talk about it again? If we don't like it, we can change.

FIRST DAY OF SCHOOL—DISCUSSION WITH OLDER CHILDREN

Teacher: Boys and girls, perhaps you know that every teacher has to submit a lesson plan to the principal each week. I haven't made mine yet because I was hoping that we might make some of these decisions together. Could we take a little time and talk about it?

Pat: What do you mean?

Teacher: I mean that, in some respects, you could help me plan our activities in class. That is, if you want to. You see, since I teach spelling, reading, and social studies in the morning, it's entirely up to me to decide upon the time when to teach what, as long as I teach these subjects. I could start the morning with reading, followed by spelling, and then go to social studies, or I can reverse the process. I could also change the procedure each week. It would depend on what you like. It seems to me that we could plan better if we do it together. What do you think?

Tony: You mean we can decide such things?

Lester: You're not kidding?

Teacher: I mean that we could decide together.

Alex: Could we leave out spelling? I don't like that subject.

Teacher: What do you kids think? Can I leave out spelling?

Jim: Yes, let's do that.

Teacher: That isn't what I meant. I meant, is it up to me to have or not to have spelling?

Janet: I guess not. You have to teach spelling. Everybody has to learn how to spell and teachers must teach it.

Teacher: You're right. I must teach it whether I like it or not. The question is whether you want to start the morning with spelling.

Helen: I'd rather start with reading and have spelling later.

Teacher: How do the others feel?

Jane: Let's vote and find out.

Teacher: Good idea. How many of you would prefer starting the morning with reading? Most of you seem to prefer it, so we'll start that way. If we don't like it, we can always change. What do you want next?

Janet: I'm always through with spelling before anyone else. I don't need that much time for spelling.

Lester: Me neither.

(Many children voice similar opinions.)

Teacher: Perhaps we ought to discuss what those who wait for the others could do in the meantime.

Liz: Are we allowed to take dictionaries to our desks?

Teacher: Yes.

Tommy: Maybe we could look up new words and add them to our spelling list of words for that day.

Joe: I don't want to do this.

Teacher: How many of you would like to work with the dictionary? *(Some hands go up.)* Those who like it, may use the dictionary. Would you care to hand in your additional work for me to see or would you rather not do it?

Many children: Hand it in.

Teacher: Good. What about the children who don't care for the dictionary, what do they want to do?

Bill: Could we just sit and do nothing?

Teacher: Yes, you could, under one condition. I wonder if anyone knows what I have in mind?

Alex: Not to bother other children.

Teacher: Right. You don't have to do anything as long as you let the others and me do our work.

Helen: Could we play checkers while we wait?

Teacher: I haven't yet put out the games, but I will as soon as the class has been organized and as soon as we work well together.

Liz: Could several of us pull up our chairs in the back of the room and read like we do with you in a circle?

Teacher: By all means. I'd like that.

Janet: What will we do after we finish spelling?

Teacher: I was just coming to that. We must choose between reading and social studies.

Roy: I think reading, because in social studies we sometimes have a lot to say and we run overtime and then if we didn't already have our reading, there would not be time for it.

Sally: I agree with Roy Let's have reading first.

Teacher: How many want reading first? *(Some do and some don't.)* There are about the same number of children who prefer to have reading first as there are who prefer having it later. What shall we do?

Helen: Maybe we could have reading first one week and then change off.

Alex: Yes, that's a good idea.

Teacher: It's all right with me. How many like this suggestion? *(Most hands go up.)*

This is but one example of how a teacher can unite a class for a common purpose and start a discussion the first day of school. The type of discussion will depend on the ages of the children. Older children may be interested in discussing what they enjoyed and what they did not like in school procedures the previous years. If possible, the teacher and they may find ways to change unsatisfactory procedures. If this is not possible, it is always helpful to discuss it with the group and to help them realize that a teacher is not always free to do what she wants to do. In this way, children begin to see the logic and necessity for certain rules and procedures. This must be done in a friendly manner, letting the students do most of the talking.

TRAINING OF CHILDREN FOR EFFECTIVE DISCUSSIONS

Children need specific training for participation in group discussions. Training in itself is not vital, training for specific purposes is. Group discussions are a means to train students in responsibilities; duties are then turned over to the group. During the training period, the teacher must participate actively as the leader of the group, as well as providing a model of how a leader should relate to the group. Natural leadership will usually emerge from the group so that the teacher within several weeks can relinquish leadership to certain members of the group. (See "Class Council," p. 148.) The teacher must act as listener, advisor, and as co-participant with the children. She should help the group decide on issues it wishes to discuss, to clarify issues, and to plan procedures. She also needs to remind the group to remain conscious of time limits and thus help them to focus their discussions more sharply. The teacher acting as a consultant is not expected to make a speech or to monopolize the discussion but rather to give direction. Helping children to participate is her major job. She sets the stage and becomes the scene shifter. Through gentle guidance, she helps the children to accept various roles and responsibilities so that each fully participates; she helps the non-cooperative group members become cooperative in the interests of group progress.

The ultimate goal is to develop a classroom organization where responsibilities are shouldered by the class. There are a number of considerations in training children for group discussions.

Establishing Game Rules. The first step in training children for group discussion is to talk about what it means to have a friendly discussion and what is involved. When individuals come together as a group, some kind of standards seem to evolve as a natural result. In these first training discussions, the group comes to realize that just as rules of a game exist for all the players to bring about fair play, so certain guidelines need to exist for the welfare of everyone. Guidelines help to protect the rights of everyone and to prevent unfair members from interfering with the rights of others. This type of planning together is friendly, cooperative, and peaceful. It guides the members of the group in their conduct toward each other and helps them to work together in solving problems.

The guidelines which are established should be simple, few in number, and cooperatively planned by the students and the teacher. Therefore, the field in which each group operates would not necessarily have the same limits or rules for participation as the group next door or the group down the hall or across town. The rules for group discussion are unique within that group.

At the end of the first or second week of school, the teacher and the group should take inventory of what has been achieved, how things are going in general, where things might have been poorly planned, and how they could be improved. The group should then formulate plans for the future.

Insuring Total Group Participation. The second step is to encourage each child to contribute in any way that he can, within the limits of his capacity.

Here the teacher may then introduce simple problems for discussion such as going to the lavatory, order in the hall, playground activities, taking care of school belongings, procedures in the cafeteria, and so forth. The problem should be of such nature that most children have an opinion and would respond if asked to voice it. The teacher should invite each child to give suggestions or express opinions.

It is usually easy for the verbal child to volunteer, but not so easy for the one who is more reserved. A way needs to be devised to stimulate the reserved child who seldom volunteers. One should not wait until the discussion has dragged on before asking such a child to respond. The teacher could say to a shy child, "What's your opinion, Sarah?" or "We haven't heard from Otto yet." "Let's hear what he has to say." Suggestions should be well accepted. The teacher should never ask children for advice or suggestions unless she is prepared to take them seriously. Questions should be directed back to the students for consideration. Comments such as the following are an example of what the teacher could say: "That is an interesting statement, Suzie. Do you have any evidence to support it?" "Your point is well taken, Wayne, perhaps you would like to explain it further?" "Would you like to tell us, Claudia, how you think this problem should be handled?" Not only should each child be asked for his opinion, but others should be invited to comment on what has been suggested.

The Teacher as Group Leader. The third consideration concerns the teacher as a group leader. She must not use discussions to express merely her own ideas. This usually results in preaching and is not considered a "discussion." Children soon stop listening to preaching and rarely know what the teacher has been saying. The teacher should also refrain from contradicting or speaking critically of any child's offering. If the teacher feels that a child is mistaken in his thinking, she could ask the other children what they think of what was said, whether they agree or disagree, and have them explain why. This type of intervention gives direction to the discussion and keeps things moving smoothly. To lead a group effectively, the teacher should help the children to think through their own experiences, to learn how to question, evaluate what they have heard. She should guide them in reaching a conclusion or solution to the problem at hand, while at the same time refraining from over-directing the discussion.

Handling Touchy Problems. The fourth consideration for the teacher is to keep the discussion focused on constructive thinking; she should not allow nonproductive or meaningless discussion. Never should she permit a child to humiliate another. If a child does make a derogatory remark, the teacher should let the group handle the situation as shown in the following example:

For several days, the teacher had received complaints about a child who was calling other children ugly names. The teacher suggested that this problem might be solved through group discussion and role playing. ("Role Playing," p. 136.) Three groups were formed, each consisting of three children. These groups acted out this problem in the following manner.

GROUP 1

Danny: *(To David)* You stink, and so do your father and mother.

David: You say that again and I'll break your jaw. Your mother and father probably stink themselves.

Danny: You just said that because I said it first. Your mother and father and you stink, and besides you look like an ape.

Joan: Don't take this from him Davy. Let him have it.

DISCUSSION:

John: It's silly to call people names, and it's babyish.

Mary: Yes, but he did call him a name and nobody likes to be called names, especially if they call your mother and father nasty names.

Raymond: Yes, but fighting doesn't help any. They should at least apologize and make up.

Teacher: Let's see how the second group will handle the problem.

GROUP 2

Helen: I hate you, you stink and so does your mother and father.

Van: Oh, is that so? I hate you too. My mother told me not to play with you, anyway. You're a dirty stupid girl.

Thelma: Aren't you going to do something, Van? Helen insulted your parents.

Helen: Yeah! Aren't you going to do something about it? You're a coward.

Van: *(Crying)* I will tell the teacher on you and I will tell my father. Just you wait and see.

DISCUSSION:

Sally: I liked it better than the other group because Van did not get into a fight.

Tom: But he shouldn't cry and he shouldn't have his father fight his battles for him.

Mary: I think Van was right in not calling Helen's mother and father names. That is not nice. And anyway, they didn't do anything to Van, so why call them names?

Janet: But it's all right to tell the teacher, maybe she could bring it up in the group discussion.

Teacher: Now, let us hear how the third group would handle the same problem.

GROUP 3

Jerry: Gilbert, you're a pig and you stink, and your father and mother stink, and your whole family stinks.

Gilbert: I don't stink. I take a bath almost every night. Why do you insult my parents? They did you no harm. They were very nice to you when you came to my birthday party. Weren't they? Now tell me, weren't they nice to you?

Jerry: Yes, they were nice. But you stink just the same.

Anna: Jerry, you don't mean that. Why are you so nasty to Gilbert? He is your friend. If you are angry at him for some reason, why don't you discuss it with him instead of acting so nastily?

Jerry: I'm sorry I called your parents names. I didn't mean it, really.

Gilbert: That's all right. Why are you so mad at me?

Jerry: You pushed me when we were going downstairs.

Anna: Yes, you did, Gilbert. I saw it.

Gilbert: I'm sorry, Jerry. I didn't even know that I pushed you, so you see, I didn't really mean to push you.

Jerry: That's all right. I'm sorry too.

DISCUSSION:

Tony: I think that worked out all right.

Mary: I still think that Jerry should not have called the parents bad names.

Alex: But he said that he was sorry, so he knows that it wasn't nice. I don't think that he would do that again to anyone.

Nancy: I think that this group learned from the other groups that getting into fights and insulting each other does not help, and besides, everybody realizes that one shouldn't call parents bad names.

Jim: I think the best way would have been to just walk away and not discuss it with Jerry.

Molly: No, I think it was better that they talked about it. This way all of us learned something.

In this way, the teacher is helping the children to see the significance of what they are using this particular experience for, that is, to clarify the concepts which are being considered. This type of direction can be used to help the children discover the goals of misbehavior and uncover ways of helping children to change their behavior. (See "Goals of Misbehavior," p. 17.)

When the discussion strays, the teacher may lead it back to its original purpose by interjections such as: "We were discussing why Larry is getting into frequent fights. Some other time we may discuss the fights which you, Harry, have with your brother." Or, "Could it be that Richard felt left out and therefore he changed the subject to———?"

If a child talks forever without getting to the point, the teacher can direct him and bring him back to the original problem. For example:

Karl tells of a fight he had with his brother and his report goes something like this. "My brother called me stupid, and so I said, 'You are stupid yourself,' then he said, 'No, you are stupid,' and I said, 'You are.'" At this point the teacher may interrupt asking, "Karl, how often do you fight? Where are your parents and what are they doing when you are fighting?"

114

In time, the children learn some of the reasons for their behavior, their goals, and why they pursue them in the particular manner they do. The teacher gets to know the interrelationship between the members of the family and the purpose behind their behavior.

Stimulate Ideas. When the children have some idea of what it is like to participate in a discussion, and have gained some freedom of expression and some skill in the processes of problem solving, the teacher may suggest problems which require observation, evaluation, and conclusion on the part of the group. Such problems could be of a more personal nature such as getting along with brothers and sisters, getting along with parents, fighting, and so forth. She might say, "I'm thinking of people who have difficulties in getting along with others, in doing their work in school, being orderly, behaving in class, and so on. I think that we could help children who have difficulties if we talk about them in a manner which would not make them feel that we criticize them, but that we are interested in helping them. Sometimes, you may wish to talk about something that *I* don't do the way you think it should be done. Teachers have difficulties too, and I would be grateful to you if you could help me."

The following example is one in which the class is critical of the teacher. The discussion took place during a class council session. (See "Class Council," p. 148.)

> Joan: I'd like to bring up something that the teacher does that sometimes disturbs me. Everytime a teacher comes into our room, they stand by Mrs. X's desk which is right in front of mine, and they talk and disturb me. I can't do my work.
>
> Peter: I have noticed this too.
>
> Joan: Maybe they could go outside the room and talk there and this wouldn't disturb us.
>
> Chairman of council: How many like this suggestion? *(All of the children hold up their hands.)*
>
> Teacher: I'm so glad that you brought this to my attention. I should have realized this myself, but I didn't. I am truly sorry if I disturbed you, and I'll try to remember to walk out whenever somebody from outside comes in to talk to me.

Another example:

> Scott: Everytime the teacher dismisses the class, she lets the first row go out first. I don't think that this is fair. She should let each row have a turn in going out first.
>
> Many children: That's right. This is not fair.

115

Teacher: You are right, and I shall change this procedure immediately. From now on, each row will have a chance to go out first. We shall alternate each week. This will be easier to remember than if we alternate each day. What is your opinion?

Children: Agreed.

Once the children discover that others have the same problems they have, that these problems can be solved by cooperative action, that they can come to know and to share their experiences, the teacher will be amazed at the freedom with which the children will express themselves, as well as the spirit of cooperativeness and helpfulness they will display.

Group Decisions. The sixth consideration has to do with making group decisions and then learning to live with the consequences. In the classroom, groups are making decisions constantly. The teacher needs to be aware of how these decisions will affect all class members and also whether the consequences are really what the group had in mind. The group must be able to tolerate and appreciate differences of opinion. It is important that one does not confuse conformity with cooperation. Sometimes a minority opinion is the most valuable contribution and can stimulate real thinking.

Group decisions are hard to undo. Sometimes it may be necessary to reconstruct the discussion in order to understand how a decision was reached. In this process, the group may see implications of their previous decision. At this point, the group may wish to withdraw the decision and initiate another course of action.

Summary and Evaluation of Progress Made. The seventh consideration concerning group discussion has to do with evaluation and assessment of past performance and making plans for the future. It is important that the group take time to evaluate how far they have gone, and to determine what needs to be done how they are going to do it. Reviewing what the group has done helps to give the group a feeling of accomplishment and also helps to modify goals with the added insight. The use of direct questions is one way to get the group to evaluate itself. "What have we done?" "Has it been of value? In what way?" "Why wasn't it so good?" "Did we leave out anything?" A teacher could say, "It seems as though we understand and agree about————." "We seem to need more discussions about ————." "We seem to be working well together on————." As a teacher works with her group, she will find other ways of stock-taking which will fit into her particular needs.

Group discussions play an important role in the child's learning experience. Through group discussions and gentle guidance from

116

the teacher, the child is able to understand how his demand for attention is going to affect the class. The challenge of handling matters of behavior becomes the responsibility of the child and the group. As a result of this experience, children become adept at reaching decisions and accepting responsibility for their own behavior.

CHANGING ATTITUDES THROUGH DISCUSSION

Presenting "a problem" to the class and letting the children "guess" why this problem exists and what kind of person may have such a problem often develops into a most interesting and stimulating discussion. Such a discussion helps children gain insight into cause and behavior and into their false deductions in regard to what kind of behavior will bring them success. For instance, a teacher may say to the class:

> I'd like to discuss with you a problem that I had last year. One of my students was always late coming into class after we returned from recess. Let's take a moment and think about this problem. Why, in your opinion, would a child behave that way? What kind of child might do this? Of course, we can only guess, but guessing is fun and it helps us think through a problem and come up with some very good explanations why anyone behaves in a certain way. Who would like to start this discussion?

The following discussion, transcribed from a tape, is based on this kind of technique.

Problem: *A boy took money out of his mother's purse, without telling her, and then bought candy which he gave to other children.*

Teacher: Let's take a few moments and think about this problem. We don't know much about this boy, yet I'm sure that we have some feelings about him and his behavior. Why would any child do such a thing, and what kind of child might this boy be? Let's guess and see what we may come up with.

Mike: I think that maybe the children asked him to get them some candy, and that is why he did it.

Bob: I think that this boy probably was afraid of the children and that is why he did it.

Teacher: What do you mean?

Bob: I mean maybe they told him that they would get him after school and he was afraid.

Teacher: Do you mean that they threatened to beat him up unless he gave them candy?

Bob: Yes.

117

Teacher: How do the other children feel about this?

Judy: Maybe this boy promised them the candy and he had no money so he had to take it from his mother. Maybe his mother didn't want to give him the money.

Bill: He stole the money, and that is not right.

Teacher: Do you mind if we don't discuss now if what this boy did is right or wrong, but talk only about the reasons a child may have to do such a thing? If you want to, we may discuss the problem from a right or wrong point of view later. All right?

Sandra: Maybe this boy wanted to make friends with these children.

Ann: I think that he was probably a lonely boy and he wanted friends. I agree with Sandra.

John: I think that probably his mother wasn't home and then he is the boss in the house, so he doesn't have to ask his mother for permission to take the money. He probably had only twenty cents of his own and that wasn't enough, so he took what he needed.

Betsy: He must be a very spoiled boy.

Girl: John said that he is the boss when his mother isn't home. Is this boy grown up, like a man, I mean?

Teacher: This boy is 10 years old. John, did you think that he was already a grown man?

John: Well, I think it makes no difference. I mean when his mother isn't home, if he is the only boy in the family, then maybe he is the boss—when his father isn't home, I mean.

Helen: I don't agree with you that he is the boss just because he is a boy and his father isn't home. Why should he be a boss when he is only a child? Anyway, he should ask permission before he takes money from his mother's purse.

Jane: I agree with Helen. Maybe there are other children, and even if they are girls, I don't think that they would like it if he made himself the boss.

Ann: If you let him be a boss in the family, then maybe he would like to be a boss all the time.

Teacher: Can you explain what you mean by that?

Sandra: Well, if he thinks that he is a boss at home, he may want to be the boss when he is outside or in school.

Bill: I think that John said this because he is the only boy in his family and maybe he is the boss when his father isn't home.

Teacher: Please, children, we are not discussing John now. We are discussing a problem, somebody's problem, a boy we don't even know. Let us try and discuss the problem. What kind of child would have this problem?

118

Peter: I think that he is trying to make friends. He probably has no friends.

Teacher: Do you have friends?

Peter: Yes.

Teacher: Do you have to give them candy or other presents to be your friend?

Peter: No.

(The teacher asked several children if they had friends and if they made friends by giving them candy or other presents. All children said that they did not.)

Teacher: All of you tell me that you have friends and that you do not have to bribe them. Peter tells us that this boy tried to make friends. Let's discuss this a little further.

Jim: If he tried to make friends that way, the children will like him only for a little while and then they won't be his friends anymore.

Teacher: Why not?

Jim: Because they will always want him to buy them candy, and if he doesn't always have the money, they won't be his friends.

Frank: That's right. They won't be his friends. You would have to buy candy all the time.

Tony: He should play with them and maybe ask them to come over sometime and play at his home, then he may make friends.

Teacher: Why doesn't this boy have any friends? Let's see if we could guess what some of the reasons might be.

Mary: Well, if he is like John said, that he is the boss, I don't blame the children if they don't want to be his friend.

Kevin: Maybe he is not very friendly.

Linda: He could be a nasty kid and that's why he doesn't have friends.

Patsy: Maybe he is new in the neighborhood and that's why he has no friends.

Bill: But even then he could make friends without taking money from his mother.

Sandra: I think that maybe he wants his way all the time and that's why he has no friends.

Teacher: You have come up with some very good ideas. Everything you said may be the reason why this boy behaved as he did. We are not sure, but that is not important. You see how many different reasons there are why some people behave in one way and others behave in a different way in the same kind of situation. Each one of you has friends, yet each of you made friends in a different way than this boy did, or tried to do. Did you learn anything from this discussion?

Bob: Yes. I learned about how to make friends.

Ann: I did too.

Judy: I think that the teacher told us this problem so that we may think about why some people have friends and some don't.

Teacher: Yes, you are right. Some other time we may discuss a different kind of problem. How many of you enjoyed this kind of discussion? *(Most hands go up.)*

Some readers may wonder why the teacher did not discuss the moral aspect of this problem and the ethics. This may be done at another time when the focus of the training is on values. In this discussion, the focus was on understanding behavior. It would take too much time and be too confusing if the teacher were to concentrate on both, morals and training, for understanding of behavior at the same time.

During such a discussion, the teacher may observe that some children lower their heads or listen with an expression of extreme intensity. This is usually a recognition reflex. Probably these children identify with the action and motivation behind the behavior of this boy.

In the case of John, the teacher gained great insight into his position at home, being the only boy of several children. Although the teacher discouraged the group from discussing his position in his family and his interpretation of what his rights were because of it, John was indirectly exposed to the children's feelings of such behavior, and, we may assume, that he gave this some thought.

From this example, we can see that any discussion that is thought provoking, if skillfully led by the teacher, has possibilities for training children to understand behavior and draw conclusions. The teacher must be on the alert to know when and what kind of questions to ask so as to provoke further logical thinking. Interpretations must come from the children themselves. If none are forthcoming, she may bring up some of the comments made by the children in regard to this problem and continue the discussion at another time.

TRAINING CHILDREN TO UNDERSTAND BEHAVIOR THROUGH THE USE OF STORIES

If the teacher feels that the group is not yet ready to discuss their own behavior problems, she may train the group to analyze and understand behavior through the reading of stories in which the characters have problems in social adjustment. In such a situation, the children feel freer to express their ideas and feelings since this is not threatening to them personally.

The teacher, on the other hand, is able to discuss the problem with

120

the class from a psychological point of view without fear of putting a specific child on the spot. As she and the class talk about behavior in general, the child learns to accept that everyone has some kind of problem. The following example will illustrate this point.

Teacher: Boys and girls, I will read to you a story about a French poodle. Later we will discuss how you feel about this little dog.

Bo, The Ball Player[7]

Bo was a beautiful, young, silver-gray French poodle. He was friendly, liked to play ball, and quickly made friends with everybody.

Bo had two very nice masters, father and mother Johnson. They had many friends who often came to visit. Bo was a fine ball player. He could catch a ball rolling across the floor on the first bounce, or even high in the air. He would carry it back in his mouth and toss it into the lap of anyone who looked like a ball player. Bo thought everyone looked like a ball player.

Whenever father and mother Johnsons' guests met Bo for the first time, they always said, "What a cute dog, and how clever he is to catch and bring the ball." Bo wagged his short little tail. No matter what direction they threw the ball, Bo would scramble and catch it. Everybody admired Bo.

But Bo never seemed to get tired. Nobody could quit playing ball because Bo wanted everybody to see how well he played. He played ten minutes, a half hour, or even a whole hour. Everybody got tired of playing with Bo. They had come to talk and have fun with father and mother Johnson. But Bo tossed the ball on their laps, wagged his tail, sneaked up on the ball, and even turned half circles in the air when he jumped for the ball.

Teacher: How do you feel about Bo?

The group will discuss Bo from various points of view. Most of the children usually see him as a very lovable dog, one they would love to have themselves.

Teacher: Do you like everything about Bo? Do you always like his behavior?

Usually, the children pick up this clue. A number of them will question whether he should insist on playing with the Johnsons' guests when they want to talk.

[7]Maurice L. Bullard, *The Use of Stories for Self-Understanding* (Corvallis, Oregon: Maurice L. Bullard, 1963).

Teacher: Can you figure out why he wants to play all the time, and for what other purpose he might be bothering the guests?

Some child will point to the fact that Bo wants attention.

Teacher: What is wrong with wanting attention?

The children will point out that he wants too much attention, that he should let the people talk and enjoy themselves, especially after they did pay attention to him for quite a while.

Teacher: Are little dogs the only ones who want so much attention and who don't let parents talk when they have guests? Do you know somebody who behaves just like Bo when the parents have company and want to talk?

The observant teacher will notice many recognition reflexes. Some will giggle, some lower their heads, while others will openly admit that they often behave like Bo.

Teacher: Do children ever behave like Bo in the classroom?

The discussion will now turn to the classroom situation when children want undue attention and, through their behavior, disturb those who want to work.
Since this story is geared to younger children (Kindergarten through third grade), the entire discussion should last no more than fifteen to twenty minutes. The questions should be brief and to the point. As soon as a child responds with the answer which shows psychological understanding, the teacher should move on to the next question.
A similar story may be used for discussion at a later time.
Gradually, the children begin to identify the problems in the stories with those they have themselves and they start to talk about them. Stories, therefore, are a link in the transitory process from discussing general problems to dealing with personal ones.
A teacher need not wait until the group is well trained in discussing personal problems if she has a student whose disruptive behavior prevents her from teaching. In such a case, she must consider the welfare of her class rather than the reaction of the child. She may have to discuss right away why and for what purpose this child is behaving as he is and what they can do about it. Example:

Teacher: Boys and girls, please leave your work for a moment, I need your help. I am having a problem with Hank. Does anyone know what I am talking about? The children will know and they will point out that the problem is that Hank is whistling or tapping.
Teacher: Everyone is aware of what you are doing, Hank. Could it be that you want everyone in class to pay attention to you?

Such disclosure of the child's goal will usually keep him quiet for a while.

Teachers who cannot find appropriate stories in their reading textbooks may write their own stories to fit specific situations.

An excellent story for a group discussion is *Ricky Goes Fishing.* It is a story of a young boy who promises his father not to fish from the pier while the father goes deep-sea fishing. This discussion usually takes in the following form:

Ricky Goes Fishing[8]

Teacher: What do you think of Ricky?

    Child: I like him.

Teacher: Why do you like him?

    Child: Because he does not disobey his father.

    Child: I like him too for the same reason. His father told him not to fish from the pier and he doesn't.

Teacher: Doesn't he want to?

    Child: Yes, he wants to very much, but he promised his father that he wouldn't do it.

Teacher: Couldn't he fish anyway? After all, his father is too far away to see him and he may never find out.

    Child: But that wouldn't be nice if he gave a promise.

    Child: I don't think that he should do this just because his father isn't there to see him.

    Child: What's the use giving a promise if you're going to break it?

Teacher: How many of you agree with these children that promises should be kept? *(Most children raise their hands.)*

Teacher: Could we apply this example to a school situation?

    Child: I don't understand what you mean. We don't fish in class.

Teacher: Let me explain what I mean. Is there ever a class situation which is similar to Ricky's? *(No answer)* Assuming that this is a family, who in class could take the place of Ricky?

    Child: Do you mean one of us?

Teacher: Is one child my class?

    Child: You mean that we are in class the same as Ricky is in the family?

Teacher: Exactly.

    Child: Then we, all of us, are like Ricky to you.

Teacher: Right. Who is the father?

[8]"Ricky Goes Fishing" in *The New Streets and Roads* (Chicago: Scott, Foresman and Company, 1958).

123

Child: You are.

Teacher: Do all of you follow this?

Child: How can you be a father?

Teacher: We are just trying to set up a similar situation. You may think of me as the mother if this helps you.

Child: But you don't go sea fishing.

Teacher: The father in the story goes away and leaves Ricky behind. Right?

Class: Right.

Teacher: Doesn't a teacher ever go away and leave her children behind?

Child: Yes.

Child: I see what you mean. You go away just as the father does in the story, and you leave the class just as he does Ricky.

Teacher: That's right. Let's recall what happened between the father and Ricky before he left.

Child: The father asked him not to go fishing from the pier.

Teacher: And what did Ricky say?

Child: He said that he would not go.

Child: I know what the teacher means.

Teacher: What do I mean?

Child: When you go out you ask us not to talk and not to leave our desks.

Teacher: And what does the class say?

Child: We always promise not to do it.

Class: I understand now too.

Teacher: And what happens when I leave?

Child: We start talking and we get out of our seats sometimes.

Teacher: Do you think that Ricky is a likeable boy because he keeps his promise to his father, but that you don't have to keep your promise?

(No answer)

We call this "double standard." That means that we don't stick to our opinions, or that we think that other people have to behave in a certain way, but we don't have to. What do you think of this?

Child: I think that we mustn't leave our seats if the teacher leaves the room.

Child: We mustn't promise to be good when we don't keep our promise.

Child: I agree. If we promise, we should keep our promise.

Teacher: Think about it. A teacher has to leave the class many times. So there will be plenty of opportunities to find out how you really feel about this situation now that we have talked about it.

Such a discussion ends right there. There are no references made to any specific child in class. At a later time, the teacher may, in connection with a child's problem, bring up Ricky's case.

The third grade reader, *The New Streets and Roads,* has a number of stories which lend themselves to discussion. They indirectly touch on problems that many children will recognize as their own. "Whizzer's Purple Tail" for example, is an excellent story use as a basis for a discussion of people who will go to any length of behavior in order to maintain a special position in the family or in any group.

Whizzer's Purple Tail[9]

This is a story in which a young mouse received more attention than the others in his family by disregarding the wishes of his parents. He receives the status of a king in the family when, by accident, he dips his tail into purple paint. Purple is the sign of a king, according to his father. When the paint begins to wear off, Whizzer is mortified lest he lose his royal status, and deliberately dips his tail into the paint again.

Whizzer's position in the family could be discussed from an objective point of view. Questions could be asked, such as, "Would you like to have him for your brother? Why not? Why is it so necessary for Whizzer to be different in an unpleasant way? Is this the only way he could get attention? Did Whizzer believe that he could be liked and accepted by others if he were not any different?" The extent to which Whizzer went in order to maintain his position of being something "special" could be discussed. The group could be asked if they know people who behave similarly to Whizzer, and for the same reason.

Now and then, a child offers voluntarily that this is precisely what he has been doing. Many children occupy "royal" status because they are different from their sisters and brothers in one way or another: they may be the only boy or girl among siblings of the opposite sex, they may be an only child, the oldest or youngest, more talented in some area, and the like. They too have fears of losing this status and become difficult the minute they sense any threat. Once a child makes such an admission, many others have the courage to speak about their faulty behavior. These discussions never fail to have an effect on children and do bring some results.

Other stories that can be used include: John Steptoe, *Stevie* (New

[9]Polly Curren, "Whizzer's Purple Tail," *The New Streets and Roads* (Chicago: Scott, Foresman and Company, 1958).

York: Harper & Row, 1969); Charlotte Zolotow, *The Quarreling Book* (New York: Harper & Row, 1963); and C. Bethgoff, *Where Is Daddy?* (Englewood Cliffs, N.J.: Prentice-Hall, 1969).

Almost every story lends itself for a discussion involving social relationships and analysis of the character's motivation to behave as they do. The teacher skilled in conducting discussions will succeed in bringing out the points which would touch upon the problems existing in the class without putting the student on the spot at this particular time. The focus is more on the problem as it affects everyone and less on the individual child.

Through the discussion of characters in stories, students can be trained to question and understand their own and other children's behavior. As they learn to accept the fact that everyone makes mistakes, that mistakes can be rectified, that one should not feel embarrassed to discuss one's problems, the teacher may start bringing up for discussion specific problems of specific children in the class.

When a problem needs discussing, but the teacher cannot find a story which deals with such a problem, she may write her own story. The following story was written to train children to understand behavior:

Carmen

Carmen was in the second grade. She was a very smart girl according to everyone who knew her. She liked to go to school, but she did not do any work in class. She spent most of her time drawing, walking about the room, or talking to other children. This made the teacher angry, and she often scolded and punished Carmen for her behavior. The parents were also very angry with her; they could not understand why she behaved that way, since they were always very good to her and gave her everything she asked for.

The following discussion developed:

Teacher: What do you think of Carmen?
A Child: Well, she sure doesn't act right.
Teacher: What do you mean?
Child: She is not nice.
Teacher: Why not?
A Child: She should be doing her work in class just like everybody else.
Teacher: Yes, she should, but she doesn't. Why doesn't she?
Child: Maybe the work is too hard.
Teacher: Do you believe that the work is too hard for Carmen?
Child: Maybe not.
Another Child: I don't think it's too hard for her.

126

Teacher: How do we know that the work couldn't be too hard for her?

Child: She is very smart and everybody thinks so.

Another Child: Yes, she is smart, but I think that she is just stubborn.

Teacher: What do you mean by that?

Child: Well, she must have her way.

Teacher: How do the other children feel about what X just said? Many children will agree that Carmen probably must have her way.

Teacher: Why is it so important to Carmen to have her way?

Child: I think that she is spoiled.

Teacher: Could you explain to the others what you mean by being "spoiled"?

Child: Well, at home she gets everything she wants.

Teacher: Is there anything wrong with this?

(Many children will say "no" and many will say "yes." This develops into a discussion concerning family inter-relationship and merits and disadvantages of being spoiled.)

Child: I think that she thinks that she must get her way in everything because if she doesn't, she thinks that the people don't love her.

Teacher: Do you think that people could love Carmen and that she could get attention in a different way—a way in which it would make living with her more pleasant?

Child: Yes, I think she could.

Another Child: She could if she tried.

Teacher: What could she do?

A Child: She could be a helper to her mother and get attention.

Another Child: She could even help other children who are not as smart as she is.

Another Child: Yes, and this way she would be helping the teacher too.

Teacher: I see that you all have very good ideas of how Carmen could get attention. There is nothing wrong with wanting attention. We all do. It's a question of how we get it. How should one get attention?

Invariably, someone will mention that we must get attention in such a way that it is pleasant to us, yet doesn't hurt others. As the teacher listens to the individual members of her class, and as she begins to understand their problems and their concepts of how they can solve them; as she gets the picture of the relationships among students, she can plan more successfully for the individual student, establish shared values, and raise the morale of the entire group. This requires confidence in the group, self-assurance, and inner freedom, so that the teacher can function without concern for her own prestige. Only then will she succeed in guiding the child to the successful development of his innate abilities and his social potential.

Following are examples of illustrative stories written by teachers for use in their classes.

KINDERGARTEN THROUGH PRIMARY GRADES

Gary, The Snatcher

Gary is a little boy of 3 who is always getting into mischief. He especially enjoys snatching something from other children or from his father, running off with it and laughing. Of course, the children and the father run after him and try to get back what he has taken. Gary only laughs. When he thinks that he will not be able to hold on to the object, he throws it away and laughs still harder.

Gary seldom takes anything from his mother. Once when he took her slipper and tried to run off with it, she threw him the other slipper too, and kept on reading her book, never even glancing up. Gary stood for awhile, not knowing what he should do. Then he took both slippers and put them by his mother's chair.

Questions:
1. What do you think of Gary?
2. Why is he taking the things from everybody except from his mother?
3. What does he get out of this behavior?
4. What would you do if you were his father or a child from whom he likes to take things? How could you stop him without getting into a fight?
5. Do you know of any behavior which is similar to that of Gary but is happening in a class?
6. What could we do in such a case?

Quiet Janice

Janice never got in anyone's way. She always saw to it that she was the last in line for recess, for lunch or to go to the library. Of course, if someone else wanted to be last she didn't care.

When Janice came to the reading group, she would wait until all the other children were seated before she would slide silently into her chair.

One day, the teacher asked Janice to read. She began to read, but as usual, she read so softly that no one could hear her. The teacher

128

and the children did everything they could think of to get Janice to read loud enough for all to hear, but they just couldn't get her to do it.

Questions:
1. What do you think of Janice?
2. Why do you think she was always so quiet?
3. Could she have read louder?
4. Why didn't she read louder?
5. Was she getting people to notice her?
6. How did she do it?
7. Do you know people like Janice?
8. What other ways could Janice get attention which might be better?

Tap, Tap, Tap

Marion's pencil was going, tap, tap, tap on her workbook.

"Who is tapping?" asked Mrs. Saltz.

Several children looked at Marion, hoping that she would admit that she was the one, but she had no such intention. She stopped tapping just for a while and then started all over.

"Will the child who is tapping please stand up?" said the teacher.

Marion grinned to herself, but remained in her seat. In a few seconds, she started tapping as before.

Questions:
1. What do you think is going to happen now?
2. Why is Marion tapping?
3. Why doesn't she admit that she is doing it?
4. How does it make her feel when she can fool the teacher?
5. What else does she get out of this?
6. How many of you sometimes behave just like Marion?
7. What do you suggest that the teacher should do if this should happen in our class?

I Wish I Could

Bouncy was a little red fox who liked playing and eating more than anything else.

"Today I am going to run all the way to the brook," he said to himself as he woke up. He stretched, and yawned, and edged over to the opening of the den. It was a lovely day. The sun was shining and a light wind rustled through the grass.

"Perfect for running and turning somersaults," he thought to himself and he moved closer to the opening. Just as he was about to squeeze through the hole of the den, he remembered what his father and mother had said to him and his brother, Lazy, before they left the den this morning: "Don't leave home until we return. We will try to be back soon. We're just going over to Farmer Brown's to get a fat chicken for breakfast. Do not leave the den."

Bouncy's head was almost outside, but he pulled it back. He did not know what to do. Should he go out or shouldn't he? If he went out and ran down to the brook and right back, his parents would never know.

He moved closer to the opening again and looked out. A chipmunk was chasing a butterfly. When the little chip noticed Bouncy's face peeping out of the hole, he called, "Come out and help me chase this butterfly. It's so much fun."

But Bouncy shook his head and pulled back. He curled up and went to sleep.

Questions:
1. What do you think of Bouncy?
2. Why do you like him?
3. Couldn't he have gone out for a little while? Would his parents have found out?
4. Do you think that he didn't go out because he was afraid that his parents would find out? Could he have had another reason?
5. How can we compare this story with what sometimes happens in class?
6. Who would take the place of the parents in class? (Teacher)
7. Who would take the place of Bouncy in class? (The children)
8. What kind of situation would be similar to the one that Bouncy had? (When the teacher leaves the room)
9. What happens when the teacher leaves the room?
10. Why do you like Bouncy and think that this is the way to behave and then do the opposite in class? Isn't it the same situation? I'm going to leave the class in a few minutes. Let's see how many can live up to what they believe.

STORIES FOR THIRD AND FOURTH GRADES

Paul

When Paul entered his house he called, "Jane, hey Jane, where are you? I need you, Jane, come here!"

"Not so loud, Paul," said his mother, "Dad is taking a nap."

Paul yelled even louder, "Jane, I'm calling you. Come here this minute. I'm in a hurry."

At this moment, Jane came up from the basement. "All right, Paul. What is it you want?"

"I can't find my bat, Jane, and the boys are waiting outside for me. Find it quickly. Hurry up!" He ran into the kitchen and yelled, "Mom, make me a sandwich to take along. I haven't any time to eat it now. Don't give me cheese, as you did yesterday. I hate it. Give me ham."

Jane came in with the bat. "Honestly, Paul, I wish you would find your own things, you never even try."

Paul grabbed the bat and ran out of the house.

Questions:

1. What do you think of Paul?
2. What's wrong with doing what he did?
3. What is his attitude toward other people?
4. What would you do if you were his sister?
5. How do you think he might behave with the boys when he plays with them? Let's guess.
6. How many children do you know who behave just like Paul?

Be Nice

"Did you do your workbook?" asked George.

Samuel shook his head. "That darn workbook. I haven't touched it in days." He pulled out the workbook and opened it. "So many questions!" he said to himself, "and so many different answers to each question! How am I to know which is the right answer?"

Without reading any of the questions, Samuel started to underline the answers. After a while, he turned to George. "Hey, George," he said, "is this right?"

George shook his head and pointed to the line below.

"Thanks, George," said Samuel as he erased his own answer and underlined the one George had pointed out.

Next he tapped Pamela on the shoulder. "Hey, Pam, what's the right answer to question number two?"

Pamela opened her workbook and showed him her answer.

"Oh, thanks," said Samuel as he drew a line under the same answer.

He noticed that Jimmy who sat in back of him was also working on the same page. He turned around and looked at Jimmy's workbook.

At this, Jimmy covered the page with a piece of paper. "Do your own work, Samuel," he whispered. Samuel stuck his tongue out at Jimmy.

Questions:
1. What do you think of Samuel?
2. Who likes him? Why?
3. Who doesn't like him? Why?
4. What's wrong with what he is doing?
5. What does he get out of this behavior?
6. Why isn't he doing his own work?
7. What do you think of George and Pamela? Are they good friends of Samuel?
8. Why "yes" and why "no"?
9. What would you do if your neighbor acted like Samuel?
10. What should a teacher do?
11. How many of you agree with this suggestion?
12. Shall we try to do this in our class if this problem should arise?

He's Such a Nice Boy, But . . .

"Stanley," called Mrs. Cruz, "please come to my desk for a minute."

Stanley looked up for a moment and then went right back to tracing the picture on his book cover.

"You mustn't put pencil marks on a book," said Mark who was sitting next to him.

But Stanley paid no attention to Mark and continued his tracing.

"Please, Stanley, I want to see you for a minute. Please come here."

Stanley picked himself up very slowly and sauntered over to his teacher's desk.

"I did not get your arithmetic for today. Why didn't you hand it in when I collected the papers?"

Stanley just stood there without answering.

"Please, Stanley, I am trying hard to understand you, but it is hard for me if you don't tell me why you never do your work. You're such a nice boy, always neat looking, and you have such a pleasant face, but you're lazy, Stanley, you know that. Laziness will get you bad grades. You know that Stanley, don't you?"

Stanley did not answer. He looked away from the teacher as if he did not want to have anything to do with her.

"I tell you what, Stanley," continued Mrs. Cruz, "I won't put any grade in my book for today if you promise to hand in your work tomorrow. Remember, this is a promise. I expect your work tomorrow. You may return to your desk now."

Stanley angrily returned to his desk.

"Stan," whispered Mark, "I did part of the arithmetic for you. All you have to do is just finish the last few problems. That can be done in a few minutes."

Stanley took the paper and put it into his folder. "She said 'tomorrow,' I'll hand it in tomorrow." He took out his comb from his pocket and began combing his hair.

Questions:

1. What do you think of Stanley?
2. What kind of boy is he?
3. What might be his problem? Let's guess. It might be any number of things. What is his goal?
4. How does he get to his goal?
5. Why is he angry at the teacher?
6. Do you agree with the way the teacher handled the problem? Why "yes" or why "no"?
7. How does he try to make up for his "deficiencies"?
8. What about Mark? Does he help Stanley?

Huh?

"Edgar," said Mrs. Murphy, "can you tell the class the characteristics of birds?"

"What did you say?" said Edgar who was playing with a piece of string under his desk.

Mrs. Murphy repeated the question.

"I wasn't in school on the day we studied this lesson," replied Edgar.

"We have been studying birds for three weeks now. You were in class most of the time, Edgar," said the teacher.

"What did you say?" said Edgar.

"I think you heard what I said," said Mrs. Murphy angrily.

"Huh?" answered Edgar.

Mrs. Murphy asked that the children who heard what she said raise their hands. All but Edgar raised their hands.

"Look, Edgar, everyone in the class heard what I said. I think I'll let you stand until you recall what my question was," said Mrs. Murphy.

"You said that we have been studying birds for three weeks and that I was here most of the time," said Edgar.

Questions:
1. What do you think of Edgar?
2. What is his problem?
3. You say that he doesn't listen. Is this true? How do we know that he hears what people talk to him about?
4. Why does he say, "What did you say?" all the time?
5. Does he get anything out of this?

Peter

Peter took out paste, scissors, paper, and crayons and put them on the kitchen table. He started to work on a May basket for his teacher. He worked for a while and then left everything and went into his room where he played with his new engine.

Later, when his mother needed the table, she put everything away where it belonged.

Questions:
1. What is the point of this story?
2. Is there anything wrong with Peter's behavior? What might be the reason for this behavior? Does this story tell us anything that might be a clue to why he doesn't take care of his own things?
3. In your opinion, how old a child would behave that way? (2 to 3 years)

I'm Hungry

Mother was busy preparing dinner when Theresa entered the kitchen. She went straight to the refrigerator, took out the apple pie which mother had baked in the morning, and began cutting off a piece.

"What are you doing, Theresa?" asked her mother.

"I'm hungry," said Theresa.

"But you can't have any pie. It's for dinner. Father will be home in ten minutes and then we will eat." Mother seemed to be annoyed when she said this.

"Well, I'm hungry now and I don't want to wait until later," answered Theresa and she bit into the pie.

Her mother rushed over to her and tried to take the pie away from her. Theresa pulled away from her mother's grip and ran out of the kitchen laughing.

Questions:
1. What do you think of this situation?
2. Do you believe that Theresa is so hungry that she can't wait a few minutes?
3. What is her main reason for running off with the pie?
4. How does she feel about the other members in the family?
5. If you were Theresa's mother, what would you do in such a situation?
6. If your mother were to do to you what you just said that you would do, would you think that she is right? Would you accept this or would you be angry?

Recommended Stories for Effective Group Discussions

Andersen, H. C. *The Emperor's New Clothes.* New York: Oxford University Press, 1945.

Andersen, H. C. *The Princess on the Pea.* New York: Oxford University Press, 1955.

Andersen, H. C. *The Ugly Duckling.* New York: Oxford University Press, 1955.

Berghoff, C. *Where Is Daddy?* Englewood Cliffs, N.J.: Prentice-Hall, 1969.

Bollinger, Max. *Joseph.* New York: Delacorte Press, 1967.

Bullard, Maurice L. *The Use of Stories for Self-Understanding.* Maurice L. Bullard, 333 N. 6th St., Corvallis, Oregon, 1963.

Curren Polly. *"Whizzer's Purple Tail."* In *The New Streets and Roads.* Chicago: Scott, Foresman, 1958.

Elkin, Benjamin. *The Loudest Noise in the World.* New York: Viking Press, 1954.

Epstein, Samuel. *George Washington Carver.* Garrard Press, 1960.

Geisel, Theodore Seuss. *Horton Hatches the Egg.* New York: Random House, 1960.

Geisel, Theodore Seuss. *Horton Hears a Who.* New York: Random House, 1954.

Geisel, Theodore Seuss. *Thidwick, the Big-Hearted Moose.* New York: Random House, 1958.

Grantoff, Christian. *The Stubborn Donkey.* Aladdin Books, 1969.

Gudrum, Thorne-Thomsen. *The Giant Who Had No Heart in His Body, A Book of Giant Stories.* New York: Dodd, Mead & Co., 1926.

Moore, Lillian. *The Terrible Mr. Twitimeyer.* Eau Claire, Wisconsin: E. M. Hale & Co., 1952.

Steptoe, John. *Stevie.* New York: Harper & Row, 1969.

Zolotow, Charlotte. *The Quarreling Book.* New York: Harper & Row, 1963.

In the literature taught at high school level, we find many characters whose personalities can be analyzed from the point of view of their "social interest," that is, their concern or lack of concern for others, and the underlying goals of their behavior. Newspaper articles and movies make excellent topics for group discussion.

ROLE PLAYING

Role playing is especially useful in solving relationship problems among two or more persons. It allows a child to stand aside and look at his problems through the eyes of someone else. It also helps a child to understand the situation of another child who feels rejected, picked on, blamed for everything, unloved, and unable to handle his frustrations in an acceptable manner.

In role playing, the child is assigned a specific role or character which he then interprets as he understands it. In this respect, it is spontaneous, for nobody tells him what to say or how to interpret the character he portrays.

There are several different techniques and methods used in role playing. The first technique that we are going to explore is known as *reporting through role playing.* This is a technique that will produce recall—not only of a given incident, but also of the emotional charges that fired those who participated in it.

We have all heard the expressions, "He did it," "It wasn't my fault," "I didn't do anything," "He's always bothering me."

When some incident happens, there we are—the big teacher—right in the middle trying to explore the facts, trying to listen, trying to figure out who did what and who started it. The teacher then becomes the judge and jury.

Reporting through role playing is one way in which the teacher can profess ignorance of the incident in question and can insist upon being shown what happened as shown in the next two illustrations:

Scene: *A group of children are sitting at a table working. Teacher is helping someone at the other side of room.*

Incident: *All of a sudden there is scuffling. Marilyn and Betsy are hitting each other.*

Betsy: *(Running to the teacher)* Make her stop. Marilyn hit me. Make her stop. She's a bad girl!

Marilyn: *(right behind Betsy)* I didn't start it. She hit me first.

Teacher: OK, show me what happened.

Both girls: Well, she hit me and—no, she poked me—and. . . .

Teacher: No, girls. Show me. What props do you need?

Betsy: We need to sit at the table and be working.

Girls: *(Arrange themselves at the table)*

Teacher: *(Waits expectantly)*

Marilyn: We need Guy.

Guy: *(Moves to the table)*

Teacher: Show me.

Guy: *(Gets up and goes to sharpen his pencil, pokes Betsy on the way back, and gets very busy working)*

Betsy: *(Starts to hit Marilyn, but catches herself, everybody looks at Guy)*

At that moment, the students and the teacher realized what had happened and started to laugh. The girls realized that Guy had "set them up," and they had almost gotten into trouble. At this point, one could drop the incident, as this teacher did.

Quite often role playing can be used to settle everyday episodes that occur involving only two or three children who were interacting:

Several fourth grade boys were working on their individual projects at the round table. All of a sudden, Jack came screaming to the teacher saying, "Fred hit me. Make him stop."

The teacher said, "All right, show me what happened."

Both boys started to *tell* what had happened.

The teacher said, "No, don't tell me, show me."

Jack was the first aggressor, and then Fred retaliated. Jack said, "But I was only playing. I wasn't angry."

No more was said.

The next day Joe and Jack had an argument. Again, Jack came crying to his teacher. She said, "All right, show me."

Joe was the first aggressor in this instance and Jack hit him back. Joe said, "But I was only playing."

Jack said, "O-o-h, I see, just like me yesterday with Fred."

Through this kind of role playing, the children gain insight into their own behavior and begin to recognize what starts conflicts, and how they become involved in them. This way, the teacher is able to play her own role: to be ignorant of the episode, and to insist upon being *shown* what happened. The end results are rewarding to the teacher, to the children involved, and to the class as well. Role playing allows the child to recognize himself; the teacher does not get caught in the trap of lecturing, chastising, passing judgment, or trying to sift out truth from fantasy.

The second technique to be explored is called *problem solving*. It can be used effectively to deal with a problem that might have several possible solutions.

If the problem is a fight between two or more children, the actors first act out the fight as it actually happened, using the same words and the same movements. In a group discussion, the students give their own feelings concerning what they think about the problems and where the mistakes were made. The teacher then asks for a new set of actors to act out the same situation, but to come up with a different solution. The class then compares the two solutions to see which they think is the best and to express their feeling about which would be more helpful.

Another group may act out the same situation and give its interpretation and solution. The class again discusses the various solutions which were presented and decides which of these would probably be the most effective one and why. Remember, in role playing, there is no *right* solution, but an exploration of many solutions.

The teacher will invariably learn a great deal about the child as he portrays the role assigned to him. The role playing situation will offer clues to the child's own adequacy in dealing with difficult problems and will reveal his personal goals. (See "The Four Goals of Misbehavior," p. 17.)

The following examples may help to further clarify the nature of role playing:

Incident: **Keith is crying because Henry tore up his arithmetic paper. Henry claims that Keith was copying from him and that he was cheating. He had asked him once not to copy, but as Keith continued copying, he snatched Keith's paper and tore it.**

Role Playing *(first time): Helen acted the part of Henry, and Margo took the part of Keith. They acted out the situation exactly as it was described by Keith and Henry.*

DISCUSSION:

Teacher: Let's first discuss what you liked about the way this problem was handled.

Maria: I liked the fact that Henry asked Keith first not to copy before he tore his paper.

Stanley: I think it served Keith right because he always used to copy from me.

138

Teacher: Stanley, please, let us now discuss only what happened today.

George: I think it was all right for Henry to tear up Keith's paper because it will teach Keith a lesson.

Teacher: What do you mean? Could you explain this more clearly?

George: Well, I think that from now on, Keith won't cheat any more because he knows what will happen.

Teacher: What do others think of George's feelings?

Anna: I don't agree with George because it won't teach Keith anything.

Howard: I didn't like the way Henry tore up the paper because it made Keith angry and that might lead to a fight later on.

Dorothy: I don't think that Henry had a right to tear up somebody else's paper. He could have told the teacher about it and she would have talked to Keith.

Henry: Yes, but I did not want to get the teacher involved.

Teacher: We have heard many opinions. How many think that they could handle this situation in a better way?

(Many hands go up)

Teacher: Kenneth, will you please take the part of Henry, and you, Gary, take the part of Keith.

Role Playing *(second time):* *Kenneth pretends to do his arithmetic and Gary pretends to look over his shoulder and copy.*

Kenneth: Please, Gary, don't copy my arithmetic.

Gary: I'm not copying. (*Continues looking over Kenneth's shoulder and copying. Kenneth takes a piece of paper and covers up his work.*)

DISCUSSION

Teacher: What did you like about the way Kenneth and Gary worked out this problem?

Michael: I liked the whole thing much better because Kenneth didn't make Gary angry.

Stanley: I guess I'm changing my mind. I think it was better too.

Teacher: What do you think, Lydia?

Lydia: I don't know. I guess I liked the second time better.

Teacher: Would you tell us why you liked it better?

Lydia: Well, Kenneth didn't make Gary angry and he didn't tear up his paper.

Teacher: I'm glad to know how you feel.

Dorothy: This is a good way of stopping somebody from copying without getting into a fight.

Teacher: I see Danny shaking his head all the time. It looks like he disagrees with you. Let's hear what you have to say, Danny.

Danny: I don't agree because it doesn't help Gary, I mean Keith, at all.

Teacher: Could you explain what you mean by this?

Danny: It's nice that they didn't make each other mad, but Keith is cheating because he can't do the work, and this way we don't help him any.

Teacher: I'll tell you what, Danny. Let's act this out once more, and you take the part of Henry and show us how you would solve this problem.

Role Playing *(third time)*: **Danny takes the part of Henry and Sandra takes the part of Keith. Danny pretends to be working while Sandra looks over his shoulder and copies.**

Danny: Need help, Sandra?

Sandra: Yes, I just can't get these problems.

Danny: Maybe I can help you; I know how to do them real well. Do you think the teacher would mind if we went over to the blackboard and practiced?

Sandra: Let's ask her.

Danny: *(To teacher)* Sandra is having a little trouble with these arithmetic problems. May we go over to the blackboard and practice? I think that I could help her.

Teacher: That would be very nice, Danny. Thank you.

Danny: *(To teacher)* If it takes long I may not be able to finish my arithmetic in time.

Teacher: Don't worry about that, Danny. You do the best you can.

DISCUSSION

Teacher: What is your reaction?

Maria: I can see now why Danny disagreed with us before.

Miriam: I like this solution best because Danny helped Sandra. If nobody helps her she will always have to cheat because she wouldn't know how to do the problems.

Albert: That's what Nina and I do all the time. Sometimes, when I don't know something, she helps me and when she doesn't know something, sometimes I help her.

Danny: Maybe Henry wouldn't mind helping Keith tomorrow when we do arithmetic.

Teacher: I think we have found a very good solution to this problem. Maybe it won't ever be necessary to discuss this any more. I'm very happy that you realize that you don't have to copy if you don't understand how to do the work. Anyone who understands it will be glad to help you. How do you feel about this, Henry?

Henry: Well, I think this is a good solution, and I'm sorry I tore the paper.

140

Teacher: I'm sure Keith and the others have already forgotten what you did.

The final solution to this problem will work with children who cheat because they do not know how to do the work and are eager to hand in the assignment. However, this approach may have little, if any, effect on the child who is passive, destructive, lazy, or one whose goal is power, and who has to defeat the teacher. In such a case, role playing alone would not be sufficient.

It is not necessary to role-play all situations the second or third time. The following example provides insight concerning a particular child's behavior. The setting for the situation and the assigning of roles is very structured.

Background information: Harry, 9 years old, the oldest of four children and the only boy in the family, constantly disrupted the class through his unique behavior. He had partial paralysis in both legs and had to wear braces as a result of polio. From his first day in school, Harry's behavior was impossible. By the time he reached third grade, his school folder consisted of scores of letters and complaints from teachers and parents of children whom he had molested and hurt.

In spite of his braces, Harry was very agile; he could run and climb, roller skate and ride a scooter. He was very daring in all physical activities, outdoing many normal children. He was very determined to succeed in whatever goal he set for himself, disregarding how it affected others. If he decided to be first on top of the jungle gym, he would simply push off anyone who was in his way, kicking the children with his braces and stepping on their hands when they were beneath him. Upon reaching the top, Harry would look around and grin. He did the same when he wanted access to a swing or other playground equipment.

In class Harry did not work. He sang or whistled, tapped his foot, let himself deliberately drop from his chair, or went to the window to look out. To add to his problems, Harry's nose was always running. When he was sent out of the room as a consequence of his behavior, he would merely continue making noises and would disturb the other teachers as well.

Harry was disliked by his peers. They pitied him because of his physical handicap, but not a single child reached out to him for friendship. No one chose him in a sociometric test. Nor did he make any effort to form any friendships.

When the teacher asked Harry to do some of his school work, he would laugh loudly and reply, "Try and make me. I never do my school work. You can ask the other teachers." He was usually tee-

141

tering in his chair during this interchange and would suddenly topple, sprawling himself out on the floor where he remained for some time.

Situation and assigning the roles: Harry liked to act and he always begged for a role in role playing. Here, as in his personal life, he was destructive, vicious, and vindictive. When this was pointed out to him by the group, he laughed with satisfaction. Once Harry volunteered to play the mother of a girl who was having problems in class. The teacher assigned Betty to play the role of the girl and privately instructed Betty to behave the way Harry behaved in class, with all of his classroom disruption. Harry asked for a part in this role playing and since the teacher could not let him play himself, she assigned him the role of the mother and he was to act it as he felt.

The teacher wanted to mirror to Harry his own behavior in class in such a way that the problem could be discussed in general terms and in such a manner that Harry would not feel that he was personally being criticized, but that he could see how this kind of behavior affected everyone in class.

Presentation: In the presentation, Betty pretended to come home from school and the mother inquired how things were going. When Betty replied that she was always naughty and that the teacher was annoyed with her, Harry (the mother) replied, "Don't let this bother you, dear. I don't care if you make them miserable."

Discussion: During the discussion which followed, many children expressed outright anger at Harry's solution; they felt that no mother could ever act as he had. For once Harry did not laugh; he became angry and shouted, "I don't care what you say. My mother hates teachers and so do I."

Additional evaluation and follow-up by the teacher: This outburst made the teacher suspicious. Perhaps there was some truth to what Harry had said about his mother. The teacher had tried numerous times to have a conference with her, but she not only refused to come to school, she ignored many letters and did not reply to the teacher's invitations. She decided to investigate, and with the cooperation of the principal, the mother was told about Harry's outburst; she admitted that he was telling the truth. Her own school life had been a miserable one; she had been made to stay after school almost every day and her parents never took her part, but punished her in addition. Without realizing it, this woman had taken revenge on all teachers through her child.

As the teacher worked with the mother and as the home situation changed, Harry's attitude and behavior changed toward his studies and in his social relationships. In time, he took more interest in his studies and became a more cooperative boy. Although this is a most unusual case, the fact remains that the teacher would have remained ignorant about this situation had it not been for role playing.

As we have seen, role playing provides an interesting situation in which to study children's perceptions. The teacher can learn a great deal from the type of role that children choose for themselves or others. It is not uncommon for a shy, frightened child to insist on playing the "bad" one who beats up everybody, or for the group to assign the role of a "father" to a boy who is strong and bold.

From the child's own choices, and from the way he plays his role, his teacher can learn not only about how he sees himself, but also how he would like to be seen by others, how he sees the world around him, and how children take on the values of their parents.

Probably the most important value in role playing is the fact that an individual is given the opportunity to see how another person feels in certain situations and to discover for himself that certain behavior doesn't solve his problem. This brings us to the third technique known as *role reversal*.

Sometimes an incident is quite complicated and one child may say that the other child is not playing the part correctly. The teacher may need to intervene and remind them that each should play his part as he remembers it. Upon completion of the incident, it may be quite evident that something was left out or that an error was made. At this point, it may be necessary to let different children take one part or even both parts, or perhaps let the two children exchange roles. It is very important that the teacher meet all objections of "That's not the way it happened" with the same comment which is, "Show me." The following is an example of role reversal:

Incident:

Kathy: Teacher, José took my lunch.

José: I did not. You big liar.

Kathy: Yes, you did. You erased my name from the bag and you wrote your name on it. I saw you.

José: Prove it. You have no proof. You just want to get me in trouble.

Teacher: José, please show us your bag.

José: I hate you too. You always stick up for the girls. I don't have to show you nothing.

Teacher: If you haven't taken Kathy's lunch, you have nothing to fear. You just said, "Prove it." I can't prove it if you don't let me see your bag. Please, give me your bag.

José: I don't have to and you can't make me.

The teacher realized she had fallen into the trap of arguing in a power struggle. By having everyone switch roles, the solution became obvious.

Role Reversal: *José plays the part of the teacher. Kathy plays the part of José. The teacher takes the part of Kathy.*

Kathy: Teacher, José took my lunch.

Teacher: José, is that true?

José: No, I didn't.

Teacher: Kathy, how do you know that José took your lunch?

Kathy: I saw him take it and then erase my name from the bag and write his own name on it.

Teacher: José, please let me look at the bag. This is the only way we can solve this argument.

José: I won't do it and you can't make me.

Teacher: José, if you talk that way, everybody will think that you took Kathy's lunch and that she is telling the truth. Why don't you let me look at the bag?

José: I hate you and I will not give you the bag.

Teacher: I think that you are afraid to let me look because you probably did take Kathy's lunch. If you didn't, you wouldn't be afraid to let me look. If you're so hungry that you must take other people's lunch, you should tell your mother to give you more food for lunch. If you won't do it, then I'll have to ask your mother to give you a bigger lunch. What do you say?

(José hands the bag to the teacher. Kathy's erased name is clearly visible.)

Teacher: Thank you, José.

This example illustrates how José's perception of the situation changed in the moment he saw the problem from the role of the teacher.

The steps in role playing as used by most teachers are few. First, a simple situation to role play; second, setting the stage and assigning the roles; third, the presentation of the situation; and fourth, the discussion and evaluation of the solution. Sometimes role playing may take five minutes and other times it may take half an hour, depending upon the situation and also how role playing is being used. If it is being used as a learning situation for the entire class, then more time will be needed.

There are many other role-playing variations, such as soliloquy, mirroring, monologue or multiple role playing, replaying, chair auxiliary ego, audience reaction, auxiliary ego, double technique, and others, which provide insight, skill practice and release of tensions. Since they are usually not used by the classroom teacher, they will not be dealt with.

The following principles of role playing should be kept in mind:

1. *Role-playing atmosphere.* One of the most important factors in role playing is the atmosphere that is created by the teacher. It should be conducive to realistic role playing. The teacher should convey to the group that many problems are not easy to solve; many need to be an exploration into different solutions with no one right solution, and that everyone does get into difficulty sometime. The teacher guides the group and works for open-ended exploration. After presenting the problem story, she should pause for a minute to give the children time to think. She might then ask, "What did happen?" "What is the problem?" "What is the situation?" This process is known as the warm-up to the situation or problem. Invite ideas from the children. The teacher will have more to work with if a number of solutions are offered. Sometimes both socially acceptable and antisocial solutions are proposed.

2. *Selecting the actors.* The teacher needs to be aware of who is responding and who seems to be identifying with the various roles. Usually, youngsters are ready for role playing. If possible, the teacher should select for the first enactment children who show impulsive or antisocial solutions so that they may be explored for their consequences. However, the teacher should not choose actors whose natural role is like the one to be portrayed. Also, one must be careful that the class does not "type" a particular child by proposing him for that role.

The teacher needs to help the characters get the "feel" of the role by asking them questions such as: "What is———like?" "How does he feel?" In this process, the "warm-up" deals with the actors getting prepared for their roles. They have to be able to step out of their own roles and assume the role of another.

3. *Setting the stage.* Very little equipment is needed for role playing. Usually, a few chairs, a table, and space for action is all that is needed. The teacher could ask such questions as: "Where will this take place?" "What time of day is it?" "What are the various characters supposed to be doing?"

4. *Enactment.* The teacher decides when to cut the enactments, guides the players, and selects which solutions are to be portrayed. Sometimes a child may get lost in his role, become silly, not knowing what to do. The teacher should stop the role playing and refocus the child by asking such questions as, "Are you really playing this character?" "What kind of person is ———?" "We're not really working on this problem, are we?" The teacher should avoid scolding a child about his performance. She must also allow the child to work out his idea of the role and not let the other members of the class tell him what to do. They will have a chance to work out their ideas later.

145

Keep the focus on how true to life the enactment is. Help the children to be aware of the different feelings and ideas. Give recognition to those who contribute to the experience and encourage others to do so the next time.

Sometimes the role-playing session does not work out. Perhaps the problem was not conducive to role-playing, but would fit better in group discussion. At this point, the teacher could bring the role playing to a close by simply saying, "We will discuss this later," or "That will be all for this time."

The teacher also has to instruct the rest of the class to be observers of the actors. Through the process of observing, the rest of the class becomes involved. The teacher asks the observers to see if the actor is playing his part for "real," or could this really happen; what feelings are being portrayed; and what other solutions come to mind.

5. *Discussion.* The discussion that follows the enactment is of the greatest significance. In the discussion, the children learn to analyze situations and find support and opposition among their class members in considering the various consequences and solutions. The observers are able to give a broader perspective and are able to see more alternatives. They are also more objective and can see the consequences to the solutions more clearly. Such feelings are explored as: "How do you suppose———felt while Sally was talking?" "Why do you suppose———said that?" Through these kinds of discussions, children learn about anger, frustration, tenderness, etc.

6. *Reenactment.* New actors are selected and the situation is reenacted, with a different ending. The situation may be reenacted any number of times with many different solutions. The children then understand that there are several solutions to most problems. They gain insight into their own behavior and the behavior of others as they move from the role of observer to actor and back again. After each enactment, a discussion period should follow.

7. *Generalization.* The role-playing session needs closure and a time for generalizations. Through this process of shared experiences, children discover the principles for social living. They realize that they are closer to each other as their problems are shared, that they are able to make decisions and choices, and are consciously developing a different value system.

The following bibliography can be helpful for readers who want to learn more about role playing and psychodrama:

Adult Education Association of the U.S.A. *How to Use Role Playing and Other Tools for Learning.* Chicago: 1955, p. 49. Leadership Pamphlet No. 8.

Benne, Kenneth, and Bozidar Muntyan. "What Is Role Playing?" and "The Use of Role Playing," in *Human Relations in Curriculum Change*. New York: Dryden Press, 1951, pp. 223–249.

Blake, R. R. "Experimental Psychodrama with Children," *Group Psychotherapy*, 1955, pp. 347–350.

Boniface, J. "Role Playing in Kindergarten," *Grade Teacher*, Vol. 76 (October 1958), p. 31.

Boyd, Gertrude A. "Role Playing," *Social Education*, Vol. 21 (October 1957), pp. 267–269.

Brunelle, Peggy. "Action Projects from Children's Literature," and "Indirect Approach to Intercultural Relations in Elementary Schools," *Sociatry 2*, December–March 1948, pp. 235–243.

Graham, Grace. "Sociodrama as a Teaching Technique," *Sociatry*, December 1960, pp. 257–259.

Haas, R. B. *Roleplaying in Guidance*, 16mm. film, black and white, sound, 14 min., 1953, Department of Visual Instruction, University of California, Berkeley, California.

Jennings, Helen Hall. "Sociodrama as Educative Process," in *Fostering Mental Health in Our Schools*, 1950 Yearbook. Washington, D.C.: Association for Supervision and Curriculum Development, pp. 260–285.

Kean, Charles. "Some Role-Playing Experiments with High School Students," *Group Psychotherapy 6*, January–March 1954, pp. 256–265.

Klein, Alan F. *How to Use Role Playing Effectively* New York: Association Press, 1959.

Klein, Alan F. *Role Playing in Leadership Training and Group Problem Solving*. New York: Association Press, 1956.

Lippitt, Rosemary, and Catherine Clancy. "Psychodrama in the Kindergarten," *Group Psychotherapy 7*, December 1954, pp. 262–273.

Martin, C. P., Jr., "Role Playing in the Classroom," *Grade Teacher*, Vol. 73 (November 1955), p. 63.

Nichols, Hildred, and Lois Williams. *Learning About Role Playing for Children and Teachers*. Washington, D.C.: Association for Childhood Education International, 1960, p. 40.

Shaftel and Shaftel. *Role-Playing the Problem Story*. New York: N.C.C.J., 1952.

Shaftel and Shaftel. *Role Playing for Social Value*. Englewood Cliffs, N. J.: Prentice-Hall, 1967.

Solt, M. A. "George Wanted In," *Childhood Education*, Vol. 38 (April 1962), pp. 374–376.

THE CLASS COUNCIL

After the class has had some training in group discussions, the teacher might suggest that they have their own government in the form of a class council which would meet once or twice a week. At this time, they could discuss anything they wanted to. This suggestion is usually received with great enthusiasm. The class council usually works out successfully, but only after some trying weeks. There is considerable confusion at first which may discourage teachers who do not have sufficient confidence in children.

Two or three members are selected by the class to form the council for a certain length of time. Usually, every two weeks the group elects a new council until all children in the class have had a chance to be leaders.

Grievances and suggestions of all types are brought to the council. The council brings these problems up for discussion with the entire class. The opinion of the council carries more weight than the opinion of the teacher alone. If the council discusses the disturbances John creates by tapping his pencil on the desk, the problem is invariably solved more satisfactorily than if the teacher had reprimanded him.

It takes time before the children are trained to conduct their discussions in an orderly and democratic manner. As the child learns to accept the values of the group, and as his concept of himself and his relationship to others changes, then he sees a solution to some of his personal problems.

During the first part of the year, the teacher must participate actively as a member of the group. When discussion strays, she may have to lead it back to its original purpose. She may point out to the class council that some children have not been called on to express their views, or that they have let some child talk too long. Sometimes, the teacher may have to call a special meeting with the members of the council in order to point out specific problems existing in the group which they need to bring up for discussion.

A teacher must be a good listener. She must sit *with* the children, not behind the desk doing some paper work while the discussion is in process. If the teacher gives her full attention, the children will do likewise. If she lends only half an ear, some children may become disinterested and withdraw from participation. If the teacher observes listlessness, she may invite a child to voice an opinion concerning the topic of discussion, or she may ask the speaker to stop the discussion until everyone pays attention. The class council meetings must be held at regular times, and must be considered as an important part of the general school activities.

148

Some people may ask what sort of grievances children bring up. Children should be able to bring up anything that concerns them and that occupies their thinking. This may include situations which are threatening to them, as exams or the teacher's conference with their parents about their misbehavior, the teacher's handling of situations in an unfair manner, punishment, situations on the playground, cheating, etc.

The better the relationship the teacher has with her class, the freer the child will be in bringing up for discussion anything that bothers him. It takes time before a class is sufficiently trained to conduct discussions in an orderly and cooperative manner.

Some children bring up problems they have at home. The following are but a few of the problems that can be discussed in class:

> Patsy asked the class whether she should invite a girl to her birthday party even though this girl did not invite Patsy to her party. Patsy was advised to disregard what the other girl did and invite her if she would really like her to be there. Patsy took the advice, and later reported that she and the girl became close friends and had good times together.
>
> Reynold wanted to know how much work the other children had to do at home. He thought that his mother demanded too much help from him. This developed into a discussion about family belonging and responsibility. The conclusion was that we cannot compare the amount of work children do in their respective homes since each home is different; in every case we must do our share, according to what is necessary.
>
> Sue wanted to know if it was fair that she should have to go to bed at the same time that her younger brother did. During the discussion it became evident that she made a big scene at home every time she had more work to do than her brother. She demanded that the chores be divided equally. The group felt, under those circumstances, she had no right to demand special privileges for herself in the evenings. If she wanted to be treated as the older, with more rights, then she must also assume more responsibilities than the younger. Sue promptly discussed this with her parents, and accepted the group's suggestion.

The following are minutes taken from a third grade class council in action.

Third Grade—Class Council—Organization Meeting

> Class agreed that the council should be elected by a *secret ballot*. It should consist of three members, one of whom should be the chairman. The student council should be changed every two weeks

and no person may have a second turn before everyone in class has served. The chairman's duties are to present to the class any suggestions which may come up for new activities, criticism of activities in process, other complaints such as fighting, cheating, etc.

The student council should meet from 1 p.m. to 1:30 p.m. every Monday, Wednesday, and Friday. The chairman should first discuss the agenda of the next meeting with the council and together they should decide how much time to allot to each case or problem they want to discuss. If in doubt, they should come to the teacher who will assist them. The teacher will normally sit with the class and participate just as any other member of the class. However, she will assist or direct the discussion if it should prove to be necessary.

The teacher will write the minutes until the class names a member to take over this duty.

First elections of student class council: Michael M. (chairman), Susan, and James.

First Meeting (October)

As was decided at the previous meeting, teacher read the rules of the student class council meeting.

Michael brought up the fact that only two children had come to the council with ideas and problems to be discussed during the meeting. He accused John of having had a fight with another boy from a different class and that John was arrogant when the council suggested that this fight should be discussed in class.

Susan said that when he told him that the council would bring it up anyway, John called her "stupid" and other names.

Michael said that the first thing they would like to discuss was why hardly anyone came to the council all week.

Sandra said that probably most children forgot about the council since they are not used to this new setup yet. The other children felt the same way.

Michael asked that John tell why he had the fight with the boy. John claimed that he had already forgotten why. James suggested that they call in the other boy to tell his story, but John said that he now recalled what happened. He told the class that this boy picked on him all the time. Then he started to cry and said that now the council is also beginning to pick on him. Michael said that this is not the case, but that it was agreed that all fighting must be discussed in class.

Susan said, "If you say that we pick on you when it isn't true, how can we be sure that the boy picks on you? Maybe this is just as true as your saying that we pick on you?" (Many children supported this feeling and demanded further explanations, but John kept crying.)

150

Teacher asked the class if anyone could explain why he was crying since nobody did anything bad to him.

Jane said that he probably felt sorry for himself.

Paul said, "Maybe he feels guilty?"

Michael said that John doesn't fight clean. For instance, why did he call Susan names when all she did was ask him a question? This is just like dirty fighting.

Teacher suggested that the class should concentrate more on helping John to find out why he feels so unfriendly toward others rather than elaborate on the accusations.

Larry said that he thinks that John is jealous of the good students. He also said that he thinks that John called Susan "stupid" to show her that she isn't as smart as she thinks just because she serves on the council.

James asked John if this was true. John did not reply, but everybody felt that James had a point.

Michael explained that this is just the first council and that everybody will have a turn in time.

Time was up and Michael asked Mary to present her suggestions for a spelling bee. She suggested that we invite the two best spellers from every third grade class and to prepare a list of words, then have the five best spellers from every room compete for some prize.

Helen objected to giving a prize because being a winner was enough.

Cedric did not like the idea of choosing the "best spellers" because the other children would never have a chance.

Michael asked for a vote by showing hands. Most children were against it, and so this suggestion was dropped.

Next, Michael brought up Elsa's complaint that Danny is always copying from her. Since time had run out, the council postponed discussion of this until the next meeting.

Second Meeting (October)

Michael suggested that we discuss Elsa's problem first.

James said that the council had discussed it among themselves and that they had observed Danny during the last two days and did not notice any copying.

Danny claimed that he copied once from Elsa and ever since, she claims that he copies from her.

Judy suggested that Danny's desk should be moved away from Elsa.

Teacher asked if anyone could explain to Elsa why she brought up this complaint.

Ermelene said that one doesn't learn from copying and that Elsa felt that it was bad for Danny to copy.

Michael agreed with Ermelene.

Teacher asked if the children thought that Elsa is really concerned with what is good or bad for Danny.

Most children felt that she was not concerned.

Teacher asked again that the children try helping Elsa to understand why she made the complaint.

Larry said that Elsa is trying to show everybody how smart she is.

Teacher said that one should not make definite statements, but that some people in class might wonder if Elsa made the accusation in order to show the class how good a speller she was.

Michael asked Elsa if that was true. Elsa replied, "Maybe."

Irene said that she did not have to get others in trouble just for that.

Teacher suggested that Elsa could get the recognition she wanted by pinning her spelling paper on the bulletin board.

All agreed that this would be better.

Irene complained that Harry went out to play during recess although he had not completed his work.

Patricia said that we had decided to apply natural consequences, but did not do it in Harry's case and demanded to know why not.

Susan said that the council will still have to work on this; that they do not know how to apply natural consequences.

Teacher reminded them that the class must decide that, not just the council.

Judy asked for suggestions.

Patti suggested that Harry stay in the next day and do the work he was supposed to do today.

Gloria didn't think that he should stay in during recess, but should come in ten minutes earlier each day at lunchtime until he had made up his work.

Harry said that he would like that better, too.

Bill asked if the two other children and he who were practicing a puppet play could put it on for the class. It was agreed that they could do so on Friday afternoon.

Frances wanted to know what children should do with found money which nobody claimed. Class decided to put such money into a box and use it for special purposes.

Third Meeting (October)

Michael mentioned that Charlene was playing on her way to school and was tardy later on. She had been tardy for three days in a row.

Charlene said that she was tardy because she had a long walk from home.

James said that he and John saw her on the street playing with other children. So did Danny.

Michael asked the class what should be done if children are tardy. The class agreed that we should add up the time of tardiness and as soon as it amounted to 15 minutes or more, the child would have to make it up during lunch time or after school. Unanimous vote. Class discussed the Halloween party. It was decided that children should come in costumes. Those who could not get a costume could make it at school with the teacher's help.

1. The following committees were elected: Refreshment Committee—Violetta, Mary Lou, Gus. Clean-up—Mickey and Charlene. Room Decorations—Michael Young, Cedric, Tom, Helen, Patricia, Gloria.

2. Parents would be invited.

3. Program would consist of: a. Songs. b. Puppet play. c. Games. Further details will be discussed at next meeting.

Fourth Meeting (October)

Class decided on the following songs: 1. "Jack-o-lantern" 2. "The Witch" 3. "Halloween Night" 4. "Come Out, Come Out" Games: 1. Who Started the Motion? 2. Electricity. 3. Simon Says. 4. Hide the Keys.

Michael said Charlene was seven minutes late after lunch. This brought up her tardiness to twenty-one minutes. Michael suggested that Charlene should make up her time the following day.

Harry said that Charlene was tardy on purpose so as to be alone with the teacher.

Teacher explained that she will go out for lunch and Charlene will be supervised by the playground supervisor.

The student council brought up the following complaints that they had received:

Sandy D. asked why the teacher had changed her seat the other day. She was not happy in her new seat because she did not like to sit between two boys.

John said that he thought that the reason Sandy's seat was changed was on account of her constant chattering with Helen. He reminded Sandy that the teacher had given her fair warning that this would happen unless she stopped talking so much.

Teacher asked why Sandy disliked sitting between boys.

Sandy replied, "I don't like boys. My brother is the meanest thing and I hate him."

James reminded Sandy that these boys were not her brothers and that they weren't mean.

Sandy cried and said that they were all mean.

Teacher asked Sandy if she would like to be a girl or if she would like to exchange places with her brother, if this were possible.

Sandy did not reply.

Teacher asked the question again.

Sandy said that this couldn't happen anyway, so why talk about it.

Teacher asked the children what they thought.

Irene said that she knows how Sandy feels because she would like to change places with her brother.

Teacher asked the girls how many of them would rather be boys. Of twelve girls, five raised their hands including Sandy.

Teacher asked if anyone would like to tell why she would prefer to be a boy.

Irene said that boys don't have to help in the house.

Mary claimed that most parents like boys better because they will be men when they grow up, and that parents are prouder of boys than of girls.

Patricia said that she would like to be a boy because she could play football and other sports.

Frances said she wanted to be a boy because she wouldn't have to help in the house and because boys "get away with everything."

Teacher asked the children which one of these reasons sounded the most plausible one.

Michael said that he must help in the household. Other boys made similar statements.

Danny said that he thinks that parents prefer girls because they are not so naughty and don't mess up the house.

Helen said that she believes that the girls who want to be boys are always the kind of girls who have brothers and are jealous of them.

Sandy yelled at Helen saying that she too would be jealous if she had a brother who was a rat.

Teacher asked Sandy if one is usually jealous of rats, and if it could be that she thought her brother was preferred by the parents because he still required a lot of attention. (Brother only 3 years old.)

During the discussion, the children expressed feelings that many older children are jealous of younger siblings, girls or boys, because the parents, especially the mother, spends more time with them.

Teacher asked in what way older children get more attention than the little ones.

Time up—discussion postponed.

Fifth Meeting (October)

Michael brought up the unfinished discussion of last meeting. He said that he, being the oldest of three children had many privileges the younger ones did not have. He received a larger allowance, he could stay up thirty minutes later at night, and he could go to the show with the boys. The younger children could only go with a parent.

Teacher asked if Michael would exchange places with a younger sibling and he said that he would not.

Michael asked Sandy if she would exchange places with her brother.

Sandy who did not answer the same question last time, now replied. "Well, I'm sure you will laugh at me if I told you my answer so I won't tell you."

It was obvious to all that she would rather be in her brother's place.

Teacher asked Sandy to tell the class the things she liked about being a girl and about being older than her brother.

Sandy said that she liked her dresses, her dolls and doll house, and her long hair, as she would not like to wear her hair short like a boy. As for being older, she liked to be able to watch T.V. in the evenings when her brother was already asleep. She liked to go to the store for her mother, to go to school, and she liked staying with her grandparents (who live in Chicago) for two weeks during the summer. Her brother had to stay home.

James asked if she would give up all these things in order to be younger. Sandy said that she wouldn't like to change these privileges, that this is not what she meant. She admitted, when questioned further, that she liked being what she is, wanted to keep what she had, but at the same time, also would like to have what her brother has.

Harry said that she can't be two people at the same time, and that she would have to make up her mind.

Irene said that she would not like it if Sandy were a boy because she and Sandy are friends and she would hate to lose her.

Teacher asked Sandy if she still wanted to have her seat moved away from the boys.

Sandy replied, "No, I'll stay here."

Danny said that she'll see that boys are not rats.

Sandy said she was sorry she called them "rats."

This problem, the teacher suggested, would be discussed again some time in the future.

James said that Elsa looks into other children's desks and takes out pencils.

Helen claimed that she too saw Elsa do that.

Michael asked Elsa to give her explanation.

Elsa claimed that she borrowed a pencil from Ermelene's desk and later returned it.

Ermelene did not miss her pencil.

Teacher suggested that children be very certain before they make accusations.

Sixth Meeting (October)

Michael asked for a discussion.

James said that he was pleased with the way the Halloween party went, except that the children who did the puppet play forgot their lines and giggled.

Judy felt that it didn't matter, that the group who presented the play did a good job.

Cedric complained that he got only one cookie when all the other children got two.

Michael suggested that next time, Cedric should get an extra cookie.

Teacher asked the class to evaluate the first two weeks of the council meetings, this being the last day of this council.

Helen said that it was fun talking things over.

Susan said that she liked them too, except that the time went too fast and some children did not have a chance to talk.

Michael said that these children should be the first to talk at the next meeting.

James said that during the meetings of the three children who comprise the council, Michael takes over and doesn't give the others a chance to talk.

Michael said that this is his right since he is the chairman.

Harry did not agree with Michael. He said that the chairman is supposed to be a leader but not take over everything himself.

Ermelene agreed to this.

Danny suggested that the three children on the council should have equal opportunity to speak, but that the chairman should lead the discussion.

Teacher reminded the class that this was their first student council and that in time they would correct their mistakes. The next group would probably do it better. She complimented this council for doing a good job. The class applauded.

Michael said that if ever he should be chairman again, he thinks that he will be able to do a better job.

First Meeting (November)

Cedric (Elections chairman), Charlene, and Gloria.

Paul said that next time, the class should elect two boys and one girl since this time there was only one boy on the council.

Cedric said that this was not in the rules that the class had made up.

Irene said that it did not matter how many girls or boys were on

156

the council, that whoever will be elected, will serve.

Harry said that he wouldn't like it if only girls were elected.

Other boys felt the same way.

Teacher suggested that they can add to or change their constitution.

There were many, "Yes, let us," so she suggested that the chairman have the children raise their hands if they wanted the council always to consist of girls and boys. The count was 14 against 11 in favor of a mixed group.

Second Meeting (November)

Cedric opened the meeting by telling the class that his father said that he was proud of his son because the fact that class elected him chairman proved that they liked him and trusted him. Many children called out, "We do." Cedric brought up the question of homework.

He said that the student council had discussed this and that they thought that all children should get homework.

Gloria asked for a show of hands. Sixteen children raised their hands.

Cedric asked the teacher what to do.

Teacher suggested that she will prepare homework for these sixteen children.

Larry asked if he could change his mind and also vote "yes."

Ermelene also said that she had changed her mind.

Charlene asked Cedric to take a second vote. This time twenty-one children raised their hands.

Cedric asked the teacher what would she do about the children who do not want homework.

Teacher said that she would not force them. However, she hoped that they would change their minds too someday. If they do, they should let the council know about it.

Gloria reported that a number of children played in the puddles although the teacher had asked them not to.

Irene asked who these children were, but Cedric said that the council had decided not to reveal names the first time, but that they will do so if those children do it again.

Larry got up and announced that he waded in the puddle and that his mother gave him a licking because his shoes and socks were wet.

Teacher asked Larry why he was grinning when he told class that his mother gave him a licking.

Larry said that he didn't know but he shook with laughter as he said it.

Gloria said that he was only trying to get everybody's attention.

Judy said that if her mother spanked her, she'd be ashamed to tell it to anyone.

Frances said that Larry probably likes to make his mother angry.

Larry said that this wasn't true.

Teacher asked the class what the children did when Larry told them that his mother spanked him.

Gloria said that everybody laughed.

Mary asked if Larry said this on purpose to make the class laugh.

Teacher asked the class how Larry could get attention from the children in a different way.

Paul said that Larry is the best runner of the boys and that he wins every race. So, he does get attention.

Michael said that probably Larry doesn't think that this is as important as being a good reader and that Larry is jealous of the children who can read better.

Teacher asked the class what they thought of Larry's ability to learn to read. Did they think he could or could not learn?

Gloria said that she was sure that he could if he wanted to.

Teacher asked the children if they believed that Larry doesn't want to learn how to read. Most children thought that he didn't want to.

Teacher said that she was not so certain of that.

Paul said that maybe he thinks that he cannot learn.

Frances asked how Larry could even know if he can or cannot if he didn't try. She said that he did not give himself a chance.

Sandra said that once she thought that she would never learn how to read but when she tried, really tried, she found that it was not as hard as she thought.

Larry said that he did want to be able to read.

Teacher said that she believed Larry. She asked him if he thought that he could learn it.

Larry said he didn't know.

Teacher asked class who of them thought that Larry was a very smart boy and could learn how to read.

Everyone held up his hand.

Teacher suggested that she would work with Larry every day for 10–15 minutes if he really wanted to.

Larry said that he would like it.

Teacher asked if Larry would like to have someone in class also read with him for 10 minutes a day and he chose Jane. It was decided that Jane would read with Larry every morning from 10:15 to 10:25 and that Larry should decide which book and story he wanted to read.

Third Meeting (November)

Gloria opened the meeting. She told the teacher that a few children had asked the committee to ask her if it would be all right for the class to go out for recess four times a week and, one time, stay in and dance.

Teacher asked the chairman to see how many children were in favor of this. All the girls and two boys raised their hands.

Cedric suggested that those who wanted to go out should go out and the others should stay in.

Ermelene reminded the class that the teacher must be with her class at all times.

Teacher promised to think about this problem and see if it could be solved.

Cedric said that except for this one request nobody had come to the committee for anything. He asked if anyone had anything that should be discussed.

Michael mentioned that some children never participate in the discussion, as for instance, Elsa, Mary, Jim, Bill, and Catherine.

Harry said that they must be scared.

Gloria said that there was nothing to be scared of, that everyone has the same right.

Teacher suggested that the chairman draw these people into the discussion. That they need to be encouraged.

Cedric asked Elsa if she would like to say something.

Elsa said "no" at first, but then she said that she did have something she would like to bring up. She complained that John often copies her work.

Cedric asked John if this was true and he replied, "Sometimes."

The class decided that for one week John would have to sit by himself at the reading table. Then, if he should copy again, he should sit by himself for two weeks.

Cedric asked John if he thought this fair, and John said that it was.

Teacher asked John what kind of work was so hard for him that he couldn't do it by himself.

John said that he copied mostly when he had to subtract with borrowing.

It was decided that John should get some extra help from teacher and that Cedric should help him too, since he could do it very well.

Cedric asked if Gloria could be chairman for the rest of the period. No one objected.

Fourth Meeting (November)

Cedric said that the class was wondering about whether they would have a Thanksgiving party.

159

Teacher reminded them that they could have only three parties a year, and that they had already had one. If they had a Thanksgiving and a Christmas party, they would use up all the parties and there would be nothing left until June.

Bill suggested that the class should have only the Christmas party and have one left over for spring.

Cedric asked for a show of hands.

Everybody agreed to Bill's suggestion.

Gloria reported that Susan was kissing the boys on the playground.

Teacher asked if the boys were agreeable to this. Many called "No." She asked chairman to have boys hold up their hands if they liked to be kissed by Susan or any other girl. No one raised their hand. Cedric said that since no one of the boys wanted to be kissed the girls mustn't ever do it.

Teacher explained that there are many other ways by which we can show that we like a person. She asked for suggestions.

Irene said that we can be friendly and play with the other child.

John said that we share toys and other things.

Mary said that children can do things together after school.

Danny said that we cooperate with people we like and don't insist on having our own way.

Harry said that his mother told him that we kiss only those people whom we love very much, like parents and sometimes friends on their birthdays or special days.

Michael accused Jim of tripping him on purpose when they went home at lunch time.

Jim said that Michael tripped him first.

Cedric asked for witnesses. Danny claimed that both boys argued about who knew his spelling better and that Jim then tripped Michael.

Jim cried and said that Michael had called him a dummy.

Gloria said that Michael boasts about being the best speller in class.

Teacher asked how many of the children could do as well in spelling as Michael if they really tried. Many children raised their hands. Teacher pointed out that how well they do is entirely in their power, that Jim could do as well as anyone else if he should so decide, however, that we do not help others by criticizing them or by boasting how good we are.

Frances said that Jimmy is better in writing than most children in class.

Cedric suggested that Jim and Michael should not go out together. Teacher asked if the two boys would like to step out and talk it over before the council made further suggestions. The boys liked the idea. Susan said that Cedric is noisy in the corridor and that this sets a bad example for the other children if the council member breaks school rules. Cedric said that he doesn't do it any more. Danny confirmed this. Larry asked if he could bring treats the next day since it was his birthday. Children said they'd love it.

Michael and Jim returned and said they were straightened out and were friends.

Time was up.

Fifth Meeting (November)

Gloria was absent, so Cedric acted as chairman.

Charlene said that Helen wanted to announce something to the class.

Helen announced the birth of her fourth sister. She said that her parents were hoping for a boy, but that the other girls, except her oldest sister, wanted another girl.

Teacher asked why she wanted another sister.

Helen said that boys mess up the house.

Teacher asked if she had other reasons.

Helen could not tell.

Paul said that maybe Helen was afraid of a boy. When the teacher asked why be afraid, he added that if there are five girls in the family they might be jealous of a boy.

Sandra said that she would be jealous in Helen's place.

Teacher asked if they could think of reasons why it could be nice to have a boy also.

Larry said that it is more interesting when there are boys and girls.

Irene said that it's nice to have a brother.

Teacher said that it was also very nice to have five sisters, that there were few families where there are five girls and no boys, but that if we know how to get along, it makes no difference how many boys or girls.

Paul said that he had two younger brothers, and that he would like to have a sister instead of his brother Dick who comes right after him.

Teacher asked why he didn't like Dick.

Paul said that Dick starts fights and then tells the parents that he, Paul, started it and they scold him.

John said that the same thing happens in his family.

Patricia said that she, too, has the same situation.

Teacher asked why it is that we run into this kind of situation so often.

161

Cedric said that the younger child wants to bring the older into trouble.

Irene said that the older children are always stuck up and blamed the younger ones for starting the fight.

James said the oldest think they are much smarter and can do everything.

Michael said that this is not true, that the older children are always smarter. Sometimes the younger ones are smarter than the older.

Teacher asked why it is that the oldest and the one next to him or her usually fight. Why doesn't the oldest fight with the youngest?

Patricia said that the youngest is no trouble.

Teacher asked if this was really true.

Mary said the younger is trouble sometimes but in a different way.

James said that the youngest and the oldest do not do the same things and that the youngest, especially if he is very young, doesn't have to do anything, but the oldest and the middle one must do things at home and at school.

Teacher explained the word "competition," and what we mean by "competing."

Michael said that the oldest and the middle one compete more.

The class understood and realized that these two compete.

Teacher asked why they compete, and whom they want to impress.

Susan said that they want to impress the parents.

Danny said they want to show who is better.

Frances said maybe Paul didn't like his brother, Dick, because he wants his parents to love only him.

Teacher pointed out that the council had run seven minutes overtime.

The discussion was postponed for next meeting.

Sixth Meeting (November)

Gloria asked Cedric to be chairman since she was absent last time and did not have a chance to read the minutes.

Cedric reminded the class that this was Election Day and that the student council had only twenty minutes.

Gloria proposed that they hold elections first.

The new council will consist of: Irene, Jim, and Harry as chairman.

Teacher asked for an evaluation of the student council and of what the class achieved during these two weeks.

Mary said that Gloria made a good chairman because she gave everybody a chance to talk.

Ermelene noticed that the children talked more than in recent meetings than they did with the first council.

Michael pointed out that there was hardly any fighting among the children.

Cedric pointed out that almost everybody was now doing his homework except two children.

Teacher asked if anyone noticed any changes in Larry.

Charlene said that Larry does not want so much attention any more.

Teacher asked Larry what he thought.

Larry just smiled, but did not say anything.

Class applauded the council

First Meeting (December)

New Members: Harry, chairman, Irene, and Jim.

Harry suggested that the class continue the discussion that was not finished the week before, why Paul doesn't like or get along with Dick.

Paul said that he was getting along better now.

Teacher asked him to tell the class how this happened.

Paul said that he let Dick squeal on him all he wanted, and he never said anything bad about Dick to his parents. He told Dick that this is what he would do from now on. At first Dick didn't believe him, but then when he saw that Paul kept his word, he also stopped squealing.

Teacher asked if the two boys did anything together for fun.

Paul said that they play checkers.

John said that he tried not to tattle on his younger sister, but that she told lies about him to their parents and he got a spanking.

Irene said that John should talk it over with his sister and show her that he is her friend.

Patricia said that John should not give up so easily.

Teacher asked who could tell whom John's sister wanted as her friends.

Judy said that she wanted John as a friend.

Gloria said that John's sister wants to have the parents' friendship more than she wants John's.

Teacher asked what John's sister is really trying to tell her parents when she tattles on John.

Harry said she wants attention.

Frances said she wants them not to love John, but only love her.

Teacher asked why John's sister believes that if she tells on him, the parents will not love him.

Susan said, "Because he is bad."

Paul said, "She wants to tell them that he is bad, but that she is always innocent."

Teacher pointed out that this is usually the reason why one tattles, to tell how bad the other is and how good the one is who is telling the parents or the teacher. She asked if anyone can tell her how the children do the same thing in school in order to tell the teacher how good they are as compared with someone else.

James said, "By tattling."

Judy said, "By complaining."

Teacher asked how they complain and about what they tattle.

Michael S. said that they tattle if someone copies his work.

Michael M. said that our best example is Elsa who always complains that people copy from her.

Teacher asked why Elsa would want that kind of attention.

Gloria said that maybe she doesn't think that the teacher likes her.

Harry said that she wants to tell the teacher that she is better than Bill, that he copies from her, but that she doesn't copy from anyone.

Teacher asked what does this make Elsa and Bill.

Sandra said that this suggests that Elsa is better than Bill.

Teacher urged them to think about this situation and discuss it again soon.

Second Meeting (December)

Harry brought up a problem that the student council had while meeting by themselves. Jim felt that the council should do something about Cathy, who was slow in finishing her work. Irene felt that Cathy was improving and doing much better than before, and she should be let alone.

Harry and Jim agreed on calling Catherine to account for her slowness.

Harry presented this problem to the class and asked for their opinion. Sandra agreed with Irene. Gloria also expressed her belief that Cathy was improving. James said that Cathy was doing better, but that she still talked and played around instead of finishing her work.

Teacher pointed out that Cathy was making an effort, but that she cannot change entirely in just a few weeks—that we must give her more time.

Teacher suggested that they *ask Cathy* how much time she will need.

Cathy said that she didn't know, but that she would try to finish all the work.

Teacher suggested that they wait until Christmas before evaluating Cathy's progress.

All agreed to this.

Third Meeting (December)

Harry suggested that we plan for our Christmas party since we had only two and a half weeks left. He asked for a show of hands to see how many would want a special committee to do the planning. The majority voted for a special program committee.

Program Committee: Ermelene, Danny, Bill, Susan, and Teacher.

Irene told of a complaint that Frances had against Patsy. She claimed that Patsy took her crayons home and now borrows crayons from other children. Patsy admitted taking crayons home. (The crayons are school property.)

Harry asked for suggestions for natural consequences.

Patsy said that she would bring them back.

Class agreed that she would have to be without crayons if she didn't return them.

Jim accused Cedric of going to Rubens during lunch hours. As this was the third time Cedric broke this school rule, class decided on having Cedric take the consequence.

Elsa suggested that Cedric's parents should be notified and told not to give him any more spending money.

Paul said that this would be unfair, that Cedric must not go to Rubens, but that he should be allowed to buy something in the cafeteria.

Harry suggested that Cedric should give his money to the teacher and she would appoint someone to buy the things in the school cafeteria that Cedric wanted.

Teacher appointed Michael S. for one week. During this week, Cedric would not be allowed to do any buying by himself.

Harry asked for a vote on this.

Accepted by majority.

Cedric cried, but he said that he considered it fair.

Fourth Meeting (December)

Harry called on the program committee to give their report.

Danny reported that the committee decided that the program should last forty minutes and consist of:

a. Five Christmas Carols (to be decided).
b. A Christmas play based on *Paddy's Christmas*.
c. Helen should play something on the piano.
d. Gloria and Susan should do a tap dance.
e. Someone should read Moor's "T'was the night before Christmas . . ."

Next we should have refreshments and play games at the end.

Irene said the director could choose the characters. Class agreed.

Judy said that she had directed a play before and would like the job.

Larry said that he too had experience. Both Larry and Judy were elected.

They will pick characters and start rehearsing. Rehearsal should take place in the hall, daily from 2:00 to 2:30 p.m.

Paul, Sandra, and Catherine were elected to prepare any scenery or costumes that might be needed.

The following is a tape recording of a third grade class council during the last month of school.

Christine: Will the class, please, come to order because the student council will begin. Today, we will record the class council meeting. The members of the class council are Morton, John, and I, Christine. I will read the list of things that the children want to talk about today. James wants to talk about Debby P.; Quentin wants to talk about Katy; The class wants to decide what we should do with the money we have left over from our party; Tommy wants to talk about the playground. Some children want to talk about the class council— Gale, James, Danny, and Kenny.

James: I want to talk about Debby because she is doing so well in arithmetic and spelling.

Christine: Carmen!

Carmen: Everytime Debby can't do her work, she feels sad. I think Debby is trying hard to do well in her reading and in arithmetic.

Christine: What's your opinion, Debby?

Debby M.: Some people in class don't like to learn, but Debby likes to do her work.

Teacher: Debby, will you tell who you are because your name is Debby too. People might think that we are talking about you.

Debby M.: My name is Debby M. There are two Debby's in this class.

Christine: Kenny.

Kenny: Every time I look at Debby, she is always doing her work. She is never playing around like some of the kids are.

Teacher: I'd like to know why you picked Debby to talk about. Is there any special reason why you feel that you would like to compliment Debby?

Christine: Gail.

Gail: I think that Debby has been working hard this year to try to catch up with what we are doing.

Christine: But we want to know for what special reason did we choose Debby to talk about? Inez!

Inez: She's not smart, but she's trying very hard to learn. I'm sorry. She's smart, and she's trying very hard to learn. Some people are smart, but they aren't trying to learn, but Debby does.

Teacher: Would you say that Debby needed those compliments?

Christine: Yes, because nobody ever paid any attention to her, and I think she's happy because we put her in the student council and somebody is thinking about her. Tommy, what do you have to say?

Tommy: Debby is getting better, and she doesn't bother anybody. She hardly gets up, and when it's recess, she just sits and does her work.

Teacher: Do you think that's wise? Tommy, what's your opinion? Do you think she should be *working during recess?*

Tommy: Nobody asks us.

Teacher: Should a person work during recess?

Tommy: No!

Teacher: I don't think so either. So, maybe you better tell her next time that she doesn't have to work during recess. Does she?

Tommy: No.

Teacher to class: Do you think that she has to work during recess?

Class: No!

Teacher: Christine, shall we change now?

Christine: Now, we go on to the next thing. Quentin wants to talk about Katy.

Quentin: I want to know why Katy is late all the time before school.

Christine: That's what I would like to know too.

Danny: Well, she always walks to school with Joyce, and sometimes she messes around with Joyce on the way.

Christine: But why does she do that?

Candy: Joyce says she was late because the alarm clock didn't ring. Katy says something else, but they come to school at the same time together.

Christine: What would be a natural consequence for this kind of behavior, Mike?

Mike: I think if they should come in late, the teacher should put them in a corner or something.

Teacher: Do you think that this is a natural consequence?

Class: No!

Teacher: That's not a natural consequence, Mike.

Christine: Paul, what do you think?

167

Paul: Well, everytime they come late, the teacher could have them make up the time after school.

Christine: How many children agree with that? Almost everybody. Joyce and Katy, what do you think?

Teacher: Since we're talking about it, Katy, you tell us what you feel about your coming late? Tell us how you feel about it.

Katy: I think I should stay after school and make up the time.

Teacher: Do you think that's fair?

Katy: Yes.

Teacher: Joyce, what do you think?

Joyce: I think that I should stay after school and make up time.

Christine: We'll go to the next thing now. The class wants to decide what we should do with the money we have left over.

Teacher: Christine, would you explain what kind of money you are talking about because anyone listening to this would not know what we are talking about.

Christine: We have party money—some party money left over—and we would like to know what we should do with it.

Candy: Last year, we had some money left over from a trip or I think it was from a party, no, from a trip, and we bought a book last year. And maybe we could buy instead of a book this year, maybe we could buy something else.

James G.: I think that we could buy some things that would go with Science and we could use it.

Christine: Morton, you can take over now. (Morton is the other chairman of the class council.)

Morton: All right. James I.!

James I.: I think we could buy something that goes with the sea.

Christine: We could buy sea horses and maybe some sea fans and different things.

Quentin: I think on the last day of school we should have a party.

Morton: You're out of order.

Christine: You're out of order. We're talking about buying things for the class next year—for the ocean. You're just going off the subject.

Morton: Tommy wants to talk about the playground. (Morton refused to let Quentin talk about having a school party because he was out of order. However, he allowed Tommy to talk about an entirely different subject than the one the class was discussing. The teacher brought this to Morton's attention at a *later time*. It could have been discussed right there and then with equal effect.)

Tommy: Well, we discussed this a few weeks ago and hardly anyone listened. When somebody gets a swing, they keep it until we go in from recess. The other day, Gail had a swing, and she wouldn't give it away for the whole hour. I don't know if she gave it away for the whole hour, but she had it for almost half an hour. I asked her if I could have it for five minutes, because we discussed the fact that we were supposed to have it for five minutes then give it away.

Christine: I think, when we are on the playground, *everybody should share* the playground toys and whatever is outside and then we could be a happy class. Then we'll all have a turn to swing and slide.

Milagritta: We think that we should share the swings because some of the people want the swings and some won't give them to other people.

Morton: Do we think that everybody will cooperate? Who doesn't think that we will cooperate?

Teacher: You don't think they'll say that they won't cooperate. I am so glad that Tommy brought this problem up because I noticed it too. It's not just the swings. We did talk about it. So, please, let's remember that there are just a few swings and that everybody wants to have a turn. If we don't go on, we'll never finish, John. Is there something that someone still wants to say about this? (The teacher was eager to finish the discussion because the music teacher was due in class in a short while. However, the children ignore the teacher's mild suggestion that they come to a close, and continue the discussion. This may be discussed during the next class council meeting if the teacher so desires. She would then have to sign up with the Chairman in order to be called upon just as the other members of the class are.)

Debby P.: I want to say something because I never get a chance to swing. When I asked Connie, she is nice to me, and she shares with me.

Tommy: I haven't had a swing now for about a month.

Teacher: Let's go on. See what is the next thing on the program.

Morton: Some students want to talk about the class council and what they got out of it.

169

Gail: One time in the class council, they were talking about me, and that night my mom had to go to the hospital for a foot operation, and I helped her a lot. I did mostly the things I had never done before. I liked it because she couldn't. She was going to have a foot operation, and I was doing my best to help her.

Teacher: Gail, what does this have to do with the class council? You said that you were going to talk about the class council. Did the class council help you in your decision? Will you tell us?

Gail: Well, the class council helped me a lot when they talked about me.

Teacher: How? In what?

Debby: Because they talked about me and I learned a lot, and I got better in school, and I love school very much.

Morton: Danny, do you have something to say?

Danny: The class council, helped me to finish my work on time.

Teacher: What else did it do for you, Danny? Are you happier now than you were before?

Danny: Yes.

Teacher: Nothing changed at home?

Danny: At home, I help my mother a lot.

Teacher: Didn't you do that before? Say "No," don't just shake your head. People can't see you shake your head.

Danny: No.

Teacher: Now, you help?

Danny: Yes.

Teacher: Do you have more friends now, or did you have more friends before?

Danny: I have more friends now.

Teacher: I'm glad to hear that. (This may seem like coaxing from the teacher. She was anxious for Danny to talk because at one time he was considered "a holy terror" at school and at home, and was very much disliked by his teachers.)

James I.: The class council helped me a lot because I cheated a lot when I was checking my work. The teacher said to raise your hand, but I never did, I just changed the answer. And at home, my mom tells me to do the dog papers, and I do it. Before, I didn't.

Teacher: I am glad to hear that, James.

Christine: I think that James I. was very honest. We were glad to hear what he said because I don't think that anybody else would say that they used to cheat and change the answer.

Teacher: You're proud of him?

Christine: Yes.

Teacher: I am too.

Kenny: I had a lot of problems. One time, I had a problem with Van and I went to the class council and I discussed it with them and it all went right. It's also helped me at home because, before, everytime my mother asked me to get something for the dog or something, I'd never do it.

Teacher: Do you do it now?

Kenny: Yes.

Teacher: Did it help you with your work at school?

Kenny: Yes.

Teacher: Will you tell us about it?

Kenny: Well, before, in my arithmetic—way back in second grade, when we didn't have a class council, I didn't admit to the teacher when I had something wrong.

Teacher: Why is it necessary to admit, Kenny. Could you explain it, do you know why we should admit when we make mistakes?

Kenny: Well, because when you admit you won't get punished as much.

Teacher: Is that the reason?

Class: No.

Christine: Well, if you tell, then whoever you tell will help you, then you can learn from what they tell you, and then the next time you won't make the same mistake.

Teacher: Kenny, did I ever punish you for making mistakes?

Kenny: No.

Teacher: What did we say, when we make mistakes, we. . . .

Preston: Well, you learn from that mistake because it teaches you so you won't make it again.

Teacher: That's right. Now, is there anything else?

Christine: We'll have one more question and then. . . .

Teacher: Let's call on somebody who didn't say anything.

Christine: Diana.

Diana: I think Kenny is getting better in his arithmetic.

Teacher: Milan, you weren't here. (He had just come into the class). Would you like to say something. You have lots to tell about yourself. Did the class council help you?

Milan: Yes. The class council helped me. At first, I didn't like getting my name all the time up there. So they started

171

teaching me a lesson. I mean, the class council helped me in a dozen different ways, like finishing my work, and teaching me from my mistakes.

Teacher: Milan, do you remember how you used to behave at the beginning of the school year? What did you do all the time?

Milan: I used to fight, I used to hit everybody. I used to have a dirty face. My nose used to be running like it is now.

Teacher: Is it running now?

Milan: A little bit.

Teacher: No, it isn't. I haven't seen a running nose on you for months. Have you, class?

Class: No.

Teacher: It always used to run. How about fighting, Milan?

Milan: Very little.

Christine: This is all we'll have today. The class council will have another meeting Friday afternoon, after lunch.

This example clearly indicates the power of the group. Without the help of the group, the teacher could not have achieved such drastic changes in the individual children's behavior.

Such training of the group did not happen in just a week or two. It took time, persistence, and belief in the children's ability to learn and to change, as well as a belief in the method applied.

THE DEMOCRATIC VERSUS THE TRADITIONAL CLASSROOM

Wherever an autocratic school community still exists, the traditional methods of motivating children through reward and punishment, through pressure from without, are usually sufficient to achieve the limited results that the teacher desires. All the teacher has to do is to teach; the children's obligation is to learn. This is no longer true in a democratic setting. The pressure from without has lost its significance. It has to be replaced with stimulation from within. We can no longer run schools for the children; we have to take them in as partners, win their support. This cannot be done without introducing democratic approaches in each class. Failure to do so is responsible for the growing deficiency in our schools to develop the potential of our children, to make them cooperate in the learning process.

A democratic atmosphere does not imply anarchy and permissiveness; order cannot be established by domination. In a democratic society, freedom and order are necessary, unlike an autocratic society where the two are mutually exclusive. Permissiveness invariably leads to anarchy, while force and power often induce rebellion. The reader may ask, does this mean that the adult has to abdicate altogether? On the contrary, he must and can exert leadership and guidance. What must change is the manner in which he exerts his leadership. Children want guidance and someone to lead them; however, today they do not accept imposition and dominance. Neither are they satisfied with an adult who lets them run wild.

The question arises whether students should be given the right to decide whether or what they will learn. This is no longer a question since children are already taking this decision upon themselves, and the teacher is in no position to force a reluctant student to learn.

Once the principle of sharing responsibility is understood by the teacher, she will not find it difficult to apply. At the present time, teachers vacilate between imposing their will on the children and letting them dominate them. We hear that one should teach children what they like to learn. Such an approach means abdication. Currently, one tries to make the children learn what they are supposed to learn. This is autocratic domination. Neither of the two approaches will get satisfactory results. The democratic way is to help the children to enjoy learning what they ought to learn. The crux of the matter is: what should they learn? This cannot be decided by the children, nor by the authorities. Children are more than willing to accept guidance from adults if ideas are not imposed on them, if they feel that their opinions and suggestions are taken seriously. This does not necessarily mean the obligation to do what they suggest. It does mean the necessary process of discussion, of coming to conclusions by considering the issues from all sides. The curriculum should, however, be flexible enough to give students and teachers a chance to follow the inclination and interest of the class.

At the present time, the curriculum is usually rigidly imposed on the teacher. Even under these circumstances, she still can have a democratic class if she shares her obligations—and her frustrations—with her pupils.

> In a co-ed home economics class for senior boys and girls, the teacher briefly outlined the units of work that were required by the State Board of Education. The students and the teacher cooperatively planned which unit would be studied first, second, and so on. They also figured the approximate time allotment for each unit and scope of each one.
>
> Later in the year, as each unit was introduced, the students were again involved in planning the specifics of the course. Such planning made it their and not *her* or the Board of Education's course.

One of the most frequent objections of students is the boredom of a teacher. Often they refuse to study for such a teacher. Let us consider what would have happened if their grandfather had told his father that he didn't want to study because the teacher was boring. He would have gotten a spanking and, "What's the idea? You want to be entertained by your teacher?" But this is changed today. Boredom is the greatest hindrance to study on the part of children who are concerned only with what they get and not with what has to be done.

Today, however, the teacher has the obligation to make her class interesting, to evoke enthusiasm, to integrate the class and unite all in a common educational purpose. By her actions and her attitudes, she affects the morale of the whole class. Each class, like any group, has its own configuration, its own specific atmosphere.

Although teachers claim that they have a democratic atmosphere in the class and that they treat their students with respect, they are often not aware of how they violate this principle the moment their prestige is at stake. These two examples illustrate this point:

> I had to see a principal of an elementary school. They talked about the present dilemma of the schools. Mr. X seemed very enlightened: he suggested that students should have a bigger say in policy making; that we should listen to children more than we do, etc.
>
> The bell rang, and the children were going home for lunch. Mr. X excused himself, stating that he always likes to stand at the foot of the stairs as the students come down. I went with him. The children came down in a very orderly fashion, single file, with their hands folded across their chests.
>
> Suddenly, Mr. X pulled a child, a boy around 9 years old, out of the line, held him firmly at one shoulder until all children had passed. He then turned to the boy and asked, "How many feet apart from the child ahead of you must you be?" Keeping his hands in the pockets, and without looking up, the boy replied,
>
> "Three."
>
> Mr. X went on, "Hands out of your pockets when you talk to me! Understand?"
>
> The child mumbled an "O.K."
>
> Mr. X became angrier at each answer. At this point, he shouted, "When you talk to me, you say 'Yes, sir' and not 'O.K.' Understand?"
>
> While we do not condone impudent behavior by a child, we cannot approve of the manner in which this principal handled the situation. If he accomplished anything, he probably provoked this uncooperative boy to feel even greater resentment against him. In

his heart, he may have wished the principal dead or to break a leg while his lips were saying, "Yes sir."

An effective way of dealing with such disrespect would have been an immediate disclosure of the goal to the boy, or an informal discussion with the entire group about mutual respect, what it means and why it is necessary. Children think nothing of showing disrespect for their elders, yet feel very hurt and unjustly treated if the latter tell them to "Shut up," or "Don't lie to me," "Don't be stupid."

> The playground, where teachers stand around watching their students while they play, is usually the place where teachers discuss their experiences of the day and express their feelings.
>
> While the writer was standing on the playground, watching her class, she observed the following: A teacher just coming out of the building, shook a child by his shoulders, repeating over and over, "How dare you?" It turned out that this boy, having noticed the teacher munch on a cookie before leaving the classroom, reminded her that chewing in class was against school regulations. The boy defended himself. He reminded her that she had often taken cookies away from, and even punished, children who were caught eating them. The teacher shook a threatening finger and shouted, "Don't be fresh or I'll send you back to your room!"
>
> The child shrugged his shoulders in complete lack of understanding.
>
> The teacher then turned to the writer and remarked, "See what I have to put up with?"

This example is not an unusual one. Teachers who insist that their students never eat in class, often munch on something when they feel hungry. They believe that the children won't notice if they eat behind the door of their coat closet or by stepping into the corridor. Children are very much aware of what the teacher is doing. They often discuss this practice by the teachers among themselves.

Teachers also have the right to go to the teachers' rest room and smoke a cigarette, or have a cup of coffee—rights which the students do not have. Can we imagine what would happen if a student, feeling the urge to drink milk or a coke would go to his locker and proceed drinking whatever he brought from home?

Teachers should have an understanding with their students that at a certain time of the day, she goes to the teachers' room to have some refreshment while the children are allowed to have a snack in class during this time.

The writer observed a fourth grade class during a social studies lesson. The class was studying the history of Chicago.

175

The teacher asked a girl to tell two factors which contributed toward the development of the city.

The girl answered, "The lake and the cow that kicked the bucket and started the big fire."

The teacher looked at the girl quizzically, as if she didn't believe what she had just heard. "And what has the cow to do with it?" she asked.

The girl explained, "Well, after the city burned down, they had to build it up again, and they made it bigger and nicer."

The teacher stared at the girl for a moment, and then asked another student to give two factors.

He said, "The lake and two Indian trails which ran through this territory." The teacher praised him for his good thinking.

An imaginative teacher, not concerned with getting the exact answers to her questions, would have used this opportunity to encourage the girl to be independent in her thinking. She might have said, "I never thought of this, but it's very plausible. I'm glad you thought of it. Can you think of another factor to add to the two you gave me?"

Teachers who insist on the exact answers that they prepared or the ones that come from the book are dull teachers, responsible not only for the boredom of their students, but for many discipline problems that come up because of a rigid, stale, and antiquated method of teaching. It is not uncommon to find children who, because of such teaching, decide that they don't like social studies or arithmetic, and so on.

Kurt Lewin,[10] in his famous Iowa Experiment with Boy's Clubs, established three types of a social climate. He trained leaders to be either autocratic, democratic, or anarchic, and he observed the behavior of the boys in each class. In the anarchic group, they accomplished little; in the autocratic and in the democratic group, the achievement was similar, but not the relationship between students and teacher. The autocratic group could function only when the leader was present. Without him they fought and quarreled. The democratic group could function without a leader, and got along outside the class.

Many important lessons can be learned from these experiments. First of all, the anarchic group is not democratic. Too many teachers assume that they become democratic by merely not being autocratic. By doing so, they become anarchic, not democratic. This misconception about the nature of democracy is unfortunately deeply

---

[10]Kurt Lewin, *Resolving Social Conflicts* (New York: Harper & Row, 1948).

embedded in our culture. Any one who asserts his influence over others is automatically stamped as being an autocrat. Democracy seems to mean that everybody can do as he pleases. This is anarchy, not democracy. The democratic group requires a leader; without him, the group cannot function well. But the leader does not have to be an autocrat. The distinction between autocratic and democratic leadership has to be clearly understood, as well as the consequences of the two opposing types of leadership.

The influence which the democratic or the autocratic leader has on the group became most dramatically revealed when a leader changed his role. When the democratic leader became—on instruction—autocratic, nothing changed perceptively. He had won the cooperation of the boys, and they went along with him, and soon behaved in the typical way of an autocratically led group. That was quite different when the autocratic leader suddenly became democratic. The boys had not learned to function without the pressure of a dominant authority. They ran wild. It took about a week to bring them back to an orderly function.

This observation has far-reaching significance for our whole culture. Wherever children move from an autocratic into a democratic setting, they become "free," but do not know what to do with their freedom. Freedom carries responsibilities. This holds true for adults as well. We are going—internationally—through the process of changing from an autocratic past into a democratic present. Many of the events of our times, the confusion, misused freedom, and lack of responsibility, validate the observations of Kurt Lewin.

Observing our present generation of teachers, we will find that they are neither fully autocratic nor democratic. Today, even the most dictatorial teacher cannot be as tyrannical and forceful as she could have been in the past. Many so-called democratic teachers are inclined toward anarchic-permissiveness, and fall back into autocratic methods if the children abuse their freedom. Both teachers and students should be given a choice by exposing them to either alternative. It makes a deep impression on students when they are given this preference. Most teachers prefer the democratic approach. Many are not sure that it will work and that students would do their part if discipline were not imposed on them. To have a boss is easier; one does not have to take responsibility oneself.

In training teachers to be autocratic or democratic, we use two sets of approaches, distinguishing one from the other:[11]

---

[11]Rudolf Dreikurs, *Psychology in the Classroom,* 2nd ed. (New York: Harper & Row, 1968).

Autocratic	*Democratic*
Boss	Leader
Sharp voice	Friendly voice
Command	Invitation
Power	Influence
Pressure	Stimulation
Demanding cooperation	Winning cooperation
I tell you what you should do	I tell you what I will do
Imposing ideas	Selling ideas
Domination	Guidance
Criticism	Encouragement
Faultfinding	Acknowledgment of achievement
Punishing	Helping
I tell you	Discussion
I decide, you obey	I suggest and help you to decide
Sole responsibility of boss	Shared responsibility of team

The left column indicates pressure from without; the right, stimulation from within. This list of democratic and autocratic approaches could probably be enlarged. It permits each teacher to use it as her own "democratic index" if she takes the description of procedures as a guide to evaluating her way of handling her class.

In this scheme, punishment is clearly recognizable as an authoritarian method. Only in an autocratic setting is punishment, the pressure from without, effective. In today's classrooms, it is not only ineffective, but harmful. Punishment does not stimulate a cooperative attitude on the part of the students. A teacher who shares the responsibility for conducting the class with her students does not need this personal display of her authority. Unless she can create a team spirit, she cannot integrate the class nor unite its members in cooperative efforts. Only by integrating everyone into one unit, can all be influenced and advanced.

This is the reason why the competitive spirit has to be replaced with one of cooperation serving the common interest. In such a setting each child is important, a prerequisite for harmonious function within the group. Instead of providing a sense of worth and equality for each student, competition makes one student feel superior and another inferior. In such a situation, no cooperation or team work is possible.

Let us take the question of grading. Grades are a typical system of reward and punishment. They are neither needed nor effective. The only children who respond to grading are the good students who could be stimulated to progress without grades. The poor students often shrug them off as a new proof of their hopeless condition. What can an individual teacher do to offset the detrimental and discouraging effects of poor grades? She can refrain from presenting them as her verdict. She can make the grading process, unpleasant and humiliating as it is, a common task. All can work together, not only on what grades each child should get, since the teacher is obliged to grade, but on helping the poor student to avoid low grades.

> In the senior coed class, the students turned in a written evaluation of their own work weeks before grading period. During the following week, brief conferences were held with each student and agreement was usually reached as to a fair grade.
>
> The slow or low student had been encouraged prior to this time both by the class and the teacher. The faster students served as tutors to the slower students. The entire class benefited from this arrangement. Not only did the slow student learn faster, but the fast student learned more and the course grew in depth and scope.

This is in sharp contrast to most classes where the good students lord it over the poor, and push them further down in esteem, status, and achievement.

In this cooperative spirit, being a good student or being very bright and ahead of everyone else does not mean "glory"; it entails a responsibility to help others and to be of service. The student learns to curb many of his personal desires and interests and to use them for the benefit of others.

Sharing responsibility is possible when the teacher is confronted with certain demands from the administration which would contradict any democratic procedures. Usually, teachers are inclined to pass the pressure which they receive from the principal on to the children. We recommend that the teacher ask the children to join her in carrying out her obligations by accepting reality as a given fact. Whenever she appeals for help to the students, she is more likely than not to get it, particularly when she has demonstrated her sincerity and proven to be trustworthy and not an enemy.

One reason why a teacher may find it difficult to win her students as equal partners in all activities is a general tendency to underestimate the ability of children, their intelligence, and their capacity for responsibility. True enough, they do not demonstrate these qualities when they are at war with the teacher. But the defiant, those who consistently negate a common educational goal, have to be drawn in. Planning and decision making cannot be left solely to the teacher or her allies in the class. All pupils can participate in the planning of activities that meet both the needs of the curriculum and of the students. At any age, they can work creatively on all school problems, provided they know that they have the respect, cooperation, and support of their teachers. The crucial point is the inclusion of every member of the class and of all classes within the school to participate in the planning of the whole educational process.

Under the impact of a new democratic social order, schools are beginning to have student councils. However, in most cases these are only a fake representation of the students, usually used by the administration as a tool to implement of their own decisions, often to decide penalties and carry them out. If planning is permitted, it usually concerns very minor and extracurricular activities; the potential dropout or delinquent student who needs to be involved in the discussion with the administration is usually excluded. We are witnessing an upsurge of student rebellion against administrations that do not ask their opinions nor consider their wishes. This system leads to war and open rebellion of the students.

The schools should involve themselves in the training of cooperative leadership among the students. Leadership quality consists of more than popular support. It should consist of the ability to resolve conflicts and to reconcile opposing interests. Differences of interest and opinion will always exist. Without such differences, progress would not be possible. The democratic process requires leaders. Without them we have no democracy, only anarchy. At present, are our schools concerned with development of leadership qualities in the students? One can safely say, "No." Whatever leadership emerges is usually for selfish purposes and more often directed against the school system and the administration than in support of it.

Such leadership training has to begin at the grass roots level, in each class. It is not enough to have a class president who is elected by popular vote. We know some school systems that gave a different meaning to this office. Students were elected to the office for one function: to keep the class functioning while the teacher was absent. In other words, this student had to be capable of taking the responsibility of being a leader of his peers. If he was not capable of doing so, he was replaced by someone else who was able to do so. Eventually, several students emerged who could fill such an assignment; however, they did not have personal authority. If this student tried to use his office to intimidate, to denounce, or punish, he would not gain the cooperation of his classmates for very long. He was the helper and not the boss.

The recognized function of the school is to prepare children for life, for responsible adulthood. This obviously requires more than teaching subject matter and increasing the academic knowledge of students. Since there is no other agency in society which has the same potential, the school needs to concern itself with the values on which youth operates, and this is done primarily through group involvement. Leadership training is one aspect of the development of values needed in a democratic society. One may question to what extent our present school systems are prepared for this task. The highly competitive spirit in our schools reinforces the students' concern with selfish interests, personal glory and status, and disregard for the next fellow, who is mercilessly pushed down by the ambition of the successful. We have to recognize the obligation of schools to be a value-forming agency. If the schools are capable of functioning on a truly democratic basis, then they can discharge their responsibility of providing a whole generation with the knowledge and skill of how to live democratically, as equals among equals.

SPECIFIC DEMOCRATIC PROCEDURES

We live in a democracy. We believe in it. We know we would not want to live under any other system. But how many teachers manage their classrooms in a democratic manner?

Those of us who live in a democracy have some important beliefs that act as the foundation stones of democratic living and governing. Briefly, these beliefs can be stated as:

    a. A belief in the worth and dignity of every person.
    b. A belief in the equality of all people.
    c. A belief in freedom of decision making.
    d. A belief that people can be trusted to make wise decisions concerning their common welfare.

These beliefs form the basis for a democratic society. Democracy is more than a form of government. A democratic society requires an atmosphere of freedom and mutual respect.

In a democratic classroom, pupils and the teacher are united in planning, organizing, implementing, and participating in their common activities. The teacher, as the expert, provides a broad base. She has the duty and the responsibility to give direction, to help each child to increase his ability to take part effectively in group settings and to be able to make and carry out group decisions.

In order to have democracy work effectively, the children will need to be trained. It is important for the teacher to take a few days at the beginning of the school year to talk over democratic methods with the students and get to know how they think and what their values are. A teacher who takes time at the beginning of the year to train her children and to involve them in planning will find that as time goes on she will need to spend less and less time fighting with her children. She will also find that most of the children are willing learners and become more or less self-motivated. So, while training does take time in the beginning, it pays off in the long run.

The question is often asked whether a teacher can have a democratic classroom in a school system which is essentially not democratic. What characterizes a democratic classroom? It does not mean taking votes in deciding what should be done. It does imply participation in decision making. This, then, shows that even in an autocratic school system, the teacher can proceed with democratic methods.

First, a democratic classroom presupposes a democratic atmosphere. Cooperative action depends on good will, sincere mutual interest, respect for each other, a good relationship and democratic procedures. In a democratic school setting, a child cannot live at peace either with himself or with others unless he recognizes his being equal to every other person.

To most adults, it seems preposterous to consider a child as an equal. The adult views the child as smaller in size, limited in physical ability, limited in responsibility, and too unskilled and unsophisticated to be given the stature that equality and respect imply. Lack of qualities or abilities should never deprive a person of respect and of equal voice. Unfortunately, the adult frequently believes that he can maintain this fair attitude only as long as he is not threatened in his own status. Furthermore, few adults treat the child as they would treat another adult. The mere assumption that children should be treated as their equal is a preposterous idea to them. But children exert their equality by being unwilling to accept the dictates of adults.

> In the senior coed class, each student had the same value and worth as any other class member, including the teacher. The fact that Mrs. P. happened to be the teacher did not exclude her from being a class member. Also the fact that Toby's father was a lawyer, Linda's father was a doctor, Ron's father was a drunkard, Tim's father was in prison, and Toni's mother was a prostitute, made absolutely no difference in the students' value persons or in the manner in which they were treated.
>
> As Toni so aptly put it, "For the first time in my life, I feel that I am worth something and that I *do* count. You don't know how bad it has been—always to be considered dirt."

182

Each class member had equal rights. Equal rights in this classroom meant having the right to express his opinions to a teacher who listened and treated each student with respect, to an atmosphere which was friendly and conducive to learning, to having a voice in class discussions and decisions, to individualized materials and instructions commensurate with the student's ability, and to the opportunity to stretch his interest and span of knowledge.

The teacher was responsible for providing leadership, direction, materials, enthusiasm, and for giving the students plenty of room for independent functioning with trust and without fear. The class members who were the fast or able ones, served as aides to the slower students. Corrine, who had difficulty in reading, was assisted by Greg and thereby was able to understand the theory of house planning. However, during the assignment of drawing side elevations, it was Corrine who helped Greg and others, as drawing was her forte.

Cooperation in the democratic classroom is based on consideration for the other's rights and interests while standing up for one's own rights. In such an atmosphere, one does not concern himself with what others do, but must accept responsibility for what *he* has to do. Neither imposing on others nor letting others dictate is the formula for equality.

The principle underlying this type of classroom implies mutual respect—respect for the dignity of others, and respect for oneself. Mutual respect means treating each member with respect, recognizing the worth of his ideas, accepting his plans and contributions, and also, when necessary, to reject his contributions as being of no value in a particular situation, while at the same time not rejecting him.

Respect implies that the other person has something to offer as well as the right and the ability to offer it. Mutual respect is based upon acceptance of the equality of human beings, independent of individual differences, of knowledge, information, abilities, and position.[12]

Essential to a democratic classroom is a combination of firmness and kindness expressed in the teacher's attitude to her class. *Firmness* implies self-respect, *kindness* implies respect for others; neither alone achieves a harmonious relationship of equals. We can resolve our conflicts without either fighting, or yielding; by both respecting others and respecting ourselves. This is the founda-

[12]R. Dreikurs, *Social Equality: The Challenge of Today* (Chicago: Henry Regnery, Co., 1971)

tion upon which satisfactory classroom relationships are built.

Firmness is not meant to threaten. Quite often, the limits are the product of group decision. The teacher's firm support needs to be present at all times. Firmness helps a child to feel secure.

Throughout this chapter, we have discussed various methods and techniques which a teacher could use in order to have a democratic classroom. Briefly, the ground rules are as follows:

1. Order is necessary under all circumstances, that is, also in a democratic setting. A group cannot run democratically without order and ground rules.
2. Limits are necessary. School rules and school policies may not be correct and adequate and may need revision; but as long as they exist, they must be followed. They are reality.
3. Children should participate in establishing and maintaining rules necessary for functioning in an orderly group.
4. The group needs leadership and the teacher needs to know how to exert democratic leadership.
5. Without trust and faith in each other a class cannot function democratically. It may require efforts to establish mutual trust between students and teacher.
6. The teacher must know how to win cooperation of the students. She cannot demand it.
7. A spirit of cooperation has to replace competitiveness in the classroom.
8. A classroom atmosphere conducive to learning cooperation and mutual help is essential for solving problems through democratic transactions.
9. The teacher needs the skill to integrate the class for a common purpose; each child has to have a sense of belonging to the whole class.
10. The pattern of relationships existing in a class is usually established during the first few days. It requires the full attention of the teacher to give each child a feeling of belonging.
11. Group discussion is essential in a democratic setting. It does not consist of chit-chat, but of listening to each other, understanding each other, helping each other, and solving the common problems in the classroom.
12. The democratic school setting requires class and school councils in which all segments of the school population are represented.

The teacher needs to learn not only teaching methods, but also principles of motivation. She also needs to remember that if she feels her status is at stake, she will not have a good relationship with her class. Any time a teacher tries to establish a free atmosphere in her classroom, she must use democratic methods. She must establish limits and give the children freedom within those limits.

4
coping with specific problems

CHANGING THE CHILD'S GOALS

The goals of a misbehaving child have been discussed throughout this book, and the means of coping with deficient and maladjusted children have been presented. In this chapter, we will focus on the immediate corrective steps possible in a classroom situation. One must keep in mind that the response to the child's disturbance in the moment it occurs is only one aspect of corrective efforts. Teachers need to develop skills of responding to the immediate problem in a constructive way. Most teachers, even the most experienced, feel at a loss when the child disturbs, defies, refuses to cooperate, and so forth. Often what she does may do more harm than good, for if she is not familiar with the child's goal, she unwittingly reinforces his

186

erroneous behavior. Also, teachers have a tendency either to overlook the disturbance because they do not know what to do, or to make some critical or threatening remark that does not resolve the disturbance except, perhaps, for a short moment.

An interesting study was conducted in Germany that probably could be duplicated with similar results in the United States.[1] Forty-four teachers were observed in fifty-one periods, during which the frequency of disturbances needing the teacher's intervention, and the kinds of intervention were studied.

It was found that on the average, each teacher had to interrupt classroom procedures every 2 ½ minutes in order to take some corrective step, and that 94 percent of all interventions were autocratic and ineffective; only 6 percent of the interventions improved the situation.

In discussions with teachers, almost all proceed in the same way. They enumerated the kind of disturbances in their classes and wanted immediate answers.

UNDERSTANDING THE CHILD'S GOALS[2]

Let us briefly review the procedure of diagnosing the child's goals. First, we can observe the consequence of his disturbing behavior. Second, we can verify our impressions of his goals when we watch his reaction to corrections, what we call corrective feedback. Third, we can notice our own emotional and practical response to the child's disturbance. For instance, when we are annoyed, it is probably goal 1., a bid for attention; when we feel threatened and provoked, it is probably goal 2., power; when we feel hurt, it is goal 3., the child seeking revenge; and when we feel like giving up, we are probably faced with goal 4.

The following is an example of a teacher who gets himself involved in a conflict with a child without being aware of how she is falling for the child's provocation and into his trap.

Teacher: Johnny, stop talking and disturbing the students around you.
   Johnny: I wasn't talking.
Teacher: Why are you bothering everyone?
   Johnny: I am not doing anything.
Teacher: Pass your paper to the front.
   Johnny: *(Does not pass paper, later the teacher asks about his work.)*
        You did not tell us to pass our papers.

[1]Anne-Marie Tausch, *Besonere Erziehungssituationen des praktischen Schulunterrichtes*, Haufickeit, Veranlassung und Art ihrer Losungen Durch Lehrer. Zt. f. Exper. und angew. Psychologie. Band V/4, Verlag F. Psychologie Goettingen, 1967.
   [2]See Table 1, p. 16.

(Teacher asks what to do with a child who never admits that he is at fault or wrong.)

It is obvious that the teacher does not realize the power play in which she let herself be drawn. Without recognizing it, and using some effective methods of counteracting it, she has no chance to get anything from the child, except continued defeat.

Sometimes the diagnosis of the goal is not as simple. Here is a description of a behavior type that does not fit easily into one of the four goals:

> Quite often in our classroom, we are faced with withdrawal tactics and a display of incompetency in the academic area. Stalling behaviors include a whole host of self-stimulatory behaviors that are relatively quiet, and not on the bothersome noise level. Sometimes the child is just sitting and doing nothing; playing or fiddling with an object (a piece of fuzz, a pencil, a piece of paper, a little rock, string, leaf, bug, or the like); playing with mouth, face, hands, ears, hair; swinging foot, crossing and uncrossing legs; continuous movement, wriggling, and so forth; blinking, squinting eyes, screwing up face, licking lips; scratching self, rubbing self, hugging self; daydreaming (a form of mental masturbation that keeps him occupied and happy); or continuously losing or misplacing something, usually a pencil. These behaviors are usually paired with nonacademic performance, commonly known as studied incompetency. The assignments given the child are well within the child's abilities. Stalling behaviors are the bane of every teacher's existence. For what purpose do children stall? After looking at the various methods employed by the youngsters and the reaction of the teachers, many of these behaviors are still difficult to peg in their goals.

It is obvious that we are dealing with difficult children. Some consider similar behavior patterns as expressions of mental or neurological disorder. Such children may be autistic, minimal brain damaged, or suffering from neurogenic learning disabilities. These considerations of organic causes of the behavior neglect the movements that such children make within the given field of their activities. Regardless of their organic and physical condition, they have a private logic that has to be understood. We shall go deeper into this aspect when we discuss learning and reading difficulties. Severely disturbed and especially psychotic children are determined to have their own way; their pathological condition is part of such a determination whereby they completely defy any social demands. One often calls these children emotionally disturbed. Basically, there is nothing wrong with their emotions, only with their intentions; they create the emotions

188

they need for the directions they take. When they move against adults, against the order of living, it is only natural that their emotions will be destructive.

Let us continue with an exploration of the goals of the children as described by the teacher. The following are some examples of her students:

> Kevin, age 6, was given the assignment of matching the printed color words on a card to the color and color word on the chart. He had accomplished this task successfully earlier in the day. He raised his hand and the teacher went to his desk. Kevin said, "I can't do it." The teacher walked away. Kevin started making noises with a pencil, wallowing on his desk, and whining in a high shrilled voice, "I can't do it. I can't do it."

What was Kevin's goal? At first it may appear that he was discouraged and really tried to impress the teacher with his inability (goal 4); but he did not want to be left alone, as a very discouraged child would. The question is now, did he want attention and service or to show his power? From the intensity of his disturbance, one may consider goal 2, that he wanted to defy the teacher's demands. However, his reaction to her approach clearly indicated that he wanted attention from the teacher (goal 1).

> The teacher continued to ignore the situation, and Kevin increased his disturbing behavior. At this point the teacher said, "Either do your task or go stand on the mat." Kevin chose the mat. When he noticed that his group was working on a project he usually enjoyed, he quickly raised his hand and asked to be allowed to return to his seat and do his work. He had no difficulties doing the assigned exercise.

It is questionable whether ignoring him was the right procedure, as there are better ways to respond, which will be discussed later. At any rate, the teacher gave Kevin a choice that had been set up as a logical consequence. Kevin's response permitted a corrective feedback, supporting the diagnosis of goal 1. Logical consequences are only effective in children with goal 1; in a power conflict, the child usually gets worse. (See p. 197.) Kevin responded to her approach, realizing he would not get anywhere with his tactics, and therefore, stopped his annoyance.

> Wendy, age 8, used withdrawal tactics and studied incompetency. When confronted with an assignment she does not particularly like, she uses a rash of stalling behaviors. She has the capacity for using a dead pan or expressionless face. She refuses to do her work and

stares straight ahead. When given assistance, she indicates that she does not understand or does not know how. She is so good at her game that the teacher did not know for some time whether Wendy really could do her work.

The description of the girl and of the teacher's reaction makes it clear that Wendy is in a power conflict. The teacher seems completely lost as to what to do with Wendy, and feels defeated. Two elements enter into her defeat, namely Wendy's refusal to do the work regardless of what the teacher does, and the teacher's admitted ignorance in knowing whether Wendy really could do the work. Wendy's behavior takes on a violent passivity, and she is challenging the teacher with "Try and make me and I'll show you what I can do to you."

It is important that Wendy's goal is understood by the teacher, and by the class as well, for the group will have to help the teacher with Wendy's problem. This is usually done in group discussion. When one teacher introduced the concepts of the four goals of disturbing behavior to her class, the children themselves recognized the category in which they belonged. One teacher helped her students in understanding the goals of a child by asking them to bring a short description of a child's behavior to the class for discussion. She did not ask the children to describe their behavior in school, but also at home. It is there, in the family constellation, that each child develops his own movements in finding a place, but his mistaken goal may not be the same in school as at home.

Here are some examples of the children's illustrations of goal-directed behavior in a class of fourth graders:

> Carmen brought up the story of Sheila. She did not like to get up when her mother called her. Mother came again and again, telling her to get up, "You will be late for school." But Sheila did not get up. When she finally got up, mother was worried and helped her to get dressed and washed. Then Sheila did not like the dress her mother picked out for her. When her mother told her to pick out her own dress, she didn't know which to pick. But when her mother picked another dress, Sheila did not like it again. Then there was not time to pack a lunch, so her mother had to give her thirty-five cents to buy lunch in school.
>
> After Carmen read her story, a discussion followed. All children agreed that Sheila liked to keep her mother busy, and she gets a lot of attention. The children felt that the mother gave into Sheila; that she should wake her up, but then leave it up to her to get up and dress by herself. They also felt that her mother should not pick out her dresses. There was some disagreement in regard to the lunch

money. Some children felt that mother was right in giving her the money; others felt that she should have gone hungry.

Emil described himself. Emil is 9 years old and he goes to fourth grade. He is not a good student like his brother who is in sixth grade. Emil and his brother fight all the time. Emil always starts the fight. Sometimes he changes the TV station while his brother is watching. When his brother turns it back, they start to fight. Then his mother yells at his brother, because he is older and should know better.

In the discussion, the children said that Emil did not want to grow up. He acted like a baby. Maybe he thought that his brother was smarter and that his parents were prouder of him. Emil wanted to get more attention from his mother and that is why he was fighting. All children felt that the mother should not mix in, and that it would serve Emil right, if his brother took a poke at him. But they felt that this would not solve anything. They suggested that the brothers talk it over and share the TV time.

Thelma reported about Kim. Kim never does any work in class. She always plays with something in her desk, or she talks. The teacher reminds her many times to do her work, but she just does not do it. She is always angry with everybody and tries to push other children around.

The children felt that Kim tried to show the teacher that she could do what she wanted. They felt the teacher should not remind her to do the work, but should bring it up in Class Council. Pushing the children around made Kim feel big. They also felt that Kim was not a happy child, or she would not be angry all the time. Maybe she thought that nobody liked her, and therefore, she wanted to punish and hurt them.

It is obvious that these children were trained in understanding psychological dynamics. Does this make such discussions less valuable? Anything we learn must be fortified through repetition, and since the children whose cases were presented were in the group, such discussions may have helped each to become more aware of his behavior. It was interesting to note that one child presented his own case. One can be certain that he was not fully aware of his goal.

The same behavior of two children may serve entirely different goals. For example:

Arnold raises his hand whether he has something to say or not. Then the teacher calls on him. He stands up and talks about something completely irrelevant. He knows this, but it does not prevent him from continuing this behavior. All he wants is attention. When the teacher revealed this to Arnold, he smiled; for some time he was satisfied.

Roy, who behaves the same way, looked at the teacher angrily when she asked him if he seeks attention; he continued interrupting by talking nonsense. When the teacher asked him, "Could it be that you are trying to show us that you must be the boss, and that I can't stop you from talking whenever you feel like it?" He grinned and he stopped interrupting for some time.

The child's reaction to interpretation usually indicates his goal. When the disclosure was correct, he responded with a recognition reflex. The more violent reaction of Roy indicted his power conflict, which was absent with Arnold.

TECHNIQUES OF CONFLICT SOLVING

Whenever a child disturbs, actively or passively, a conflict arises. This tests the teacher's ability to resolve it. Without such skill, the conflicts continue even if a temporary peace has been established. The principles of problem solving in a democratic transaction are so important that each teacher should, almost automatically, be able to apply them.

Conflicts are inevitable whenever people live together. In the past, conflicts could only be resolved through a contest; the stronger person won and decided the outcome. This is no longer possible in a democratic setting. Recognizing the child's goals and helping him to change them is an integral part of problem solving. When the basic principles of resolving conflicts are outlined, we will see that some of them have already been discussed, while others need further clarification. What are the principles?

1. One can no longer resolve any conflict by either fighting or giving in. Fighting or imposition violates respect for the child, and giving in, or permissiveness, violates the respect for the adult. In a democratic setting, conflicts have to be resolved by mutual respect.

2. To resolve a conflict requires pinpointing the issue. Regardless of its content, it always implies a disturbed relationship. Although opponents may argue about a specific issue, they use the content of the conflict only to fight each other. It is always a question of who gives in or wins out, of status and prestige, of personal advantage or abuse. To be more specific: the real issue behind any conflict with a child is one of the four goals of his disturbing behavior. Unless the teacher realizes this, she cannot understand the conflict. If she looks for causes behind his behavior, she cannot understand him or the nature of the conflict.

3. All transactions between any two people are based on communication and cooperation. There is never any breakdown in com-

munication or a lack of cooperation. When you want to fight with someone, you first have to communicate to him your desire and then get his cooperation, otherwise there will be no fight. Whatever goes on between any two people, be it positive or negative, it requires full agreement. When a mother complains about what her child did, we immediately ask her about her reaction. Only when we know what the mother did, can we understand why the child transgressed. Although we have no power to change what our opponent does, we can change the situation if we change our part. Unfortunately, nobody knows the part he plays, he only knows what his opponent does, and that makes no sense. In most cases, everybody complains about the others who are responsible for their predicament. Only when we begin to think about what we can do, do we become aware of the tremendous strength and power that we all have and exert. Once the teacher stops passing the buck—blaming the child, his parents, and the system or society for her difficulties with the child —she can become aware of the many ways and means by which she can change the relationship between herself and the child and improve his deficiencies.

4. The actions we take to resolve a conflict has to take into consideration the need for letting everybody participate in the decision. The teacher alone can no longer exert her influence; she has to share the responsibility with the children. Part of her strength is her ability to utilize the group in discharging her responsibility.

The first and last steps in resolving a conflict have already been discussed as part of the establishment of democratic procedures in the school and in the classroom. Points 2, 3, and 4, require a clear understanding of how to deal with the four goals. In evaluating a teacher's effort to cope with a conflict situation, the points made above can serve as a yardstick. They indicate effective approaches and explain failures due to violation of the basic principles of conflict solving.

ATTENTION-GETTING DEVICES

The teacher who is confronted with a child's demands for undue attention has it in her power either to continue to present agreement by which she accedes to his demands, or refuses to give in by ignoring his efforts. However, the question of ignoring his disturbing behavior poses a dilemma: when is it effective? Here is a typical example of how ignoring the child's disturbing behavior was sufficient for the child to discontinue it:

> After a workshop with the faculty of a school system, a teacher reported the perplexing effects of ignoring the child. In her kindergarten class, she had one boy and one girl who always demanded

special attention when the group sat in a circle for storytelling. The boy always flopped down on his belly, and she had to tell him to sit up which he did, but not for long; the girl always interrupted with silly questions. During the workshop, she found out how children manipulate teachers with their demands for attention, and she got angry when she realized how the children had outsmarted her. She decided then and there that she would pay no attention to the boy's antics and the girl's questions. Next day, when she came to her class, she could not believe what happened. The boy did not lay down once, and the girl did not disrupt with questions once. How did they know that the teacher would no longer respond? Children, especially when they are very young, know exactly when the jig is up. There was no sense in continuing the disturbing behavior if the teacher would not respond. The ability of young children to size up the situation correctly and to know what the adult would do is unbelievable. Children are excellent observers, which is the reason they deal effectively with adults, while adults do not know how to cope with them.

Ignoring the child may bring the desired result; however, in some cases the child continues his efforts for a while. At this point, continuing to disregard the child's behavior may be inadvisable as it disturbs the class atmosphere and the learning procedure.

The teacher can give attention to the child who seeks it, but in a way which does not mean yielding. Each teacher must experiment and, depending on her own resourcefulness and temperament, establish her own technique. Often it suffices to call a child by name, but without any comment, just looking at him (eye contact). Humor helps. If a child whispers something to his neighbor in a disturbing way, the teacher can express her curiosity, but without a trace of anger and annoyance, which the child expects. If a child is inattentive, it is a passive way of demanding attention. The teacher can ask his opinion about what has been said either by her or by another child. In this way, she draws the child's attention to the class procedure without scolding him about his inattentiveness. If a child clowns, one can stop and invite the class to watch him perform. This does not mean that one encourages clowning; it deprives him of his success in annoying the teacher.

One technique has often brought immediate and sometimes lasting results. The teacher may have a little talk with the child, privately. After confronting him with his goals, in the way described before through a sequence of questions (p. 34), he may respond with a recognition reflex. Then she can ask the child how many times he may want special attention during the next hour. To that, the child usually responds with, "I don't know." Then the teacher may suggest perhaps ten or fifteen times, depending on the frequency of the child's disturbing behavior. He usually thinks that this is too much because he really does not know how often he disturbs. After an agreement is reached, the teacher responds to each disturbance by merely counting, "Johnny, number 1," and so forth. Although no method works every time, and no child responds equally well to the same approach, this procedure has usually been found effective.

It is interesting to note that sometimes a teacher is unsuccessful with this method, and does not realize how she defeated her own purpose. One unsuccessful teacher revealed her procedure. She told the child, "Johnny, this is the first time I have to remind you," and soon afterwards, "Johnny, this is the second time I have to remind you;" and the child enjoyed this procedure thoroughly and kept the teacher going. Why was she ineffective? First, she talked too much, and second, she scolded. Both are certain to make the teacher fail in her efforts.

Teachers do numerous things that spoil their effectiveness. One teacher made a deal with a child by writing on a piece of paper whenever the child disturbed. Of course, he loved that, and kept her busy writing, until she no longer could stand it, and blew up. Another teacher put a mark on the blackboard whenever the child disturbed. He liked that very much. One may question the difference between putting a mark on the blackboard or calling his name. The difference is that the child has the satisfaction of keeping the teacher busy writing on the blackboard. It is the undue service he wants and gets. Merely calling his name and a number is a limited action. Experience shows that that is not the kind of attention the child wants.

The following examples are illustrations of attention-goal 1:

1. When the class returned from recess, April remained in the corridor. When the children brought this fact to the teacher's attention, she told them that this was April's pleasure and that the class should not spoil it for her.

After a few minutes of waiting, April walked into the room, stood at the door long enough for all to see her, and then walked out again into the corridor. She repeated this procedure several times. During all this time, the teacher went about her work, paying no attention to her.

April made a few entrances and exits and then returned to her seat and proceeded with her work. When the teacher passed her desk, she merely complimented her on her neat writing.

2. Adeline, a fourth grade student, surprised and shocked the children in class because of the long, dangling earrings she was

195

wearing. At first, the teacher decided to ignore this, hoping that the children would soon ignore it also. However, the subdued but excited noise continued. Everyone wanted to see and touch the earrings. The teacher then invited Adeline to come up to the front of the class, so that everyone could see her. She inquired where Adeline got the earrings and learned that they belonged to her older sister, and that she had borrowed them without her sister's knowledge. The teacher suggested that after wearing the earrings for a while, and if Adeline wanted to, she would be glad to put them away for her in a safe place and return them when the children go home. After an hour, Adeline handed the earrings to the teacher.

Both of these incidents might have developed into major problems, taking up much of the teacher's time. These children's erroneous concepts of how they could receive attention would only have been fortified by such action.

There is a principle that one can follow. A disturbing form of demanding attention can be turned into a constructive one, passive into active, until the child no longer feels the need to receive special attention in order to have a place. He can receive recognition for useful efforts and accomplishments, but until that is accomplished, one must be careful not to fall for his provocations. Any scolding, reprimanding, or threatening, violates the first principle of problem solving since it expresses warfare. It prevents the teacher from helping the child to overcome his feeling of inadequacy and to gain self-confidence about his place in the group, which is a prerequisite of his enjoyment in participating without concern for status. To function for the satisfaction of usefulness is the basis for social adjustment and academic growth.

Here is an important point of which few teachers are aware. A special bid for attention does not have to be made through disturbing behavior. Many children succeed in getting special attention through constructive means, by being excellent students, well behaved and cooperative. They study not for the enjoyment of it, but for the recognition they receive. In many cases, they are the teacher's pet. Her enjoyment of a pleasant child is particularly ill advised when the child gets special attention through passive means, just being charming, clinging, or cute, without really contributing.

In our competitive society, we inevitably make a big fuss over the achiever, not realizing how much harm we do. Many teachers fall for such efforts without realizing the damage to the child. Many excellent students are highly vulnerable. They can only function when they receive recognition and are on top. If they run into obstacles in playing a superior role, they may give up altogether. Many underachievers are overambitious and give up studying when they believe that they cannot excel. In order to feel important, they may switch to other, and often destructive, means.

STRUGGLE FOR POWER

If it is difficult to resist the child's provocation when he seeks attention, it is even more difficult to restrain oneself when he strives for power. An ever growing number of children defy the teacher both in their behavior and in their refusal to learn, and very few teachers are able to cope with them. They are not prepared personally, emotionally, or ideologically to stay out of a power struggle with a child who threatens their authority and prestige. They are too deeply steeped in an autocratic tradition which prescribes that one must show the children that their behavior will not be tolerated. Unfortunately, present methods of dealing with children convey to them that they can get by with any behavior they choose and that no one can stop them. Thus, the warfare between adults and children becomes more intense as the children, in their sense of equality, are no longer willing to submit to dictates.

Teachers may be surprised to read that nobody has to fight with a child. Many believe just the opposite, that one has to assert one's authority. Few teachers realize that they do not lose status if they openly admit their defeat. We must accept the fact that the power of the adult over the child is a matter of the past. It does not work in our present society where children have gained new freedoms. Therefore, it stands to reason that they will not respond to traditional methods of discipline.

The first obstacle toward a solution of a conflict is the widespread assumption that one has to subdue the defiant child and make him respect adult demands. The second stumbling block is the teacher's personal involvement in a power conflict. One cannot extricate oneself if one has a feeling of inadequacy and is concerned with one's own prestige. No conflict can be resolved as long as one is afraid of being humiliated, taken advantage of and personally defeated. If one can free oneself from such considerations, one can see how amazingly simple it is to resist the power of a child who wants to force us into a struggle. It is obvious that certain personality types have greater difficulties with such children. One teacher accepts the challenge, fights back, and is defeated again and again; another remains calm and composed, and eventually wins the child's cooperation.

After a teacher has decided to avoid both fighting and giving in, which is the first step toward conflict solving, she can concern herself with the issue at hand. What makes a child strive for power? A power-drunk child is always ambitious, but his ambition is directed almost exclusively to the defeat of the power of those who try to suppress him. It is more difficult for an overambitious child to be on top academically or socially, but his success in defeating the teacher brings him considerable status among his peers. It is, naturally, a mistaken idea about how to be significant, but the frantic efforts of authorities to suppress any sign of defiance and nonconformity only provide greater gratification to those students who clamor for what they consider their rights.

The next step in an effort to solve conflicts is the realization that we cannot demand changes from the children as long as we are determined to fight it out, which, in a sense, is a subconscious agreement to fight. The degree of rebellion is usually in direct proportion to the degree of autocratic imposition; both parties are alike and equal in their destructive endeavors. It is almost comical when one compares the complaints of teachers about their students and the complaints of their students about their teachers. Each one sees what the other one is doing wrong, and neither has any idea of what he could do about it. In our communities, we find a strong division of opinion and approach to the problem. Many people side with the authorities who hold on to authoritarian principles, then there are those who side with the students and support them in their demands. The classroom teacher is either asked by parents to bear down on the reluctant learner, or condemned for her punitive strictness.

Each teacher has to resolve this conflict within herself. Instead of blaming the students and their parents for her difficulty, she can explore all the means she has at her disposal to change the situation. We already have discussed the need for participation in decision making, for changing the values of her students through group discussions that also can help to establish agreement about what to do in conflict situations. The crucial question is, however, what can a teacher do in the immediate situation when she is challenged by a defiant and power-bent child? We can distinguish between the need for immediate action and plans for resolving the conflict.

The first step is to avoid a fight. The teacher can admit her defeat openly. This, far from increasing the child's desire to fight, will make him more willing to give it up. There is no sense in challenging an authority who does not feel challenged. The teacher can use group pressure to quiet a troublemaker. The pressure of peers is more potent than the pressure of the teacher. If the whole class is out of hand, the teacher can even leave the room and tell them to call her when they are ready. This, naturally, requires the consent of the principal. It only works with younger children because teenage rebellion is usually so pronounced that such a simple method will have little effect.

198

In order to avoid a fight and to be effective, teacher and students must find a new agreement. Although this cannot be accomplished through demands, it may well be possible through open and frank admission by the teacher that she needs help. Actually, she is at the mercy of the individual child and of the class. She can have private conversations with the child, explaining to him that she does not intend to fight. This often disarms the child. An appeal to his intelligence, sympathy, and assistance is usually more effective than any threat or display of authority. When the teacher can point out the child's own goals to him, she removes from him the conviction that he is just a bad child, and opens avenues for alternatives. Children rarely realize the predicament of the teacher or how they provoke her. Making the child feel that he has it in his power to help the teacher in her difficult task, can give the child a sense of significance and power in a constructive way.

The same procedure is necessary with the entire class. A disturbing child is not only a problem to the teacher, but to the whole class. At the present time, most teachers, whether they are aware of it or not, intensify the friction among their students, particularly between the good and the bad, and the slow and the advanced. How to cope with any one child can be decided through class discussions. The teacher, as a leader, has to help the members of the class in finding a constructive solution.

GOAL-DIRECTED BEHAVIOR

Attention and Power: During a music lesson, while the teacher tried to demonstrate the rhythm of a song, Joel took two pencils and proceeded to drum on a book. The teacher stopped playing and demanded to know who was drumming. No reply came forth, so she resumed her playing. This very instant, the drumming started again. The teacher, who had been on the alert, caught Joel in the act. She scolded him and asked him to put his pencils in his desk. Joel made no move to obey her order. She asked once more. This time Joel put his elbows on his desk, grinned, and held up the pencils for all to see. In a rage, the teacher snatched the pencils, threw them in his desk, and demanded that he wipe the grin off his face. Everyone watched the spectacle with tenseness and expectations. Joel continued to grin. Once more the teacher ordered him to stop grinning. She threatened to take him to the principal if he continued to be disobedient. Since he showed no inclination to change his behavior, she took a firm hold of his arm and tried to pull him out of his seat, demanding that he come with her to the principal. Joel stiffened and resisted. A tug-of-war began between teacher and the boy.

In this incident, the situation might have been of minor significance, but it turned into a major episode due to the teacher's inability to understand Joel's behavior and to her incompetence in handling him. The skillful teacher would have had very little trouble with Joel. She might have handled this episode using any of the following techniques with the likelihood of better results.

1. The teacher might have asked Joel if he would demonstrate the rhythm by using his pencils as drumsticks. She could have suggested that he use the real drum in a closet.
2. She might have suggested that he beat the rhythm right along with her—she on the piano and he on the drum or with his pencils.
3. She could have suggested that they alternate, he on the drum and she with the pencils.

An unexpected and friendly reaction might have taken all the spice out of the satisfaction Joel derived from defying the teacher; he may have been quite satisfied with the attention of the teacher and the class.

Assuming that the attention alone would not have sufficed, and Joel continued his disturbing behavior in spite of it, a teacher who understood the goal-directed behavior of the misbehaving child would have realized that he was out to show her, and everyone in class, that he was going to be the boss in the situation. With this realization, she would have immediately withdrawn from any power contest, telling Joel that she was powerless to stop him.

What else could the teacher have done? She might have said:

> "Joel, let's see if we can figure out a way that you can do what you want to do without anyone disturbing you, and I can do what I want to do without being disturbed. This way, no one will impose on anyone. Why don't you take your pencils and the book, go out into the corridor and drum until you have had enough. Then, please come back and join us."

She could have stopped the lesson and told the class that she would wait until Joel tells her to go ahead. In this manner, she would have placed the responsibility of whether or not the class would have music into Joel's hands. Although this is not always successful, in many cases, the child responds favorably because he feels the indirect group pressure. This ceases to be his private battle, but one concerning everyone in class.

If none of these approaches works, the teacher may appeal to the entire class. She may say:

200

"Boys and girls, I'm powerless. I'd like to continue with my lesson but I can't. You may be more successful in handling this situation than I. I'm going to leave it to you. I'll be outside while you discuss this problem. When the class is ready to go on with the lesson, send someone to call me."

Leaving the room may depend on the rules of the school. It is always more effective if the teacher leaves the room. If she is not allowed to leave her class, she may sit down and wait.

By withdrawing from the provocation, the teacher automatically takes all the fun out of Joel's play. By handing the problem over to the class, she makes the children aware that this is everybody's problem, and that all share in the responsibility of solving it.

Some teachers may argue that this procedure may give Joel a sense of victory. Such an argument only confirms the theory that often teachers are more concerned with their prestige than with the need to train children to understand the cause and effect of behavior, as well as the power the group has over the individual. The more the teacher is concerned with her own need to show the child who is in command, the more the child will resist. In the end, the teacher is usually the loser.

The power struggle between teacher and student can take many forms. Very often children look down at the teacher, for whatever reason, to show their superiority. This is difficult for the teacher to tolerate. She is supposed to be superior. Here is an interesting example:

Chip, a senior in high school, must outsmart every adult with whom he comes in contact. His need to feel superior is so strong that he spends hours plotting how he can achieve this goal. He goes to the library to look up definitions and information of irrelevant subject matter, and then confronts the teacher with questions like, "What kind of dress did Josephine wear when she married Napoleon?" Since the teacher cannot answer this question, Chip proceeds with his information and proves his superiority to the whole class. He shows his power also by refusing to spell correctly because, "no one has the right" to tell him that a word must be spelled in just one way. He argues that somebody made up the spelling once upon a time; this person, however, had no right to impose it on others. He, Chip, has just as much right to make up his own spelling of words.

Here the rejection of rules and order is preposterous; even more ludicrous is his way of demonstrating his superiority to the teacher. Any effort to reason with him is hopeless, as he will outsmart anybody intellectually. The only way of dealing with him is by making him aware of his exaggerated need to be superior and to acknowledge his success. There would be little pleasure left for him in trying so hard to prove a superiority that is not contested. More important, however, is his form of justification for not accepting order, that is, the rules of spelling. This is the more serious problem because many children and adults alike assume that democracy means everybody can do what he wants. This is not democracy, but anarchy, and out of such perspectives comes the anarchy found in many classrooms. This is a test of the teacher's ability to withstand powerful pressure, be it in action or words. She has to acknowledge the right of her students to participate in setting rules, as far as the situation permits, but she also has to lead them to recognize the limitations of reality. Such discussions can have a considerable effect in shaping the value system on which the children operate. This can be done only when the teacher refuses to be drawn into a power struggle.

Seeking Revenge. Desire for power and for revenge can easily overlap. If a child is convinced that he has the right to do whatever he pleases, and anyone who tries to stop him is his enemy, he may decide on revenge. This is more probable if the teacher has responded to his bid for power by punishment, then the child will come to the point of punitive retaliation. Coping with a child bent on revenge constitutes one of the most serious problems for a teacher. Such a child is almost inaccessible to reason. Convinced that he is hopelessly disliked and has no chance within the group, he responds with deep distrust to any effort to convince him otherwise. The teacher is exposed to all kinds of well-designed provocations, which makes it difficult for her to convince the child that he is worthwhile and can be liked.

In such a situation, the class group can be of great help, but it also can be a dangerous accomplice. Good pupils will eagerly identify with the teacher in a consolidated front against the troublemaker. Too often, the teachers accept this alliance because of their own sense of failure in dealing with such provocations. In this way, the attitudes of the good students aggravate the problem instead of solving it.

Can one treat the revengeful child with respect? This seems almost preposterous to expect. On the other hand, we can solve problems only on the basis of mutual respect. Here the cultural setting is decisive. In our competitive society, we look down on everybody who is wrong, and in our schools, particularly in the ability groupings, we create a new class of intellectual and moral snobs. One cannot help a revengeful child unless one realizes how much he suffers. The hurt he feels prompts him to hurt others. For this reason, the teacher has to generate an attitude of understanding and assistance. It may be difficult to evoke, but it is essential not only for the sake of the disturbed child, but for the morale of the whole class. Instead of pitting one against the other, we have to teach children that each one is his brother's keeper.

One pitfall for the well-meaning teacher is to treat the disturbed child with preference in order to show him that he can be liked and appreciated. In this way, she may exert a good influence on him— but at what expense. She intensifies the rift with the rest of the class, which resents such preferential treatment, and she makes it impossible for any other teacher to be acceptable to him unless she too gives him special attention.

The teacher can solicit the help of a pupil (see "Billy," p. 91), preferably one with high esteem, to take special interest in the outcast, drawing him into the group and demonstrating appreciation. In this way, it is often possible to build a bridge across the hateful and fearful barrier the child has put up between himself and society. A sociogram may often help to produce better relationships. Teachers and children need to give each other moral support in this endeavor so they will not become discouraged. The antagonism a revengeful child shows in the face of friendliness and kindness is understandable, but it is difficult to withstand. To convince someone that one wants to be his friend when he is convinced that he cannot trust anyone, requires fortitude and persistence. Often, in the moment when one believes one has gained the child's confidence, he puts you to a test in the most outrageous manner. Here is an example:

> Tom, age 15, was a holy terror and notorious for that in the community. His destructiveness was so well designed that it always occurred in a crucial moment. The children were giving a play. The night before, he destroyed the piano, or on another occasion, the stage sets. After consulting with the staff, it was recommended that the teacher concerned with theater productions befriend Tom because his acts of destruction showed his interest in the theater. The teacher should let Tom help him in stage designing and so forth.
>
> For a while this really seemed to turn the trick. Tom was interested in what they were doing and kept out of trouble. Then something strange happened. The teacher could not understand it. While she was working with Tom, she put her watch on the table next to him. Suddenly Tom grabbed the watch and put it in his pocket. The teacher did not know what to do. So she told Tom that somebody must have taken her watch. Tom was furious; how could anybody do something like that? The teacher then proposed they look around for someone who may have taken it. So they went around

the school trying to find out who had taken the watch. Finally, Tom could no longer stand it and returned the watch saying, "You knew all the time that I took it." That was the last provocation. But what did it mean?

This was a well-designed test, which the teacher passed with flying colors. Normally, one would have asked Tom to return the watch immediately, which would have started a big fight. Tom would have denied it, despite the obviousness of his act, and the teacher would have insisted and threatened, perhaps, to get the watch forcibly, and all the good work she had done would have been lost. In dealing with such children, one must be prepared for such tests.

Children who pursue goals 1 or 2 are usually not aware of the purpose for their behavior, whereas children who feel hurt and disliked are often very much aware of their aims. They do not know, however, that they view almost every situation with suspicion and the conviction that they will, again, be the victims. They always feel unfairly treated. They disregard experiences pointing to the contrary, and they do not know that they provoke the experiences to which they respond with hostility. In provoking others to abuse them, they display a kind of moral superiority, looking down on those who are wrong and who, by their actions, are responsible for their own misbehavior. Then they become firmly convinced that they are right in their convictions and justified in their retaliation. These are psychological factors which the teacher can and should discuss with her class.

Displaying Inadequacy. Overcoming a child's discouragement is the most common and urgent task for the teacher. In almost all poor performances, be they academic or social, the child expresses his discouragement.

An assumed or real disability or inadequacy is used by the child to protect himself against the demands of life. The child employs a cloak of inadequacy in order to be left alone. This behavior may characterize all actions of the child or it may only appear in situations where he feels deficient and wants to avoid certain activities.

Many times a teacher gives up easily when her first few attempts in trying a new technique end in failure. So it is with children who are having difficulty socially and academically.

Children who are extremely discouraged, defeated, and have assumed the role of being "a blob" usually operate from three premises:

1. Overambition: cannot do as well as he wants to do.
2. Competition: cannot do as well as others.
3. Pressure: does not do as well as he ought to do.

204

Frustrated overambition is perhaps the most frequent cause for giving up. The desire to be superior may bring about an amount of despair where the child sees no chance to be as good as he wants to be. The feeling of personal superiority sooner or later gives way to cold feet. If he cannot be first, have the best grades, be mother's favorite child, be the leader of the group, or be the homecoming queen or the football hero, he will reach the point of giving up and will refuse to put forth any effort.

> Frank, age 7, was working on his writing assignment. His paper was not the best in the class, but was fairly neat and legible. However, he erased his work, redid it, and erased it again. It was not done well enough to suit him. Consequently, he never finished his assignment. As a first grader, Frank gave up and refused to put forth any effort.

The child, who assumes disability because of his overambition, will not participate in an activity that does not provide him with the opportunity to prove his superiority. For this reason, many teachers find it difficult to accept a psychological interpretation of overambition in a child who does not try at all. The only way to help such a child is by making him aware of how he defeats himself, specifically labeling his actions.

The competitive child is convinced that he has no chance to do as well as others. This child has always been impressed with the fact that he is not good enough and has always been pushed to do better. Teachers and parents, in trying to motivate the competitive child, constantly say defeating things:

> "When I had your sister in my room, she was an A student."
> "Why don't you get higher marks, like Mary?"
> "Are you stupid or something?"
>
> Jenny, age 10, felt that she was "no good" and "stupid." Her mother said to her, "You can't learn, you are too stupid." Jenny was convinced that she could not learn and therefore would not try. When a request was made of her, she would reply, "I can't, I'm too dumb."

Some children may respond by withdrawing as they are actually unable to keep up with others. The sense of being less than others and the conviction of not being good enough bears no relation to the child's ability.

The pressured child who is constantly criticized by parents and teachers, finds that whatever he does is not as good as others think it should be. Passing the course or making a *B* is not enough for some teachers and parents. They often make defeating and discouraging remarks.

205

Rich, age 8, was having problems in school. He could not accept making mistakes. He also did not like to participate in sports. His mother told him, "Why can't you do as good in school as Steve. He always gets a 100 on his papers, and you always miss one or two." His father told him, "You shouldn't have missed that ball, Steve wouldn't have missed it. I know you stopped two sizzlers, but you should have gotten that other one."

Some teachers also discourage the pressured child at a nonverbal level. Their facial expressions and shoulder shrugs are as defeating as their remarks.

Teachers need to convey to the child that he is "good enough" as he is. They need to remove the pressure by being less critical, less faultfinding, and less picky. They need to give the child time to solve problems and to perform at his own speed. They need to allow time for the child to learn a skill so that he can improve his rate of performance.

Our present educational system, with its mistake-centered orientation and its competitive strife, makes it difficult to encourage the children who need it the most. The technique of encouragement, which the teacher has to learn, has been described previously. It may be difficult for the teacher, but it is essential to her corrective ability that she watch for every critical, condemning, disapproving, and impatient sign in her reactions. The difficulty lies in the fact that the discouraged child is prone to impart his conviction of inadequacy to the teacher. Any deficiency must be met with methods that will not perpetuate or increase it. To avoid this, the teacher must be aware of her contribution to the deterioration of the child's ability. Recent studies have shown the tremendous influence exerted by the expectations of the teachers about a given child.[3]

Students who fail, instill in their teacher the anticipation that they will fail again, which in turn, confirms the student's doubt in his ability and hinders his progress. At the present time, we are exposed to an avalanche of organic explanations for the learning deficiencies of children that are bound to increase in frequency and degree.

THE SLOW LEARNER

Many children with normal and even high intelligence are labeled mentally retarded, slow, uneducable, because they do not perform on tests according to standards, or because they do not learn in

[3]Robert Rosenthal, *Experimenter Effects on Behavioral Research* (New York: Academic Press, 1969).

school. Perhaps we need to see how most experts differentiate between the slow learner, the underachiever, and the mentally retarded. The term slow learner is used to describe those students who are scholastically retarded and who have low normal or dull normal intelligence, that is, IQ's in the 75–70 range. It is usually in the intellectual sphere, in the highly complex mental operations or reasoning processes, where the slow learner falls short. It is poor reasoning and poor reading that makes him slow in many instances. Underachievement is a form of unsuccessful school living, that is, individuals are not learning as they should according to their ability. They can have any IQ. The mentally retarded are those students who cannot function sufficiently enough to be served by the regular school program. The usual IQ break-off point is 70.

Some children behave in a manner that may well give the impression that they are incapable of learning. Winnie is an example of such a child. (See "Billy," p. 91.) He convinced his mother and his teachers that he was hopeless and that nothing could be expected of him. True, this was not done consciously, but this does not alter the fact that his fallacious belief in his incapability reinforced his self-image because of the way he was treated.

Many children are afraid of appearing stupid in the eyes of others, yet they almost deliberately use slowness as a means to avoid exposure and certain tasks. (See "Peter," p. 223.) By and large, the bright students as well as the not so bright are subject to this fear and humiliation. School, and society in general, make such a fuss over the bright and the gifted, that the average child, and certainly the below average one, is automatically placed in the position of a second-rate citizen, deserving less consideration and less respect. Parents, even more than teachers, dread the idea of having a stupid child, and they often convey to him that he is bringing disgrace upon them. In turn, this convinces the child that he is a failure. The fear of being considered dumb is often an important factor in the child's withdrawal from intellectual participation, especially in older children. It is a safeguarding device, for it is easier to accept being regarded as lazy rather than stupid.

Some children learn that telling the teacher what they think she wants to hear is safer than expressing doubts, asking questions, or making original deductions and coming to one's own conclusions. This too may be regarded as being not so bright. Thus all creativity, independent thinking, and enjoyment of learning is being stifled for the sake of not appearing stupid.

Every child, no matter what his innate intelligence, feels, perceives, and makes deductions from his experiences. It is not always a question of what we say to him, but also of what we convey without using

207

words. Our facial expressions, sarcastic remarks, and gestures, as well as ignoring hs presence in class, will express the message. Teachers often make such a student the target of ridicule. Such remarks as "Let's ask Tommy. He's so smart and always knows the answer." Or, "Tommy, what do you have in your head instead of brains?" are usually followed by laughter from the class.

> Once a teacher introduced a student as her "goose," saying that a goose probably had more upstairs than this girl. She said it loudly, in front of an entire class. The children promptly started to laugh, while the "goose" glared at the teacher with hatred in her eyes.
>
> At another time, during a science lesson, the teacher posed a question, and a number of hands went up, among them the hand of a boy who was considered stupid. The teacher called on this boy saying, "What do you know, our genius has his hand up. Well, let's hear what you have to say. I'm sure that I'm wasting my time with you, but let's hear you." The boy dropped his hand and remained silent. All eyes were on him. After waiting for a few seconds, the teacher burst out laughing. "That's my genius," she said.

This is not an unusual situation but one that occurs many times in classrooms. Some teachers sincerely believe that ridicule and embarrassment of the child will spur him on to greater efforts. Most teachers are oblivious to the ways in which they contribute to the child's stupidity.

There are many factors that contribute to a child's backwardness, intelligence being just one of them. Unfortunately, the school's evaluation of his ability is based primarily on his performance on tests which measure his mastery of reading, writing, and arithmetic, or by IQ. Normalcy is measured by how well or how poorly he performed according to prescribed standards and norms.

Do these tests tell us more than how the child performed during the time he was tested? They do not measure the child's ability to perform at another time, under different circumstances. Testing children who perform poorly in class and who show no interest in learning, who are poor listeners, who daydream, and who are on the warpath with authority is inconclusive and a sheer waste of time. These children do not behave differently during a testing situation than they do at other times. Some do not hear the tester's directions and underline the first thing they see; some feel uncomfortable with the stranger who is talking to them and have only one thing on their minds, to get out as fast as possible. Others try to feel superior to the psychologist and deliberately pull his leg, as Michael did when he told him that a horse had five legs. Michael thought it was the greatest, and he told everybody what he did and why he did it. When the test results were read, the psychologist had written that Michael was not very observant.

Tests may follow a child from first grade through high school and often through life. In this respect, the school started the child on a career of deficiency.

True, there are individuals who, in spite of having been "retarded" in school, have made a very good adjustment to society. Some achieved high positions in industry while others became successful and even famous in the performing arts. In comparison to the many who turned out to be failures, the few successes are of little consequence. Yet, we know that many of the "retarded" children are actually highly intelligent. Why have we failed them?

We recognize that backwardness has little to do with tests and performance. Studies of slow children indicate that the seemingly slow child often develops slowness as a technique to avoid tasks, and as a means of drawing others into his service. Some children withdraw from class activities because school is too dull for them, some use it as a subconscious means of getting even with overambitious parents or with teachers who push and make them work. Still others have been so beaten down by their previous experiences, which always spelled failure, that they gave up trying. (See "Jerry," p. 225.)

> Betty's IQ was 68, and she was to be placed in a special class for the mentally retarded. At the suggestion of her teacher, she was allowed to remain in a class of normal children and was to be retested at the end of the school year.
>
> There were six children in Betty's family. The oldest two were married and lived away from home. A 12-year-old sister was in seventh grade and a good student. Betty was 10 years old and in third grade. (She had repeated the first grade and was then promoted because of her age.) Her 9-year-old sister was also in the third grade. She was an average student, but she was an accomplished tap dancer and had twice appeared on television. The youngest child, a boy of 7, was in the second grade. He was asthmatic and frequently absent from school. From this family situation, we can see that every child, except Betty, occupied a special position in the family. She was squeezed out by two successful sisters.
>
> Betty's mother told the teacher that at home, her daughter kept to herself. She helped with the chores, but was not very smart.
>
> Betty was also withdrawn in class. She liked to draw and to paint, and to spend most of her time with these activities. Many children knew her from previous classes, and they accepted the fact that nothing could be expected of her. She was ignored.
>
> As the class became aware of the differences in people, of prob-

209

lems that some children have, and of how the group can help to solve some of these problems, the children started to pay attention to Betty. Those who lived close to her home, walked home with her, some invited her to their homes, while others offered to help her with her school work. Gradually, Betty began to show attentiveness, especially during group discussions. Now and then, she offered a suggestion or asked a question.

One day, after a lesson on the characteristics of mammals, she asked why an elephant was not smarter than a human being, considering that the mother elphant carried her baby much longer than the human mother. She reasoned, that the elephant's brain would be better developed, having had more time to do so. Since the brain determines intelligence, it would follow that the elephant be more intelligent.

This was the first time that Betty had expressed an opinion in more than just a few words. The other children were very impressed with her reasoning, and they told her so. The fact that she was not right in her conclusion, did not diminish their impression.

Betty lost her fear of saying something dumb. When she was retested, her IQ had gone up to 97.

Robert was also a mentally retarded child, his IQ being under 70. He was the oldest of three boys, all of whom had spent most of their lives in foster homes. The parents had abandoned the children when Robert was 5 years old. He could not remember them. Robert lived with a family of many children, all younger than he. He had to help with the household chores, babysit for the children, and take frequent punishment for not having done the right things at home or for neglecting one of the little ones. His nickname at home was "Moron."

Robert spent most of his time in class daydreaming or looking out of the window. He was no behavior problem. He was very attentive during class discussions, but never participated.

One day a boy asked the class to help him with a home problem. He said that their tenants complained that his family was too noisy and that they must stop making so much noise. This boy felt that since it was his parents' house, they had a right to make all the noise they wanted, and he wanted to know how the rest of the children felt about this problem. Suddenly Robert got up and shouted, "You have no such rights. Nobody has a right to make others unhappy. I don't care if this is your house or who you are, nor how smart you think you are."

Everybody stared at Robert. Suddenly they saw a different boy in him. Many children agreed that Robert was right, but they asked him why was he so angry. One child said that perhaps Robert felt the class had not treated him right, and he was angry not only because of the problem discussed, but because of his own situation. Other children expressed similar opinions. A new life in class had started for Robert. At the end of the year, his IQ had gone up to 91.

Children live up to our expectations of them. A teacher who assumes that the child cannot learn, or one who accepts the child's passivity and poor performance because "What can you expect of this child?" will find that she will get nothing from him. This convinces her that she was right in her assumption, and in turn, it convinces the child that he too was right in his belief that he is too dumb to learn. It becomes a vicious circle.

> John, age 8, was considered uneducable. He could not sit still, had a short interest span, and was constantly disturbing. For this reason, the school decided to expel him. The mother came for help. John was the youngest in the family. He was sickly as a baby and consequently overprotected by his mother. Although he refused to accept any order and limitations, he succeeded in putting everyone in his service. One sister, a few years older, was, in contrast, the good cooperative child. The mother was willing to accept guidance. She stopped treating John as incapable and deficient, stopped giving him the service he demanded, and he improved in a relatively short period of time. Then we tried to get him back into school. It was a hard struggle because the principal and the teacher did not believe that in such a short time he could have changed enough to be able to function in the class. Eventually, the school was persuaded to take him back on a trial basis. The teacher reported that he really had improved a great deal, but still, he was not quite capable of cooperating during the whole school day. He was cooperative for two periods, but in the third, he could no longer sit still and fell back to his previous behavior. The teacher thought that it was too much of a burden on him to be restricted for more than two periods.

Is it possible for the boy to have only enough energy or ability to work for two periods, and too much energy to sit still thereafter? What the teacher did not know was that she did not believe that he could sit quietly for such a long period, and he acted in accordance with her expectations.[4]

A teacher who believes that a child performs according to his inborn intelligence, will not try to find out whether she is right or

[4]Robert Rosenthal, "Self-fulfilling Prophecies," *Psychology Today*, 2, 1968, pp. 44–51.

wrong. She is so concerned with his limitations, that she overlooks his potential. Surprisingly enough, the opposite is found with equal frequency. The teacher recognizes the child's potential because of high scores on tests, and then cannot understand why he does not come up to his potential. Consequently, very gifted children often find themselves in the same predicament. Their unwillingness to perform leads to the same discouraging experiences, that is, the despair of a discouraged teacher who does not believe in her own ability to succeed in her teaching and corrective efforts. Why should a gifted child refuse to learn? We have a growing number of these underachievers from the third to fifth grades in our schools. Their discouragement is a consequence of their overambition. (See "Changing the Child's Goals," p. 186.) They can only function when they are on top, when they are excellent, and when they are treated as someone special. They want to be the best or they become the worst. Their lack of interest in their studies is the result of not receiving any significance from studying, while they may find quite a place for themselves in athletics or the arts, or they may switch to the useless side and then find some nonproductive way in which they can excel. It is so much easier to be something special through disturbance than through academic effort.

Separating children into homogeneous grouping, as some schools do, does not solve the problem of the slow learner nor does it help the gifted child. Taking gifted children out of the regular classroom situation may be harmful to both. The complaint that the gifted child is held back or that he begins to dislike school because he is bored indicates the teacher's inability to integrate her class.

A gifted child would not become bored if he were stimulated to find intellectual outlets and interesting activities within the class. In fact, being on his own or with other children, he can explore and make his own discoveries, and then share them with the other pupils. This stimulates his independence and his creativity which, in the long run, has greater value than the teacher-directed activities we usually find in special classes for gifted children.

The drive and the competition in the class for the accelerated is often more than some children can endure. Many children become tense and nervous, while others break down under the strain. In this respect, the school system fails the gifted child as much as the impoverished program does the slow child. School becomes a drudge for both.

Some people argue that mixing gifted children with slow children may add to the anxiety of the latter, for in comparison to the bright one, they become more painfully aware of their own shortcomings. This, in turn, only adds to their discouragement, and may happen in

212

a highly competitive class atmosphere. As pointed out, it even happens to some of the gifted children in a special class. It is not likely to occur in a class where a democratic spirit prevails, where children are guided to accept and respect individual differences on all levels, and where they assist one another and solve their problems together. This requires unification of the class for a common purpose with positive social interaction. In such an atmosphere, the self-esteem of the slow child is bound to be raised by the acceptance of those whom he admires and envies. Earlier in this chapter, we showed how Betty was helped by the acceptance of the group, by their encouragement, and by their appreciation of her.

Children who are grouped according to ability are often deprived of the stimulation derived from the interrelationship with other children who come from different socio-economic and cultural backgrounds. Such stimulation broadens their horizon; it helps them to develop healthy values, and it prepares them far better for life than an enriched program in mathematics or science. Every class should have an enrichment program for all children according to their interests and abilities, but without separating them. It is a pity that so many children come in contact only with other children of the same background and interests. How often do we hear teachers say, "He is a fine student but he is poorly adjusted." Adjustment referring to social living. Of what value is his intellectual achievement if he is not well adjusted?

If the teacher wishes to group the children within the classroom, there are several ways open to her, none of which is based on IQ. Grouping for special talents or skills is usually not connected with IQ or intellectual reasoning. A particular student may have a talent for making artistic arrangements and, at the same time, have a reading difficulty. (See "Corrine," p. 183.) She could function very well as the organizer for the showcase displays and be made to feel that she was really contributing to the program as a whole.

Interest groups are usually arranged so that those who wish to develop along specific interest lines can function as a group, and gather materials to present to the class. Such groups could be a mixture of rapid learners and slow learners, as each would have something to contribute.

Grouping according to interests is one of the easier ways of handling the problem, as the students are anxious to acquire the skills they need in order to stay within the group.

Sometimes there is a need for grouping by teams, either mixing or matching ability levels, as the rapid learner could help the slower student with practice in a particular skill. Other times it may be to everyones advantage to group a fast team and a slow team. No decision should be made without discussion and agreement of the students. Whichever way the class is grouped, the end result seems to be that each student has a contribution to make and that each student can contribute to the other's knowledge and skill.

The teacher must always keep in mind that groups are formed for a purpose, that a student can learn to look for assistance from someone other than the teacher, that the specific goal of each group should be clearly understood, and that youngsters should have some experience in working with groups in which there is a wide range of ability.

Most young children are eager to learn and they look forward to going to school. Yet, we see so many children who resent school after being there for just a few weeks. Undoubtedly, poor preparation by their parents toward social living and toward independence plays a part in this, but the fault is not only with the upbringing of these children, it is the school that fails them. A good teacher can overcome all the damage done by the family and the community because she has the group with which to work. Also, as the power of the adult diminishes the influence of the peer group increases.

The increasing number of children who do not learn and who fail particularly in reading and writing is a vivid and striking expression of the bankruptcy of our learning institutions. Unfortunately, this fact is now systematically denied by some leading figures in the field of education who use their research methods to excuse teachers for their failure to teach children. Various so-called scientific findings are presented to explain the failure of the teacher. (See "Reading Difficulties," p. 216.) First, there was the concept of the intelligence quotient. Then came the idea of the slow development of boys that prevented them from being ready to read and to learn at the age of 6. In recent years, the concept of dyslexia, perceptual deprivation, neurogenic learning disabilities, sidedness, and minimal brain damage were offered as excuses to explain why 20 to 25 percent of all children could not learn to read and write properly. We will discuss the significance of such alibis when we examine the problem of reading difficulties.

Let us consider some of these deficiencies that are to blame for the child's inability or slowness in learning. There is the question of intelligence. Naturally, a retarded child will not be able to accomplish as much as a normal or average child, but how do we know whether a child is retarded. Tests show a child's IQ, that is, his intellectual abilities or deficiencies. But is a test a reliable basis for judgment? Contrary to what is generally believed, it is not. It is reliable only in the upper score. A child with a tested IQ of 135 certainly has to have the ability for such performance, but a low score is unreliable. Even a normal child can decide to be dumb and then act as such. One educator points out the test is not taken into account alone, but only in connection with the general function of the child. A child who is really convinced of his stupidity, as many Head Start and culturally deprived students are, can play stupid in all areas.

Adler suggested one sign of severe mental retardation, that is, the inability of a child to form a life style, to set his own goals. Most retarded children do not fall into this category. They may be retarded as far as the academic process is concerned, but in most instances, they have enough intelligence to manipulate adults, as well as to put them in their service. If they learn that, why could they not learn other things as well? They may be slower, but we can assume that as our teaching methods improve, the learning abilities of retarded children will increase.

The teacher needs to participate with the students in the process of learning, accept the gradualness of their progress, and extend her own assistance, suggestions, and interest. She needs to make a critical transition from her world, her standards, and her goals to a consideration of the slow learner's world, his view, and what he regards important.

She can provide concrete, meaningful experiences that will help the slower student to become a self-reliant, worthy individual. She must never lose sight of the fact that individuals grow and develop within a context of interpersonal relationships. The explanation of what goes on, of how and what the individual learns, can be found in his relationship to his teacher and peers, both of whom can further or retard his progress. Whenever learning occurs, an individual changes his concepts.

One cannot evaluate the child's intellectual deficiencies until one first succeeds in stopping his parents and teachers from reinforcing them. Such reinforcement takes place when parents and teachers succumb to the child's schemes and let him convince them of his stupidity, as any intelligent "retarded" child can easily do. Additionally, all the special attention, help, coaxing, and pushing has the opposite of the desired effect, it only stimulates the child to continue playing for special attention and service. The child may also play dumb to defeat adults as we have stated before. All this has to stop before the real intellectual capacity of the child emerges. Presently, none of this is done before a diagnosis of mental retardation is made. Originally, one assumed that the IQ measures the innate intelligence of the child. This, at least, has been given up. Evidence indicates that the IQ can go up or down and is by no means an indicator of the child's native ability, but only of his present performance.

215

READING DIFFICULTIES

The increasing number of children who never learn to read and write properly presents a serious cultural dilemma. It is estimated that about four million Americans are poor readers, although they have no mental or physical handicap, and their intelligence is often above average. Reading ability is the basis for any academic progress. The inability to impart this knowledge to all children is an indictment of our present educational setup. Parents and educators are duly alarmed and looking for explanations and remedies. We cannot hope to improve the situation as long as the causes for the predictment are in dispute. This awareness has brought forth numerous books and hundreds of articles dealing with "Why Johnnie can't read." New theories in regard to teaching methods as well as to the causes of poor reading habits come up every few years. They become popular for a time only to be displaced by a new theory a few years later. The confusion of the teacher in coping with the increasing numbers of nonreading pupils is equaled by the confusion shown by the experts in their conflicting findings.

Before we can turn to the psychological aspects of reading difficulties, the prevalent assumptions of the inability of many children to learn to read must be considered. Some experts present a picture that makes our problem insoluble. What are some of their theories?

There is a list of causes based on a deficiency psychology, which is shared by many. According to them, the child is disadvantaged, deprived, and, therefore, unable to learn. He suffers from cultural or perceptual deprivation and a dysfunction of the brain. They describe the nonlearner as having peripheral and central nervous system disorders, sensory deprivation and handicaps, neurophrenia, dyslexia, aphasias, disgraphias, intrasensory and intersensory disabilities, deficiency in auditory perception and disorders of auditory comprehension, problems with visual imagery and special visual distortions, and many other similar disorders. The fundamental principles that experts suggest the teacher should consider are the integrities, deficits, tolerance levels, number and types of sensory modalities to be activated, types of involvement, levels of involvement, relationships between reception and expression, nature of verbal and nonverbal disturbances, states of readiness, and the need for assistance with total integration. They conclude, "The teacher must develop the greatest possible degree of balance among the behavioral functions by individualizing the program for each child or each group of children."[5] Experts expect the

[5]Doris J. Johnson and Helmer R. Myklebust, *Learning Disabilities* (New York: Grune and Stratton, 1967).

teacher to "diagnose the nature of the learning problem, the deficits, the integrities, the levels of function in spoken, read, and written language, and the nonverbal and medical aspects."

At a time when too few teachers understand the problems of the normal child who is disturbing or deficient, how can we expect, in the foreseeable future, to train sufficient teachers in the diagnosis and specific remedial procedures for the 20 percent of all our school population who supposedly are afflicted with dyslexia, and, therefore, cannot be taught the customary way?

Another aspect of such "expert" opinion is even more disastrous. Since one can now expect every fifth child in the class to be affected by such disorder, we provide an opportunity for all boys to behave badly. One can visualize the consequences of this development. Boys, at the present time, show all the disorders, reading inability, delinquency, psychosis in approximately the same ratio to girls, 4–7 to 1. All kinds of intellectual gymnastics can be found in the literature to explain this ratio. One suggestion is that girls are playing house while boys are scouting territory. They say that it is difficult for nature to make a male to develop territoriality, and boys who cannot attend this task become nonlearners, disabled readers, school dropouts, and delinquents. Another peculiar suggestion is that boys have larger heads and, therefore, suffer greater birth trauma. A typical example is the assumption that the slow development of boys is responsible for the fact that many do not show reading readiness at the age of 6. Thus, it was seriously considered to postpone reading instruction for boys to the age of 8, notwithstanding the fact that in other cultures all boys learn to read at the age of 4.

This whole question of reading readiness becomes even more confused when we have evidence that children can learn to read at the age of 3. Why then are most of them ready to learn only at the age of 6? Because that is what is expected of them. This still leaves it up to some children to learn to read earlier, particularly if there is a brother or sister who is slow in learning. Other children may decide not to be ready to learn until the age of 8, and some never learn.

Fortunately, one hears many voices who object to this trend. "The methods in perceptual training and visual-motor coordination have not yet been proven to have any direct effect on the learning of reading. The various methods are presented sometimes with the partisanship and finality that seem to preclude alternatives."[6]

John Money continues, "It is fashionable today to talk of minimal brain damage in relation to reading disability. This is really begging

[6]John Money, in *The Disabled Reader* (Baltimore: Johns Hopkins Press, 1966), p. 33

the question. In the majority of cases, no kind of brain damage can be demonstrated by today's technique. EEG's do not support the hypothesis of minimal brain damage in retarded readers. There are minor EEG anomalies, but the same are seen in children with different or with no diagnosis. They merely indicate a maturation anomaly. Disability specific to reading is rare in cases of brain pathology in childhood."[7]

According to Eisenberg, "Competent investigators have been led to contrary conclusions about the role of handedness, heredity, perceptual handicap, and the like. Incomplete cerebral dominance does not account for reading problems. The determination of laterality is not so simple a matter as what one thought, nor is brainedness so readily to be inferred from handedness."[8]

All the assumptions of neurogenic learning disabilities and similar organic explanations for reading disabilities will continue and probably increase in number and kind as long as teaching techniques do not catch up with the way young children learn before they enter school.

Nobody denies that children may have brain damage, but brain-damaged children do not behave in the same manner as minimal-brain-damaged children. Their hyperactivity is not a consequence of brain damage, which cannot be proven, but a behavior problem. It can be stopped through firm but kind restrictions. Still worse is the assumption of perceptual disadvantage. We know of children with a form of aphasia where they cannot identify what they see. However, this is a rare condition. Today the diagnosis of perceptual handicap is made for thousands of children. In those children with whom we worked, and who were diagnosed as "minimal brain-damaged" or "perceptually handicapped," we found no such evidence. Their behavior, which led to the former diagnosis, was based on their playing dumb, since it brought them satisfaction of one kind or another. Here is one dramatic example:

> A mother came in with her 14-year-old daughter who suffered from perceptual difficulties, and was in a special class to remedy them. This girl read on a fourth-grade level when she was in third grade. Suddenly she stopped in her progress, both in reading and in comprehension. What caused this sudden change? When we looked into this matter, we found that a little brother was born into the family. She had been an only child before. As we investigated further, we found that the brother was a hyperactive and brain-

[7]Money, p. 33.
[8]Eisenberg, Leon, in *The Disabled Reader* (Baltimore: Johns Hopkins Press, 1966), p. 8.

damaged child. The girl, who was a good child, and who was appreciated by her parents for it, could not rebel openly, as this would make her bad in the eyes of her parents. She could avoid taking such a risk by displaying an inability to read, which was the worse thing she could do to her highly sophisticated and overambitious parents. We felt that she probably could read as well as before, in fact, even on a higher level as she did before. We conveyed our feelings to her parents. The mother then told us that her daughter loves to read mystery stories and that she was reading them all the time. This confirmed our suspicion. She certainly could not have read such stories if she had not understood what she was reading. It was all a pretense.

When the girl was questioned, she was asked whether she can read. Her reply was, "Yes, if I am interested." We suggested that she be removed from the special class, put into a regular class, and to let her navigate by herself. The parents were advised to stop all pressure, and to stop feeling embarrassed and ashamed because of their daughter. When the true motives for the girl's regression were explained to her, she acknowledged them. She soon regained her ability to read and comprehend.

Some claim that the kindergarten is to blame for the poor preparation the children receive in regard to the acceptance of responsibilities toward academic learning. They claim that reading readiness is either not taught at all or poorly taught, and that this automatically carries over to the child's attitude toward reading.

Some claim that the root of the problem lies in the poor reading instruction children receive in first grade, and that these children are sent on to the next grade without mastery of the fundamentals. This social promotion then continues until the child finds himself in the fifth or sixth grade where the teachers become alarmed. At this stage, it is exceedingly difficult to help the child.

Some are convinced that the child is not motivated because of the poor textbooks the school system imposes, the content of which is either not stimulating or completely foreign to the child's experiences.

There are those who attribute reading failures to a bad experience during the child's first attempt to read, at home or at school. They contend that the first experience has discouraged the child to such a degree that he wants no part in reading from there on. There are those who believe that the key to teaching reading is phonics, and that the schools of today do not emphasize this technique sufficiently.

Then there are those who see a high correlation between reading difficulties and an emotional disturbance in the child. This theory has been much emphasized during the last decade, although this relationship had been pointed out earlier.[9]

It seems that the method of teaching reading is of less importance than the child's individual personality development; the cause of his difficulties is peculiar to him alone, although there may be other children with similar difficulties. Thus, it becomes a matter of understanding the child's academic and social development in order to understand the underlying cause of his problem. Without this understanding, the teacher is in no position to help the child to overcome his handicap. Unfortunately, there are still many teachers who cannot understand that there is a relationship between a child's inability to learn how to read and his psychological development. More deplorable is that the teachers who do accept this theory, cannot convey it to the parents. This lack of understanding, both by the teacher and by the parents, prompts them to push harder, force the child to read, and often punish him for his lack of progress.

In some schools, the teacher refers the child to special remedial reading classes. Many children attend remedial reading classes for years without improving their reading skills, and without any basic change in their attitude toward reading. Remedial reading usually consists of specific teaching techniques, such as drills in the various reading areas. It does not direct its approach toward the change of the child's negative attitudes, which are of a psychological nature. Corrective efforts should, therefore, be aimed at the child's unwillingness to learn and toward the acceptance of a friendly attitude toward reading. Only after the child has made this fundamental change can remedial reading techniques be applied successfully. The teacher should never say, "A child can't," all she knows is that the child *does not* learn.

Organic or physiological concepts lead to an underestimation of the psychological factors of reading difficulties. Even when cultural or social factors are taken into consideration, they prevent rather than facilitate an understanding of the child's problems. Without comprehension of his goals, the significance of his disfunctions and deficiencies cannot be determined. Corrective measures require an understanding of the child's concepts, private logic, and goals. (See "Private Logic" and "Four Goals," p. 17, 186.) Even if he is physically deficient or culturally deprived, it is his reaction to the conditions that explains his behavior. What a child has is less important than what he does with it.

[9]Rudolf Dreikurs. "Emotional Predisposition to Reading Difficulties." *Archives of Pediatrics,* 71, 1954, pp. 339–353.

We can distinguish three groups of functions that are disturbed in a nonreader or in a child who is unduly slow in his reading development. First, he obviously displays a disability. His accomplishments are far below par. He cannot do what other children of his age group can do. This disability has to be understood in its function. Is it a means of getting special attention, of defying the demand of adults, or is it an expression of goal 4, of his conviction that he cannot learn to read, and, therefore, gives up.

Second, the retarded reader usually has poor working habits. They result from inadequate training. Even if the child makes an effort, it is spotty, sporadic, and erratic.

Third, the retarded reader has difficulty cooperating with others, particularly with adults. He often displays disdain for and defiance of order. Despite personal affection he may have for adults, he is usually unable or unwilling to follow directions, to accept responsibility, or to do as he is told. The reading difficulty appears then as merely one facet of disturbed interpersonal relationships resulting in social maladjustment.

Reading and writing are the two subjects most affected by the child's reluctance to accept rules and to conform to them. No other subject is as closely related to order. Arithmetic, for instance, also requires the recognition of rules and order, but a child who has difficulty with arithmetic is less impressed with the aspect of order than with the need to solve his own problems. He feels unable to do so, usually because he depends too much on others to solve his problems for him. In contrast, spelling is most difficult for a child not trained to observe order. He spells, as the spirit moves him, the same word in different ways. Poor script also reflects defiance of order, and reading deficiencies are the strongest rebuffer to the academic demands of adults.

Too often the reading disability is not regarded as a symptom, but as the real problem. Such a mistaken approach is inevitable as long as the teacher does not understand the child's psychological dynamics, and, therefore, does not direct any efforts toward changing them. In this way, the teacher is involved unnecessarily in an uphill struggle. Her own discouragement, puts an additional handicap in the way of the child's progress. His apprehensions and fears, instead of being relieved, receive additional fuel through the tedious and often tortuous practices imposed on him. Remedial courses, designed to help the child, may easily undermine his spirit, his self-confidence, and his self-respect, unless he has the good fortune to have an especially patient and understanding teacher. But often enough, such a teacher falls for the child's demands for special attention and service, and by indulging him with sympathy and pity, deters his progress.

221

The elements necessary for an adequate corrective approach are self-evident. Remedial teaching requires not merely a specific teaching technique, but it must be directed toward changing some deeper psychological dynamics of the child, stimulating a change in motivation. Instead of involving the child in the laborious practice of reading, the teacher has to assume corrective functions of a psychological nature.

1. The teacher cannot ignore the faulty values on which the child may operate, like the fallacy of constantly comparing himself with others, of being more concerned with success than with learning. Such distorted ambition often leads to the assumption of being a failure. The child may need a better concept of order and usefulness. The teacher can and should enhance the child's comprehension of social living. Such teaching should not be incidental to the practice of reading, but rather be the essence of remedial teaching. This can be achieved through individual and particularly group discussion, since most students in remedial classes share similar deficiencies in their value system.

2. The basis for effective educational endeavors is a proper interpersonal relationship. Children in need of special instruction have not been able to establish such a relationship in their families. Otherwise, they would not be academically and socially deficient. The teacher will be put in the same role the mother, father, and other authority figures played in the child's family, unless she makes deliberate efforts to recognize such faulty patterns and to correct them. This collusion of adults against the child is only fortified if the teacher tries to involve the mother in supervising the child's reading efforts.

3. The teacher has to free herself from the assumption that the difficulty in reading permits any conclusion about the reading *ability* of a child. Presently, the real ability of children in this regard is grossly underestimated by the majority of teachers.

4. Children will not learn rather than cannot learn. The child is opposing and sabotaging efforts at instruction. Corrective efforts must be aimed at his unwillingness to learn, although the child may display a pretended desire to learn to cover up his real intention. "The mind of such a child is full of resistance and must be emptied, in contrast to the prevalent opinion that his mind is empty, waiting only to be filled."[10]

Do present techniques in remedial reading provide such stimulation? This is a question every remedial teacher may ask herself. Present methods are often anything but stimulating. They may be dull,

[10]Willard Beecher, "A New Approach to Remedial Reading," *American Journal of Individual Psychology,* 10, 1952, p. 5.

uninspiring, repetitious, and mechanical. Unless the interest and enthusiasm of the child is evoked, little can be accomplished, despite much work and effort.

The teacher who concentrates her efforts toward the elimination of previous failures and discouragements, and who builds up the child's strength and ability, will find that he will learn how to read with any method she may apply or with the method to which he responds best. For there is no one method to which all children respond equally well. This requires a flexible program, a willingness and know how by the teacher.

The cases that follow are those of children who made no progress in reading in spite of years of remedial help, but who learned how to read within a comparatively short time once their not-learning tendency was removed, and once their self-image was changed.

Peter was an only child of elderly parents. He was small and underweight until the age of 4. Both parents constantly worried about him and gave in to him in order not to upset him. When he could not have his way, Peter screamed and threw anything that was near at his parents. When they gave in to him, "he was lovable" and very affectionate which both parents adored.

Peter was not sent to kindergarten. The parents were afraid that he might catch diseases from the other children. They were equally afraid to let him go out and play with other children. One of them took him to the park every afternoon where he would sit on a swing while a parent pushed it. The mother insisted that Peter loved it that way since he never asked to be allowed to play with other children.

When Peter entered first grade, he cried and would not let go of his mother. She promised to stand outside where he could see her through the window. After some time, the teacher insisted that the mother go away, which she did, only to wait for Peter around the corner. She brought him to school and picked him up at noon and in the afternoon every day for two years in spite of the teacher's appeal to allow the boy to walk home alone or with other children.

Peter made no progress in first grade and had to repeat the grade. This seemed to have no effect on him or his parents. At the end of the second year, he was promoted to second grade although he had not learned any more than during the first year. Thus, he was promoted again into third grade. Here he spent most of the time either at the window or going back and forth to the washroom or to the drinking fountain. He seemed not to hear when the teacher spoke to him.

While still in third grade, Peter's mother had a fatal accident. This changed his entire life. The father worked during the day; he left the house before Peter had to leave for school. Not being able to afford a housekeeper, Peter was forced to shift for himself. He had to walk to school either by himself or with other children. After school, he waited for his father in the home of a neighbor who had young children.

The first few weeks were, indeed, pitiful. Peter was too stunned, or else he understood that tantrums would not help him. He walked as if in his sleep. For a while, the children in class overprotected and pampered him. They took him to the cafeteria where they sat with him, they walked him from and to school, and they invited him to their homes to wait for his father. Gradually, he formed relationships with them, and he discovered that he could hold his own quite successfully. This change carried over into his attitude toward everything that concerned school and school activities. By the end of the school year, he could read and write as well as many of the students in his class.

Percy was the younger of two children. His parents were divorced when he was 3 years old. Each parent took one child; Percy remained with his mother.

Percy's mother ran a small grocery store where he spent each day. He was a very fearful child, afraid of lightning and thunder, the dark, animals, and strange people. He refused to ride a tricycle because he might fall off. He slept in the same bed with his mother until he was 11, when she was helped to understand that she was holding him back with her overprotection.

Percy's school attendance was most irregular. Usually he skipped mornings, but often did not show up for many days in a row. In class, he was generally well behaved and showed considerable interest and knowledge in science. He lacked the most rudimentary reading skills. Whatever he learned in his remedial reading class, he forgot within minutes.

When Percy was 11 years old, his mother became alarmed about his reading disability, and she came to the teacher for help. This was unusual for this woman because she had never kept any appointments with the teachers of any grade.

The mother was helped to understand how she had deprived Percy of a normal development by making him the center of her life, by giving in to him and by serving him as though he were incapable of learning to be responsible for himself. She was helped to see the connection between what she did and his school retardation. She was an intelligent woman and desperate enough to follow the teacher's advice. It was a very difficult task for all of them—the mother, Percy, and the teacher. Although Percy was prepared for the changes that would take place at home, he threw tantrums, broke dishes, refused to go to school, and so forth. The mother was desperate and ran to the teacher for help almost daily. Her biggest difficulty was in knowing how to show love and affection for the boy without being his slave. Both of them required frequent counseling, the mother by the teacher, and Percy by the teacher and frequent reassurance by the group. In this way, both of them were reeducated and slowly formed a new relationship. Percy's school attendance became more regular, and he began to form social interrelationships with some of the children. The teacher assigned to him the lead in a Christmas play. This required the memorization of lines. Percy had to depend on other children to read the lines for him, which he did, but in the process he developed a feeling for reading for the first time, reading seemed to make sense, and he could see the need for it. It was then that the remedial instruction that he had received for over two years took on importance and meaning. He progressed rapidly.

Jerry was classified as a nonlearner after four years of individual instruction. At age 11 he still looked like 8 and people who did not know his age would often ask him if he were in first or second grade. He never answered such questions, but hung his head or looked away. Whenever he was confronted with such a question in front of his mother, she would quickly reply that he was in fifth grade, which was not true, and she added that he was very shy.

Jerry was the second child of five children. His older brother died when he was 3 years old. The other siblings were born when he was 5 and already in kindergarten.

After the death of his brother, the parents doubled their vigilance and protection not only of this boy, but of all of their children. Jerry was kept at home on rainy days. He was never allowed to join his class on field trips or in energetic activities in the gymnasium.

In class, he was very talkative but in a sly, underhanded manner. When the teacher looked at him, he assumed an angelic expression, but the moment she took her eyes off him, he started talking to his neighbors. Usually, he brought some object to school to show off or to play with under his desk. Whenever the teacher called on him, he got up in a daze. He hung his head so low that it would almost touch his desk. He often remained in this position in spite of the teacher's invitation to sit down. The children looked at him with pity, and those near by often pleaded with him to sit down. Jerry could never find his pencil or his scissors. His desk was crammed with unwritten papers and with the various objects he brought from home. He could neither read nor write, and he showed

225

no interest in any subject. Whenever the teacher tried to help him, he shook his head and mumbled, "I can't." Nevertheless, Jerry never missed going to his remedial reading class, he never had to be reminded.

During an interview with the mother, it became obvious that the parents accepted the belief that Jerry was retarded physically as well as mentally, and that he needed their protection. It was impossible to persuade these parents to try a different approach. They were convinced of Jerry's retardation and reproached themselves for having children, as one of the father's brothers was mentally retarded and in an institution. They blamed Jerry's condition on heredity.

During one of the class discussions, it was brought up that sometimes it pays for children to play "dumb" even though they are quite intelligent. Jerry, who had never taken obvious interest in those discussions, raised his hand for the first time. He asked that we explain what one could possibly get out of playing dumb. He said, "If you're dumb, you're dumb. You don't play like you're dumb because you get nothing." The group disagreed with him and gave him many examples how it pays off for somebody to play dumb, how people are forced into their service, how nobody expects anything of such children, and how they get out of assuming responsibilities for themselves. One child said that it may pay off while one is young, but when one grows up, such a person will have a hard time because he won't know how to do anything for himself. Nobody mentioned Jerry's name, but he suddenly got up and in a clear voice announced, "But I'm not playing dumb." The teacher asked him to explain this comment, but all he could say was, "I'm not playing," over and over. For several seconds one could hear a pin drop. Nobody said a word, but everyone looked at Jerry. Finally one girl remarked, "How do you know, Jerry? Maybe you're much smarter than you think but you never try to find out. You don't even try to walk home by yourself like the other kids do."

After class was dismissed, Jerry stopped at the teacher's desk and timidly asked if she would speak to his parents and ask them to allow him to come to and walk from school by himself. This was Jerry's first step toward independence. After he learned to walk to school by himself, he asked to be permitted to walk to the park by himself. Next, the teacher induced the parents to get him an alarm clock and to let him get up in the morning and get ready for school by himself. Each time Jerry made the slightest progress, the parents were instructed to show appreciation. In class, the children complimented Jerry and showed their interest in all of his achievements.

As the parents' and the children's attitude toward him changed, so did his self-evaluation. When asked a question, he no longer hung his head, he answered without fear. He did not always know the answers, but he showed no sign of fear or shame.

Jerry's school progress was unbelievably fast. His dormant ambition now came to fore, and he set high goals for himself, like completing a reader within one month. He did. At the end of that year, he had successfully covered three years work.

In this case, we see a reverse process, namely of a child changing the attitudes of his parents. This is possible only when the teacher understands how to redirect the child's wrong concepts and how to use the group to encourage the child. Without the help of the group, this would have been impossible.

Dick, 11 years old, had a deaf twin brother and a younger sister. Dick was supposed to be in the sixth grade, but was reading on a second grade level. His parents bought reading books and tutored Dick in long stormy sessions each evening.

Dick had been in a classroom that was set up with strong remediation techniques. He was diagnosed as having weak phonic skills, reversals, substitutions, and omission of letters and words. Dick did not improve in his reading. The teacher and others who worked with him were very concerned with Dick's inability to learn to read.

At this time, Dick was transferred to another classroom, where they had a general discussion about reading, and Dick said, "Reading is a bore." The teacher said she enjoyed reading and that it was fun. She would like to go many places and meet different people, but since she could not, the next best thing was to read about them. At this point, Dick looked at her as if to say, "Man, you are trying to sell me something." The teacher let the subject drop and asked the parents to come in for a conference.

The parents were both concerned and upset over Dick's lack of progress and wanted to know if they should enroll him in a private reading clinic. They further stated that Dick kept their household constantly upset, and they were beside themselves.

The teacher suggested they follow a plan she had in mind, for about six weeks. She asked the parents to remove all pressure from Dick about school and his work. To emphasize this point she said, "Please do not even mention the word *school* as this may seem like pressure to Dick. Do not ask him to read or to do any other academic related task. Since school and especially reading is so important to you, Dick is probably using this method to defeat you." The parents agreed to do this although they felt that it would be difficult for them.

During the next few days, the teacher did not give Dick a reading assignment nor did she mention it to him. When he approached the teacher about his reading lesson, she shrugged her shoulders and indicated that she was not interested. A couple of days later, Dick again asked the teacher about his reading assignment. She half-heartedly said, "OK, if you think it is necessary," but she did nothing about it that day.

The next day, Dick asked if she had figured out a reading assignment for him. She said she had been thinking about it and thought they should use a fourth grade book as the stories were interesting. Dick thought that was a good idea. He read the fourth-grade book with a great deal of proficiency.

About two weeks later, the teacher forgot Dick's reading assignment again for two days. He was very concerned and wanted his lesson. The teacher said she had been thinking again and had looked at a sixth-grade book, and it had more interesting stories than the book he was reading. He eagerly exchanged books and found he could read it with relatively few errors.

The parents came to school for their six weeks conference. They were pleased with the change in Dick's behavior at home and in the community. They were amazed at Dick's progress in the classroom. They were now able to see how they unwittingly contributed to and reinforced Dick's reading difficulties. At this time, they agreed to continue to keep the pressure off. They also agreed if he brought homework from school, they would not help him and, furthermore, they would not remind him.

Dick became responsible for his own work and began to read library books for fun.

We can see that a teacher trained in psychological methods can recognize the discouragement of the child and the reasons for it, and that she can offset much of the discouraging influence. We may say that remedial reading should take on the aspects of therapy and must never be merely incidental to the general reading program with some children. This can be done through individual counseling or through group discussion.

Some children have reading difficulties because of poor eyesight or poor health. This has to be established first by a physician. Even in such cases, counseling is of greatest importance. We know that physically handicapped children are able not only to compensate, but to overcompensate for their deficiencies if properly guided.

FIGHTING

There are many kinds of behavior problems that have to be dealt with daily. One of the most common problems which confront teachers is that of fighting or quarreling. Many children have difficulty in accepting the demands of certain situations. Many teachers get themselves hopelessly entangled with children who are in conflict.

Every teacher has, at one time or another, heard these familiar cries: "He hit me." "Teacher, Jimmy hit me as we were going home. I don't know why. I didn't do a thing to him." When we ask Jimmy, he insists that it was the other child who started the fight, and that he only hit back in self-defense. This, "You did" and "I did not," could go on endlessly if we permit it. (See "Role Playing," p. 136.) Some teachers even call for witnesses. Usually one or the other of the culprits or both produce witnesses to testify to their innocence. In this system, there has to be a winner and a loser, and no one is satisfied, not even the teacher who feels compelled to give the verdict and give out the punishment. If a teacher would take time to observe the start and the development of such quarrels, she would usually find that both children are equally guilty—guilty of keeping the teacher occupied with them.

A teacher should not permit herself to become the referee in such quarrels. If the fight is in the classroom, the teacher and the class will need to know how to respond. Together in weekly group discussions, they need to decide what procedures and policies to follow. One such solution could be to ask the fighters to leave the room and not return until they have settled their fight. It has been found that quarrels stop very soon when there is no interference from adults. As soon as children realize that the teacher has complete confidence in their ability to manage their own affairs, they lose incentive for this kind of disturbance.

> During a sixth grade study period, Judy and Jolie got into a biting, wrestling, hitting fight. The teacher looked up from working with a group of children and said, "If you girls wish to fight, go out into the hall. We are busy here." The other children continued working. There was a shocked silence between the two girls, then sort of a giggle as they quietly went back to work.

As to the time it takes for children to come to an agreement, one will find that the majority return almost immediately. Children, especially young children, take little if any pleasure in staying out of class when they are sent out by the teacher. In most cases, they feel foolish. Sometimes they ask to be permitted to remain in class.

Many teachers would hesitate to let a fight go on. They think that

229

a child may get hurt, particularly when a weaker child is beaten down by a bully. They worry, "Doesn't he need the protection of the teacher and does the school not have the responsibility to prevent a child from getting hurt?"

This question deserves careful scrutiny. Regardless of the vigilance of the teacher, children can get hurt while she is looking in another direction. The chances are reduced when the children learn to settle their own fights, particularly when they begin to understand the reason why they fight.

In the next class discussion, the teacher may discuss the reason why children fight. Fighting could be a means of seeking attention, power, or revenge. Some children fight because the situation (or life) seems unfair, they feel threatened, or they seek superiority.

ANGER

Anger enables the child to express his objections with the end result of fighting in some form. For many, fighting is the only way to resolve a conflict. Some children prefer anger and fighting, and its message, "No one is going to push me around," rather than settling conflicts without fighting or giving in.

Bullying is a familiar form of fighting. It grows under forceful and punitive discipline. The child may think he has the right to do as he pleases and will punish anyone who gets in his way.

Provoking to be abused is a frequent stimulus for a fight. If the child is hurt, this proves his conviction that life is cruel and unfair.

There is also the youngster who provokes another child, uses his fists and then comes running to the teacher for protection (after he has gotten in his licks) before the second child retaliates.

THE GALLANT CHILD—HELPING OTHERS IN DISTRESS

Quite often children become involved in fights that are none of their concern. A child may receive praise for his willingness to help others. In some instances, he may be told to mind his own business next time, but rarely will he be helped to understand the true motives behind his gallant behavior.

When questioned by the teacher, such a child may reply, "I pounded Harry because I saw him hit Mike." He feels not only justified in his action, but expects that the others will look at him with admiration for having done a good deed, and "hasn't he stuck his own neck out in order to protect somebody else?"

Should we discourage children from helping others who are in distress? Should the child receive no recognition for having stuck out his neck in order to help somebody else? That would depend on the situation or his goal. As previously stressed (See "Goals of Misbehav-

230

ior," p. 186), each child and each situation is unique and should be evaluated in its own light. If we do not recognize the quest for power when he plays the gallant rescuer, we may only encourage his mistaken goal by approval and encouragement. How can a teacher help him to understand that his goal is wrong? By pointing out his true aim, not at the moment, but in the class discussion.

> During group discussion, the teacher said, "I wonder if Larry is interested only in helping the other child. Let's examine my notes and see when Larry got involved in other people's fights. He was in three fights two weeks ago, two fights last week, and this is the second time he tried to help somebody this week and got into a fight. What do you think? Could Larry have had another reason for getting into these fights?"
>
> Through a process of leading questions, the group suddenly recognized Larry's goal which was to be in a revered position, receiving admiration from everyone for being the great hero. The teacher pointed out to Larry that these are the only times when he wanted to do something for others. For instance, the other day, Larry bought three taffy apples for himself when the high school girls came around to sell them. Yet, Sam, for whom he "risked himself in a fight" could not afford to buy one. Larry never thought of sharing his apples with Sam. The group also reminded Larry of the time that he twisted Sam's wrist until Sam cried, which showed how little he really liked Sam.

Let us consider Larry's situation and some possible consequences. If the fighting usually occurred after school, then the logical thing is for Larry to stay about ten minutes after the other children have been dismissed. They are already home or have such a head start that Larry would not come in contact with them. On the other hand, if the fighting occurs mostly during recess time, then perhaps Larry should remain in his classroom. Another solution would be for Larry to remain by the teacher's side during recess time for several days.

Boys Cannot Touch Girls. A common and frequent type of quarreling is that between boys and girls in which the girls usually insist they have been picked on. Of course, in this case, as in the previous one, no one takes the blame. It is always the other who started the fight. Upon careful observation, we may find that the girls, having been brought up to believe that their sex protects them from being hit by boys, frequently provoke them to a point where even an angel would lash out. The girls abuse and dare the boys in every possible way, yet, the minute a boy retaliates, the girls come screaming and crying, and demand that the teacher consider "their rights as women," namely, protection and revenge.

231

Juliana is a typical example. Hardly a day passed when she did not complain to the teacher that a boy hit or pushed her for no reason. When the boy accused her of having provoked the fight, she denied it vehemently, always demanding the teacher punish the boy. When the group discussed this problem during their discussion period, she carried on and demanded, "Won't you punish him, he is not supposed to touch a girl." References to "girls shouldn't be touched by boys" made the teacher suspicious. She decided to observe Juliana more carefully when the children were out on the playground. Not long after when the class went out for recess, the following incident took place. As soon as the class reached the playground, Juliana gathered a few girls around her, and instructed them on the positions and the strategy they must take. Next, she placed herself close to a boy who was playing ball with the others, snatched his cap, ran off with it, and threw it to one of her accomplices who in turn threw the cap to the next girl in line. When the cap reached the last girl, she threw it over the fence. All this time, the boy was frantically trying to retrieve his cap. Juliana was hysterical with laughter. When the cap was thrown into the street, the boy demanded that Juliana go and get it. She told him to get it himself and kicked him in the shin. In the meantime, the other boys had gathered around the two children. They too demanded that Juliana should get the cap. One of the boys took her by her arm and tried to lead her toward the gate, she, in turn, pushed him so hard that he fell. During this time, she continued laughing and telling the boy that he can do nothing to her. When the boy picked himself up, he knocked Juliana down. This was the signal for which she was waiting. She came running to the teacher, sobbing, showing her dirty dress, and insisting on having been unfairly attacked by the boys. When the teacher told Juliana that she had watched the incident from beginning to end, and that she had seen how Juliana went about organizing her group of girls, and how she had provoked the boys, Juliana replied, "Anyway, they are not supposed to touch me. My mother told me so, and I will tell my mother how they beat me up."

In Juliana's personal folder, the teacher found evidence that she had been in similar fights before. However, none of her teachers had recognized Juliana's real problem. One of her teachers wrote, "Juliana is a sweet girl and is generally liked by the girls. She is not accepted by the boys. They often hurt her." Another teacher had written, "Juliana's social adjustment is generally good. She gets along better with girls. The boys like to tease her because she is a pretty girl."

232

Juliana's is not an isolated case. Many girls tease and provoke the boys, hoping that the latter will not retaliate because "boys are not supposed to touch girls." If they get away with it, it gives them the feeling of being superior, of having special rights and privileges. If the boys retaliate, the girls capitalize on getting the sympathy of those who share their belief, be they children, parents, or teachers. Frequently, a teacher will tell a boy that a gentleman never touches a woman, no matter what she does.

This situation can be changed only if the children are helped to understand the meaning of democratic living, of what is and what is not fair. During class discussions, Juliana began to understand the reasons for her behavior:

> When the teacher asked the class how many of them thought that it was right and fair that boys should never strike a girl "no matter what she does," none of the boys raised their hand, and out of seventeen girls, only two raised theirs. In further questioning like, "Why isn't it fair?" the class began to consider and to talk about democratic living—equal rights, fairness, respect for others, and the like. (See "Democratic Classroom," p. 172.) Juliana participated little in the discussion, but when she was asked what she thought of giving everybody the same rights, and of the unfairness of hurting others, she admitted that she too thought it wrong. When the teacher raised the question why Juliana took such great pleasure in making the boys angry, most children understood Juliana's goal. Some said, "She wants to make herself important and show the boys that she has more power than they." Some said, "She gets a lot of attention from everybody, the whole class and the teacher." A boy added, "And from her mother because she will go home and complain that we are after her for no reason, and then her mother will think she is right." Juliana's best girl friend said, "Juliana wants people to feel sorry for her and then everybody will be nice to her."

> Juliana, it may be interesting to know, was very small for her age; many people thought she was in first grade when she was already in third grade. She was also the second of five children, all girls. She told the teacher that every time her mother was expecting a child, the parents hoped it would be a boy and each time they were disappointed. Since having a boy was of so great importance to her parents and since her wish to be a boy was so strong, she was going to show everybody that she could be better than any boy by raising her status to an "untouchable," something the boys could not claim. She felt, indeed, very sorry for herself.

FIGHTING THROUGH HYPERSENSITIVITY

A fight is not necessarily of a physical nature. Some children express their hostility in their display of hypersensitivity to any situation in which they feel slighted, criticized, or simply one that they cannot dominate. This hostility expresses itself in continuous silent withdrawal, crying, clamming up to a point where a teacher can not get one word out of them, taking on a hurt look, feigning illness as well as other manifestations that should make the teacher feel guilty for "what she has done" to them. In all these manifestations, the child may show unbelievable endurance and will not budge until the teacher makes up to him.

> Claudette is a good example of the child who cries for hours until the teacher comes over to her to wipe her tears away and to tell her, "Now let's forget all about it. I am no longer cross." Claudette buried her head into her arms and whimpered like a hurt dog. It was a painful sound to all in the classroom. For a while, one or the other child would go over to her and try to comfort her. This would only increase Claudette's crying. When asked for the reason for her tears, she would only shake her head without giving any reply. Every now and then, she would look at the teacher imploringly, as if to say, "Be nice to me, see how I suffer."

> Lizzie behaved similarly when the teacher reprimanded her for some misdeed or poor work. After crying for a while without getting the desired sympathy from the teacher, she would slip a note on the teacher's desk that usually read as follows: "I know you don't love me. You love the others but not me. I love you very much. Answer immediately if you love me or not. I get a headache when I cry." Or she would say, "I loved you yesterday but today I don't. You are mean to me."

> Michael retaliates by sulking and throwing angry looks at the teacher. He refuses to talk and actually holds his hand over his mouth to make sure that no word will escape him. Neither teacher nor classmate can get a sound out of him. He may easily keep this up for several days. Yet, during all this time, he may be doing his work, even finish in time, something he normally does not do. However, he refuses to let the teacher check the work. He also refuses to join in the oral reading.

What can a teacher do to help such children? In the first place, the teacher must recognize that all of them are fighting and trying to punish the teacher by their method of nonparticipation and by their silent accusation of being rejected. The worst thing a teacher can do is to get into a power contest with these children, insisting that the child do as he is told or else. If any consequences are to be applied, then they must be those of leaving the child alone, not scolding and not punishing. The child, however, must be helped to understand the reason for his behavior, what he is trying to achieve. In most cases, such children use their hypersensitivity in order to control through their passivity. If they have been successful in making their parents submit to them by applying this method, they will try the same trick at school. The group can be of greater help to such children than the teacher.

The teacher may ask the class if anyone could tell why Michael or Lizzie are crying and refuse to talk.

Child: "Because he is angry."

Teacher: "But why is he angry?"

Child: "He is angry because he had to do over his spelling."

Another Child: "He is angry because you don't pay attention to him."

Teacher: "Do you really believe that doing over his spelling would bother him so much? Could there be another reason?"

Child: "Maybe he thinks that if he cries long enough, he won't have to do it over again."

Teacher: "You mean because there won't be any time then?"

Child: "No, because you will feel sorry for him and you will tell him to stop crying and not to do the work if it makes him so unhappy."

Teacher: "How does he try to make me feel?"

Some Child: "Bad."

Teacher: "Would you say that he tries to make me feel guilty, as though I did something wrong?"

Child: "That's right."

Teacher: "How does he try to make all of you feel?"

Child: "He wants us to feel sorry for him."

Teacher: "What else is he trying to get out of this, besides not to do the work? What did Lucy do several times when she went over to Michael."

Some Child: "She spent a lot of time with him trying to cheer him up. He probably wants this from you and he wants to get attention."

Teacher: "Can you tell me why anyone would want to make another feel guilty when he is really the one who is guilty of noncooperation?"

Child: "Because we want the other to feel bad and make up to us."

Teacher: "Make up how?"

Child: "Make up by letting him do what he wants."

235

Sooner or later somebody will hit the real motive behind this kind of behavior. When the teacher asks Michael if it could be true that he wants to have his way all the time, he may deny it, but his facial expression usually betrays him. If the conversation is conducted in a friendly manner, Michael, or any child, will usually admit that this is the true reason.

> The teacher may then speak directly to Michael and say, "You see Michael, you don't know why you behave that way and I don't blame you. However, I would like to show you how unfair you are and how much you hurt yourself and others. I treated you like I do everybody else. If I didn't, then you may justly think that I don't care about you. I do care very much. By not letting me help you, you sort of push me away from you. I know you don't mean to do that, but if you think, you'll realize that's what happens. Unless, you would rather I'd not bother with you and allow you to make all the mistakes."

It is very seldom that a young child will accept such a proposition. He may want to eat the cake and to keep it at the same time, This too, must be pointed out to him in a friendly manner. He must see the impossibility of this. If the child continues to sulk, however, the teacher may tell him to take a day or two and think about the discussion. There should be no further discussion or attention given to the child's crying until he, of his own accord, changes his behavior. At this point, such a child should receive praise from the teacher. This is the time to give him the desired attention. The teacher may say to the class, "Isn't it wonderful that Michael did not immediately agree to everything we said, but took time to think it over and to come to a decision. Michael, I am so happy that you have decided to be one of us. And you know, it takes a great deal of courage to admit that one did the wrong thing. I am very proud of you."

JEALOUSY

Jealousy is closely related to the need for excelling. The jealous child feels inferior to others, especially to those who get recognition and attention because of their good academic performance. He compares himself with the others, never being able to measure up to them. This may be the cause of fighting and punishing those he considers superior.

> Cecil was such a child. Every time he performed poorly, regardless whether in a subject matter, sports, or games, he retaliated by beating up the child who was ahead of him. The children were aware of this, all but Cecil. He argued that during the game, the other had cheated or made fun of him. He could never admit that he was at fault. Finally, the group appointed a student to record

236

Cecil's performance in class. Thus, they could show him that in each case he punished the child who had been a little more successful in an area on that particular day. When confronted with these facts, Cecil had no argument. He claimed that he did not realize that this is what he always did. He was right, he did not realize it until that moment. Gradually, his fighting subsided.

Not every case brings results as quickly and comparatively smoothly as that of Cecil. Some children require longer and more intense work. In almost all cases, the child will change his method of obtaining his goal as soon as his behavior is mirrored to him. As we succeed in convincing the child that we are interested in him personally, that we accept him for what he is and not for what he is trying to be, he may change his negative approach to a positive one, namely that of trust, cooperation, and enjoyment of being a member of a group with equal rights.

This does not mean that we should discourage children from wanting and from trying to better themselves. On the contrary, children need constant encouragement and recognition for every step they take, but they must be helped to enjoy going forward for its own sake and not as a means of controlling or surpassing others.

THE CHILD WHO MUST BE FIRST

The child who must be first is another form of subtle fighting that is seldom recognized by adults. One child is good in order to show others how bad they are in comparison. Another child is jealous and ambitious in order to be first. A child never allows himself to use his own judgment and act on it, if he thinks that it might displease the teacher. We may expect that sooner or later such a child will stumble into situations that cannot be controlled by him, then his hostilities may come to the fore. The course of aggression will depend on the child's goals and the amount of success he has had with similar behavior patterns at other times, when things did not go according to his expectations.

The following example may serve to illustrate such behavior:

Mary was an excellent student from the very first day she entered school. She was known to all of the teachers as "the exceptionally bright girl." She was the envy of many children who openly admitted that they would like to be like her. At home, she was placed on a pedestal; nothing was ever denied to her because of the honor she brought to the family. Mary was always friendly. She never refused to help another child, but she made no special effort to make close friends. During recess, she preferred to stay in class and read or do some other work. She did not refuse to go out when the

237

teacher asked her to, but each day she requested again to be allowed to stay in and work. She had few friends outside of school. Her mother insisted that she join the Brownies, so she did. However, she never talked about her experiences there as did the other girls. The children expected and accepted that Mary's work was always perfect. They talked about her to their parents, and it was not unusual that some parent would ask the teacher to point out that wonderful child to them.

One can imagine the shock every one experienced when, one day, Mary threw a tantrum when she missed three words in a spelling test. There were two other students who had perfect scores. First, Mary tore up her paper, then she proceeded to tear up the spelling book, throwing the pages at the other two students. She screamed that the others cheated, that she was always the best, and always will be. It was impossible to quiet her down. Since she was always so good and cooperative, this was a unique situation for the teacher who felt self-conscious for having to insist that Mary leave the room until she calmed down.

Mary did not understand any more than did her schoolmates what had happened to her and why. This was a situation where teachers who lack the understanding of children's goals, might have said, "The child must have been ill; she was certainly not herself."

Mary needed an understanding attitude from the teacher. She needed to be helped to understand that she was concerned with the attention she received in being first, and if that was impossible, she got it through her tantrum. Apparently, she felt secure only as long as she occupied this position, and she felt entitled to it. She had to be helped to understand that one did not need to be on top in order to have a place. She also had to see the terrible strain she had put on herself by having to be ahead at all times and at all costs.

Later, when this was discussed in the group, not just as Mary's problem, but one found in many children and adults, one could actually observe the relief on Mary's face. During the discussion, the teacher helped the children see and understand that strong competition is really a form of pushing others down, because we want always to be in a superior position.

> Teacher: "You have been so wonderful in understanding the reasons for our behavior, I thought that it might be a good idea to talk over why people who are always very good in everything, suddenly show anger and sometimes even meanness."
>
> First Child: "Well, if somebody is always good in everything and if then he isn't, he thinks it's unfair to him."

238

Teacher: "What is unfair?"

Child: "It is unfair that he should not do well if he is always good."

Teacher: "Do you all agree with this?"

Second Child: "I think that if a child is always good in everything, he thinks that he will always be good in everything, and then if he isn't, he is mad."

Teacher: "At whom is he mad?"

Child: "I guess he is mad at those who did better?"

Teacher: "Could he be mad at somebody else also?"

Third Child: "He might be mad at himself why he didn't do any better."

First Child: "He might be mad at the teacher because she marked him 'wrong.'"

Teacher: "Do you think a good child would be satisfied if the teacher marked him right even though he is wrong?"

Third Child: "Maybe not, but he is probably mostly mad at himself to have made mistakes."

Teacher: "Do you think that a person must be good at all times, and that he must never make a mistake?"

Many Children: "No."

Teacher: "Let us think for a moment, why would somebody always want to be the best in everything?"

One Child: "Because everybody likes you better and your mother sometimes buys you something if you are the best. My mother gave me a dollar when I had a good report card."

Another Child: "If you are the best in everything, you think that you are smarter than all the others and that nobody can do better than you."

Teacher: "And if somebody does better, how do you think such a person may feel? I mean in addition to being angry."

One Child: "He may feel scared that now he is 'no good' any more."

Another Child: "He may feel that now people won't like him as much any more."

Teacher: "Yes, I think that this may be true, that anyone who is used to being first all the time may feel that making a mistake is a threat to him. Can anyone explain why this is threatening?"

Child: "Well, it is like you threaten somebody that if he doesn't do what he is supposed to do, he will be punished."

Teacher: "That is right, such a person is afraid that people may not look up to him as much as before and may not admire him as much. Can you tell me how this might affect him at home? Let's think of how most parents behave when their child is always the best and how they might react if their child is not the best any more."

One Child: "The parents are proud of you, but when you are not the best any more they are not proud of you."

Another Child: "I don't think that this is true because if you are not the best that doesn't mean that you are bad. Besides, you may not be the best one day, but be the best the next day."

Teacher: "I am so glad that you brought this up, Gloria. Nobody can be the best always, and nobody should be because no one else would have a chance to be 'best' oncè also. But do we really have to be best?" Let's see, if we want to be best, then how do we want the others to be?"

Child: "Bad."

Teacher: "Perhaps, not bad, but something else."

Other Child: "We want the others to be less good than we are."

Teacher: "Yes, we want the others to be worse. We don't feel happy as long as somebody else does better than we do. Isn't that foolish, especially when we do quite well? Just give yourself a chance to do the best you can, and you will see that you won't mind if somebody else does better than you do once in a while. At home, too, you will be happier if you don't always have to show how bad your brother or sister is. Why don't you try it and see for yourself."

The discussion may be resumed after a few days. The teacher may ask the children if they have thought any further about the discussion they had the other day. If any children raise their hands, she may ask them to state their conclusions. She may even casually ask Mary what her opinion was of this discussion.

A teacher may ask a show of hands of children who threaten their parents that they will drop in their schoolwork if the parents do not give in to some of their demands. Hands always go up. The teacher may ask children to tell the class how they have threatened their parents and how it has paid off.

This gives the teacher the opportunity to show how they use punishment in an unfair manner. It is also a chance to talk about the merits of learning for ones own sake. A teacher may ask, "For whom do you study, Jim?" Invariably he will answer, "For myself." The teacher may then ask, "Do you really? Just think, if you fall behind in your work because your parents wouldn't let you watch television, whom do you punish?" It is seldom that a child does not see the point.

It helps if the teacher can work with the parents to help them to understand the importance of changing their attitude toward the child's schoolwork and toward curbing their own ambitions. Behind every overambitious child we will find overambitious parents, or one parent whose attitude toward being first has instilled distorted values about achievement. It becomes a question of helping the parents as well as the child in changing this attitude.

The teacher may ask the class if they can think of other ways children sometimes punish others, without mentioning specific names or situations. Together, they may point out that sometimes children punish others who do better in tests or better in general work; and that they punish other children because they have toys or other things they themselves do not have. The child to whom this applies takes in the conversation. One can notice a pensive look on his face, and yet nobody is talking about him specifically. At another time, when a child is guilty of such a misdeed, the teacher may ask him, "Do you remember the discussion the class had about why we sometimes punish others? Could it be that you lashed out at Susan because she had a higher score than you did in arithmetic?"

Again, we must remember to show the child that he is not being evaluated by the score he makes on tests, but by what he is as a person. We must encourage him to do well in his work, especially if we know that he is capable. But we must discourage the kind of competition that leads to the goal of having to be better than the other or else learning is not worthwhile.

STEALING, LYING, AND SWEARING

Stealing occurs frequently among children of all ages; among the poor as well as among the wealthy; among those who come from culturally esteemed parents as well as those who come from culturally deprived families.

Most children have stolen at one time or another. A child's attitude toward stealing depends on the culture in which he grew up, on customs, traditions, religion, and training. In some groups, stealing by children is not considered as delinquent, especially in communities where people are poor. If a child steals food from the market and brings it home, he may be praised for the act. When a child steals in our society, we are shocked and frightened about his character development and may feel honor-bound to return the stolen goods. We all know of a number of cases where children have been severely punished, humiliated in front of others, deprived of food or special

241

privileges because they were caught stealing a nickel out of mother's purse or a candy bar from a store.

Respect for property is a product of social conventions that have existed for centuries. We are not born with the inherent sense that "what is mine does not belong to someone else" or the reverse.

Respect for property has to be learned. Children who have a great need to own property often find it difficult to respect the property rights of others. A child learns about what is "mine" when another child takes one of his toys. After a child learns about "this is mine," he becomes aware of and can make the distinction between mine and yours. Sometime after this distinction is made, the child recognizes that he cannot have everything he wants. Shortly after this, the child learns a lesson in elementary economics, which is, if you want something, you have to pay for it. He then knows what is fair, although he may act against his better judgement.

Owning property and enjoying property rights are two different things. Usually we give a child a toy, a record player, or some other object, and then proceed to tell him what to do with it. How can we expect the child to respect property rights of others if we do not respect his rights?

At school, we use equipment and other supplies as a class, and everyone in the room uses the record player, a game, balls, and the like. The manner in which they are used, and the condition they are kept, affects everyone, and the group may have somethng to say about how equipment is used.

> One day Marie was marking on a new table in our room. Mike said, "Teacher, Marie is marking on your table." I replied, "My table, it's no more my table than it is your table or Marie's table. The table belongs to this school and more particularly, to this classroom, so it is our table." A few minutes later, another child started marking on the table. At this point, Marie turned to him and said, "Well, I'm not going to clean your old marks off this table." So they both cleaned off the table together.

The above example is a subtle lesson in respect for property and property rights. The more we let children assume responsibility for property, for property rights, and for their actions, the more they will respect property in general.

Learning to respect the belongings of others must be developed in the child as it is an essential part of growing up. It must be taught through the building of proper attitudes, of appreciation for others and their rights, by training not only what is right and wrong, but the willingness to do what is right.

Every teacher has had experiences with students who have taken possessions of others. In most cases, these children were reported to the principal and to the parents. A conference generally followed during which the child was faced with the facts, and he was told by the school authorities that if this behavior were repeated, he would face grave consequences. Often, the mother cries, assures the principal and the teacher that this has never happened before, that she does not know from whom her child learned such bad behavior, and that he will suffer the consequences when she gets him home. Next the teacher writes up the episode and places it in the child's folder as a constant reminder to the future teachers to be on the alert.

> Scooter arrived in my room during the middle of his fifth-grade year. In his folder was a page listing six books that he had returned to the school that fall. These books were second and third grade readers he had kept at home for a year or more. This report was placed in his folder so future teachers would know that Scooter was not to be trusted with books. The fact that he had later returned the books was insignificant.
>
> In checking Scooter's reading level, it was found that he operated on a low third-grade reading level, below the reading level of his classmates. I gave him a series of low ability, high interest reading material. During the next year and a half that he was in my room, he checked out and returned every book..

This example may be of help to a teacher who has a child who is already a delinquent and who may need more help. In most cases, especially with the young child, stealing is an expression of the child's mistaken goal, of his right to have his own way, to defeat the demands of others, or even of his desire to get even.

When a person says, "My child steals," his statement tells us nothing. We know that people steal for a variety of reasons. Consequently, we need to look at stealing from various angles. What prompts it? How is it reinforced? What are the consequences of the act? Is there a feeling of being poor and deprived? How does the child view himself? What is his background? How is he in school? How can we help him to find his place in the social order? We also need to know and recognize the difference between the first timer and the habitual thief. We need to look for the child's theft pattern.

> A group of preadolescent boys developed a clever technique of how to smuggle books out of a public library. Their justification was that the library had enough money to replace the books. Superficially, it looked as if these boys would not know the difference between honesty and theft. For them, stealing seemed to be proper. Did they know the difference between mine and yours? Apparently

not. When they were asked what they would do if somebody stole something from them, they all had the same reply. They would not tolerate such a thing and *get* the thief. In other words, the boys knew that one should not steal, but they had the right to disregard such rules when it suited them.

In looking for the reason for stealing, it is well to keep in mind the different types of stealing.

A mother came to school one afternoon to tell me about Tom. She burst into tears and told me that Tom had been picked up by the juvenile authorities for shoplifting. As she continued to sob, she also blurted out that her husband was in jail for stealing.

Here we have an example of a child who imitated the masculine pattern of his family. Children pattern themselves after impressive parental figures, learning takes place easily by watching others. It is impossible to say, "Do as I say, not as I do."

Miriam was a freshman in high school and came from a financially secure family. For several months, Miriam had been shoplifting from various stores. She never wore the articles, but merely stuffed them in her dresser or closet. Her friends thought Miriam was the greatest, because she could snitch things without being caught.

Miriam had been dropping hints about shoplifting for several weeks. She would say, "I saw the prettiest sweater, I thought about taking it, but I didn't." "Oh, Mother, they have the best smelling perfume at the store, would you believe it, I just swiped a bottle of it." After making these kinds of statements, she and her Mother would laugh the incident off as though it were a big joke. When this tactic did not work, Miriam left some of the stolen articles on the dining room table where her Mother could not miss them. At this point, they had a talk and came in for help.

Here we find a girl who stole because she wanted attention from her family, peer recognition, and "for kicks." Now the parents pay more attention to Miriam. Before the father was busy making money and the mother was a professional, and neither of them took much time to enjoy their daughter.

A 4-year-old stole a piece of licorice from the store. No one was looking when he took it from the shelf.

This child has not as yet learned to accept property rights. He merely saw a piece of candy, wanted to eat it, and did so.

Bernard was a second grader who stole money only from his mother. His mother quite often left change in her coat pocket. Ber-

244

nard would sneak nickels, dimes, and quarters. His mother noticed this and told him that "he was mother's bad boy." She no longer left change in her coat, and he started taking money from her purse. Mother would chastise him saying, "You bad boy, you have been in mother's purse again. How much did you take this time? Now you won't do that again will you?" She would hide her purse in different places and tell him that he could not find her purse now. But he always did!

This is an example of a child who has learned to defeat his mother. His mother reinforced Bernard's actions by constantly giving him opportunities to outsmart her.

These examples show different types of situations. It is impossible to put all these children into the same category and to treat them in the same manner. One child was following the parental model, a girl stole to get attention, a toddler took a piece of candy to have his own way, and another child to defeat his mother.

The act of taking something should be examined differently, not as black or white, or as good or bad. It can mean many things to the child. Stealing has strong consequences, and we need to substitute other behaviors for our customary reinforcement and to show the child alternatives for finding his place in life and for feeling important.

What other ways are there of getting peer recognition? What other ways are there to deal with family conflicts? What are other ways of providing gratification, and how can we reinforce different behavior patterns? In each of the preceding cases, the answers would be different, and dealing with the child should be different.

Briefly, the usual reason for stealing is for kicks. Stealing for kicks includes peer recognition and status, irritation of a parent or other adult, a means to defeat them, to get what one wants regardless of the consequences. It gratifies the desire for excitement, prevalent in our children and youth. However, stealing may also be a means of survival.

One of the most common motives for theft among children is to bribe others with gifts to win their love and affection. The child wants to be the center of attention and has a strong urge to make himself noticed. Since it seems impossible for him to achieve his goal in positive or useful ways, he tries another.

Harold stole money in order to buy cigarettes for a group of somewhat older boys who would not accept him otherwise. When his father discovered this situation, he made Harold smoke an entire package of cigarettes, lighting one from the other, until the boy was so sick he could not sit up. However, this experience did not cure him. His need to belong and to be accepted by the group of older boys was stronger than his fear of punishment, so he continued to steal for them.

Harold was only 10 years old, but he was tall and broad and looked like 14. He was embarrassed when he had to tell people that he was only in the third grade. He had failed twice, and was still a poor student, despite his considerable intelligence. The children in his class ignored him, mostly because he kept away from them and acted aloof. He boasted about his friends who were already in the seventh and eighth grades, and often told them about their meetings and escapades.

Fortunately, this came to the teacher's attention only a few weeks after school started. The parents were cooperative. They soon realized that they had made some grave mistakes in dealing with the problem, and changed their attitude and tactics. They were helped to understand that more than anything else, this boy needed to feel that he is somebody, that he had a place not only in school, but at home as well. With the help of the parents and the classroom group, Harold no longer felt the need for the friendship of the older boys. He became an integral member of his class, and there was no longer any need to steal.

In the next example, we can see how a child's stealing and untruthfulness in general is an expression of the struggle for power over the mother. We can also see the child's desire to punish the mother for what she had done. When the girl discovered the power she held through stealing and lying, she used these means to reduce her mother to helplessness and despair.

At the age of 10, Marsha was already a proficient thief. She stole mostly from five-and-ten-cent stores, taking candy, cosmetics, and knickknacks. She distributed the items among her friends, especially the candy. She hid the knickknacks in her bed, playing with them and fondling them in the evening.

Eventually, Marsha was caught a few times, but in each case she was allowed to go free after getting a long lecture from the owner of the store or the salespeople. When the teacher learned about Marsha's escapades, and when this was first discussed in class, Marsha not only laughed, but called the other children stupid for not availing themselves of many commodities and goodies that were so easily accessible to them. "What are you afraid of?" she said, "Even if the police should catch you, they would never do anything to a child. They may punish the parents and hold them responsible, but they will let you go free. Besides, it is loads of fun to fool the salesgirls, and when you pretend that you are sorry and you cry, they even let you keep the things you took."

Marsha was an only child of middle-aged parents. She was adored by them and spoiled. When she was 5 years old, her father died in a car accident, after which her mother clung to Marsha and gave in to the child even more than before. When she was 8 years old, Marsha's mother fell in love with a man who did not take too well to the girl. He was willing to marry the mother only if Marsha were to live away from home.

Thus, Marsha was placed in a boarding school. Here she became the despair of the staff, for she was not only aggressive, disobedient, and hostile, but also extremely cunning and shrewd, evading all problems, and inducing other children to do her dirty work, so when discovered it seemed as though they were more guilty than she. Several times, when her mother called for her during the weekend, Marsha hid and could not be found. A few times, she ran away from her mother after they had left the institution, and the mother became desperate, unable to find her daughter, and fearing the worst.

Marsha was helped after some very trying months. She was helped mainly through group discussions during which she began to understand the dynamics of her behavior, the goal she pursued, and the means she used to attain it. The members of the group, understanding her problem, reached out to her and so did the teacher. As her attitude and behavior improved, she was better accepted by her stepfather. Marsha became much easier to live with and eventually was able to leave the boarding school.

An unhappy child, deprived of the pleasures that most children have nowadays, such as a few cents to buy candy, or go to the movies, or to buy trinkets and toys, may take the money from wherever it is easily available. They feel entitled to get more than they have.

Debbie, the oldest of five children, who came from an economically deprived family, and who felt that her mother disliked her, was constantly bringing presents to the teacher and to the children in class. It turned out that Debbie, when leaving the class to go to the washroom, searched the pockets of all the garments in the cloakroom, and took whatever she found. The children discovered this act of hers long before the teacher knew anything about it. They tried to protect Debbie, knowing her terror of her mother and that she was an unhappy child. Debbie pleaded with the children not to tell anyone because then her mother would find out and would surely kill her.

It turned out that Debbie's fear of her mother, as well as her feeling of being rejected was justified. In spite of letters from the

247

teacher and from the school authorities, the mother refused to come to school. The teacher decided to pay this mother a visit.

When the teacher arrived, she heard terrible screams, which she recognized as Debbie's. Entering the house, she saw a woman running after Debbie, hitting her with the buckle end of a belt. The mother was punishing the child because she caught Debbie in the act of using her powder. The mother told the teacher what a liar and a thief Debbie was, how she could not be trusted, what a disgrace Debbie brings upon the family, and how she would like Debbie to live with her paternal grandparents, who liked Debbie. She did not have one good word to say about her daughter.

Here we see a child who was spoiled by her grandparents, who gave Debbie the feeling that she could get whatever she wanted and also that her mother was unfair. Debbie provoked her mother. She continued to do as she pleased, defeating her mother's demands, and also those of society. She was able to get support for her actions by making others feel sorry for her, as she did with her grandparents.

The teacher was unable to obtain cooperation from the parents as the mother refused to listen, and the father was working two jobs in order to support the family. There was only the group to come to the rescue. As in the situation with Marsha, the children, through their understanding and acceptance of Debbie, helped to bring about a drastic change in her behavior. The children did not ignore her when she walked home from school, as they did before. Many invited Debbie to their homes and gave her recognition whenever they saw a realistic occasion. This changed Debbie's life to a great extent, and nothing was ever missing from the class for the rest of the year.

Stealing is sometimes an attempt to escape a stronger person or a devious way to catch up to him. Some children steal for excitement and for the satisfaction of getting the better of somebody, especially if this person is superior to them, like a parent, a teacher, or a storekeeper. The child's goal is the attainment of superiority and power.

Ben was an 18-year-old high school senior whose father was the president of a large corporation. From the age of 14, Ben had been stealing cars and driving them until apprehended. His father would move in and pay damages, if any, and was able to keep Ben's record clean. At the age of 17, Ben stole cars and drove them to another city where he sold them. His father continued to make restitution, and there was never any scandal involving his family. Finally, Ben peddled a stolen car in another state, this became a federal offense.

In conferences with his father, several people suggested that he allow Ben to suffer the consequences or at least let Ben sit it out in jail, for three or four days. The father was most reluctant to do this, but finally agreed. Ben had to wait four days in jail before his father bailed him out. This ended Ben's car stealing career.

It has been noted that acts of destructiveness quite often accompany the act of stealing. Destructiveness is usually a kind of hate or revenge in action. It also brings excitement. Many children who have suffered an injustice or feel slighted, may want to take revenge on others by being unfair.

A group of high school girls from well-to-do families organized a social club outside of the school activities. The prerequisite to membership was the shoplifting of an expensive piece of clothing from one of the better stores. The girls went to the stores in twos or threes to observe that the new recruit did not pay for the merchandise.

After initiation into the club, the requirements were that several articles were to be stolen each week and brought to the "bonfire party" every Saturday. At this time, all articles were burned and plans were made for the following week. Under no circumstances were the articles to be worn, given away, or used in any manner.

These girls were brought up with little or no supervision from their parents. Usually, the only times they were really noticed was when they were in the way or when some social event was coming up, then the parents worried about whether their daughters would have escorts or made arrangements so their daughters would be included.

Generally, the goal in stealing is to enrich oneself and to feel important by possessing more. There is also the feeling of being poor and deprived even if one is wealthy in a material sense.

There are children who steal because they are trained to do so by their parents. Yet neither of them is aware of this fact.

Ronnie was a fifth-grade boy who had been taking the children's milk money. When the teacher mentioned this to the mother during a conference, the mother became unreasonably upset. She insisted on punishing Ronnie in front of the entire class. She said that her husband would beat Ronnie with a stick. All of this time the mother was sobbing bitterly.

Later during a class discussion, Ronnie told the class how he stole tomatoes from a neighbor's garden. When the children asked him why he would do such a dishonest thing, he said that his mother

always sent him to steal from the gardens when neighbors were away from home.

This is not unusual when we consider the number of parents who instruct their children to tell a peddler or bill collector that they are not at home, or to tell lies when someone calls on the telephone, and they do not wish to talk. Also consider the case of Ben's father in bribing the police officers. Under the guise of making things easy for his son, the father was really unable to face what people might think about him as he would lose status.

As mentioned earlier, stealing also includes stealing for survival and has quite a different meaning in some low socioeconomic areas. There are also those people who roam from place to place and steal food as they have no job or no money.

> Ike, an off-beat boy in high school, could hardly wait until he graduated and intended to go on the road until the draft got him, which he did. He cruised the United States, never worked a day and never starved either. He begged food and lodging, slept in empty houses or buildings and stole food.

Most adults become upset if their child steals a nickel or a balloon. Yet how many adults cheat on their income tax or try to smuggle something through customs? Most adults, however, make a distinction between stealing from an individual and stealing from an organization. They are most hesitant to steal from an individual, but think nothing of using the office stamps to mail their two hundred personal Christmas cards. Most children who steal will not make such a distinction, they steal when the opportunity offers itself.

One of the problems we face today is the attitude some store owners take toward petty thievery among children. In the example concerning Marsha, she confidently stated that "They won't do anything to a child." It is very difficult for parents and teachers to train children in morality when it is taken so lightly by people in the community. A child's sense of right and wrong comes from the attitudes of those with whom he is closely associated—first his immediate family and then the community.

Many teachers find themselves in a tough spot when some children in their class complain that something was stolen. Most are inclined to investigate. They feel obliged to find out the culprit. When they have some idea, they struggle to have the child admit the theft and to return what was stolen. Many teachers find it helpful to stay out of such struggles. When they leave it to the children to find the thief, and the missing item, they usually settle the matter by themselves.

LYING

Lying is an intentional falsification of facts, with a purpose. Lying does not occur alone, but usually in conjunction with other types of misbehavior. Many children manage to use a lie successfully. Sometimes it goes with stealing because stealing requires that one get out of the situation somehow.

Children pattern themselves after their parents or other important adults. They may learn to lie from their parents, when they want to escape responsibility or punishment. Sometimes parents perpetuate a family lie in order to make Johnny a good boy, or to preserve the family picture. Children may lie for different purposes: to be left alone, to get attention, to impress or fool others, to get out of a situation, to hurt others, to respond to pressure, to excuse oneself, to reduce one's own anxiety, to make an honest error, to flagrantly lie, or to fantasize. How is a child to distinguish between legitimate and illegitimate lying?

In most cases, adults cannot tell what is true or what is not true. There are whole areas in which we cannot be sure the child is lying or telling the truth. We do not have control over reports, and we have no evidence if we do not observe the behavior. The consequences for lying are so uncertain. Sometimes we punish for telling the truth, and sometimes we reward for lying. Sometimes, too, a parent's concept of a lie or the truth differs considerably from the child's concept.

Severe parents and teachers give children abundant reasons for lying. Untruth is then a simple method to escape unreasonable punishment. A lie would have no meaning unless the truth was felt as dangerous. Children who do not fear to tell the truth, that is, who do not get punished by those who have power, rarely lie. Children will tell the truth if they feel sufficiently strong. Children lie out of fear or out of a need to appear superior in the eyes of others and compensate for their own feelings of inadequacy or inferiority. Here is a detailed case description of a boy, named Jimmy: One day, a boy entered my classroom and asked if I would allow him to "show and tell" something to my class. I granted my permission, thinking that he had to make an announcement. To my surprise, he pulled out a rock from his pocket and proceded with a very interesting and competent lecture on gold mining. He said that he had visited several gold mines and that he had made a thorough study of the subject.

> Comments: **Our first impression of this boy, would, no doubt be, that here is a kid with a lot of guts and self-assurance, interrupting a teacher in what she was doing. In spite of the interruption, we may be inclined to admire him for his competency and for sharing his knowledge with the entire class. However, the teacher, trained to**

examine motivation of behavior and to analyze the goal and purpose the child had set for himself, would immediately recognize that this child was taking the stage in order to be the center of attention.

There are two forms of attention children may seek. Some children, who do not yet believe in their ability to gain a place among their peers without the support of an adult, will seek the attention of the adult. Others are primarily concerned with getting attention from their peers. In this case, we see that this boy wanted attention from the group, and that he had the ability to get it.

He thanked me for giving him permission to talk, adding that, although he took much of my time, it was not lost time, since the students learned something about gold mining.

Comments: This last remark makes us wonder if attention is all that this boy wanted. In a very subtle way, he tried to place the teacher in a position where she had to be thankful to him. There is an element of superiority in this remark, and it may indicate a need for power, although, at this point, it is limited to intellectual level. His approach was well planned and well executed. There was no question in our minds about the intelligence of this boy.

He gave his name as Jimmy, a seventh grade student. The boy aroused my curiosity, and I asked the seventh grade teachers about him. None had him in class, nor did they know who he was.

The following year, Jimmy's name appeared on my class list. I was surprised because I taught a class of children with learning difficulties, covering the subjects from first to fourth grade. At first I thought that perhaps Jimmy's name was put on my list by mistake, since he was supposedly in the seventh grade the previous year. When I checked with his teacher, I discovered that he was only in the fourth grade the previous year; that he had repeated second and third grade, and that he was classified as a nonreader.

Comments: This was our first important clue to Jimmy's problem. Why has this intelligent boy not learned how to read? We know that children who are not actually mentally defective can learn how to read. They may not, and usually do not, understand what they are reading, but they can learn to decipher the printed symbols, and may actually read fluently. Children who do not learn how to read have excellent private reasons for not being willing to learn. We must investigate why this boy does not want to learn how to read. So far, we do not yet have enough information about Jimmy, but we may speculate, and set up tentative hypothesis. Is this boy an overindulged and dependent child? We know that there is a high correlation between dependency of children and their subconscious resistance to reading, unwilling to function independently.

We may also suspect a younger brother or sister who is doing very well in school as a discouraging factor. But, so far we do not know.

I also learned that he had accumulated a great deal of knowledge of various subjects with which he likes to show off whenever he has a chance.

Comments: We can see that this is an ambitious boy. He seeks recognition and status. It would also appear that he is overcompensating with an accumulation of knowledge beyond what the other children have. But where and how does he get it since he can't read?

On the first day of school, when the students introduced themselves, Jimmy made approximately the following statement: "You are probably wondering how come a boy of my age happens to be in this class. All I can say is that I have had bad luck. I was sick most of my life, and I was in and out of hospitals most of the time. As you know, there are no schools in hospitals where one can learn how to read and how to spell. But there were many doctors in the hospital. They used to come and talk to me for hours, and from them I learned more about sickness and medicine and even operations than the nurses did." When the children asked him what was wrong with him, he said that he had a rare disease, unknown to medicine before, and that his case will go down in history. When they asked what symptoms he had, he replied that this was still a secret; that he was not allowed to reveal anything about his illness, but that his case would soon be published, and then everybody will be able to read about it.

Comments: There is now no doubt in our minds that this is an over-ambitious child with a strong drive for superiority. He must be something "special"; being equal, and certainly being inferior to those around him, is unbearable for him. With such a belief he can never accept himself for what he is or gather enough power to move forward on his own. We may assume that he has been exposed to suffer social humiliation over a long period of time. He may have been teased by his classmates and criticised by his family for his lack of progress in school. Perhaps he was also shamed by teachers. Jimmy is trying to overcompensate for these humiliations by carrying the kind of prestige that none others do. He must safeguard himself against further disgrace, even if he has to resort to cunning and lying.

There is something very pathetic in his defensive explanations for his school retardation. We sense his discouragement in spite of his exaggerated report of his importance.

253

If such a child is to regain his self-confidence we must remove any pressure in regard to learning.

It was obvious that Jimmy was trying to get the admiration of the whole class. It was also obvious, to the other children, that he was telling tall tales.

Comments: It is possible that Jimmy is aware of this also, but at this moment he has the center of the stage, which is so important to him.

I asked the class if we could put Jimmy in charge of washing and bandaging minor bruises and cuts, since he knew so much about medicine. They thought that it was a good idea because it would save the school nurse a lot of time.

Comments: the teacher is trying to induce the entire class to give Jimmy the experience of being needed and appreciated. This is her first opportunity to encourage him.

The following day, Jimmy came to class with a white band and a red cross over his arm. I found him surrounded by children, explaining the meaning of the Red Cross, and where and how it started. Again, he was well informed. When I asked him where he gathered so much information, he replied that he had read about it, but he immediately corrected himself, saying that his uncle had told him about it. Evidently he suddenly remembered that only the previous day he had told the class that he could not read. I complimented him, saying that some day he might become a great scientist.

Comments: We can see that on the one hand, Jimmy lacks self-confidence, but on the other hand he is constantly seeking and finding ways to be in the center of attention. We also notice a quality for leadership. This is no small success, having the entire class listen and pay attention to him.

It seems that the teacher succeeded in giving Jimmy a feeling of being welcome. She ignored his deficiencies and in this way opened the door to his feelings of belonging to the class. It was her determination to use every opportunity to show respect for and a belief in him, something he may have never experienced before.

Background

Jimmy was the oldest of three children, and the only boy. His grandparents had immigrated from Greece when his father was a young man.

Comments: This is further important information which will hopefully lead to a better understanding of Jimmy's problem. We know that the position a child holds in the family constellation is a great factor in his personality development. Jimmy is a first born child and a male. This is an important consideration, especially the fact that father and the grandparents came from a patriarchal society, where the man is the boss of the house, and where a male child automatically inherits certain birth rights not granted to girls. Much is expected of this boy.

Our next piece of information is that he is dethroned by a girl. Unfortunately we do not know for how long Jimmy was an only child. However, we may assume that as the first born, he may have been pampered and indulged. Before the first girl was born, he may have been treated like a prince by the entire family. The father became a very successful businessman. He married an American girl—a school teacher. In addition to the immediate family, there lived in the house his mother's brother, a chemist, and his paternal grandparent.

Comments: Jimmy may have been the center of attention of many adults. In a sense, he had more than one set of parents. There is a strong possibility that he was exposed to different influences and values; his grandparents and his father coming from a different cultural background than his mother and his uncle.

The mother was a very sick woman had who spent a great deal of time in the hospital. His two sisters were very close, leaving Jimmy out of their relationship and activities. Both of them were good students. The sister next to him was a grade higher in school than he was.

Comments: Our first assumption seems to be confirmed. Jimmy was defeated by a younger sister who not only dethroned him but also surpassed him in school. This is very threatening to any first born, especially to a boy of Jimmy's cultural background.

The grandparents favored the girls, who were affectionate, helpful in the house, and "smart." They considered Jimmy as stupid, a liar, and lazy.

Comments: Most children find support in their grandparents. Usually, they are indulgent and gentle with their grandchildren, no matter what the children may do. In this case, even the grandparents fail Jimmy.

The father was very much disappointed in his son. He made no secrets of his feelings. He told Jimmy that he would never amount to anything, and he threatened that he would not leave the business to a "good-for-nothing son."

Comments: Here is an abundance of significant data from a psychological point of view. We notice a very definite struggle with father. Both of them are discouraged. The father seems to have given up all hopes of making a MAN out of Jimmy; a man with

255

self-confidence and with a sense of responsibility toward the family and toward the future.

Jimmy may be as overambitious as his father is, and therefore afraid that he will not be able to live up to his standards. He doesn't feel that he is a man. He is a male, but he doesn't compare with his father. This increases his feelings of inadequacy. But he is a first child, and he must maintain his position by all costs. We see that Jimmy cannot compete with his sisters, so he gives up. But he had to find something which will bring attention from his father, and he became a problem child, thus keeping his father continuously busy with him. We now see that he is acting intelligently but for the wrong purpose.

We see that Jimmy is creative and resourceful. He operated with a wide range of purposes. At times he is seeking attention, at times he is involved in a subtle power contest. Surely, he could change his behavior at home and at school if, subconsciously, he would not resist pressure. We may also suspect an element of revenge, especially against his father. From his point of view, opposing his father has brought him success.

During a conference with the father, I learned that he blamed Jimmy's difficulties partly on inheritance from his wife's family, and partly on his wife who "pampered and spoiled the boy." I also found out that Jimmy had a close relationship with his mother; that he spent much time with her, amusing her with funny stories, and that he always cried when she left for the hospital.

Comments: This warrants further speculations. We notice an unusual alliance, namely between mother and son. Probably an alliance against father. We may assume that the father is also disappointed in his wife who is sick so often; that he neglects her. Although we have no details about the home situation, we may assume that Jimmy is siding with her against his father. We don't know to what extent mother may plead with her husband not to be so strict with the boy, thus protecting him. Since she is a sick woman, he may yield to her, but not without resentment against both of them.

It is interesting to note to what extent Jimmy has been a focal point of opposing forces within the family—grandparents, father and sisters against Jimmy and mother. We still don't know the role the uncle plays in this family, but we may assume that he too is on the side of Jimmy.

Jimmy cries when mother goes to the hospital. This is our first indication that he tries to get attention by inducing pity toward himself. But knowing father's values and attitudes toward the male sex, he may only feel more contemptious over such display of weakness.

I learned that Jimmy was always a healthy boy He had never been in a hospital.

Comments: It is possible that Jimmy obtained his information about hospitals from his mother.

His school records showed that he was a show-off since kindergarten, and that he was frequently absent from school.

Comments: Jimmy probably felt that he had no status in class.

Jimmy's Position in My Class

Jimmy was the oldest student in my class. At first, he was very conscious of this fact. He used every opportunity to remind us that he was in this class only because of the years he had spent in the hospital.

Comments: Being that much older than the other children is an unfortunate strike against him. His discouragement is two fold; he doubts that he can do the work as well as the other much younger children, at the same time he must show that he is superior to them.

Once, after he had again brought up the subject of the years he spent in hospitals, I asked the class why Jimmy gave this matter so much thought, and why he used every opportunity to remind us of it. This developed into an animated discussion. Some children said that Jimmy must feel very much ashamed to be so far behind in school, and this is how he justified it. Some said that Jimmy thinks that by telling us about the hospital, we will feel sorry for him and we will not be so critical. Others said that he wants to be noticed and admired. Jimmy denied that he wanted any of these things. I asked the class if, in their opinion, Jimmy got anything out of this kind of behavior. Some felt that it served as an excuse for not doing any work, but the majority of the children felt that Jimmy was so afraid that nobody would notice him that he forced their attention by telling stories in which he is something special.

Comments: The teacher takes the first step to solicit the help of the group, discussing Jimmy's behavior not from a critical point of view but to help Jimmy and all children in class to look for purposes in behavior. It is interesting to notice how well the children understood that Jimmy was safeguarding himself by telling that he could not read because he was in the hospital, and thereby hoping that his failure will be excused without having to assume the fault of it. I asked the group if Jimmy could get attention in any other way, and if so, could they tell him in what way. The children said that they admired him very much for his knowledge in science and for his ability in sports.

257

Comments: Frankly, Jimmy's ability in sports surprises us. We would have expected that such realistic achievement which puts him ahead of his class would suffice to flatter his ego, and that it would be this area that he would exploit in order to have status with his peers. For this very ambitious child, being good in just one area is, evidently, not sufficient. He does not think that he is good enough unless he is exceptional. There were other children in class who were also good in sports. Jimmy can stand no competition.

Jimmy, who was sulking until then, looked up and smiled for just an instant. He quickly resumed his angry expression.

Comments: At this point, Jimmy is determined to show us that we are wrong. Perhaps, he is continuing in the classroom the power contest he has with his father. He tries to defeat both by his display of obstinacy. Smiling openly would to him be an admission that we were correct in our evaluation.

I asked him if he knew that the children admired him, and he shook his head. When I asked for a show of hands of those who admired and liked him, most of the children raised their hands. I asked Jimmy to look up and count his friends, but he refused. He was angry for the rest of the day.

Comments: This supports the above supposition. He does not give in easily. However, the possibilities are that this experience had encouraging effects. Probably Jimmy never before experienced open display of acceptance by his peer group.

I decided to build Jimmy up through sports since this required no reading.

Comments: The teacher was careful not to choose a subject or activity in which Jimmy might possibly fail or do poorly. She is trying to build on his strength.

I discussed this with the students one day when Jimmy was not in school. All thought that this was a good idea.

Comments: Some may argue that this was not a spontaneous and natural reaction of the class, but that the teacher plotted, using the class in her endeavor. This is absolutely true. However, it does not diminish its effectiveness. If any, it demonstrates that basically, children are good and eager to be of help to others provided that we lead and motivate them in this direction.

The next time the group met for the regular class discussion meeting, one of the students suggested that the class should form a baseball league with Jimmy as its leader. They also suggested that they invite another class to join them. Jimmy liked this idea very much, and he went to work immediately. He went into the other classroom to talk to the teacher about our suggestion. When he returned, he looked radiant. He had managed to organize the first match. The children showed open amazement and admiration.

Jimmy soon became the leader of both groups. He practiced with them after school, and he reported daily to the children in class.

Comments: The significance of this example lies in the fact that the teacher spotted Jimmy's one advantage—his ability in sports, and acted upon it. She moved him from a minus to a plus position. He is moving into active participation.

From that day on, Jimmy participated in all activities which did not require reading. No one made any point of this fact. When the children read, Jimmy either listened or he occupied himself with something without disturbing the class.

When I suggested to him that he could be helped by any student he might like to work with, he refused such help. He did, however, agree to let me work with him for fifteen minutes each day.

Comments: This is the first breakthrough leading in the right direction. Discouragement was counteracted by his first experience of success. But this is only a start which may, or may not develop further. We hope that this is a turning point for this child. The teacher has succeeded by now in winning Jimmy's cooperation, but this does not indicate that she has also succeeded in changing his general outlook nor his goal.

Every now and then, the children began asking him to join any reading group he would like; they assured him that this would make them happy, that they would like to help him, also that they could help him if he would let them. But he still refused.

Comments: It confirms our feeling of Jimmy's obstinacy. A child who feels that life is worth living only if one is ahead of others will stay away from activities that do not provide them with the opportunity to prove their superiority. They lack the courage to be imperfect.

One day I told the children the story of the boy who wanted very much to know how to swim, but he refused to go into the water until such time when he knew how to swim. At this, Jimmy burst out in uncontrolable laughter. He said that this boy must be very stupid to think that he could learn how to swim without going into the water. I agreed with him that this boy would never learn how to swim in this manner but I did not think that this boy was necessarily "stupid." I then asked the class to think of a reason this boy might have for not going into the water. Most children felt that he was afraid that he will probably never learn how to swim but did not want other people to know this. By saying that he must first learn how to swim before he goes into the water, this boy thought that he could protect himself from showing his real reason. The children emphasized that what this boy felt and what he did was not exactly smart,

259

but that was no indication that he was dumb otherwise.

I asked Jimmy if he knew anyone who behaved in a similar way to this boy. He did not reply to my question.

Comments: It is interesting to see how a child, not understanding the behavior of another person, assumed that the other is "stupid," whereas he never associates his own behavior with such an interpretation. Whereas children are quick to understand the purpose of other people's behavior—when they personally are not involved, this does not hold true when it concerns their own. Such children must be helped to understand the ficticious goal they have set for themselves.

At the end of the day, after the class was dismissed, Jimmy stopped at my desk and he told me that he realized that I had meant him when I asked him that question. I agreed with him and I asked if he intends "to go into the water." Jimmy cried for the first time. He said that he was ashamed that the children would laugh if they heard his halting reading.

Comments: Did Jimmy cry in order to get the teacher's sympathy or was this a first admission that he might be wrong? We are inclined to believe the latter. If so, this would indicate his first courageous step.

In a mirror technique, the teacher succeeded in showing him how silly his actions were, without shaming him in the process.

I told him that I did not think so, but that he would have to find out for himself. He said that he wanted to wait a little longer.

Comments: So far, Jimmy always declined all friendly invitations to try. Although he wants to wait a little longer, he is not actually refusing. This gives us further hope.

It is important to notice that the teacher made no promises to Jimmy, not only because she is in no position to make such a promise, but more so because it is important for Jimmy to learn to take chances. It is his fear of failure that paralyzes him, therefore we must concentrate on removing such fears, even at the risk of failure.

As the students progressed in their reading, and as they started to give book-reports, Jimmy's mood showed changes. He appeared gloomy and absentminded. He also started to cut classes.

Comments: What might be the reason for this change? There is definitely a sign of new discouragement. Possibly the fact that the other children are being successful and receive attention, especially when they give book-reports. Too little attention is now being paid to him. This kind of reversal or regression is not rare in overambitious children when they think that they are losing ground.

One day he announced that the club to which he belonged (which he had never mentioned before) was sending him to New York City to play in a baseball tournament, and that he would be absent for three days. Everyone was very curious about this trip, asking many questions. Jimmy was once more in his element. He did not show up for three days. When he returned, he gave a full report of the events and of the places he visited in New York—Times Square, Radio City, and other known places. Again he was well informed and could answer most of the questions posed by the curious students.

Comments: We see how ingenious this boy is; how well he lays plans and executes them.

Suddenly it occurred to me that I had not asked Jimmy to bring a statement from the parents regarding his taking off from school, and that this may have been another of his tall tales. I called his home and learned that he had never been away from home; that every morning he left as usual when he goes to school, not returning until at the time when he normally would return.

Comments: This should not surprise us. He was driven by his need for being "special."

During our next discussion meeting, I asked the class if they could figure out why children tell "tall tales." I did not mention what I had learned about Jimmy. Most children felt that tall tales are used by people who don't believe that they could find admiration from others in any other way. They also brought out that these people never give themselves a chance to find out if they are right; that they often operate on false assumptions. Jimmy did not participate in the discussion. I asked him if he would like to comment but he shook his head and remained silent.

Comments: It may sound that the teacher is demanding too much of small children. Many teachers may question the advisability to involve the class in the problems of an individual child. This would indicate a lack of confidence in the children's ability and eagerness to understand behavior, and especially to be helpful to others. Children want to solve their problems, and school is the best, if not the only place, where such training is possible. We must be careful not to extend our adult anxieties and inadequacies to children and thereby teach them to avoid facing problems and finding solutions to them. At all times, we must refrain from fault-finding and from becoming punitive.

We notice that the teacher did not make any fuss, nor did she confront him directly with his lie. She did not even mention Jimmy's name during the discussion. In a way, the teacher was put on the

261

spot, having transgressed a school regulation which requires that children bring notes from home whenever they want to take off from school. The average teacher probably would have reported the incident to the principal, etc. How different this situation might have turned out had she done so. All that was gained would have been destroyed and she would have lost the friendly relationship which she had established with the child. The children understood that the goal of one who is bragging is to hide feelings of inadequacy.

The following morning, Jimmy came to school somewhat earlier than usual. He came straight to my desk and told me that he had heard that I had called his father. He demanded to know why I had done it. He appeared very angry.

Comments: It is not uncommon that children who operate on power, consider anything that may indicate disapproval by others as unfair. Perhaps he was trying to get the teacher involved in an argument.

I told him that, I violated a school regulation by not asking for a note; that for my own and for his protection I needed confirmation from his parents that they gave their approval for his absence. I also added that I liked him and that I wanted to do all I can to help him. However, in order for me to know what to do, I had to know the facts. I also pointed out that the children in class felt the same as I do, and that he must surely have noticed it. I reminded him of the discussion the group had the previous day, regarding discouraged people. I told him that I felt that he was such a person, afraid of failure to such a degree that he would not risk the chance of trying and finding out if he is right or wrong. I asked him, "Could it be that you feel worthless unless you occupy a 'special' position, being different and superior to others?" Jimmy's mouth began to twitch and tears, filled his eyes. I told him, further, that he was waiting for a miracle from heaven in regard to his reading as well as in regard to feeling accepted for what he was. I said, "Jimmy, haven't you noticed that all of us like and respect you for what you are? For us you needn't be anything else."

Comments: This may sound like a lecture. In a way it is. However, there are times when private counseling is necessary. The teacher actually indicates understanding and even sympathy for the fact that he avoids reading. She appeals to his ambition but at the same time points out how unimportant it is to be exceptional, that he is liked for what he is. She put no cloak of moral indignation over his lying to her, in fact, the lie isn't even discussed.

Jimmy answered that he realized that he was only fooling himself not others. He said that a number of times, only the fear of being laughed at kept him from joining a reading group. Again he asked me to promise him that nobody would laugh if he read. I told him that I could not give him such a promise; that it takes courage to find out for himself and to face such a possibility. I added, "I am sure of one thing though. The children will have more respect and admire you more for having the courage to try, no matter how poorly you perform, than they will if you continue being 'different.' This is a decision that must come from you alone." He said that he would think about it and tell me in the morning.

The next day Jimmy pulled up his chair and joined a reading group. All the children smiled; some waved at him. The boy next to him put his arm around him. When Jimmy's turn came to read, he blushed, hesitated for a moment and then started pronouncing the words he could read. The teacher jumped in quickly whenever she anticipated a word which he might not know. When he had finished, he blew his chest and in a boisterous way said, "Well, I did better than I thought. In fact, I think that I did rather well."

Comments: The teacher did not get into a power contest with Jimmy. She did not argue nor did she make promises. But she proved to be his friend. As a consequence, he cooperated with her; mustered up his courage. She had succeeded in restoring Jimmy's confidence in himself and in others.

We notice that in Jimmy's remark there is more of a humorous bravado than sincere belief in what he is saying. His old pattern is still visible, but not so deeply entrenched as before.

Conclusion

Frustrated overambition is often the main reason for giving up. Jimmy had to learn to believe in himself and to respect himself as he was before anyone could help him. The teacher and the group gave Jimmy the incentive to overcome his disbelief in his own ability and to have the courage to accept the fact that in some areas others were superior to him, without feeling humilated or rejected because of this. The teacher went to a great length to provide him with proof of the fallacy of his original thinking. However, without the help of the group, she might have not succeeded. We see in this example that the group was being used to influence the child not only toward wanting to learn and to exercise self-discipline but to exercise a corrective influence of the child's attitudes and behavior. At all times, we must remember that when the teacher or the group can convince the child of the futility of his goal, and can show him alternatives, he is likely to consider and change it. He then turns to constructive direction.

263

Appendix; Years Later

It may be of interest to the reader that Jimmy is a television actor, and is frequently performing. His basic life style has not changed. He is still the center, and the spotlights are on him. However, he is using constructive, socially acceptable means to achieve his goal.

Interestingly, he chose a profession which requires constant reading.

Sometimes children lie when their imagination runs away with them. Sometimes they confuse fantasy with reality. If we accuse these children of deliberately lying, we run the risk of making real liars out of them.

Herman, a fourth grader, was always telling the class about his Great Dane. He told the class about Timber, the tricks he could perform, what a wonderful watchdog he was, and how Timber would protect Herman. Each week he would come to school and tell about the wonders of Timber.

As it turned out, Herman did not own a dog and none of his relatives or close friends had such a dog.

Would you say that Herman was lying or would you say that Herman had a very active fantasy life, or that he did not know the difference between truth and fiction? These are sometimes quite difficult to work out. In Herman's case, this was probably a truthful account of what was going on in his fantasy life.

What is a flagrant lie? How does one distinguish this kind of lie from another kind? How do you know it is lying?

Hank was a third grader who had a consistent pattern of telling lies. The teacher might make a simple request, such as, "Hank, please clean the apple cores out of your desk." Hank would say a few minutes later, "I cleaned my desk and put the apple cores in the wastebasket." In checking his desk, the apple cores would still be there.

Another time the teacher might say, "Hank, your coat is on the floor, please hang it up." A few minutes later Hank would say that he had hung up his coat. In checking the coat, it would still be on the floor.

There was never an excuse of any kind given. It would be a direct lie that could be checked. Is the child's goal to be deceptive? If the teacher thinks so, then she should label it lying. Many children lie just in order to put something over on the adults.

Some children lie because they are curious to see what will happen. Usually, this is of short duration if we pay little attention to those lies or make jokes of them. Unfortunately, most adults make a big fuss and thus show the child that his method works.

There are times when a lie may put a teacher into a situation where she does not know what to do. Doing the opposite of what the child thinks or expects is very effective. You may say to the child, "People could always fool me. I guess, I'm a sucker for lies." This takes the enjoyment out of feeling superior, and the child often feels foolish. Sometimes children even apologize when the teacher, without anger or provocation, admits her weakness.

> One day a teacher was called to the door of her classroom and while talking with the principal, there was some confusion in the room. Somehow the pencil sharpener had been emptied and the contents strewn on the floor.
>
> Since the teacher did not know who had spilled the shavings, she mentioned that the mess would have to be swept and picked up. The children volunteered the information that Randy had made the mess. Randy immediately stated in no uncertain terms that he did not spill the shavings. The teacher then asked for a volunteer to sweep up the shavings, and Tom immediately started to clean up the floor.
>
> At this point, Randy looked up and gruffly said, "Leave that stuff alone Tom. That's my mess and I'll clean it up."
>
> In this particular case, the teacher did not ask who made the mess nor did she respond when several children volunteered the information. Had the teacher confronted Randy, he would have denied the act, as this was his pattern, and he had already denied it. Since he was not challenged and did not get the response he expected, he was able to come forth with his statement.

We would like the child who is lying to think there is something good about our acceptance of him if he does *not* lie. We are making the assumption that the truth has some good in it. Is it possible for the child to recognize this?

There are two major ways to fight lying successfully. The first is to make the lie ineffectual in some way by undercutting the desired results. A cardinal rule is "Don't challenge a lie." It does not do any good. There are several ways to cut down the child's desired consequences. Do not pay attention to fantastic stories, do not respond or give recognition to something we do not think is correct, and do not ask for the rest of a fantastic story.

Children learn to do what is expected of them in their everyday contacts with adults. Again we need to realize that we cannot teach children by telling them or talking to them, but through showing them by our actions and deeds. Sometimes, at home, a mother can accept lies by inviting the child to a game of lying, of which he soon will tire.

We should not be afraid that the child who lies is on the road to delinquency. Lying, like any other behavior pattern, needs the understanding of the entire personality of the child, and measures to improve the situation must be taken accordingly.

SWEARING

The same theory holds true about swearing. Children feel big and smart when they use bad language, especially when they realize the reaction such words can produce. The surest way to cure a child of swearing is to let it appear insignificant and trivial. One can invite the child to show how many bad words he knows. Soon the child will see that this gets him nowhere. Sometimes, a smile or a wink from the teacher may make him realize that he is being ridiculous. Of course, helping children to understand why they like to use those words, and what they could do instead to feel important is of great help.

TEENAGERS

Adolescents have become a major problem, not only for the teacher, the parents, and society, but also for themselves.

Adolescence is the period of major change, it is the third phase of childhood. In his preschool days, the child finds his place in his own family by developing definite patterns of his personality. As he enters school, the second phase, he joins members of other families and integrates himself into the community by recognizing the general rules of behavior, work, and order. In adolescence, he becomes part of society at large. He strives for intellectual and personal freedom and independence, and looks critically at the values of adult society. He then chooses the reference group with which he shares values and ideals. He undergoes a period of psycho-sexual upheaval through which he sets his pattern of sexual behavior.

In the past, during this period, the teenager had one foot in adolescence and the other in adulthood. He slowly became an adult. He got a job, drove his own car instead of that of his father, contributed to the family income and took on the responsibility for his younger brothers and sisters. All this has changed. At present, teenagers are at war with the adult society. Their freedom from responsibility induces them to continue their adolescence far beyond the age customary for this period of life. They do not want to assume the responsibilities of adults. Teenagers have become a powerful subgroup, living in a different world, many distinguishing themselves from adults through long hair, untidiness, odd clothing, noisy music,

266

and, most recently, the use of drugs. They object to being called teenagers, as if they all were bad, irresponsible, and delinquent. In turn, they do not criticize one parent or one teacher, but always ask "why do the parents" or, "the teachers," do so and so. These generalizations on both sides are the reflection of the warfare and distrust of both groups, teenagers and adults.

The rebellion of youth is the basis of what one calls the generation gap. Our youngsters and adults do not see eye to eye, because they live in two different worlds. This warfare is so insidious that it penetrates almost every family and expresses itself in the most divergent ways. The young idealist is in the same opposition to adult society as the juvenile delinquent. What distinguishes them is the form of rebellion. At the present time, we have no evidence of any effort on the part of either camp, youth and adults, to come to a meeting of the minds. The generalized warfare gives the youthful rebels continuous fuel. The teenager and college student, who form a mass of anti-adults and anti-establishment, join the other rebellious groups. Probably, the major battle against the establishment will be fought between youth and adults, and between blacks and whites.

The "authorities" tend to pursue a course that only intensifies this struggle. On the one side, they call for law and order, which inevitably leads to more defiance, and the other faction of society, the liberals, support the rebellion of youth and of blacks as a sign of progress. Unfortunately, most institutions dealing with youth, schools and colleges, are autocratic. Youth has no voice, does not participate in decision making, neither at home, in the school, nor in the colleges and communities.

This warfare will worsen before it gets better. It will penetrate every family and every community, until we finally give up the traditional methods of dealing with youth and have the courage to start a new era and give young people a voice in all affairs in which they are involved.

In high school, teachers are often confronted with a class teeming with rebellion. The students are seldom interested in learning. Those who seem to be, usually want good grades in order to go to college, but going to college does not necessarily mean that they like to study. They go in order to get a degree, which will get them a better job. In this sense, the teacher becomes a necessary evil. One example may highlight the tragic relationship between many teachers and their students.

A high school student reported the following incident: He had a teacher who was hated by the whole class. One day the teacher

brought an elderly woman to class and introduced her as her mother. The boy could not understand what happened thereafter. The class suddenly stopped fighting with her. How could that incident have such a deep effect on this class? When the teacher came with her mother, she suddenly became a human being to them.

Often students and teachers do not regard each other as fellow human beings. The teachers do not know what they are doing to the students, or how the students feel about them. The students, on the other hand, have little idea of how much they hurt and humiliate their teachers. These situations can be eliminated if teachers conduct regular class discussions.

We have previously described the need for such discussions, to integrate the class and to promote cooperation. It is easier for the teacher to arrange such group discussions on the elementary level, as long as the instruction is not departmentalized. But who should be in charge of group discussions in the high school? We probably will have to rely on those teachers who are experienced in this approach to provide the opportunity for all students to share their problems and feelings. Every student should have such an opportunity. Although it may be more difficult in a high school or junior high to find the time for such discussions, they are crucially needed on this level.

The schools will have to become concerned with the values of their students. This cannot be accomplished through preaching and advising. It requires a real process of learning through discussion, recognizing the faulty values on which many teenagers operate, and helping them to see better alternatives.

Another expression of the utter failure of schools, to influence the values of their students, is the steady and alarming increase of the use of drugs. Unfortunately, neither home and nor community is safe from the incursion of drugs. In order to understand the drug problem, we have to realize its nature. Why do so many students fall for the temptation of drugs? It seems that there are three reasons for drug use. First, the general tendency of youth to seek excitement. Excitement has become a value in itself, regardless of cost. Boredom is intolerable, and nothing is as exciting as a "trip." It is obvious that this craving for excitement effects a large segment of our children and youth. Before one can stop the craving for drugs, one must help youngsters to free themselves from this superficial form of satisfaction in life, called fun.

The second reason for the use of drugs is the general principle on which many youngsters operate. In seeking their identity, they develop a misunderstood sense of freedom and independence. Many watch adults carefully, and then do what adults can not tolerate. The use of drugs is an extreme example. There is nothing adults can tolerate less than the use of drugs that may ruin a youngster for life.

The third factor is the most pernicious. Drugs create a temporary insanity, a sensation of freedom from the demands of reality through delusion and hallucination. This refusal to accept social obligations and restrictions is, again, a much larger issue, affecting many children and youths who easily become victims of this "freedom," but at what cost?

Helping youngsters to recognize and change their false values requires skill, understanding, and tolerance. The teacher can learn to influence the thoughts and concepts of her students. The following example illustrates how a smoking problem was resolved:

> The administrators of a high school experimented with means to help students stop smoking. The students were divided into four groups. The first group explored the reasons why one should not smoke. Smoking continued. The second group was to tell their parents why they should not smoke. They enjoyed doing it, but they did not stop smoking. The third group went about it in a scientific way. They figured out how much smoking would cost them during their lifetime, the dangers it would entail, and the discomfort they would endure if they could not smoke. Still, they continued smoking. The fourth group actually stopped smoking. How did that happen? First, the teacher discussed all the advantages of smoking: how it makes one feel important, adult, and independent; how it can defeat the demands of home and school; and the like. Only after the advantages were clearly understood, did the group discuss the disadvantages. Then, the students were given a choice. And they chose not to smoke.

This is a most important lesson. If one wants to influence children, one must first show an understanding of the motivation. What was the main difference between the first three groups and the last? In the others, the students agreed that one should not smoke. They accepted the request not to smoke, but they felt incapable of giving it up. This is characteristic for all smokers. They believed that they want to stop, but insisted they could not. Only in the last group did the students realize that it was not a question of whether one can or cannot stop smoking, but of realizing that one had a choice. Providing alternatives and choices is the only way one can help youngsters to change their ideas and their behavior. Moralizing, explaining, or dictating is futile. This is true in general; group discussion can help youngsters to understand themselves and to develop better values.

TECHNIQUES OF TEENAGE DISCUSSION[11]

Before much can be accomplished, the teacher must win the adolescent's trust. In most instances, the adolescent has a poor relationship with adults. In addition to the necessity of being honest, warm, and accepting, two other requirements are important. First, she must be able to endure the individual's calculated, antagonistic behavior without finding it necessary to defend herself against it. Second, the teacher must accept the youth as an individual of equal human value. These two attitudes go hand in hand and are necessary for a favorable atmosphere. This does not imply permissiveness, since we do not make a teenager our equal if we baby him. Neither should we fall into his trap by punishing him when he is provoking in order to prove the teacher unfair. By accepting him as an equal, we respect him and at the same time, by refusing to coddle him, we demonstrate that we expect him to respect us. Once this relationship is established the youth gradually ceases his antagonistic behavior, his practical joking, and his apparent indifference to the discussion, and assumes responsibility for maintaining order.

When the adolescent knows that he is accepted by the teacher, he must then be encouraged to find his place in the group, to feel that he belongs, and to accept its objectives as his own. Many feel unable to realize their equality with their peers and express their feelings of inferiority either by withdrawing or by interrupting the group process in such a way as to monopolize the attention of the group as well as the teacher.

Group interpretation becomes mutual understanding and empathic identification. The teacher, in order to achieve this, must respond to all members with equal interest, stressing similarities in motives and interpreting behavior in relation to movements to or away from the other members of the group. The boy who indulges in horse-play may be made aware of how he is trying to impress the group, more so than to annoy the teacher. (This is more common of teenagers than of younger children.) The teacher who is not aware of this, often takes the behavior of the individual as a personal insult and confronts the student with consequences that, unfortunately, turn him against her. Let us illustrate this point more clearly:

> After several weeks of regular group discussions with some freshmen in high school, the entire group, which was previously very difficult to handle and a serious behavior problem for all teachers, changed their behavior toward all but one teacher. The group claimed that Mr. Bunker was a mean man, that he provoked their

[11]Bernard H. Shulman, "Group Counseling for Adolescents," in *Adlerian Family Counseling* (Eugene: University of Oregon Press, 1959), pp. 69–74.

anger and disrespect, and that they could not change in their attitude toward him. When the teacher asked individual students if they were possibly acting up in Mr. Bunker's class in order to impress the other students with their ability to annoy the teacher, they denied such a possibility emphatically.

The teacher asked the individuals if they would misbehave in Mr. Bunker's class, if they were transferred to another of Mr. Bunker's classes. Each student answered that he would not. When the teacher asked why such a transfer would change their behavior toward Mr. Bunker, most students suddenly realized that they would not act up in another class because they were not sure of how the students in that class would react. After further discussion, it became clear to them that, in spite of their dislike for Mr. Bunker, they really acted up more to impress the other students than to annoy Mr. Bunker.

As soon as the group was helped to realize the true reason for their behavior, their attitude toward Mr. Bunker changed.

One of the most important functions of the teacher is to interpret to each adolescent the goals of his behavior. An individual's reaction may change when he is made aware of his intentions. One or the other of the four goals of children's misbehavior may apply here, too. However, we find additional goals in the behavior of teenagers; one of them is the desire for excitement, boredom being intolerable to them. The desire for excitement often induces them toward dangerous behavior.

Teachers must exercise great caution in how they interpret the goals to teenagers. It must be done noncritically with neither approval nor rejection. The development of mutual respect between the adolescent and the teacher provides strong encouragement toward a constructive change. Change in this setting takes place in three ways:

1. The adolescent begins to feel less criticized and is more willing to accept social demands.
2. The desire for group status and the understanding of better ways of achieving it results in more cooperative behavior which is then transferred to areas outside the group.
3. Understanding the motives for one's behavior combined with the feeling of belonging, and the increased sense of personal worth, diminishes anxiety and its attendant behavior.

The reader will notice, in the following example of a discussion with teenagers, that the teacher must be on the alert to what the individ-

271

ual members of the group are saying. Their comments should be followed up with pertinent questions which help the individual as well as the group to have a clear understanding of what is being discussed and to come to logical conclusions about the problem.

Teacher: I know that some of you have problems you would like to explore. Who would like to start the discussion today?

Brad: There's a state law against gambling at school; it should be legal to play cards at school as long as you don't gamble for money.

Teacher: Why do you think they have the law?

Brad: I have no idea. I see no reason why anyone should enforce morals, such as outlawing gambling. It should be left up to the individual whether he wants to gamble or not.

Teacher: Do any of you have any ideas to add to this?

Debbie: I think the law is good because there can be a lot of disagreements.

John: Parents are not interested in their children and don't care what they do with their money.

Teacher: The issue is, why shouldn't students be permitted to gamble and have personal freedom?

Brad: I think you misunderstood. It isn't gambling. It's playing cards, Crazy 8, and things like that, that's just as good as playing poker.

Teacher: Oh, come on Brad! Let's hear from the others and see how they feel about this issue.

Marge: I don't think there's anything the matter with playing cards unless they play for money.

Sue: I feel the same way. There's nothing wrong with Crazy 8.

Katie: Kids this age are responsible for handling their own money. I think card games are fine, but gambling should not be allowed at school.

Teacher: I want to clarify something, Brad. Did you say that there should be no law against gambling and that it should be up to the individual?

Brad: I said, I don't feel that the law against gambling is just, but there is a law against it in this state so there's not much I can do about it right now.

Teacher: Except object.

Brad: Yes.

Teacher: What is the real issue, Brad?

Brad: The real issue is, I think that students should be allowed to have cards on the school grounds and should be allowed to play

272

cards as long as they are not in class. There is nothing so evil and sinful as that projected by the administration.

Teacher: Do you play cards, Brad?

Brad: Not very often, only occasionally.

Teacher: What is your concern then? What is your interest?

Brad: I think students should be able to do what they wish on their own recreation time. I'm on a committee now to set up a recreation room for the high school and that is one of the things we want to use the lounge for, to play cards. If the students can't play cards, and can only sit and talk, then the room just won't be of much use.

Debbie: (To teacher) What do you think about this issue?

Teacher: I think Brad and his committee are in a bad spot. There seems to be no lines of communication between the student body and the administration. Somehow, the students committee and the administration need to establish a speaking relationship. What can you do?

(At this point, the teacher has to help the students view the problem from all sides. There is a variety of questions that she could ask.

1. What can the student council do about the lack of communication?
2. Is there any justification for such an order?
3. Should the students participate in making the decisions?

There are any number of questions that will permit the discussion to go a little deeper.)

Brad: We have a student-faculty liaison committee that meets twice a month. It hasn't been very effective. You go in, and there are about ten kids and six or seven faculty members. Usually, it ends up with nobody saying anything because everybody is afraid of everybody else. The administration has come to the thing where it's like "double socko," and kids can't talk back at them. You talk back and you get shot.

Teacher: Do any of you have an idea of how you go about breaking down this barrier.

Brad: Yes. Get the students not to be afraid of the administration.

Teacher: How would you go about doing that? Anybody have any ideas?

Brad: By getting out and talking to the kids, getting out and stirring them up a little bit.

273

Teacher: How do you feel about these issues?
Is there any justification for the law that students shouldn't play cards?
Why did people develop this law, just to be mean, just to deprive you of having fun?

Brad: The ruling in the school was set up because some students were playing poker for money. The principal is highly moralistic, and he thinks the kids are all losing their bread, man, and they are sinners! He says you guys can't play cards anymore and anyone with cards gets the ax, so there's no card playing. He brings it up on the premise that there is a state law in the schools against gambling.

Teacher: What do you think about that?

Brad: If there is a state law, then we shouldn't gamble.

Teacher: Then why do you rebel against it?

Brad: I'm not saying that students should be able to gamble. I'm saying students should be able to play cards. He has outlawed anyone even playing solitaire. He always says there is a state law, but he will never quote it. He never tells anybody exactly what the law says, he just says there's a law and you can't gamble. He won't clarify it to anyone.

Teacher: What do you think about what Brad said?

Sandra: If there's a state law, we are a part of the state, and most students in high school aren't old enough so that sort of leaves us out. I don't mind because I don't gamble anyway.

Teacher: But did you listen to what Brad said? How do you feel about what he said?

Marie: I agree with him. No one knows the law. I haven't been told what it says.

Teacher: What did Brad say?

Marcia: He talked about gambling and card playing. He sort of goes back and forth. He sounds like he doesn't like any rule that restricts him.

Teacher: Debbie, what was your impression of what Brad said?

Debbie: My impression is that regardless what the rule is, it is wrong.

Teacher: Okay. Keith what is your impression of what Brad said.

274

Keith: I heard him say, how come adults should be able to tell kids what to do with their time?

Teacher: Okay. What did you hear Bill?

Bill: That kids don't have any choice.

Teacher: Okay. What else did you hear? I heard something entirely different.

Mickey: I heard his reaction toward a person as much as against the rule. He reacted against the principal.

Teacher: Yes. Could you tell me more? How does he react towards the principal?

Mickey: He just doesn't like him.

Teacher: Yes, that's what I heard. The principal wouldn't quote the law, he only stated it. Brad seems to watch very carefully what the principal says so he can jump at it. How do you feel about that Brad?

Brad: That's pretty much true. Yes, I really hate the cat's guts!

Teacher: Probably, if we asked Brad about other things the principal is doing wrong, he could tell us, couldn't you?

Brad: Definitely.

Teacher: How many things do you know about him doing wrong?

Brad: Some students petitioned the student council to set up an uncensored bulletin board, like where you can pin up essays and opinions, maybe criticizing the school administration or anything you feel like. This was to be uncensored, and the principal said that's OK, that's cool, you can do it as long as I have a chance to look at everything first. It finally was vetoed. I think that students should be able to speak freely with each other and the administration, but that isn't the case. He just won't let the kids who want to talk to him, talk to him.

Teacher: Now, we know and can appreciate that Brad can find all the things that the principal is doing wrong. Why is Brad doing this? Why is the principal such a jerk? Why is he doing these stupid things? Let's hear from some of the others.

Patty: I don't think he's such a jerk. I always try to look for some good in everyone. He belongs to our church group. I was extremely disappointed because I believe he should be able to give a straight answer and know what he wants to say, but he beats around the bush mostly, and I feel kinda sorry for him. I feel he's in a tough spot and I respect him, but I still disagree with him. I think he's got a right to be a leader. He's intelligent, and he's been put in that position. I just feel sorry for him.

Teacher: Why?

Patty: Because he has so much responsibility and so much against him. I mean like about 2000 kids.

Teacher: Could it be that he is doing all of these things because he is simply afraid of the students?

Patty: No. I mean he's in a spot.

Teacher: If he would give freedom of expression, what kind of expression would he anticipate?

Patty: I don't know.

Teacher: Oh! Come on, come on!

Patty: Oh look! We have freedom of expression. I mean we have plenty of rebels and stuff.

Teacher: Yes, but you see Brad said he promised an uncensored bulletin board, and then he wanted censorship. Why? What is his point?

Patty: You can't just turn 2000 kids loose on one bulletin board. There's bound to be some kids get a little out of hand.

Teacher: Of what would you be afraid? What do others of you think about the principal and what he is doing? No opinion? Katie? Sally?

Sally: I really didn't know anything about it.

Marcia: I think he's kind of rotten because at the first of the year when I first moved here, my sister and I wrote him a note and told him what was wrong with school and stuff. We gave it to him personal and we asked him to put it in the school paper, and he wouldn't do it.

Teacher: What did you want him to put in the paper?

Marcia: We told him how bad the school was and stuff.

Teacher: And why didn't he want to put it in the paper?

Marcia: Well, I think the school is bad.

Teacher: And what do you want to do with the school?

Marcia: Well, I . . .

Teacher: To start a riot if you could, huh? Could you, would you like to stir the students up?

Marcia: No, not really, but I would like to improve the school so it would be happier.

Teacher: Does anybody have an impression of what goes on at this school particularly between adults and kids?

Tom: It seems like we have a little game going here between the principal and the power kids. The kids are trying to exercise some power, and the principal accepts this challenge and exerts some power right in return. The kids set him up so that he will exercise power, then they have an excuse to retaliate.

Teacher: Yes, agreed. But what do you think of the total situation? What is going on in this school?

Dorothy and students: A war!

Teacher: A war. And unless we realize it, we won't get anywhere. The students against the principal.

Mickey: There is something else. There is students against students.

Teacher: Whenever there is a war, you find people siding. Sometimes, there are traitors to the cause, those who side with the authorities. You don't realize that this man is frightened because he doesn't trust the kids. He doesn't know how to deal with them; he doesn't know how to influence them. He's afraid to give them freedom because with so much rebellion, they would stir each other up, and he would lose complete control. He feels responsible for the school, and he doesn't know how to discharge his responsibility because he doesn't trust the kids.

Brad: I don't think he has the right to force his morals on students. He has his morals and the kids have theirs, maybe some of them coincide, but I don't think that all the kids should be morally the same as the principal.

Teacher: Do you think schools have an obligation to develop proper morals among the students?

Brad: No, they do not. They have the right to educate the students as to the way society works and as to our language, mathematics, and other subjects. I don't think they should teach the kids morals. Your own moral stature should be figured out by yourself. I don't think the schools should try

277

and teach the students what is right and wrong. I think the things they haven't experienced yet, such as drinking, smoking, sex, marijuana, anything like that should be left up to their own experimentation.

Teacher: Brad has taken a very strong stand about moral education, which comes to the core of the problem. What do you want to do with it? He said, "Schools are here to teach subjects and that is all. Leave us alone otherwise. Don't interfere with our morals." Is that right Brad? Is that your position?

Brad: Definitely.

Teacher: How many of you agree with Brad that schools should not teach morals?

(Students vote and the majority agrees with Brad.)

How do you define morals and morality?

Brad: The kind that stops students from smoking, drinking, and gambling, and wants them to leave sex alone and be all-American kids, and this just doesn't make it.

Debbie: I think of morals and sex as teaching the law, because I am more concerned with the way kids are taught the law and respect of the law.

Teacher: The question, which Brad raised, is a fundamental question in all of our high schools. We have to come to grips with it. Why does he make this demand? Is his demand correct or not? Should the schools do it or not? This is the issue. Am I right Brad?

Brad: Yes.

Teacher: What would we do? Sally, how do you feel about this?

Sally: I think the Principal should listen at least to what the students think.

Teacher: Do you agree that adults or authorities are setting down rules for morals.

Sally: Yes they are. What they say, we have to do.

Teacher: Why does Brad take this stand? One always has to come to the principles involved. There is a principle, quite a clear principle, on which Brad seems to operate. What is the principle?

Mickey: He wants to do what he wants to do.

Teacher: OK, and why?

Mickey: I think it's equality. He wants to be equal to and respected as a human being.

Teacher: That's what he says, but when you look at his equality he wants to dominate things and have his own way. But that is not the reason why he makes this stand. Under what general premises would his stand make sense? You have to understand the significance of it. Now guess.

Bonnie: He is better than others and can make the decision.

Teacher: No, not just Brad, all the kids. You find this opinion more and more widespread. It is a misunderstanding of democracy. Democracy for him and for many others means that everyone has the right to do as he darn pleases, and that is the mistake. He doesn't realize that democracy can only function with order, that we have to have positive values in order to cooperate. His freedom about experimentation and so forth, endangers people. It is a mistaken idea of freedom. You are proposing freedom for everybody to do as he decides. Brad, am I right or wrong?

Brad: I'm not sure.

This discussion continued for several periods. It involved what is meant by democracy, and how to use democratic procedures.

In the above discussion the teacher failed to notice that Brad distinguished gambling from card playing. Brad, however, clarified it himself a little later. Even then, the discussion teeter-tottered between gambling and card playing.

It is also important to note how the teacher persisted in dealing with the underlying goals of his behavior and making Brad and the class aware of what he was doing.

Discussion with teenagers should help them to get to the issues involved and to explore all sides of the issue. Sometimes there is not a workable solution, but it does give the student depth of understanding of the problem and makes living with the problem more acceptable.

From this discussion, you can see how to get to the issues at hand, and also how difficult it is for adults to be a match for teenagers. The teacher has more responsibility as a discussion leader than merely letting students express themselves. She has to be a leader. Too often, the teacher will clamp down or give in. As Brad so aptly demonstrated, teenagers can push adults around. The teacher can avoid this trap if she sticks to the issues involved, if she helps students to view the opposite side and become aware of their underlying motives or goals.

In an earlier chapter on group discussions, it was mentioned that the teacher should get everyone to participate. In working with teenagers, it is more important to come to the issues, to face the issues, and to force youngsters to think about them. Not all issues are pertinent to all students. It is important to deal with crucial issues even though all students are not aware of the issue.

Group discussions can be held on any level. Discussing what the children really want, feel, think, and so on, helps them to clarify their relationships to each other; discover what they have in common and how they are different; what they can do; and how to come to conclusions, values, and decisions.

There are some guidelines that are helpful in leading teenage group discussions:

1. Talk about meaningful problems; about mother, father, school, and friends; and about their way of doing things. Remember, questions open the door.
2. See the total field of action, home, friends, school, and so forth.
3. Take lead questions, swing with the punches. When you find a gold mine, follow it up.
4. Watch for positive and negative statements.
5. When an individual becomes resistant, stop and ask, "How do you feel about this discussion?" (This gives the student time to relax, collect his thoughts and get his bearings.)
6. Use these techniques in making psychological disclosures: "Would you like me to tell you why I think you do this?" Explain the goal in tentative terms. When the student feels caught, it will be revealed by the recognition reflex (a grin or smile). (See "Four Goals," p. 186.)
   a. Attention: "Perhaps you want to keep the teacher busy?"
   b. Power: "You want to show the teacher that she can't stop you."
   c. Revenge: "You want to hurt others as they have hurt you?"
   d. Give Up: "You are so sure you cannot do anything and want to be left alone."
7. Questions or statements you might use:
   a. Why are you here?
   b. Any other ideas?
   c. I want you to express yourself on whatever you wish.
   d. You have something you wish to discuss.

8. You have to be a leader:
   a. You do not condone.
   b. It is not a nondirective approach.
   c. You have to bring some things to a halt and throw it back to the group.
   d. You must use a pleasant tone of voice.
   e. You must arrange a good meaningful conversation; you must listen and ask "What do you think?"
   f. The organization of the sessions is important. Arrange circular sitting whenever possible.
   g. Watch for hostility and aggression, and discuss it when it becomes apparent.

Teenagers with their own values cannot be influenced individually. They need the group because it is a value-forming agent. It is much easier to draw ten teenagers back to society than to work with just one of them.

The whole school system has to be built on discussion, on every level, in the class, in a segment of the school, among the teachers and the principals. The principal himself has to conduct group discussions with his teachers since he should not decide alone what to do. This does not mean taking a vote, but it requires the process of thinking things through and letting everyone participate.

Each school, particularly junior high and high school, needs regular meetings where students, teachers, and parents get together to discuss their common problems. One may call these sessions truce meetings. They should be on a level where participation for all is possible, and where everybody can learn to understand each other and come to conclusions about solutions for their problems. Honest group discussion is the basis for a democratic school, as democracy is not possible without such meetings.

5
parental
involvement

PARENT-TEACHER CONFERENCES

In former times, children were sent to school for only one purpose, namely to learn subjects and skills. Character formation, citizenship, values, and attitudes were the responsibility of the parents. A teacher's job was to teach, to impart knowledge, and to discipline those who did not learn, and those who strayed from accepted rules and regulations. Those who made progress according to requirements were promoted, while those who did not were flunked. This was accepted as just and proper. Parents rarely went to the teacher to discuss his child's progress or problems. The teacher was always right, at least, this is what the parents told the children.

By and large, this procedure worked, but times have changed.

282

Today, we seek the cooperation of the parents in order to help the child in school. This is frowned on by some teachers, others reject it entirely. It was much simpler for teachers when their sole responsibility was to teach and to grade.

It has become imperative that the school assume responsibility in character building. What brought about this change? The impact of the democratic spirit, now prevailing in our society, affects child-parent relationships, and as a result, the parents lose control of their children. Today, the educator has the obligation to help parents and children as well. The work of home and school can greatly benefit from the cooperation between teachers and parents. They should be partners, helping each other, but care must be taken so that the cooperation of the adults does not become a collusion against the child. Actually, it is a three-way enterprise. Parents and teachers have the responsibility to prepare a child for life, and they must pool their resources into building fruitful relationships.

Some people will reject this educational philosophy and believe that school problems and home problems should be kept apart. The former being the sole responsibility of the educator, and the latter of the parents. Their rejection is based on the belief that teachers should not be counselors; that working together with parents demands too much of the teacher's time; that parents may start to dictate school policy and procedure; that nothing good will come of it; and last, that this is not what teachers are being paid for.

Such opposition usually comes from those not familiar with modern trends in education.

WHAT PURPOSE CAN PARENT-TEACHER INTERVIEWS SERVE?

Parent-teacher conferences serve a number of purposes. Knowing the home situation, the family values, the way their child is treated, what parents expect of their child, the position the child holds in the family, his relationship with his siblings and friends, and other pertinent information, enables the teacher to plan long term procedures for the individual child more successfully. By understanding the home situation, she is better prepared to help parents in their difficulties with their children. This also proves to the child that both the parents and the teacher are really interested in him and in his welfare which, in many cases, has the effect of encouragement.

Having the teacher and the parents talk together serves to unite the two areas of the child's life, his home and his school, and enables both to plan more effectively for the child than when the teacher and parents do not know whether they differ in their methods of treating the child. The more the two understand each other, the less the child will play school against home and vice versa. To give an example:

James, a third grade student who got into frequent fights with the children in class, insisted that his father had told him to sock anyone who called him a nasty name. He conveniently interpreted the slightest offense as a just provocation to sock. When the class discussed this with him, he considered himself being attacked and criticized for doing something which his father had told him to do.

When the teacher spoke to the father, he admitted having advised his son to do so, but only in extreme cases. When he learned that James used every situation as extreme and was involved in frequent fights, he was displeased. Nevertheless, he felt that this could not hurt James in his general development, and that fighting was a healthy boyish outlet for excess energy.

In the light of James' general behavior, one may assume that he knew all along how he should behave, but he chose to use his father's advice to defy the school rules. The father, on the other hand, had no idea that his advice gave sanction to his son's behavior. He needed to realize that James had no friends because of his aggressiveness, and that such behavior does not develop good human relationships. Only after this was pointed out, did the father realize that he had given his son wrong advice. The father then told James that he had given him wrong advice. This created confusion in James' mind. For one, he could not easily accept the fact that his father had made a serious error in judgment, and furthermore, the new perspective demanded a change in his behavior that he did not like. He told the teacher, "Look what a mess my dad got me into. Now I can do nothing when the children call me nasty names." This was later discussed in class, and James was helped to understand that he was not in a "mess" unless he made one, and that there were other means of feeling important. To cite another example:

Frances, 9 years old, was a child whom we call teacher-deaf. She never heard what was said to her, never knew what the teacher expected of her in class, and consequently, never did any work. This went on for some time. When the teacher discussed this behavior with her mother, she replied, "She doesn't know what to do because you never tell her." When asked on what basis she was making this accusation, she said, "I know, because Frances always tells me that the reason she doesn't do her work is that she doesn't know what to do, that you never tell her what to do." The teacher asked her if Frances has ever mentioned that the other children in class know what to do. To this the mother replied, "I know what you are driving at, but, you see, unless you tell Frances what you want her to do, she doesn't understand you." The teacher asked, "Do you mean that I should tell Frances separately what the assignment is?"

284

and the mother replied, "I am afraid you have to, otherwise she won't know what is expected of her." The teacher learned that at home, the parents had to tell Frances many times what they wanted her to do, and even then she insisted that she did not understand or she forgot what they had told her. Therefore, she had the right to demand special service.

This example illustrates the different approach of home and school. Not only does Frances, but the mother as well, expect and demand that the teacher give the directions for the school work to Frances personally.

This is not a unique example. On the contrary, many parents accept and support the kind of behavior that Frances displayed, and in this manner fortify the child's fallacious concept of how she must act in order to receive special attention. It becomes a matter of helping parents to understand children's goals in their behavior.

In talking with parents, many opportunities arise where they give, indirectly, valuable information to the teacher about general family attitudes, their view of discipline, whether the child has any responsibilities at home, and if so, whether he carries them out voluntarily or whether he has to be forced or coaxed. If the latter, how do the parents do it and how much success do they have?

The parents, too, can gain much information about their child from the teacher. They learn about his behavior at school and the teacher's evaluation of him. They learn about the hopes and expectations she has for him; they acquaint themselves with the various rules and regulations of the school as well as those made by the teacher or by the children in class. Finally, the parent has a chance to learn something about the general program of the class in which their child spends so many hours of each day. Too many parents have no idea what their children do in school.

HOW TO INVITE PARENTS

The success of a conference may well depend on the way the teacher invites a parent to come to school. This is especially true of the parents who have come to school many times before because their children were behavior problems, had difficulties in learning, or both. These parents have been confronted with similar problems so many times without receiving any constructive suggestions, that they consider another visit to the teacher a waste of their time and resent such a request. They often feel accused. Often they feel bitter toward the teacher and toward the school in general, because they think the school has let them down. It is not uncommon for a teacher to hear some parents say, "When I received your note, I began to tremble before I even read it." Or, "What has he done this time?" Or,

"Billy came home crying. He was so afraid to give me your note. I have told him that I'll skin him alive if I ever get another note from school."

The parents anger may be the cause for a bad start. First, even the most skilled teacher may have difficulty reassuring the parent that there is no cause for alarm, especially if she, too, has had a problem with the child. Second, the parents anger may arouse angry feelings in the teacher that she may not be able to conceal. Her reaction might antagonize the parents further.

It is advisable to tell the child that the note contains nothing bad, and that there is no cause for alarm. This puts the child at ease. Often, knowing that the parent may become upset, he relieves his parents' anxiety by saying, "The teacher said that there is nothing bad in the note."

Sometimes, when one senses that a child is afraid to have his parents come to school, one can discuss this with him before sending the invitation. He can be assured that the parents' are not invited in order to accuse him, but in order to plan what they can do to help him and to make him happier. One can then ask, "What do you say? Shall we invite her?" It is seldom that the child still refuses to have his parents come. Usually, asking him for advice and consent makes him feel important and removes the fear and resentment.

If the child objects to having his parents come to school, the teacher could tell him that she will wait a while. After a week or ten days, she confronts him with the same situation. This time she tells him that she cannot wait any longer, and she would feel better if they agreed on inviting the parents. She assures him that her main concern is to help him and that she, the teacher, cannot do so by herself. Should he still refuse, she can use the group to help him understand why he refuses, and what purpose this serves. (See pp. 100–120.) This happens rarely.

The conference should be made by appointment, and sufficient time should be allowed for parent and teacher to discuss their interests and problems. Casual conferences, such as telephone calls and quick informal talks when parents drop in unexpectedly, especially during school hours, are of less value, but they should not be minimized or avoided.

Conferences in the home of the child help the teacher to see the child in his environment, which may shed considerable light on his general behavior. A home visit may be indicated if, for some reason, the parents cannot come to school. Advisedly, the teacher should notify the parents of her intention to visit the home and ask for a convenient time. Unexpected home visits, although very enlightening, may put the parents in an embarrassing situation.

A teacher recalls the time when the parents of Sarah, a very hostile and aggressive child, ignored her invitations to come to school for a conference. After receiving no answer to several of her letters, she decided to pay them a surprise visit. When she arrived, she found the home in terrible disorder, the mother was in her housecoat and with curlers in her hair. When the teacher told her who she was, the mother literally snarled at her, "What do you want? I have no time to see you." And she didn't, in spite of the teacher's protest. It certainly did not help the teacher's relationship with Sarah who witnessed the disrespect her mother showed for the teacher.

Although the teacher had also experienced pleasant unannounced visits, the experience with Sarah's mother made her more cautious. Such a visit may only add to the parent's antagonism toward school and toward the teacher, which in turn may hurt the child.

Sometimes a teacher invites a child to participate in a conference with his parents. This is a tremendous help in the case of a child who tells untrue stories at home about school. Caution should be taken so that this child will not be placed in a position where he might be shamed or scolded by the parent in front of the teacher. Usually, the teacher gets in touch with the parents and prepares them for such a conference, asking them to listen to the facts without getting angry. To cite an incident, here is the case of Peter:

Peter had told his mother that the teacher scratched his neck, and the mother was rightfully angry. When she came to school, the following conversation took place:

Teacher: I am terribly sorry that I had to ask you to come immediately, and I appreciate your coming. You seemed so angry on the telephone. Now, would you be so kind and tell me in Peter's presence the reason for your anger.

Mother: He came home crying, showing me the scratch on his neck, saying that you did it. Peter, why don't you show your teacher the scratch on your neck.

Peter: It doesn't hurt me any more.

Teacher: Peter, when did I scratch you and for what reason?

Peter: Well, when you put your hand on my neck this morning, it hurt.

Teacher: I can't recall putting my hand on your neck. Could you help me remember under what circumstances I put my hand on your neck?

Peter: When you bent over to look at my work, you touched me there and it hurt me.

287

Mother: Show her the scratch.

Teacher: I'm sorry if I hurt you, I did not know because you said nothing. But how could I have scratched you?

Peter: I couldn't sleep last night because the neck hurt me so.

Mother: What do you mean by "last night?" You said that the teacher scratched you this morning.

Peter: She hurt me when she touched me there. I think that I scratched myself at night.

> The teacher could see that the mother was forgetting their agreement and was about to explode, but a wink from the teacher helped the mother to control herself. The teacher told Peter that this was an unfortunate misunderstanding and that he should be more careful how he tells a story in the future.

The point is that without the presence of the child, this incident might have assumed serious complications and impaired the relationship with the parent.

The presence of the child is often very helpful to the discouraged child who is made to feel worthless by his parents. To such a child, it means a great deal to hear his teacher praise him in the presence of his parents. This may be very encouraging to both parent and child.

Letters to parents should impart a feeling of warmth, friendliness, and welcome. They should immediately convey an interest in the child. A letter may read:

> Dear Mrs. Cooper,
>
> I have not yet had the pleasure of meeting you. Laura often mentions you to me. She is a very likable little girl, and I enjoy having her in my class.
>
> I should like to discuss her progress with you as well as plan with you some possible steps we may both take in order to make school a happy place for her.
>
> Could you come to see me any day next week, after the children are dismissed from class? This would make talking more pleasant, as we won't be interrupted. Please let me know when I may expect you.
>
> Sincerely yours,

In contrast, letters conveying anger or anxiety, on the part of the teacher, may increase or fortify the same feelings within the parents. As a consequence, more pressure is brought to bear on the child, and it may increase the antagonism that some parents harbor against teachers and school.

To illustrate this point, let us examine the following letter:

288

Dear Mrs. Cooper;

I have written three letters to you concerning Laura's behavior at school which you ignored. Her behavior has become increasingly worse, and it has reached a point where I refuse to cope with it unless you assume your responsibility. Your indifference toward this situation is, in my opinion, an important factor in Laura's misbehavior.

I expect you Thursday at 3:00 p.m.

Sincerely yours,

What purpose does such a letter serve? Such letters are usually written when teachers are at their wit's end and do not know what to do with the child. This example is a very clear demonstration of how the teacher's reaction to the child's misbehavior reflects the same goals that we encounter in the child.

In this particular situation, we can see a teacher who feels threatened and angered by the lack of response both from the parent and the child. We can also see a completely discouraged teacher who is throwing her hands up in despair.

The mother is just as helpless as the teacher. We must assume that this child has had difficulty in school all along, and the mother had been called to school many times about the bad things her child had done. The mother has never received any insight as to how she continues to fortify the child's wrong attitudes by her response, nor has she been helped with practical suggestions in dealing with the child at home. Very often, this is why parents do not respond to the teacher's request for conferences.

Here the teacher will grab at any means to exonerate herself. Consequently, she blames the parents. This is not necessarily done on a conscious level. The general trend is to pass the buck and put the blame on the home. Although we fully recognize that the problems children have at school often started long before they entered school, and that the home is the source of the child's discouragement, we cannot and must not put the blame on the parents who, in their ignorance, do what they think is best for their children.

If teachers were better trained in child behavior, they could have helped such a child in kindergarten and eliminated the problem. In this respect, the school has failed the parent rather than the parent failing the school.

THE INTERVIEW

Before meeting with the parents, it may be helpful for the teacher to jot down a tentative list of topics she may want to discuss. She may prepare a few samples of the child's work, including pictures, stories, or a workbook. It is important that some of these samples deserve praise-worthy comments. If the child has produced absolutely nothing that merits praise, the teacher may tell of some clever or funny remarks of the child that were appreciated by the class. She may tell of an incident in which the child was helpful to her or another child. In talking about the child's work, it is important for the teacher to begin with a positive report, pointing out a child's strengths before mentioning his weaknesses. (The teacher must keep in mind that parents usually need encouragement.) For instance, the teacher may say, "Mike has a firm, clear handwriting. It is so easy to check his work." Or, "Mike has an unusually rich vocabulary." Most children have some positive qualities or have done something worth praising, either in subject matter or in human relationships.

A good place to begin may also be in telling the parent about something in which her child showed particular interest, like working puzzles, watering the plants, running errands, music, dancing, telling jokes, checking papers, or helping other children.

An interview may have a good start by asking the parents how they feel about the child's progress at school. If the parent says that the child does not seem happy in school, it is wise for the teacher not to show surprise or hurt feelings. If the child is really not happy, she would know it. She may say, "Yes, this is also my feeling, and that is one of the reasons I was so anxious to talk with you. I feel that we must find the root of his unhappiness and make some specific plans for school and for home which might help him." The parent may insist that her child is quite happy at home, but unhappy in school. Although this may be questionable, the teacher has a better chance of winning the parent by not expressing her doubts. She may ask the mother how she came to this conclusion. Inevitably, the teacher may be able to show the parent that the child's unhappiness at school stems from his inability to accept a situation where he cannot have his way, from wanting to stay at home with her, or from feeling inadequate or inferior to the others.

The main purpose of the first conference is to establish a relationship with the parents, based on confidence and the realization that both teacher and parent have a common goal. Such realization will, in most cases, lead to cooperation and a better understanding. Most parents participate actively in a conference if they are made to feel at ease and respected. The following conference took place between a teacher and the mother of a nine-year-old boy who performed poorly academically.

Mother: I am Mrs. Thomas, David's mother.

Teacher: How do you do, Mrs. Thomas. I am so glad to meet you, and I'm very happy that you could come. David told me this morning that he wasn't sure if you would be able to come. In fact, he told me not to expect you.

Mother: I wonder why he said that? I did not tell him that I might not come.

Teacher: It doesn't matter as long as you are here.

Mother: I must speak to him and find out why he told you such a lie.

Teacher: Why don't we get acquainted first, and then we'll see if it's necessary to mention this to David. Perhaps he thought that you were exceptionally busy today. He is very observant. He notices many things that most children do not see.

Mother: Yes, he observes many things. Too many, if you ask me.

Teacher: He is a very smart little fellow with a great deal of imagination. Would you care to see the story he wrote last week? He read it to the class, and we all enjoyed it tremendously.

Mother: Oh, yes, he told me about it.

Teacher: Did he? What did he say?

Mother: Oh, he came home bragging about the wonderful story he wrote and how everyone applauded.

Teacher: What did you say to him?

Mother: I don't like when he comes home bragging, especially since he is not doing so well in school.

Teacher: Did he tell you that?

Mother: Not exactly, but I got it out of him. First he told me that all is going well, but when I asked specific questions, he had to admit that things weren't so well. I always find out.

Teacher: Would you mind telling me what specific questions you asked him?

Mother: I asked him if he finishes his work on time, and he said that he finishes sometimes. Well, "sometimes" is not good enough for me, and I hope, not enough for you. I told him that if he didn't finish every day he'd be in big trouble with me, and that I will go to school to find out.

Teacher: Do you think that he might have been worried about your coming to school today?

Mother: I'm sure he was. I think that may be the reason he told you that I wouldn't come. He probably thought that you wouldn't wait for me then.

Teacher: Why is he so afraid, assuming that you did find out that he doesn't do his work?

Mother: He knows that he would be punished.

Teacher: How do you punish him? What do you do?

291

Mother: He gets it with the strap.

Teacher: Do you usually use a strap on him?

Mother: Sometimes I do and sometimes his father does. But we don't always use the strap. Sometimes we send him to his room, and sometimes we take away television privileges or other privileges. But mostly we have to spank him.

Teacher: Does he mind you then?

Mother: For a while he does.

Teacher: This means that you have to punish him often.

Mother: Oh, yes, very often.

Teacher: For how long have you been punishing him for not doing his schoolwork?

Mother: Oh, almost for as long as he has been going to school. He would have done nothing if we hadn't laid down the law.

Teacher: Have you ever tried any other method?

Mother: We have tried everything. We have given him money and toys for good behavior, and it didn't work. We locked him in his room, and it did not help. We tried almost everything. Only a good spanking will make him work.

Teacher: It may make him work for a while, as you yourself said. By forcing him to do reading and homework, he cannot develop a proper attitude toward it. Also, there is the danger that, although he does not enjoy the actual work you force him to do, he may enjoy the attention you give him.

Mother: I can see by your talking that he isn't doing well in school.

Teacher: He is doing well in the things he enjoys and for which he receives recognition.

Mother: What things? Does he read well? Does he finish his work every day? Are you pleased with his work?

Teacher: There are certain things he does quite well and which please me. He likes to write and he enjoys working with clay. He wrote several very good original stories. Would you care to read them?

Mother: Can he spell? I don't understand how he can write stories when he can't spell.

Teacher: He is not a good speller, but if I were to make an issue of it, he would give up writing his stories, and that would be a pity. He may, in time, if we encourage him to write, take more interest in spelling. We must build on the positive, and thereby encourage him to attempt to learn the things that seem to him too difficult now. If we criticize him all the time, we only discourage him further. Can you see what I mean?

Mother: I think, I understand what you mean. But what can I do to help him?

Teacher: Mrs. Thomas, would you mind trying a different approach for a few weeks? If it doesn't work, you can always go back to your old methods.

Mother: What do you suggest we do?

Teacher: Would you try not to question him about school and not make him do any schoolwork?

Mother: You mean I should do nothing?

Teacher: Not nothing. Do things with him which he will like, like playing games, singing, talking, maybe cooking or baking, anything that he will enjoy doing with you. In addition, you may start training him toward the acceptance of responsibilities at home. Does he have any responsibilities at home?

Mother: He is supposed to take out the garbage, but he forgets most of the time. We go through so much aggravation making him do it, that I decided to do it myself.

Teacher: Did David choose to take out the garbage or did you decide that?

Mother: I thought that this would be the easiest for him to do.

Teacher: Why don't you let him choose to do something he would want to do? Talk it over with him. Asking him for his consent or advice, it will make him feel important. Most children will assume responsibilities, but do not like to be pressured. You see, if he chooses his job, he assumes a responsibility, which is different from forcing him to accept one. In class, he usually carries out the responsibilities that he himself assumed.

Mother: And what if he doesn't remember?

Teacher: This could be discussed with him also. Decide on a logical consequence, something with a direct bearing on what he is doing, and then apply it. He won't resent it because he had helped you decide on what the consequence should be.

Mother: I'll talk it over with my husband and tell him what you suggested.

Teacher: Please do. I hope that he will be willing to try my suggestions. .Please, let me know what you have decided to do, and if I can help you in any way, don't hesitate to call on me.

Mother: I'll call you soon.

This is one example of an interview with a parent. The general approach and topics to be discussed will depend on the child's difficulties and on the attitude of the parents. In all situations, however, we try to win the parents, just as we try to win the child.

In this particular incident, the mother followed the suggestions, was consistent about her new approach, and had good results.

The parent's satisfaction with David at home had a direct influence on his attitude toward school. David found out that he could get attention through useful means.

If a child has difficulty in school, the parents should know about it once he has reached third or fourth grade. Difficulties do not start all of a sudden. Often parents do not know how to help their child. They are completely unaware of how their own behavior toward their child contributes or may even be ths source of his difficulties. Mrs. Thomas was unaware that her negative attention, her scolding, nagging, and punishing, intensified David's problem. Frances's mother did not realize that she was encouraging her daughter to be a bad listener by repeating her requests so often.

There are the parents who have definite ideas about how their child must be treated at school and at home, and come to the conference in order to tell this to the teacher. This holds especially true of parents who believe in strict discipline, and who challenge the teacher and her methods. They may be critical because she does not use enough discipline; other parents may think she is too strict. The former are almost always parents who have used corporal punishment for years without any results, yet expect the teacher to use the same method with results. It is easier to convince the strict parents that their methods are useless than it is those who complain that the teacher is too strict. Convinced that by allowing the children to have free and unrestricted rights because it gives them the feeling of being loved and of security, parents allow their children to rule and control them.[1] Consequently, they resent any restrictions the teacher puts on the child, and demand the child be given the same freedom in class that he enjoys at home.

The following example illustrates this kind of parent. It concerns the mother of Frank, a nine-year-old boy who was in the third grade.

> Frank was a year behind in his grade placement because the mother was reluctant to send him to kindergarten when he was five. She felt he was too young to be away from home and might pick up all kinds of diseases from other children. At 6, he went to first grade, but had to be put back into kindergarten because of his inability to adjust. In spite of this, he was no more ready for first grade than he was the year before. Because of his age, he was promoted from one grade to the next. Frank made no progress in school. In addition, he was a behavior problem in class, paying no attention to the teacher, disregarding school rules and regulations, and staying home frequently, either the entire day or half of the day.
>
> When scolded or as much as reproached for his behavior, he

[1]Rudolf Dreikurs and V. Soltz, *Children the Challenge* (New York: Hawthorne Press, 1964).

would start to cry. His crying would gradually increase to sobbing. He could keep this up for hours, until the children regretted having reprimanded him and asked him for forgiveness. This would happen even after we discussed his behavior and the purpose of his crying. They kept falling for his trap. He always succeeded in making others feel guilty if they did not act according to his wishes.

Frank was the youngest of five children, all of whom were either married or living away from home.

From his mother, the teacher learned that not only did the parents make a toy out of him, granting him every whim, but his siblings did so as well. The mother said that they all loved him so, and in addition, it was hard to refuse him anything since he was so sensitive and easily hurt. His father was especially afraid to upset Frank. He bought him many toys, went to bed with him at night and waited for him to fall asleep. Frank would not go to bed unless his father went also. Before leaving the house in the morning, Frank would tell his mother what he wanted for lunch and for dinner. If she did not comply with his wishes, his father would take him to a restaurant.

Frank's parents were completely unaware how their manner of treating him at home encouraged his uncooperative behavior at school. It took some time before his mother could understand that they had made a little tyrant out of their son, and that he now controlled their lives. It was even more difficult to convince the father that he was doing his son harm and depriving him of a normal development. However, after several conferences with both parents, they agreed to put some restrictions on Frank and to refrain from letting him dictate to them. In time, Frank's behavior changed both at home as well as in school. It was a slow, gradual process, but it went steadily uphill. This would not have happened, had the teacher held the belief that the home situation was none of her business.

The teacher must be a good listener. She must be constantly alert, picking up clues and follow up on them. For example, if a parent says, "My child is very shy," the teacher may ask, "Could you tell me how this is expressed, and what do you do?" In this way, she learns that the parent felt sorry for him and came to his aid. The teacher may succeed in pointing this out to them. If a mother says that she doesn't let her child do a sloppy job, she may want perfection from the child. This mother may set too high goals and discourage him in this way. She does not realize that a child needs recognition for merely trying to be useful. He may lose all desire to be of help again if his performance did not live up to the parents' expectations, if he should get scolded, and if his efforts are belittled. These parents need to be helped to understand that their own ambitions are hindering the child from developing pleasure and pride in the things he can do according to his ability.

If a mother refers to her youngest child as "my baby," even though he is already 9 or 10 years old, one may assume that the child is being held back in his development. The teacher must, in a gentle way, point out to the mother what she is doing. Such children often fear growing up because they are afraid to lose the position of being the "baby" and pampered.

If a mother tells of another of her children who is always good, and who never causes any trouble, it may give the teacher a clue to the difficulties her student has both at school and at home. In the competition with this good sibling, her student probably gave up and tried to have a place at home by receiving attention in a destructive way.

Many parents are impressed with the "yes" child, the one who gets satisfaction from the ready compliance that has always brought approval. Often these children fear to express any disagreement or anger because they depend so much on approval and on being liked. They frequently lack initiative and live in constant fear of displeasing others. The parents are usually not aware of this. Their satisfaction with this kind of behavior encourages the child in his fallacious convictions. He never develops the important courage to be imperfect.

If a parent comes to an interview angry about some incident or because she is convinced that coming to school is a waste of time, the teacher does well to listen until this parent has told her story and blown off some steam. Listening attentively, she may gather some information that may help her in understanding the child's present problems. Anger often fades away when it is met with a genuine wish to understand. Usually, the parent calms down as soon as she realizes that the teacher is concerned and sympathetic to her feelings. Then the parent becomes more approachable and will listen to what the teacher has to say.

In certain situations, however, a teacher may disarm an angry parent, as the following example will illustrate:

> Mr. Koda arrived ten minutes late for his interview. He stopped at the door and said, "I am a busy man, so don't keep me more than a few minutes. What is it you want to talk to me about?"[2]

Teacher: I am sorry to have bothered you, Mr. Koda. I did not know you were so busy. Besides, it wouldn't be fair to Jim if I were to take only a few minutes to talk to his father. Under the circum-

[2]Father of "Jimmy"; see p. 251.

stances it would be better if we postpone this conference. Thank you for coming. Goodbye.

Mr. Koda: Now, I'm here already. If it takes a little longer, I'll stay a little longer, just don't keep me more than necessary. I have a business, you know, and can't stay away all day.

Teacher: Yes, I know, Mr. Koda. But since a conference would be of help to Jim and to me only if we could talk without having to watch the clock, I really believe that it would be better if you came someday when you can spare the time. I will always be glad to see you. I am very fond of your son.

Mr. Koda: I'd rather stay, if you don't mind, and let's talk as long as it is necessary. Jimmy often mentions your name. He is very fond of you, too.

Teacher: I'm glad you're staying. You have a very interesting boy, Mr. Koda.

Mr. Koda: Maybe so, but I have no luck with him. I don't know what makes him so lazy.

Teacher: I wouldn't say that Jimmy is lazy. He may appear that way because he is not working in school, but this is not due to laziness.

Mr. Koda: Then what is it due to?

Teacher: I believe that he is overambitious and very discouraged. He doesn't believe that he can succeed, and so he doesn't even try.

Mr. Koda: Jimmy ambitious? I'd give anything if he had any ambition. I keep on telling him that. Why should he be discouraged: Who discourages him? Believe me, no kid ever got more from parents than he did.

Teacher: You mean that you gave him material things?

Mr. Koda: Yes, and we gave him love, too.

It was a slow process trying to explain to this man that giving everything, without giving a child a sense of accomplishment, of respect, and of parental approval is of little value, and may do harm to the child's self-concept and his general development. We discussed Jim's position in the family, the father's open disappointment in his son, the scolding and humiliation to which he exposed him, and how this undermined Jim's self-respect and sense of worth. Equally, spoiling him, whether by his father or by his mother, had deprived Jim of developing his own strength and added to his sense of being a failure. At this point, Jim did not believe that he was good enough as he was, nor did he believe that doing average work would gain him the prestige he desired. He felt that he had to be something special, far superior to the other children, and since

297

he did not believe that he could attain such a position, he gave up trying. This expressed itself especially in areas where he feared failure, such as reading and spelling. He concentrated on sports where he was sure to be successful. In addition, he manufactured deeds and achievements in order to gain status with the class.

Mr. Koda became very much interested in our discussion. He came to a number of conferences, and we discussed possible steps that would encourage Jim both at home and at school, and which would bring him recognition with realistic achievement.

If we review what happened in this interview, we see that in the first place, the teacher did not let the father throw or intimidate her with anger. She remained courteous, expressed her belief in his son, and also her regret that the father had no time to help her with his boy. Had the teacher responded emotionally, expressed her disappointment or shown anger, she would have spoiled her chances for Mr. Koda's cooperation. The teacher did not become defensive, but directed the father's attention to an objective observation of his child's potential, and the means he used to obtain recognition. She did not argue with the father because she did not want to build a wall between the father and herself which, in turn, would have hurt Jimmy.

The feelings with which the parents come to an interview differ widely. Some come with definite ideas about what they want for their child. Some have definite ideas about the kind of discipline they want, and openly criticize the teacher for being too lenient or too strict. "I want you to keep him in during lunch until he finishes his work." Or, "I don't want you to keep him in during recess or any other time when the other children go out, regardless of whether he does his work or not." Some parents will say, "I don't want you to discuss him in front of the group." Others will demand, "Shame him and embarrass him in front of the class, that may make an impression on him."

Some parents are inclined to jump to the defense of their children regardless of the incident. They cannot admit their children had done any wrong, either out of a belief that such admission may do harm to the child, or out of fear that it may put them in a bad light as parents.

Parents who believe that the teacher is blaming them for the child's difficulties in school must be reassured and put at ease as quickly as possible. The teacher could say the following to such a parent:

I am sorry to have given you the impression that you are to blame. I am sure that you did the best you could, and I hope that you feel the same way about me. Both of us are concerned about Helen, and, of course, we both want to do everything possible to help her. It is

298

for this reason that I asked you to come to school. As we talk, we may realize where either one of us has made mistakes and how they could be rectified.

During the discussion that follows, the teacher may learn about a class situation of which she was completely unaware. For instance, the parent may tell the teacher that his child feels that the teacher does not like him. This needs to be investigated. The child may have gotten this erroneous concept because of some remark or action on the teacher's part. She may learn that this child does not like to sit next to his neighbor. This may happen in spite of the sociogram the teacher administered, and then seated him next to the classmate of his choice.

In discussing this frankly with the parents, without being on the defensive, the teacher can help them to realize her genuine concern and her willingness to change her method, if need be. This makes it easier for parents to accept suggestions from the teacher.

Some parents come to complain about other children who pick on their child, and demand the teacher do something about it. This may be a clue to their child's feelings about other children, his dependency on parental protection, wanting their sympathy, or using this as a means to keep the parents busy with him.

The teacher should listen without brushing off accusations. She should listen to the parent's account of how their child behaved in other classes, with children in the neighborhood, and with his siblings. As the teacher listens, she should be able to sense the feeling of the parent, which should help her greatly to understand the present difficulties this child has in social relationships. Often the parent describes the home situation as a battleground in which both parents become involved in their children's fights, and how they have to protect Irving at home from being hurt by his sisters and brothers. The teacher may explain that such protection only weakens the child, and that many children get into fights deliberately in order to involve the parents. This may be a means of conveying to the parents "how bad the others are and how good I am." Or, "I am small and weak and must be protected," which is not necessarily true. If these children were left to fight their own battles, they would probably learn how to take care of themselves or, which is more likely, not to get into fights. The teacher must explain this to the parents, and suggest they stay out of their children's quarrels. The teacher may tell the parents of similar cases which have been solved in the proposed manner. She may offer comments and information about children in general, leading to more insight into children's behavior.

The teacher's interest in whatever the parents have to say, and her desire to learn from them, puts the parents at ease and they usually talk freely and willingly. The teacher should try to be objective and sympathetic when she attempts to see how each parent views his child.

Communication with the parent is not necessarily on a verbal level. We may easily betray our feelings of anger, discouragement, contempt for them by a severity in our voice, a critical look, a movement indicating impatience, and other signs indicating antagonism. The teacher must be aware of such possibilities. This does not imply that we must necessarily agree with what the parent is doing or share his point of view. Listening attentively is, in itself, a means of giving encouragement.

CONFERENCES REGARDING HOMEWORK,
GRADES, AND SUBJECT MATTER

Parents need a reeducation in regard to homework and the responsibility they have in this matter. This should be conveyed by the teacher as soon as the child enters school. Most parents are made to believe that they are responsible for the homework of their children. Also, they are sincerely convinced that they help the child academically when they force him to do the homework and offer their assistance with it.

The fallacy of their thinking is manifold. By taking over the responsibility of the child's homework, the child is deprived of developing a sense of responsibility, of becoming independent, and of learning from his faulty attitude.

A parent who takes over this responsibility for the child, may never be free from this servitude. In time, the parents will begin to resent this bondage and will demand independent behavior from the child, something for which he has never been trained. This will inevitably lead to conflict.

Homework may become a strong weapon in the child's hands, something he can effectively use to extort privileges, to exploit and punish ambitious parents. Therefore, parents must be helped not only to place homework in the hands of the child, but to be less concerned. Children sense the anxiety the parents have about their homework, even when they do not talk about it. The value of homework is primarily a way of training the child to work on his own and to accept responsibilities.

Helping the child may also reinforce his wrong evaluation of his capacities and of how he must act to be successful. If he has little self-confidence, it only strengthens this concept of being incapable. If he seeks constant attention, his helplessness brings him the desired satisfaction, and reinforces his belief that this is how he must act.

300

If the teacher finds it necessary to give homework, she must first win the cooperation of her students. Enforced homework has little educational value. In many cases, the time spent on imposed homework is wasted. The child does not learn from repetition unless he has first grasped the meaning of what he is doing. Mere mechanical repetition without understanding is futile. In too many cases, the children see no value in the assignment and consider their task busy work. Very often, it is exactly that. All the child learns is to hate school and the teacher. At any rate, the parents should stay out of it.

Parents can help the child by explaining to him why they will not give him much help. They must provide a place where the child can work undisturbed. An important aspect is the time for doing homework. Children will accept the responsibility more readily if given a chance to go out and play or watch a favorite TV program after a long day in school.

Often parents ask in complete dismay, "Do you mean to say that I should do nothing to help my child?" This becomes a ticklish situation requiring judgment on the part of the teacher so that it neither antagonizes the parents nor harms the child. The teacher could usually answer in the following manner:

> Of course you are concerned and want to help, and I am sure that you will be able to help your child, but not until we have helped him change his attitude toward learning, that is, not until he enjoys it and asks for help. Right now, he resents it, and being forced into it makes him fight you and dislike studies. Making him do homework is not a learning situation. If it were, you would not have to force him to do it each day for so many months. By now, he would be able and willing to do his work on his own if he had profited from your pressure. I would suggest that you withdraw from this struggle and do not force him to do any work. Discuss this with your child first. Tell him that he is old enough and smart enough to take care of his school obligations himself. It will be up to him whether he does or does not do his homework. However, when he should ask you to explain something to him, by all means, do so, but after he understands what he must do, leave him alone. When he wants to read to you, tell him that you will be glad to listen to him, and that it will give you pleasure. Won't you, please, try this method for a few weeks and then come to see me again? If it doesn't work, we may have to try something else.

As already pointed out, homework only has a value if it is done by the child out of a sense of responsibility and a desire to make progress. Parents may discuss homework policies with the child, help him decide the time he should work, and allow him sufficient time to

301

do the work. They should not interrupt the child with requests and questions while he is working. Neither should they peek in every few minutes to see how much he has done. If the child chooses to do nothing during the allotted time, then we must look for deeper causes and eliminate them before we can expect the child to do his work well and profitably.

One should never deprive children of play because of homework. Children who spend two-thirds of the day in school, where all of their activities are organized and supervised, need time when they can play or talk with whomever they please, or engage in some activity all by themselves. They look forward to coming home where their lives are different, just as much as they look forward to going back to school in the morning.

REPORT CARDS

The conventional method of reporting pupil status and progress to parents has been a controversial issue for many years. There are those who demand the report card form of summarizing the child's progress and success in his academic achievement and social adjustment. Others claim that it is an inadequate evaluation and interpretation of his progress, misleading to the parents, and that it may do harm to the child because poor grades may discourage him, whereas high grades may develop wrong values. Furthermore, it may cause friction between parents and teachers, confuse them, cause tension and worry. Finally, it can never convey what the child really knows or is capable of doing.

Reporting pupil progress to parents has been and still is one of the most frustrating and most unsatisfactory aspects of a teacher's job. Educators have tried for years to devise a new and more accurate form of reporting pupil progress, without much success. So far, no report card has conveyed to parents what the teacher wants them to know.

The parent-teacher conference is the only possible means of reporting student progress, both academic and social, to parents. Much more can be said by the teacher than can be written. Parents can ask questions about what they do not understand.

READING

Reading is one of the subjects about which parents are most anxious, and where they put the most pressure on the child. Usually parental anxiety does not develop until the child is in third or fourth grade and has not made progress. Their anxiety and pressure only increases the child's negative attitude toward reading and his feeling of inadequacy. The child dreads the time when he must read to his parents,

302

for they shame and discourage him in the process of teaching.

Some children utilize their lack of academic achievement to keep their parents busy with them. This may become a means of taking the parents away from the other members of the family, keeping mother or father all to themself.

Parents do not realize, and often cannot understand, why the child would enjoy such negative attention. "How can he possibly want this, knowing how angry he makes me and that I may even punish him?" they ask. These parents need help in understanding the child's private logic, his goal of power and the means by which he tries, usually with success, to achieve it. What can parents do to help strengthen the child's reading? There are a number of things they can do.

Probably, the most important step in developing a child's liking for reading is for the parents to read themselves. It is not uncommon to find the parents who put such emphasis on reading, rarely read a book themselves. They claim that they have no time. This does not stop them from telling their child how important it is to read, and how much pleasure they derive from it. Logically, a child asks himself, "If it is so important and so pleasant, how come my mother and father never read anything except newspapers? It can't be as important as all that." Children may pattern themselves after their parents and take on their values.

Every family should have a set reading time. If the child is still too young to read by himself, the parents may read to him, choosing a variety of reading materials, and discussing the material with him in a stimulating way. Preaching, explaining, and forcing the child to read does not stimulate him, but results in boredom and a hatred for the subject.

When a child begins to read by himself and wants to read to his parents, they should show interest and enjoyment as they listen to him. It is absolutely necessary for them to avoid any criticism when he makes mistakes, never shaming him. Parents should follow along the lines as the child reads and quickly, but casually, pronounce any word which might cause the child difficulty. This prevents embarrassment. If the child does not understand a word, they may look it up in a dictionary together. Parents can take the child to the library and allow him to choose his own books. With careful guidance, the child will learn to choose critically and wisely.

One can buy interesting books for the child and encourage him to build his own library. Parents should not insist that the children read only in their own rooms, but should make every room in the house available to them for the purpose of reading.

It is a mistake to compare children in achievement or to hold up

303

a sibling as an example. This may only drive the discouraged learner to withdraw further, as he fears that he cannot compete with his "bright" brother or sister.

HOW CAN PARENTS HELP A CHILD WHO HAS
DIFFICULTIES IN ARITHMETIC?

In general, if the child has difficulty with arithmetic or any other subject besides reading, the problems tend to be similar. There are ways by which parents can help the young child without actually teaching him. The first and most important step is planning situations in which the small child can use numbers in an enjoyable manner. They can play simple games requiring counting, matching numbers, comparing, quantity, and so forth. In helping mother set the table, the child may count the silverware, plates, and glasses. Together, mother and child may count the steps from the kitchen to the table, to the door. They may play games, such as horseshoes and parcheesi, letting the child do the scoring. Children may help to make the grocery or laundry list; they should be encouraged to buy something at the store and bring home the change. This may then be recounted with the parent. Playing ball or jumping and counting is another way to teach the meaning of numbers. In each case, one must avoid pressure. Such activities are accepted by the child only if the child enjoys them as he does playing games.

Older children who have problems with numbers are usually already discouraged and afraid of the subject. Their difficulties may well express their general inability to solve other problems in life. Helping these children with the mechanical aspect of arithmetic is of little value. Parents need to understand their part in what caused these difficulties, as well as the extent to which they have and are still contributing to the present state by trying to solve the child's problems for him, instead of guiding him to find the solutions by himself. After the child has been helped to trust his own judgment, a good tutor may help him catch up with the subject.

WHEN AND WHY DO SOME PARENTS
BECOME SO ALARMED?

The majority of parents become more alarmed when their children develop disturbing behavior than when they fail academically. Teachers, as a rule, find it more difficult to approach and help parents whose children are behavior problems. Why is this so?

There are numerous reasons for this panic. When the child has difficulty learning a subject matter, the parents may assume that this is the school's or teacher's fault, or they may blame it on hereditary deficiencies. Next, they may believe that with special help at home, either by them or by a tutor, the problem may be eased if not entirely alleviated. They may consider transferring the child to another school, especially to a private school, which, they hope, will take care of the problem. In other words, they can find a number of ways to put the blame on everyone except themselves. Behavioral transgressions, however, reflect directly on them as parents. They regard them as indictments against themselves and feel personally deficient and powerless. They see themselves as failures, embarrassed and humiliated. Some challenge the teacher to remedy the situation by disciplining the child, while others refuse to discuss the matter.

It is often extremely difficult to reach any understanding with these parents, as they do not listen to what the teacher has to say.

Sally's mother was resentful when a teacher mentioned the home situation. She maintained that home and school have nothing to do with each other, and just as she did not tell the teacher how to teach school, she demanded that the teacher did not interfere with Sally's upbringing at home. Furthermore, she was convinced that Sally would outgrow this stage. This referred to Sally's academic, physical, emotional, and health development. In reading the case of Sally we can see how her problems in school, and in life in general, stemmed directly from the home environment.

Let's consider another case:

> Rachel's mother became indignant when she was told that her daughter did not make friends at school because she called them ugly names and used vulgar speech. At first, the mother insisted that this was not true, that the children deliberately manufactured these tales in order to get Rachel into trouble. Next, she maintained that if it were true, Rachel must have picked up such language in school, for at home nobody ever used foul language. When she was assured that using such language was but a symptom of a more serious problem, she became even angrier, and shouted, "How dare you make such an accusation?" The teacher's concern was Rachel's loneliness, and how she could help her. However, it was impossible to convey this to Rachel's mother who had only one thing in mind, namely to divert the blame from herself, even though she was not being blamed.

Some parents panic because they have heard so much about juvenile delinquency, and fear that their child is heading in that direction. Their immediate reaction is, "I must take him to a psychiatrist before he gets into serious trouble." Every now and then, they actually do so, in spite of the teacher's advice to try, if only for a while, to change their way of treating the child at home. They find it difficult, however, to associate their method of bringing up their child with his behavior.

The teacher should be able to explain to the parent why their child misbehaves and what they can do to correct the situation. They can teach the child self-control through the application of logical consequences, which does not mean demanding blind obedience. Such obedience is superficial and does not last. There is little value in making children obey. Rigid discipline may develop overdependence and fearfulness of new situations if there is no one around to tell the child what to do.

The teacher should take the opportunity to tell the parents about the class council (see p. 148), and how this self-government helps the children self-discipline and understand their own problems as well as those of other children. In this way, they learn how to help and encourage one another, how to evaluate a situation, and then how to make their own decisions. This gives the teacher an opportunity to explain to the parents how they can train their children and achieve greater cooperation and harmony at home through the use of the family council (see p. 309).

WHAT OTHER KINDS OF SUGGESTIONS
CAN A TEACHER GIVE TO PARENTS?

Most parents who have been counseled are very grateful for the opportunity. Few have another place where they can take their problems or where someone will be interested in helping them. (See "Parent Study Group," p. 325, and "Parent Education," p. 319.)

Teachers can and must help troubled parents. Many of the suggestions were outlined in this chapter. Teachers must, however, be careful not to swamp parents with too many suggestions at one time, for they may become frightened and discouraged.

We should like to mention that almost every teacher, at sometime or another, has an unsuccessful interview with a parent. Even the best and most skilled teacher may say the wrong thing. The wrong gesture or the wrong tone of voice may spoil the interview and prevent the desired results.

We must be careful of how we word our suggestions. We find that it is most acceptable to parents when we invite them to try our suggestions for a while and find out for themselves. We must be careful to point out that there is no assurance that the child will immediately respond favorably, but he may. However, we may point out that other parents with similar problems had good results when they tried a new approach.

FREQUENT ARGUMENTS GIVEN BY PARENTS

I'm afraid, he takes after me. I never could stop talking in class. Don't you think that he might have inherited this trait from me? As a matter of fact, my mother told me that she had the same trouble herself.

306

I must admit, I never was much of a reader myself. I hardly ever read anything but a newspaper or magazine. My husband isn't much of a reader either. But, I insist that my children read every day.

School is nothing but a playground these days. In my days there was no nonsense. We had to study, and we did. I don't know if this is the new system that children play so much in school or if teachers just like to make it easier for themselves.

If you ask me, you are using too much psychology. I don't believe in all this nonsense. Why should my child feel insecure? He gets everything he wants. He has a good home.

What do you mean, "He is insecure?" You should see him jump off the diving board, and ride his bike without holding on. He is not afraid of anything.

I can't understand why parents are called to school so often these days. School problems are your problems. I have my own problems, and I don't bother you with them.

If you have problems with my child, it is your business to know what to do. That's what you are trained for and for that you are getting paid. I don't see why we parents have to help the teacher.

John is a sensitive child. You can't treat him like you treat any other child. I don't mean that he should get special treatment, but you know what I mean. He is different.

My child isn't used to frustrations. At home, we allow him to do what he wants to do. Why shouldn't he have all the freedom in his own home? Then at school, it is required that he do certain things at a certain time. He is restricted, and he becomes disturbed. He is used to being his own boss.

I'm sorry to hear that my Jimmy causes so much trouble. Maybe, we ought to put him in a private school.

I think that you just don't like my daughter. I must speak to the principal about it immediately. I want her out of your class.

Jimmy never had any trouble in school until he came to you.

The children in this neighborhood are a bad influence on Charles. You know this neighborhood isn't what it used to be. Some very undesirable people moved in. We try to keep Charles away from the other children, but he learned a lot of bad things from them anyway.

307

Maybe if you moved his seat away from Tommy. We never did like this boy, and we're sure that he has a bad influence on our boy.

Do you think that his thinness may have something to do with his listlessness? He is such a bad eater. He hardly eats at all. How can he have the energy to concentrate on his work.

Why don't you shame him in front of the entire class? Embarrass him in front of everybody, and this may teach him a lesson.

Why don't you use the good old paddle? It never hurt me any and it will do my boy some good. Believe me, we couldn't stand it if we didn't paddle him when he deserves it.

I'm a very busy man, and can stay only a few minutes. Now, what can I do for you? Well, I leave the upbringing of the children to their mother. This is a mother's job. Why don't you get in touch with my wife and have her come to see you?

I spoke to our doctor about Jimmy's trouble in school. He told me not to worry, that Jimmy will outgrow this stage. Frankly, I was a devil myself at his age, and I came out all right.

Teachers try to take out their frustration on the kids. This is nothing new. Any little thing they do becomes a big problem. John is a normal boy, the way I like a boy to be. A good fight now and then is good for him. It makes no difference who is at fault or who started it. Let him have his fight.

I had no idea that Sally was so bad at school. This is the first time I heard of it. If the records say that she was a problem in the other classes, I know nothing about it.

I tried everything. I promised to give him a dollar for every good grade on his report card. We bought him a special bike with his promise that he will be a good boy. He promises everything, but never keeps his promise. We don't know what to do any more.

I wish I had a dime for every time I was called to school. When John brings a note from school, I get so upset, I start shaking.

I hate to say this about my own child, but I'm afraid he is no good. I am not one of those mothers who tries to fool themselves and who shut their eyes to the truth. My husband and I have tried everything. We tried giving him much love, and it didn't do any good. We tried punishing him, spanking him, and locking him up in his room. Nothing helped.

308

Don't you believe that some children are born with a bad streak in them? I honestly think that my John was bad from the day he was born. We had no trouble with the other children, but we always had trouble with him.

John is lazy. He is the laziest thing at home. I can talk myself hoarse and he won't do a thing. I know what you are up against.

I thought that when he gets to you, you will straighten him out. Guess I was wrong about that.

I know exactly when his troubles started. In second grade, he had a very bad teacher. He had no trouble until he had her.

I can't understand why he has trouble reading and spelling at school when he does so well at home. He reads for me and I give him spelling words, and he has no trouble at all.

Wait until I get home. I'll skin him alive. No child of mine is going to behave that way.

I can't understand why Anne should have so much trouble at school. None of my other children had any trouble. After all, they were brought up exactly in the same way and in the same family.

He is not a bad boy at home. My only trouble with him is that he follows me around like a shadow. He wants to sit on my lap, and he even wants me to carry him to bed. He is getting so heavy, I can hardly lift him.

I am afraid I cannot help you. His mother pampers him to death. She makes a real sissy out of him. If I say, "No," he runs to her crying, and she lets him have his way.

He is very much like his father. He inherited his father's stubbornness and other traits which are not especially praiseworthy.

THE FAMILY COUNCIL

Teachers can help parents by showing them how the training children receive at home is reflected in their behavior in school and in the community. They train children either to conform to or defy the rules of society. Parents should prepare the child for socialized living, but they often do not know how to do it. They no longer have the power to make children behave and study, nor to stop them from being destructive. But they can and often want to learn what to do. The first step is often to set up a family council.

WHAT IS A FAMILY COUNCIL?

Teachers can help parents to establish democratic practices in the home by having scheduled family meetings. A family meeting is a cooperative discussion of topics of common interest, a meeting in which all family members sit together, encourage each other in their endeavors and reach decisions concerning family matters.

The family council is the best way to resolve the everyday problems of all family members. Regular farmily meetings encourage and promote responsibility, initiative, and cooperation. They stimulate sensitivity to the needs of others in the family. Family meetings give every member of the family a chance to express himself freely, and the obligation to listen to others and participate in the responsibilities of the family.

The family council is based on the same principles of mutual respect, trust, equality, and cooperation that were discussed in the sections on the class council and the democratic classroom. Nobody has the right to dictate, and none the obligation to submit to dictates. Consideration for other family members replaces satisfaction of personal desires. The family council has much more significance than merely to decide who will do the various household tasks.

Every member of the family old enough to express an opinion should be included. Children can help and should be able to voice an opinion in family affairs. This makes family life more enjoyable and helps to prepare youngsters for responsibility.

> "The family council, more than anything else, provides each member with a sense of equal status, both in regard to rights and in regard to obligations; in this sense it facilitates the application of democratic principles to family life.
>
> "If the sessions are used by the parents to explain, preach, scold, or impose their will on their children, then the council is not democratic and will fail in its purpose. Each parent, like any other member of the family, can merely submit his point of view to the group. The first objective of the sessions should be the willingness of all to listen sincerely to what each has to say. Before any satisfactory solutions can be found, the new routine of listening to each other and understanding what the other means has to be firmly established."[3]

The family meeting should not be a gripe session, but a source of working out solutions to problems. Each person expressing a complaint is expected to present his suggested solution.

It is important that children learn to do their part around the home.

[3]Rudolf Dreikurs, *The Challenge of Parenthood* (New York: Hawthorne Press, 1948).

Along with the rights children have, go certain responsibilities. Children need to have choices in the jobs that they do, and should be allowed to decide when to do them, taking into consideration that it should not interfere with the rest of the family members. A list of jobs could be made, such as emptying wastebaskets, taking out garbage, cleaning the basin, setting and clearing the table, washing the dishes, and the like. If the children do not follow through, this should be discussed during the next family meeting. The family must then decide on ways to deal with them.

In a well-functioning household, no one person should have to shoulder the full responsibility. If parents and the other family members are willing to accept the family meeting as the medium for working out problems, they do not need to feel discouraged if things do not always go as they should. It is more important for the children and parents to follow through with their assignments than to have things going smoothly all the time. Sometimes one family member may be reluctant to carry out his job. This requires patience. Although the daily routine may be disrupted, there is no need for discouragement or hostility. If the parents are consistent in what they are doing and let things take care of themselves, many things will eventually straighten themselves out, particularly if these problems are dealt with in the family council.

In the beginning, the family meetings could involve such things as planning family fun, evening snacktimes, parties and holiday fun, what is to be served, household chores, privacy within the family, use of the bathroom, use of the telephone, respect for property, important problems between family members, and so forth.

At times, it is impossible to reach agreement on particular problem, and it may be necessary to postpone the decision until the next meeting. Meanwhile, family members can be sorting out their feelings and ideas. A delayed decision can be an effective cooling off technique.

Most urgent decisions are not as urgent as the parents or a child may be inclined to believe. All members of the family need to acquire the patience to function under circumstances that are not to their liking. Most parents find it difficult to stand by quietly when something goes wrong or when the child misbehaves. What they can do and usually are doing may not correct the situation. However, anything seems preferable to a wait-and-see attitude. In the absence of a decision by the council, everyone has the right to do what he considers best, but no decision about what others should do has validity, unless it is approved by the council. One of the first decisions may be what to do in case of real danger. Then, on an agreed signal, any discussion should be omitted and immediate compliance guaran-

311

teed. In most other conflict situations, it is sufficient for the parent to withdraw and leave the children to their own resources, without an audience.

Once a decision has been made, any alteration has to wait for the next session. In the interim, no one has the right to impose his decision on others. On the other hand, if a decision for certain actions or functions is neglected by the children, the parents are not bound by it either. For instance, when the mother accepted the responsibility of shopping and cooking, while the children assume the task of washing the dishes, it is not up to the mother to insist that they do their part, but naturally, she cannot cook if the kitchen has not been cleared. In such a case, both parents should dine out.

For most parents, particularly for mothers, this is a difficult lesson to learn. Mothers are impressed with their sense of obligation and responsibility, and they feel negligent if they do not take care of the needs of all. As a consequence, the children have no chance to take on responsibilities themselves. If mother is willing to accept the family council as supreme authority, she does not have to feel guilty if things do not always go as they should.

Giving children a real part in the family pays off in many ways. It gives them the feeling that "This is my family," and makes them more willing to take part in it. It gives them the feeling that their parents are considering them as individuals. The family meeting gives the children valuable experiences in learning to make decisions, in taking responsibility, and in learning to handle family finances. It gives them experience in the democratic way of life.[4]

Children need training and guidance in decision making. If the child errs in his decisions, he needs to be able to follow through on his idea to discover his error for himself rather than have his idea vetoed by parents, or be faced with the I-told-you-so attitude.

> One child of 9 decided on a money-making venture. He would grow tomatoes. The area he chose was barren of good soil, rock laden, and quite small. The immediate response from the family might well have been, "Nonsense." However, they refrained from their first impulse. The youngser was treated to a dignified consideration, and it was agreed that he should go ahead. He and his dad hauled rock, dug, and seeded. The garden turned into a paradise for tomato bugs and the entire crop was lost.

Parents have to be able to let their children accept the responsibility for their decisions and actions. Children learn quickly, and in no time

[4]Thomas Poffenberger, *The Family Council . . . Kids Can Confer*, Extension Bulletin 739 (Corvallis: Oregon State College, July 1953).

at all, they will begin to make sound decisions. Children learn to sort out their ideas and thoughts in a logical and orderly fashion through practice in expressing themselves in the family group. Children also learn to evaluate the thoughts and ideas of others and give consideration to the thoughts and decisions of the group.

Steps to follow in decision making:

1. Recognize that there is a problem.
2. Present facts.
3. Analyze the facts. See the problems from the other person's point of view.
4. Think out the possible solution.
5. Agree on a solution.
6. Evaluate decision
   a. Was the decision carried through?
   b. Did it help "relieve" the problem?
   c. Should it continue, should it be changed?

HOW TO ORGANIZE AND CONDUCT THE FAMILY MEETING

Parents should discuss the concept of family meetings with all and explore:

1. *The structure.* How to structure the sessions of family meetings:
   a. What type of topics can we comfortably discuss in our family?
      Examples: planning family fun, household chores, mealtime problems, and so forth.
   b. What topics need to be reserved for parental consideration?
      Examples: financial problems, health problems, and so forth.
   c. How will we handle touchy problems such as sex, marital relationships, and so forth?
      How much freedom can we give the children in decision making, such as buying a house, buying a car, selecting paint for the living room, and so forth?
2. *Ways of starting.* There are several ways of introducing the concept of the family council to the family.
   a. Directive—Informing the children that from now on we will try to solve our problems by sitting as a family group, discussing the problem, and arriving at a workable solution.
   b. Nondirective—Wait until a problem arises for the parent to solve. At that point the parents inform the children that they will discuss this problem when all members of the family are present. When all are assembled, and without going into detail, you go about finding the answers and solutions to the

313

problems. You use the family meeting structure and procedures during the meeting. At the end of the meeting, you evaluate as a group what has happened. It is during the recap that the concept of the family meeting is explained. For example, one might say:

> The idea of having family meetings is to be able to sit together as a family and share our joys and sorrows as well as working out our problems together. Talking things over with the family group gives us more ideas on how to handle our problems and of different ways of doing things. We need your ideas and want to know how you feel about things. We know that sometimes you have better solutions than we do. We think we would have a much happier family. Family meetings would be held weekly and everyone would get to share their ideas.

3. *Setting the stage.* Choose a table where each member of the family can pull up a chair. Let the toddler join the group, he will soon learn not to disrupt if he is removed as soon as he disturbs.

   Encourage every member who lives in the home to join the group.

   Provide a notebook and pen to keep a permanent record of decisions reached.

   Have the family take their places at the table and keep these places for all future meetings.

   Rotate the official duties around the family circle. One way to do this would be according to age. The oldest child would preside at the second meeting and the person on his right would be the secretary, and so forth, until all members of the family who can read and write have officiated, and then the circle begins over again. When two children take the official roles, Mother and Dad become participating members and must abide by the general rules. The chairman has to stop the procedures as soon as the voices and the tempers rise because then nobody is willing to listen.

4. *The first family meeting.* Mother and dad should act as chairman and secretary. If mother is one who always keeps track of things, let dad be the secretary. If dad usually keeps the peace and order, let mom be the chairman.

   The first meeting should last no longer than 15–20 minutes, as this is as long as order can be easily kept in a family not used to acting jointly.

   When the family has had some experience in holding meet-

314

ings, ideas will come readily, but at first it is best for the parents to be prepared.

Call the very first meeting for the specific purpose of planning family fun. Let each have their say in what the fun will be. Mother and dad may offer suggestions, but should not force their own ideas.

The reason for limiting the first family meeting to planning for family fun is because it will encourage more members to participate, and is less threatening to all; and you will have a better chance for a successful meeting.

Sometimes a family member does not wish to participate in the family meeting. The meeting should be held without him. The absence of a member can be used to reach a decision he may not like. If he wants to change it, he will have to come to the next meeting.

5. *Suggested procedures for family council meetings.* Procedures should be outlined by the parents and presented to the family group for approval, disapproval, or revision.
   a. A chairman and secretary should preside at each meeting.
   b. The officers should rotate so that each member experiences this privilege and responsibility.
   c. A definite day should be set for the council to meet each week.
   d. When a person wishes to speak, he must raise his hand and be given the floor by the chairman. No one can interrupt or speak until he has been recognized by the chairman. The person recognized must speak about the problem or issue at hand.
   e. All members of the family are invited to participate.
   f. Once a decision has been made, any alteration has to wait until the next session. In the interim, no one has the right to decide on a different course of action or to impose his decision on others.
   g. Suggested order of business for family meetings:
      1. Call the meeting to order.
      2. Read the decisions reached from previous meeting (starting with the second meeting.).
      3. Announce activities for the coming week. P.T.A., school dance, ball game, etc.
      4. Discuss unfinished business, problems still unsolved, and decisions need to be made.
      5. Present new business, new problems, and new decisions to be reached.
      6. Discuss future plans.

315

DIFFICULTIES IN MAINTAINING A FAMILY COUNCIL

Instituting the family council requires the realization that a fundamentally new and untried course of action has begun. It requires time and effort to get all members of the family used to such procedures. Parents and children alike are not prepared for it. They do not trust each other; consequently, they do not have much faith in any project that requires cooperation. Children are afraid that this is merely another trick to make them behave and do the things they do not want to do. Parents fear demands and decisions by their children are out of place. For this reason, the council sessions are often a burden to all. Sometimes it may be difficult to start them, in other cases, the first enthusiasm may shortly disappear. Making the council effective may impose hardships on the parents for the time being. If the difficult period can be tolerated without discontinuance of council sessions, its effects should be highly beneficial for all concerned.

After setting the stage for a family council, you may encounter resistance from one or more members of the family. The father may refuse to participate because of a fear of losing his authority and importance in the family. He might also resist because of the manner in which his wife approached him. As an example, many times we have parents who are involved in a power struggle with one another. In accepting the wife's suggestions, the husband would consider this a sign of submission. In some cases, refusal to participate in a family council can be a retaliatory weapon of one parent against the other.

The reasons for a child's refusal to join a family council are the same as for the child's misbehavior. It might be to receive attention by being different, or to show the family that he will do only what he wants to do.

In either case, the family council should function with those present. If, for instance, the family decides to go to the park on Sunday, and the family member who was absent from the meeting objects to the choice, it can then be pointed out to him that had he participated, he could have influenced the decision.

Without confidence in, and respect for the other members of the family, there is no way to discuss mutual difficulties and conflicts, and no opportunity to find solutions.

Difficulty in establishing and maintaining a democratic relationship is often responsible for the discontinuation of the family council. Parents may start off with good intentions and a high degree of enthusiasm, but before long, either they or the children violate the basic premises of a democratic procedure, and the council loses its meaning and function. Maintaining a family council requires considerable persistence, a willingness to see one's own mistakes, and the ability to change one's attitude and to respect that of others. One needs courage to explore and to chart new courses, without fear and distrust, and the conviction that the others also want to live in harmony and peace, but may not know how to achieve this goal.

STUDENTS CAN INITIATE THE FAMILY COUNCIL

Since not all teachers come in contact with all parents, the teacher can suggest the students present the idea of the family council to their parents. If the teacher has been having regular class council meetings each week, the children will understand the premise and the method.

The following reports are examples of some experience from students who started family councils at the suggestion of their teacher:

1. In our home there were three teenagers who constantly bickered over the use of the telephone. There were many other areas of strife, but the use of the phone was an everyday occurrence. I introduced the idea of the family council to my family. My parents jumped at the idea. We were able to solve the phone problem by limiting the length of the calls, and by each of us having a specific time to use the phone.

2. Since my parents work, my sister and I were given several jobs to do. We both felt our parents were unfair. We used to shirk our duties, and it seemed like everyone was mad all the time. One day, in class council, I was telling how unfair I was being treated. The teacher suggested a family meeting. I talked my sister into it, and then we got our parents to go along with it. Imagine our surprise when we discovered that my sister and I were really the ones who were unfair. Our parents didn't say that. It came out in our discussion when we listed all the jobs that needed to be done at home. How could we have forgotten that mom cooked our meals; mended, washed, and ironed our clothes; shopped for groceries; cleaned house; and so forth. Dad did his share with household maintenance; taking care of our two cars; helping mom with shopping; keeping the basement, garage, and porch straightened; keeping the yard, flowers, and hedges in shape. They did all these things in addition to working fulltime.

We are now a much happier and contented family and have our meetings regularly. As a result, each family member alternates cooking the evening meal. We plan our menus for the week, and my sister and I are learning to shop. Dad is teaching me how to take care of the cars. We share many things together and even have time for fun.

3. At our house we were given an allowance, but if we didn't do our jobs around the house, our parents would deduct 10 cents here and 10 cents there. Sometimes we would end up with nothing. I got our parents to sit down and talk with my brother and me about this

317

problem. We didn't get too far, but everyone thought talking together was a good idea—at least mom and dad didn't get mad. We would have a meeting when some issue came up. After a few months, we decided to have weekly meetings, and my parents talked to the teacher and got some pointers. Since then, our meetings have been real good, and somehow our family seems closer and more cooperative. Also, we finally got the issue of allowances straightened out. Everyone in our family has an allowance that belongs to him to use as he wishes. No one can take it away. If my brother and I need extra money, we earn it by doing other jobs.

4. When I was in the sixth grade and my sister was in the third grade, we really wanted a set of encyclopedias. My teacher had suggested the idea of family meetings which my parents thought was OK. At our regular family council, we discussed the pros and cons and decided we could get a set if we all helped to pay for it. My sister and I agreed to pay a dollar a month from our allowance until the books were paid for. When I look back on it now, I know that the $12 we each paid was very small in relation to the total bill. However, I know that it was the cooperation of the entire family and the feeling that my sister and I could share in the experience of such a venture that was really valuable.

Let us briefly repeat the basic principles in conducting a family council meeting.

1. The goal of a family council is the establishment of a democratic family, in which every member shares the responsibility for the solution of every problem. It is directed toward the improvement of the relationships, the recognition of each member as an equal, giving each the opportunity to deal with all others on the basis of mutual respect, without fighting or giving in. Thus, the family council is the laboratory for the development of skills needed in a democratic society.

2. The first task of the family council meeting is to listen to each other, without arguing or attempting to change each other, even without considering the solutions of problems, until full cooperation of all is achieved. No problem needs to be solved immediately by parents who often feel that they cannot tolerate what is going on. They often can change the situation by merely doing what can be done, without telling anyone else what he should do.

3. Only after a friendly, cooperate atmosphere is established, can one begin to solve problems. Such a friendly atmosphere can, at times, be quickly established, so that the discussion will not have to wait too long. No discussion should be continued if it leads to hostility.

4. Every problem is a problem for all. Every member of the family should be invited, but not forced, to state his own interpretation of

the problem and his suggestions for a solution. Some problems will be easy to solve, but others may have to be tabled until full agreement is reached by all.

5. The family council does not provide means for a better manipulation of children, nor does it mean abdication of parental guidance and influence. The parents have to learn how to be democratic leaders.

6. Children have to learn how to function in a democratic setting. Therefore, the chairmanship of the family council should rotate. If a child is unwilling or unable to exert his influence in keeping the sessions going harmoniously, then an effective approach may have to wait until the next meeting. Thus, all unresolved problems have to be delayed (see point 2).

7. Every member of the family has the right not to participate. The only pressure which can be exerted is a decision the absent member, be it father or child, may not like. In order to rescind it, he will have to wait for the next meeting. It is essential that a decision not humiliate or hurt the absentee.

8. If a child does not behave or disturbs the session, the discussion has to stop, until the child is quiet. The power of silence is stronger than any comment, criticism, or forceful action.

9. It is not advisable to hold emergency sessions. Any problem can wait for the next session. In the meantime, the parents are not only free but obliged to act the way they see fit, and thereby to exert their nonverbal influence.

10. During the session, and only then, can parents help the children to recognize their mistaken goals. Such disclosure should not be thrown at a child, his goals should be merely suggested as a possibility. If a disclosure implies attack or humiliation, it loses its value. The children can, however, learn to understand each other and themselves. But verbal expression of such understanding should not be a family routine, but restricted to the weekly sessions. If the children use them in the interim, then such misuse has to be considered as a special form of fighting between them. The parents should treat the fight in the usual form of disinvolvement, but bring it up for discussion at the next family meeting.

PARENT EDUCATION

It seems to be well within the scope of this book to concern ourselves with the problem of parents. Among all the professional groups, the teachers are in a better position to educate parents than any other group, perhaps with the exception of the pediatrician. To fulfill this task, they must acquaint themselves with the problems of parents and with methods of solving them. For this reason, effective approaches to parent education must be part of the teacher training.

Let us face the facts. Many parents are ill-prepared to raise children. It seems that they have lost a knowledge which others possess; that is, how to raise their young. The simplest routines of family living become perplexing problems. Many parents find it difficult to get the children up in the morning and to school on time, or to bed at night, without scolding and fighting. Many families begin each day with a fight. Many young children seem to lose the natural tendency to eat. They have to be coddled and coaxed, and reminded and threatened, thus making each mealtime a torture. How to get children to keep their rooms clean, to put their toys and clothes away, is a major puzzle to which many parents still seek an answer. We take it for granted that brothers and sisters will fight for every advantage, and forget that the term "brotherly love" once implied the height of considerateness and devotion. Little of that is found in our families. The slightest contribution to the welfare of the family, such as daily chores, is fraught with conflict and frustration. The child's responsibility to study, to practice, or to apply himself, is often the source of endless friction.

The strongest evidence of a universal parental failure is our concern with parent education. If parents knew what to do with their children, they would not need books, lectures, study groups, and classes.

The reason for this predicament is the democratic evolution. Raising children was always based on tradition. With the change from an autocratic to a democratic society, the traditional methods of influencing children became obsolete. Pressure, especially through punishment, is no longer effective. It was necessary and adequate in an autocratic society, but fails in our present era. In the course of the democratic evolution, adults have lost their power over children. They can no longer control them by force, or make them behave or perform. The eternal smoldering conflict between the generations, which in the past was contained by the power of the adult, has burst into the open with the waning of adult authority. Parents and children are at war, which is the basis of the generation gap. At times, the struggle may take on subtle forms; at others it exhibits the full brutality of warfare. Misunderstanding is rampant and distrust reigns. Children feel misunderstood and abused, adults discarded and defeated. We need a new tradition in raising children, a tradition based on recognition of social equality between parents and children, and embodying mutual respect.

More is needed than a recommendation of a general attitude of

320

love and tolerance. Parents need to know what they can do and what they should not do in dealing with their children, particularly in moments of conflict and of disrupted order. They need practical information, both about effective methods and about the motivation of children. In bygone times, children posed few problems. They could be forced to do what they were supposed to do. Pressure insured compliance with demands and regulations. Today, parents need to know how to stimulate the child's cooperation, respect for order, and willingness to share the responsibility for all members of the family.

Most of the methods parents can learn to use are identical with those teachers have to know. They have been described in this book in great detail. For this reason, parents may benefit equally from studying a book for teachers, as teachers may profit from books written for parents. They are all in the same boat, but each group has certain advantages and disadvantages. The teacher can work with the whole class group in influencing the concepts and values of her students, while the parents are limited to the family group to exert its influence on each child, and often the children in the family council side with each other against the parents. This then requires more democratic leadership to withstand the pressure and to move toward a solution of conflicts. The conflicts within the family are often much more intense than in the school. On the other hand, the parents, in the sequence of so many transactions between them and the children, have many more opportunities to apply logical consequences. They need more careful study of this method to replace the authority of the adult with the pressure of reality.[5]

One of the greatest drawbacks for parent education is the difficulty entailed in stopping parents, particularly mothers, from talking incessantly. As a rule, children do not listen, since a great deal of this talk is not used for communication, but as ammunition. Why is it so difficult for a mother to stop talking? Because she does not know what else to do in a conflict situation. Unlike the teacher, she is burdened with tremendous responsibility of raising children without really knowing how to do it. This deep sense of responsibility, which most mothers have, leads to constant frustration if she cannot get the children to behave as they should. This personal involvement, this nagging fear of not being a good mother, is the reason why many teachers can get along with their students so much better than with their own children. Unlike the mothers, the teachers are not involved with every deficiency of the child, and many fathers behave like

---

[5]Rudolf Dreikurs and Loren Grey, *Parents' Guide to Child Discipline* (New York: Hawthorne Press, 1970).

mothers, although fathers usually do not talk as much and, therefore, the children listen to them.

The need for encouragement is, naturally, as great in the family as in school. However, the constant fear of being defeated, prevents mothers from exerting an encouraging influence. Most of the methods used in raising children, present them with a sequence of discouraging experiences. Either through indulgence, by doing for the children what they could do for themselves, or by the humiliating effects of scolding, coaxing, threatening, and punishing, the mothers prevent the children from the experience of their own strength. Teachers have many more opportunities to exert an encouraging influence on the child, particularly if they can win the cooperation of his peers.

We, as a society, have the tremendous responsibility of helping parents do their almost superhuman job. The schools can contribute more than any other group to the training of parents. This training should begin during adolescence. On the junior high or high School level, students can be exposed to instruction about how to influence young children. What is needed for this purpose is to make kindergarten or nursery school experiences available to them, provided that the kindergarten teacher is fully equipped to use effective methods with the children in her classes.

As previously mentioned, one of the ways to educate parents is to offer courses which prepare the youngsters for parenthood. Parent education should start before an individual becomes a parent. The following reports describe how a large metropolitan school district incorporated this type of training into the curriculum:

> The home economics curriculum in our school district offers Relationships and Child Development as a sequence of courses from the seventh grade through the twelfth. In the seventh, eighth, and ninth grades, much time is devoted to the basic principles in dealing with children. In the tenth, eleventh, and twelfth grades, the impact of the family and its relationship to the setting of values, concepts, and beliefs is stressed. The students became aware of the interrelationship among the family members and the family constellation, the use of logical consequences as a method of discipline, and the four goals of misbehavior as a method of understanding a child's actions.

> A coed course was offered to senior boys and girls as an elective. In discussing the content of this course with the students, it was noted that many wanted to learn how to improve their interpersonal relationships, how to solve family problems, how to avoid family arguments, how to prepare themselves for the business of parent-

322

hood, how to take care of simple household mechanics, how to select a house or apartment, how to artistically furnish a home, how to nutritionally feed a family, and how to mend clothing. They wanted a course in depth, and not just a course on how to select their mates or what to expect of a date.

The backbone of the course dealt with preparation for parenthood and life. In order to give the students background material, they were assigned outside readings and discussed the basic psychological needs of people. From this material and information, they developed their own concepts of basic needs and combined them with the developmental tasks of children, teenagers, young adults, parents, and the aged.

One of the requirements of the course was to observe children in various situations: on the playground, at home during different hours of the day and evening, in nursery school, at the store, and so forth. Those who were able, attended the Family Education Center on Saturdays. Students who could not attend the counseling sessions asked that tapes be made so they could listen to them. They listened to the tapes on their independent study time and used them as a basis for discussions in their small groups. Many of the students influenced their parents to attend the Family Education Center.

Three research papers were required during the year. The first one, a rather soul searching paper: "Who Am I and/or What Sort of Person Am I?" The second, "The Qualities of a Good Mother or Father," whichever the case may be (not a good parent, however). The third paper, "Essential Elements in a Good Marriage Relationship."

Many of the students learned to communicate with their parents and how they react and interact with their families. They also learned that if they changed their behavior, the other person had no alternative but to change his. They gained insight into their own reactions and could accept responsibility for their own actions. Their questions were deep and searching, and dealt with values.

In our Parent Education Centers, the whole family, parents and children, is interviewed in front of teachers, other parents, and interested people in the community. The purpose of this kind of counseling is not primarily to help any one family with their problems, but to acquaint other parents with effective methods of child rearing. There are no two mothers alike in personality, background, experience, and yet, it is hard to believe to what extent all mothers make the same mistakes. They talk too much, they do not share responsibility with the children, they get themselves involved in power conflicts, and so on. In many cases, parents learn much more from an interview with other parents than from personal counseling. As observers, they are not involved and are not defensive and, therefore, more ready to grasp the new approaches.

Such centers should be established throughout the communities, preferably within school systems. Every school should have a parent education center to which the teachers cannot only refer their difficult students, but participate in the counseling with the parent. Teacher's training institutions are beginning to include such centers for the training of teachers. In this way, student teachers learn to understand the development of children and the particular problems of the parents. Through such training, teachers become capable of helping the parents of her students.

Here is a description of a community parent-teacher education center.[6]

> The purpose of this venture is to facilitate parents, teachers, and children learning to work cooperatively and effectively in the many activities which bring them together.
>
> The function of the community parent-teacher education center is education in character. A community advisory board from the cooperating P.T.A. serves to interpret the program for the community and provides some financial assistance. A professional advisory board serves to assure the highest level of professional service possible. The center's contribution is on a community service basis.
>
> The setting for community parent-teacher education center grows out of group approach to solving problems of adult-child relationships. Parents, teachers, and other interested persons, under the leadership of the counselor, share in the solutions to problems of human relationships in a given family. The group counseling sessions are open to professional and lay persons alike. The assumption here is that all attending are interested in learning more about how they might improve their own interrelationships; thus, many may profit from the deliberations of a few.
>
> Any family experiencing difficulty in interpersonal relationships, which has as its primary focal point one or more preschool or elementary school children, is eligible for counseling. Families learn of the center from various sources. There is no planned program of announcements, public or private. Families come to the center with various motives, all of which relate to seeking some kind of assistance.

[6]R.N. Lowe, and O.C. Christenson, *Guide to Enrollees*, Community Parent-Teacher Education Centers, School of Education (Eugene, Oregon: University of Oregon, 1966).

324

PARENT STUDY GROUPS

Among the many ways by which we help parents in their difficult task of raising children, we found parent study groups most effective. There is a difference when a mother reads a book alone or whether she reads it together with a group of other mothers who discuss it.

It may be interesting to know how our study groups developed. A mother, who had attended regularly the weekly session of a family education center, had moved to another city. She missed the weekly session which supported her in a surrounding of other mothers who objected to her methods. Thus she invited a few friends to study one of our books together. Soon there were several mother's study groups in her community. They objected to professional supervision. They wanted to help each other, and this became the tradition for the study groups. They are different from courses for parents, which come to an end and leave parents to shift for themselves. At the present time, our suggested methods of dealing with the problems of the child are still controversial and find professional and lay objections. Therefore, the parents came to the conclusion that they have to help themselves, and continue to do so. Many, who had finished with one group, became the leader of another.

The book usually used by the study groups is *Children: The Challenge*.[7] We also have a *Study Group Leader's Manual*,[8] so that any parent can start a group of her own without any previous knowledge of the material.

Sometimes, parents in a larger community form an organization with coordinators to help each group if it runs into difficulty. In some states, statewide coordination has been established. If the use of one book has been exhausted, other books are available, like *The Challenge of Parenthood*,[9] or *A Parent's Guide to Child Discipline*.[10]

In many cases, study groups of parents are inaugurated by the principal of a school or by individual teachers who may start a group themselves, because they, too, are parents. Similarly, teachers may get together with their friends to study this book.

This is one of the many examples of how people are beginning to help themselves and each other. Self-help groups are becoming a strong force in our society.

[7]R. Dreikurs and V. Soltz, *Children: The Challenge* (New York: Hawthorne Press, 1964).

[8]V. Soltz, *Study Group Leader's Manual* (Chicago: Alfred Adler Institute, 1967).

[9]R. Dreikurs, *The Challenge of Parenthood* (New York: Hawthorne Press, 1948).

[10]R. Dreikurs and L. Grey, *A Parent's Guide to Child Discipline* (New York: Hawthorne Press, 1970).

epilogue

In these days of violent upheaval, each of us is confronted with a choice of despair or optimism. The teacher is in a crucial position. Not only can she influence her students in their development, but through them she can change the face of society. In our schools, children are exposed to all the injustices, antagonisms, and hostilities that presently characterize our whole world. As every trained teacher can undo the damage that parents and the community have done to the child, so she can contribute to new forms of relationships and transactions, and to the acceptance of more adequate social values.

This is quite an assignment. The danger is that it may increase the feeling of insecurity and inadequacy to which teachers are only too susceptible. They think that they have enough to do to teach the children subject matter and cannot be burdened with more responsi-

327

bility. Actually, such thinking is fallacious. We sincerely hope that the teacher who comes to this point of the book has found out for herself that there are methods to lighten her task so that the original pessimism with which she may have begun this book has given way to more hope and optimism.

There still remains the stumbling block that we all experience in our desire to help, to teach, and to enable others; this is the doubt in ourselves. Have we applied these methods to ourselves? Many people treat themselves in the same way as a "bad" teacher treats a "bad" child. We are only too prone to discourage ourselves. Teachers, trained to be sensitive to mistakes, are burdened with their own. Being a perfectionist is almost demanded from a teacher who cannot tolerate mistakes in others or in herself. The courage to be imperfect violates our mistake-oriented standards, and it is this alone that permits a teacher to put up with the many difficult problems she encounters without getting discouraged and feeling defeated. Even if she should be ready to take her shortcomings in stride, neither children, principals, nor parents, will let her forget them. The one quality a teacher needs most is *courage,* confidence in herself, in her worth as she is, a human being, bound to make mistakes, but endowed with an unbelievable strength and ability to change life around her.

index

329

71 72 73 74 7 6 5 4 3 2 1